Oil, Democracy, and Development in Africa

This book focuses on the history, key industry and policy actors, and political economic outcomes in oil-producing African states, filling a gap in the literature on resource-abundant countries by providing an optimistic assessment of circumstances in contemporary Africa. John R. Heilbrunn's historical analysis investigates the origins of how different policy makers responded to inflows of oil windfalls. In doing so, Heilbrunn illustrates how outcomes vary as a consequence of the goals of particular actors that are distinct from the activities in their country's oil sector. This contribution calls for a reassessment of how we consider the impact of oil on developing economies.

John R. Heilbrunn is associate professor in the Division of Liberal Arts and International Studies at the Colorado School of Mines. He is also a Research Fellow (Chercheur associé) at Les Afriques dans le Monde, a research unit at Sciences Po Bordeaux. Prior to his faculty appointment, Heilbrunn worked as a senior public sector reform specialist at the World Bank. At the World Bank, Heilbrunn was the anticorruption thematic group coordinator, responsible for advising country teams across the organization on integrating the then-new initiative on governance and anticorruption. He has served as a consultant to the World Bank, the African Development Bank, and the U.S. government. His many publications include articles on democratization in Africa, business associations, corruption in the oil industry, and institutional efforts to fight corruption.

For Jodi

Oil, Democracy, and Development in Africa

JOHN R. HEILBRUNN
Colorado School of Mines

CAMBRIDGE
UNIVERSITY PRESS

CAMBRIDGE
UNIVERSITY PRESS

University Printing House, Cambridge CB2 8BS, United Kingdom

One Liberty Plaza, 20th Floor, New York, NY 10006, USA

477 Williamstown Road, Port Melbourne, VIC 3207, Australia

4843/24, 2nd Floor, Ansari Road, Daryaganj, Delhi - 110002, India

79 Anson Road, #06-04/06, Singapore 079906

Cambridge University Press is part of the University of Cambridge.

It furthers the University's mission by disseminating knowledge in the pursuit of education, learning and research at the highest international levels of excellence.

www.cambridge.org
Information on this title: www.cambridge.org/9781107661073

© John R. Heilbrunn 2014

First published 2014
First paperback edition 2017

A catalogue record for this publication is available from the British Library

Library of Congress Cataloging in Publication data
Heilbrunn, John R., 1954–
Oil, democracy, and development in Africa / John R. Heilbrunn, Colorado School of Mines, Associate Professor, Division of Liberal Arts and International Studies, The Colorado School of Mines Golden, CO.
     pages   cm
Includes bibliographical references and index.
ISBN 978-1-107-04981-9 (hardback)
   1. Petroleum industry and trade – Africa, Sub-Saharan.   2. Africa, Sub-Saharan – Economic conditions – 1960–   3. Democracy – Africa, Sub-Saharan.   I. Title.
HD9577.A357H45   2014
338.2'72820967–dc23   2013040599

ISBN 978-1-107-04981-9 Hardback
ISBN 978-1-107-66107-3 Paperback

Contents

Tables

Preface

The inspiration for this book came in 1998. While on a flight to Europe from West Africa, I read an issue of *Jeune Afrique* that related a story about an unfolding investigation of grand corruption implicating senior officials with the French state-owned oil company Elf Aquitaine and a number of Central African leaders. The article was the tip of an iceberg. Collusion between Elf's executives and African presidents had been the subject of many unsubstantiated rumors. Over several years, I researched the issue of corruption in the oil sector and subsequently published my findings in an article.[1]

My research into public-sector corruption and the oil industry led me to the resource curse literature. This literature was practically hegemonic in the political science and economics work on oil-producing states. With the notable exception of Davis's 1995 article, it seemed that no one questioned the determinism of the resource curse literature.[2] However, the notion that possessing considerable natural resources was a cause of poor economic performance seemed inherently counterintuitive. How could Chad, a shockingly impoverished country, be worse off for having discovered hydrocarbons? Why would São Tomé and Príncipe be condemned to dismal economic performance and authoritarian rule? Finally, why, once the war ended in Angola, would the state have few options but dictatorship and low rates of economic growth? Such conclusions seemed both improbable and absurdly deterministic.

My reflections on these questions collided with the ostensible determinism in the resource curse literature. First, people enact policies that contribute to economic growth, stagnation, or decline. It seemed important to consider what individuals sought when they tried to manage the complex revenue streams

[1] John R. Heilbrunn, "Oil and Water? Elite Politicians and Corruption in France," *Comparative Politics* 37, 3 (April 2005): 277–292.
[2] Graham A. Davis, "Learning to Love the Dutch Disease: Evidence from the Mineral Economies," *World Development* 23, 10 (October 1995): 1765–1779.

that are evident in oil extraction and marketing. Second, oil can do nothing; it is a mineral of variable qualities and marketability. People choose how to oversee their extractive industries, and the effects of oil production are consequences of policy choices. These sentiments crystalized in a sense that only through an examination of a country's circumstances *before* the discovery of petroleum would it be possible to understand how political leaders choose to manage windfalls from oil production.

Finally, profound changes occur on multiple levels in societies that are affected by natural resource extraction. These changes take shape over extended periods of time. As factors of production shift – for example, population growth relative to capital or land – subtle changes occur that find expression in politics. Although it is tempting to consider circumstances at a particular point in time, the impact of population growth that has been continent-wide can hardly be exaggerated. As someone who began working in Africa in 1980, it is clear to me that the population explosion in Nigeria, Ghana, and other countries has consequences evident in high rates of urbanization and social upheaval. In most oil-exporting countries, these transformations have been revolutionary; they are evident in shifting authority patterns from rural gerontocracies to urban, often clan-based networks. Changes on both the surface and more subtle levels are subthemes in this book. Conclusions that flow from analysis of these changes are cautiously optimistic; African hydrocarbon exporters are developing economically and their politics reflect an impetus toward democracy.

This book unfolded over a lengthy period, and during that time I accumulated a number of debts that I would like to acknowledge. At the beginning, Lynne Rienner kindly shared some of her extensive knowledge of academic publishing. I would like to thank Amy Stanley who in her kind fashion encouraged me to go forward with the book. Muna Ndulu invited me on three occasions to make presentations to the excellent students and colleagues at Cornell University's Institute of African Development. Dominique Darbon annually hosted me at Sciences Po Bordeaux, where I made presentations on topics explored in this book. Finally, Marco Cesa at the Johns Hopkins University Paul Nitze School of Advanced International Studies – Bologna Center asked me to speak to the highly dynamic students and faculty in that program. To these friends and colleagues, a special thanks.

While I was conducting the research for this project, former colleagues at the World Bank kindly engaged me as a consultant to prepare specific studies that influenced my thinking about oil-producing states. Thanks to Julia Devlin, Joel Hellman, Anand Rajaram, and Michael Stanley for their support and encouragement. The work I did for Joel resulted in a paper on sovereign wealth funds that deepened my understanding of the permanent-income hypothesis and natural resource revenue management. That study informed another paper I prepared for Michael Stanley that analyzed revenue management in hard-rock-mining economies. Both Julia Devlin and Michael Stanley arranged for presentations at which I benefited from comments of other staff members at the World Bank and the International Monetary Fund. I am grateful for these contacts, the interactions I had with these highly talented individuals, and the confidence they showed in my thinking.

Many of my colleagues at the Colorado School of Mines have been supportive of this project. Laura Pang, former Division Head of Liberal Arts and International Studies when I joined in 2001, was highly supportive of this project. She both listened to early ideas and provided helpful funds for several research trips to Paris and Bordeaux. Eul Soo Pang was no less a sounding board for this project as it took shape. Larry Chorn, then with the Department of Petroleum Engineering, shared his deep knowledge of oil production processes. I have enjoyed numerous lunches and discussions with Graham Davis, who helped me crystalize my criticisms of resource curse arguments. Jay Straker has in his gentle manner shared concerns of how natural resources influence development in countries like Guinea, the focus of his research. Finally, James Jesudason has been a steadfast friend and intellectual critic. His input was most evident in prompting me to consider a thematic approach that I used in organizing the book.

In France, I received intellectual and financial support from friends and colleagues at the Centre d'Études d'Afrique Noire – now called Les Afriques dans le monde (LAM) – a research unit of Sciences Po Bordeaux where I have been a research Fellow since 1995. It has been a genuine pleasure and honor to be affiliated with LAM, and I would like to acknowledge the encouragement and support of Michel Cahen, Christian Coulon, Dominique Darbon, Laurent Fourchard, René Otayek, Patrick Quantin, Céline Thiriot, and Comi Toulabor. During the 2008 winter session, Vincent Hoffman at Sciences Po Bordeaux invited me to teach a seminar on corruption and natural resources. In Paris, Jean-Pierre Favennec, former Chair of Economics at the Institut français de Pétrole (IFP), generously shared public documents, information, and insights about the project. I extend my gratitude to all.

Elsewhere, I consulted a wide range of colleagues with whom I discussed the political economy of abundant natural resources. Robert Bates, Pauline Jones Luong, and Ricardo Soares de Oliveira kindly shared their insights on the political economy of oil. Bob called my attention to the importance of non-oil producers on petrostates and how they might influence policy outcomes. Rob Lempert, Peter Lewis, Michael Ross, and Nic van de Walle read and commented on early chapter drafts. I greatly appreciate their critiques that helped me think through much of what I was writing.

In the spring of 2009, Marco Cesa invited me to spend a semester in residence at the Johns Hopkins University Paul Nitze School of Advanced International Studies – Bologna Center (SAIS–BC). While at SAIS–BC, I benefited from regular interactions with the very gifted students who attend that program and lively discussions with Marco Cesa, Erik Jones, Mike Plummer, and the director, Ken Keller. Although our talks revolved around a number of topics, not all of them covered in this book, their comments and input helped me consider many of the topics that I do discuss here. Thanks to all for their inputs and comments.

I would especially like to acknowledge the support and comments of several people who were most influential in how this project unfolded. First, special thanks to Lewis Bateman, my editor at Cambridge University Press. Lew continued to support the project in spite of multiple delays on my end and was instrumental in bringing the book to completion. Second, I would like to thank the anonymous reviewers Cambridge University Press enlisted to read successive drafts of the manuscript. I marvel at the extraordinary effort they put into improving the manuscript and the final project. Their comments and suggestions for revisions were invaluable. Third, I want to acknowledge Nic van de Walle's friendship and availability to discuss ideas despite his insanely busy schedule. Dominique Darbon at Sciences Po Bordeaux commented on drafts and shared many insights on the project. My good friend and former colleague, Phil Keefer, has been a sounding board, a source of encouragement, and fount of excellent critiques throughout the project. Over the years, Phil has always been available to discuss principles of economics that I may have poorly understood. Of course, any errors that remain in the text are mine alone.

Finally, but hardly least, my family, Jodi, Jamie, and Jessica, were always sources of happiness and a grounding in priorities. Jodi read and provided comments on the entire manuscript twice. She was always supportive and tolerant of my moodiness while I worked on the project. Jamie and Jessica were sometimes impatient, but always a source of great happiness and pride.

I

Introduction: A Tale of Two Petrostates

On June 18, 2007, President John Kufuor of Ghana hosted celebrations in his offices at the Osu Castle. Amid the popping of champagne corks, Kufuor made glowing pronouncements about Ghana's newly discovered offshore reservoirs estimated to hold 250 million barrels of light, sweet crude oil.[1] He triumphantly exclaimed, "With oil as a shot in the arm, we're going to fly!"[2] "Oil," he proclaimed, would help Ghana "really zoom, accelerate, and if everything works, which I pray will happen positively, you come back in five years, and you'll find that Ghana truly is the African tiger, in economic terms for development." Kufuor dismissed critics who cautioned that mismanagement of oil wealth was an endemic problem among developing economies: "[O]il is money, and we need money to do the schools, the roads, the hospitals. If you find oil, you manage it well, can you complain about that?"[3] Two months later, Kosmos Energy, a Texas wildcatter firm, announced even more discoveries, and Ghana joined an exclusive club of African oil exporters. These remarkable discoveries promised Ghana millions in resource windfalls that would help its government develop the economy and consolidate democracy.

In 2010, the consortium of oil companies in Ghana began to lift oil from the Jubilee fields. Since the discovery of oil in 2007, the Ghanaian government proceeded with deliberation by passing legislation to manage companies operating in the sector and to limit asymmetrical growth and any negative impacts of revenues on exchange rates. They tightened fiscal policy to reduce

---

[1] The terms "oil," "petroleum," and "hydrocarbons" are used interchangeably to refer to oil, gas, and gas condensates.

[2] BBC, "UK's Tullow Discovers Oil in Ghana" (18 June 2007), retrieved from http://news.bbc.co.uk/2/hi/business/6764549.stm (accessed 2 January 2011).

[3] BBC, "Ghana 'Will Be an African Tiger'" (19 June 2011), retrieved from http://news.bbc.co.uk/2hi/Africa/6766527.stm (accessed 2 January 2011).

inflationary pressures and prevent the Ghanaian Cedi from appreciation.[4]
In effect, the Ghanaian government – whether the government of John Kufuor,
his successor John Atta Mills, or current president John Dramani Mahama –
has enacted a set of policies to mitigate the Dutch disease effects and manage
resource revenues in an efficient manner. This commentary on positive management of the oil sector cannot mask allegations of corruption and collusive arrangements between government officials and oil companies.[5] As in any
developing country with abundant natural resources, Ghana has had problems
with collusive behavior between oil companies and senior officials and inefficient revenue management.[6] However, on the whole, Ghana's experiences are
quite remarkable.

What occurred in the Central African state of Chad could hardly have
been more different from the Ghanaian experience. In 1973, Conoco discovered commercially viable hydrocarbon reserves in the Doba region. Like the
Ghanaians, the Chadians were euphoric about the prospect of becoming a
petrostate. As one individual exclaimed, "Oil! Oil! This is how we welcome
the 18th of September 1973 ... by the inauguration of petroleum wells in
Doba just five hundred kilometers south of N'Djamena.... Even my uncle has
been speaking of the future by saying, 'when our oil begins to flow'."[7] Dreams
of wealth, a release from oppressive poverty, and peace – all these hopes built
on the announcements that Conoco had found oil in southern Chad. In 1969,
Chad's first president, François Tombalbaye, had granted the exploration
license to Conoco, and his greatest hopes were coming to fruition.[8] His decision to grant the license to an American company was controversial, however. First, executives at the French national oil company, Elf Aquitaine, saw
Conoco's activities as an encroachment on their sphere of influence.[9] Second,
the American oil major's entry into a French African country annoyed officials
at the Elysée Palace's *Cellule Africaine*.[10] Given a pattern of French interventions in its former colonies, it is probable that this slight mobilized different
actors to overturn the Tombalbaye regime. Indeed, two years after Conoco's

[4] International Monetary Fund, "Ghana: Sixth and Seventh Reviews under the Three-Year
Arrangement under the Extended Credit Facility and Requests for Waiver of Nonobservance of
Performance Criteria and Extension of the Arrangement – Staff Report," IMF Country Report
No. 12/201 (Washington, DC: IMF, July 2012), 4.
[5] E. Gyimah-Boadi and H. Kwasi Prempeh, "Oil, Politics, and Ghana's Democracy," *Journal of
Democracy* 23, 3 (July 2012): 101–102.
[6] *Africa Confidential*, "Ghana: Mahama Ahead by a Hair," 53, 23 (16 November 2012).
[7] Quoted in Martin Petry and Naygotimti Bambé, *Le Pétrole du Tchad: Rêve ou Cauchemar pour
les Populations* (Paris: Éditions Karthala 2005), 21.
[8] Simon Tulipe, "Le Bassin Tchadien à l'Épreuve de l'or Noir: Réflexions sur la 'Nouvelle Donne
Pêtrole Politique' en Afrique Centrale," *Politique Africaine* 94 (Juin 2004): 61.
[9] Sam C. Nolutshungu, *Limits of Anarchy: Intervention and State Formation in Chad*
(Charlottesville: University of Virginia Press, 1996), 7.
[10] Claude Wauthier, *Quatre Presidents et l'Afrique: de Gaulle, Pompidou, Giscard d'Estaing,
Mitterrand* (Paris: Éditions de Seuil, 1995), 219–220.

announcement, rebels killed Tombalbaye in a coup d'état, and Chad spiraled into sequential civil wars. Conoco suspended production, foreign investors fled the country, the Doba fields went dormant, and warlords oppressed the Chadian people who to this date continue to live in chronic violence and poverty.

Chad's cycle of violence and poverty appeared to end in 1990 when Idriss Déby overthrew Hissein Habré, a vicious despot. Upon occupying the capital, Ndjamena, Déby announced to Chad's war-weary people, "I bring you neither gold nor silver, but I will give you liberty, democracy, and multiparty government."[11] After seizing power, Déby allowed the Chadians to hold a national conference followed by multiparty elections that Déby won.[12] After the elections, Déby began negotiations with international investors to construct a pipeline from the Doba fields to the coastal town of Kribi in Cameroon. A decade later, a consortium composed of Exxon, Chevron, and the Malaysian national oil company Petronas, in collaboration with the World Bank, completed the controversial $3.7 billion Cameroon-Chad Pipeline.[13]

Funding for the pipeline was unusual in that a minor percentage came from the World Bank's International Finance Corporation (IFC) and the International Bank for Reconstruction and Development (IBRD). Minority participation by the IBRD and IFC was a condition the consortium imposed on the Chadian government before they would fund the pipeline. The IBRD and IFC's participation meant that the loans bore a concessional interest rate and required repayment of principal within twenty years. What is remarkable about these loans is that because Chad remains one of the world's most impoverished countries, its government is therefore eligible for interest-free credits from the International Development Association (IDA), which mature decades after disbursement. Hence, for the Chadian government, the harsh terms of these loans were unprecedented; it had to begin repayment on the interest-bearing loans immediately. In order to protect its investment, the World Bank worked with the Chadian government to open offshore accounts into which revenues would be paid, as well as establish a bureaucracy to manage, to the extent possible, the new productive sector.

Because the World Bank was making a *loan* to an IDA-eligible government, its experts conceived of a novel savings and stabilization mechanism to manage the oil revenues and avoid the financial and diplomatic embarrassment that

[11] Petry and Bambé, *Le Pêtrole du Tchad*, 39.

[12] Robert Buijtenhuijs, *La Conférence Nationale Souveraine du Tchad: Une Essai d'Histoire Immédiate* (Paris: Éditions Karthala, 1993); idem, *Transition et Elections au Tchad: Restauration Autoritiare et Récomposition Politique* (Paris: Éditions Karthala, 1998).

[13] World Bank, "Management Report and Recommendation in Response to the Inspection Panel Investigation Report," Cameroon Petroleum Development and Pipeline Project (Loan no. 7020 CM) and Petroleum Environment Capacity Enhancement (CAPECE) Project (Credit No. 3372-CM), Report No. INSP/R2003–0003 (Washington, DC: World Bank: 2003), 10.

would have followed any default on payments.[14] However, disagreements were inevitable. Tensions first erupted between Déby and the World Bank in 2000 when the Consortium paid the Chadian government a $25 million bonus. Déby diverted a portion of the bonus to buy military ordinance instead of investing in social sector development, as had been a central part of his agreement with the World Bank.[15] Three years later, oil production began; two years after that benchmark, Déby's agreement with the World Bank collapsed.[16] As Pegg has noted, the World Bank had "grossly overestimated" Déby's commitment or ability to implement meaningful reforms.[17] Chad resumed its journey along a path of civil war amid the most profound levels of poverty.

This book proposes an explanation of why these two countries experienced such radically different outcomes. It poses a simple proposition that to understand the likely path of any country that discovers significant oil reserves, it is necessary to consider conditions present the day *before* the discovery. Hence, when Ghana began production in 2010, its economic and political institutions were stable. First, at the time a consortium of companies discovered oil in Ghana's West Cape offshore waters, the state possessed a legal structure modeled on British colonial laws that regulated the country's gold- and diamond-mining industries.[18] These colonial laws provided a foundation on which Ghana's parliament could pass legislation. In 1983, the then-military government established the Ghana National Petroleum Corporation Act; in 2005, the legislature passed the National Petroleum Authority Act that set forth rules for companies operating in the sector, and in 2011, the Ghanaian parliament passed the Petroleum Revenue Management Act.[19]

Ghana's experiences managing royalties, mineral income taxes, and its considerable natural resources from its gold and diamond production provided the model for its nascent petroleum sector. Its well-defined regulatory structure assured foreign investors that they were entering a low-risk environment

---

[14] For details of the law and agreements between the World Bank and the Déby government, see the chapter on revenue management in Ian Gary and Nikki Reisch, *Chad's Oil: Miracle or Mirage: Following the Money in Africa's Newest Petrostate* (Baltimore, MD: Catholic Relief Services, 2005), especially 42–48.

[15] Babette Stern, "Le Tchad a Acheté des Armes avec l'Argent du Pétrole," *Le Monde* (22 Novembre 2000).

[16] David White, "The 'Resource Curse' Anew: Why a Grand World Bank Project Has Fast Run into the Sand," *The Financial Times* (January 23, 2006); see as well John A. Gould and Matthew S. Winters, "An Obsolescing Bargain in Chad: Shifts in Leverage between the Government and the World Bank," *Business and Politics* 9, 2 (2007): 1–34.

[17] Scott Pegg, "Chronicle of a Death Foretold: The Collapse of the Chad-Cameroon Pipeline Project," *African Affairs* 108, 431 (April 2009): 312.

[18] Gilbert Stone, "The Mining Laws of the West African Colonies and Protectorates," *Journal of Comparative Legislation and International Law* 2, 3 (1920): 264.

[19] Republic of Ghana, Provisional National Defence Council Law, "Ghana National Petroleum Corporation Act 1983," PNDCL 64 (1983); Republic of Ghana, National Parliament, "National Petroleum Authority Act, 2005," Act No. 691 (14 June 2005); Republic of Ghana, National Parliament, "Petroleum Revenue Management Act," Act No. 885 (11 April 2011).

with predictable contract law and a stable, relatively independent judiciary capable of limiting executive discretion.[20] Perhaps most importantly, Ghana's active commercial and professional class provided international oil companies (IOCs) a source of local, competent employees. In the Takoradi region, for instance, IOCs are hiring and training local populations "so they are not marginalised and don't become a problem like the Niger Delta."[21] The government had reached a formal agreement with IOCs that they would train Ghanaians to assume positions of increasing responsibility.

Ghana, with its strong economic performance and functioning institutions that are the envy of other African states, provides an excellent case to assess how oil production and the resulting windfalls can positively influence development outcomes in a young African democracy. For pessimistic students of resource-abundant countries in Africa, Ghana's discoveries promise corruption, mismanagement, political instability, and autocracy. For optimistic observers, however, positive signs are evident in the Ghanaian government's ability to handle an alleged scandal involving Kosmos Energy. This scandal implicated two former insiders of the Kufuor administration in malfeasance and demonstrated the impact of Ghana's vibrant print media that exposed the immense profits reaped by the companies that discovered oil. As argued in Chapter 5, the management of this incident bodes well for Ghana's ability to enjoy positive effects from oil. It appears likely that the oil reserves may guarantee the economy's ability to grow and even embed democratic institutions in its political system. As this book shows, the actual development in other states lie somewhere between the positive outcomes Ghana experienced and the violence and instability that plagued Chad. Indeed, outcomes vary in different African petrostates as a function of the conditions before the discovery of oil and how political actors manage the windfalls.

THE ARGUMENT: OIL, DEMOCRACY, AND DEVELOPMENT IN AFRICA

This book is about the relationship between oil, democracy, and development in African petrostates.[22] It calls for a refinement of thinking about conclusions that inform the resource-curse literature. This literature argues that countries with abundant natural resources perform worse economically than those without similar endowments, and they are more likely to be autocratic regimes. However, as I show later, the determinism in much of the resource-curse

---

[20] Brian Levy and Pablo T. Spillar, "A Framework for Resolving the Regulatory Problem, in *Regulations, Institutions, and Commitment: Comparative Studies of Telecommunications*, eds. Brian Levy and Pablo T. Spillar (New York: Cambridge University Press, 1996), 5.

[21] William Wallis, "Let the Good Times Roll," *The Financial Times* (February 19, 2011).

[22] The term "petrostate" is from Terry Lynn Karl, *The Paradox of Plenty: Oil Booms and Petro-States* (Berkeley and Los Angeles: University of California Press, 1997).

literature is faulty; it is necessary to take other variables into consideration. Development signifies changes that include economic improvements for a population's physical circumstances, better social conditions, and increased political representation. Hence, both elections and representation are crucial elements of development.[23] Informing this notion of development is Sen's insightful contribution that with improved economic circumstances come greater freedom and choice.[24] Freedom encourages economic investments that lead to growth. Choice means that individuals are able to decide on their futures; poverty does not determine what people must do.

These are states that receive a substantial percentage of their fiscal revenues from oil exports; one definition is that petrostates are those states for which oil exports constitute at least 10 percent of their gross domestic product (GDP).[25] This book posits that in each of these states, albeit to varying degrees, elements of fragile democracy are present, and economic development influences outcomes. Some of these countries remain rooted in authoritarian rule and predatory economic policies, whereas others are semi-democratic polities. Some governments have lengthy experiences with the extractive industries and possess rudimentary ministries and agencies to manage resource revenues. This book explores the factors that have influenced these varying outcomes proposing that we need to assess each case according to the economic and political institutions present before the discovery of hydrocarbons.

The book uses a historical perspective to trace the preconditions in African states that were present when oil production began. It is thereby possible to analyze the arrangements that influenced responses to resource windfalls. For impoverished countries, abundant natural resources are a net benefit. Commercially viable hydrocarbons in offshore waters or onshore territories result in substantial payments that in some cases are multiples of pre-oil GDPs. The catch is that oil companies make enormous payments to impoverished countries under autocratic rulers who preside over skeletal bureaucracies with neither functioning ministries nor agencies of accountability. Authoritarian regimes have little or no capacity to manage the complex revenue streams from oil production. Leakage of resource wealth is all but inevitable.

Changes have occurred in African petrostates on various levels, which are both obvious and subtle. Payments for hydrocarbon extraction prompt increases in capital investments and alter the relative distribution of an economy's factors of production. Political leaders have incentives to impose controls over policy making as a means of gaining access to that capital. Engerman and Sokoloff find that in countries that possess substantial primary commodities,

[23] Hollis B. Chenery and Nicholas G. Carter, "Foreign Assistance and Development Performance, 1960–1970," *The American Economic Review* 63, 2 (May 1973): 462.
[24] Amartya Sen, *Development as Freedom* (New York: Anchor Books, 1999), 33.
[25] Jeff D. Colgan, "Oil and Revolutionary Governments: Fuel for International Conflict," *International Organization* 64, 4 (Fall 2010): 661.

a core elite captures the wealth and uses it to increase their political power, thereby deepening economic inequalities.[26] As Easterly observes, an entrenched elite that receives its income from natural resources has few incentives to invest in building human capital.[27] Hence, exclusivity occurred as a function both of colonial policies and the insertion of resource revenues into the economies of many formerly impoverished African petrostates.

Second, the book calls for a reconsideration of the deterministic assumption that abundant natural resources automatically contribute to poor policy outcomes. It finds useful Engerman and Sokoloff's insightful rejection of the implicit determinism in path dependency given that significant hydrocarbon endowments *influence* but do not necessarily cause specific institutional developments.[28] The task is to analyze both the subtle changes and obvious performance indicators in these states. This book argues that in African petrostates, development has varied and oil production does not determine outcomes.

Third, oil discoveries and the resulting revenues precede subtle political, economic, and social changes. Social transformations are evident in a growing middle class that imposes demands on the governing elite. This middle class may initially be small and include regime insiders, but its members adopt identities and norms of their class. Resource revenues make education and health care more readily available; literacy rates rise, and people live longer. Economic shifts are apparent in pockets of growth where revenues from hydrocarbon extraction spill over into non-oil sectors and enable the accumulation of wealth. Unequal income distribution, however, is common among petrostates. Inequalities that harken to colonial times continue in circumstances where only a few benefit from oil revenues. Despite inequitable distribution of initial revenues, the increase in economic wealth has unavoidable effects; with time, the number of people who benefit from oil production increases.

When oil prices are high, the expansion of political space to absorb new actors is a seamless process. However, when prices drop, as during the 1980s, the capacity to create new positions shrinks. Herein lies the spark that ignites demands for political change. The state can accommodate only a shrinking number of the elite and must necessarily exclude younger individuals. Competition among key social groups then increases. The exclusion of rising social groups

---

[26] Stanley L. Engerman and Kenneth L. Sokoloff, "Factor Endowments, Inequality, and Paths of Development among New World Economies," *Economia* 3 (Fall): 41–109; idem, "Factor Endowments, Institutions, and Differential Paths of Growth Among New World Economies: A View from Economic Historians of the United States," in *How Latin America Fell Behind: Essays on the Economic Histories of Brazil and Mexico, 1800–1914*, ed. Stephen Haber (Stanford: Stanford University Press, 1997), 260–304; Kenneth Sokoloff and Stanley L. Engerman, "History Lessons: Institutions, Factors Endowments, and Paths of Development in the New World," *Journal of Economic Perspectives* 14, 3 (Summer 2000): 217–232.

[27] William Easterly, "The Middle Class Consensus and Economic Development," *The Journal of Economic Growth* 6 (2001): 319.

[28] Engerman and Sokoloff, "Factor Endowments, Institutions, and Differential Paths of Growth Among New World Economies," 262.

prompts individuals to express their interests through organizations and associations. Competition for a shrinking number of coveted positions among the governing elite's children leads them to establish more formal organizations to represent their interests. An expansion of organizational behavior finds expression in political machines that may serve as nascent political parties. Increased competition therefore advances or restrains the agendas of diverse networks that are the foundations of political parties among a new generation. Although these changes are subtle, they have an inexorable impact on political economic outcomes.

Subtle changes that have occurred slowly included a nascent middle class that participates in the emerging urban political machines. These urban inhabitants use machine politics to link with rural actors and extend their authority to the countryside.[29] During prosperous economic times, people have children; their progeny mature and demand opportunities for themselves. In practically every African oil producer, increasing numbers of citizens have demanded representative government and freedoms. Although the continent-wide record is uneven, a comparison of petrostates shows that even among the poorer African oil economies, development has occurred. African oil-exporting states are forced to democratize because their citizens demand the broadened choices and improved conditions that accompany development.

Without question, hydrocarbon extraction and the resulting windfalls can cause inefficient behavior including graft, fraud, embezzlement, and other forms of corruption. After the discovery of oil, policy makers need to draft regulations, set up bank accounts, and define rules to manage this new industry. If the government has many of these instruments in place, then revenue management is more efficient. If none of these agencies and procedures exists, as in the poorest African states, then the political leaders' tasks are difficult, take years, and encounter pitfalls. It is therefore essential to consider the implications of historical arrangements in these African states and then evaluate how choices made at critical junctures influenced developmental trajectories.

One need only glance at the confidential report on the hydrocarbon sector in Nigeria that leaked in October 2012; the report details the systemic efficiencies, widespread leakage of funds, and theft of crude oil in Nigeria and presents a painful depiction of problematic behaviors.[30] However, it is also apparent from Nigeria's 2011 presidential elections, when the populace cast ballots in an election deemed to be free and fair, that the country might have moved beyond the violence and malfeasance so evident in 2007. Although the elections were not entirely free of bloodshed, ballot snatching, and other irregularities, most

---

[29] The close relationship between rural and urban authority is a central point in Catherine Boone, *Political Topographies of the African State: Territorial Authority and Institutional Choice* (New York: Cambridge University Press, 2003).

[30] Mallam Nuhu Ribado and Olasupo Shasore San, "Report of the Petroleum Revenue Special Task Force" (Abuja: Federal Ministry of Petroleum Resources, August 2012).

observers concurred that they represented a critical step forward in Nigeria's fledgling democracy.[31] As the country prepares for the 2015 elections, jockeying among factions in the dominant party and competition among various groups has turned the issues of hydrocarbons and revenue management into a political issue.

Oil revenues are hardly a curse; rather, they are an opportunity for poor states to grow economically and establish the conditions for democracy. This book's fundamental argument is that political and economic conditions present before hydrocarbons are discovered influence these countries' developmental and political trajectories for decades. Otherwise stated, to understand the impact of oil production on a state's development, it is necessary to examine what the country looked like at the time of oil discovery. The starting point when most African states begin to extract oil and receive revenues is the most effective benchmark for thinking about their development and the degree of democratization.

Table 1.1 displays the time of discovery and onset of production and the size of selected countries' reserves. Angola, Nigeria, and Gabon are three of the continent's most senior oil producers, having discovered and begun oil production before independence. Their experience is evident in arrangements that structure their domestic politics and management of their natural resource production. Nigeria and Angola are major producers; their combined daily production is close to 500 million barrels of high-quality oil. Threats of strikes or reduced production in these two petrostates have an impact on world prices. Angola, Chad, Congo, and Sudan are states in which citizens have endured relentless violence and warfare since the end of colonialism. As a functioning democracy, Ghana is in many respects a test case. Its experiences show how preexisting conditions are paramount in explaining outcomes. Conceivably, Ghana may yet develop many of the pathologies consistent with the resource curse. However, democracy has been firmly implanted in Ghana, and the test becomes whether democratic institutions mitigate poor policy choices in future years.

Oil and Democracy

Recent political events in African petrostates confirm that greater freedoms and representative government are evident in these countries. This proposition debates a large literature that argues categorically that political leaders use revenues from natural resource extraction to reinforce the institutions of authoritarian rule.[32] With little equivocation, Ross asserts: "[T]he more petroleum

---

[31] International Crisis Group, "Lessons from Nigeria's 2011 Elections," *Africa Briefing No. 81* (Brussels, September 15, 2011): 5.

[32] Nathan Jensen and Leonard Wantchekon, "Resource Wealth and Political Regimes in Africa," *Comparative Political Studies* 37, 3 (September 2004): 816–841; Michael L. Ross, "Does Oil

TABLE 1.1 *Independence, Year of Oil Discovery, Production, and Measures of Proven Reserves*

Country	Independence	Year of discovery	Year onset production	Proven reserves (Bn/Bls) BP 2007	Proven reserves (Bn/Bls) Oil & Gas 2009	Proven reserves (Bn/Bls) World Oil 2007
Angola	1975	1968	1968	9,035	9,040	9,500
Chad	1960	1970	2002	0,900	1,500	–
Congo	1960	1969	1970	1,940	1,600	1940
Eq Guinea	1968	1995	1995	1,755	1,100	1705
Gabon	1960	1957	1957	1,995	2,000	3,184 (w/LNG)
Ghana	1957	1970/2007	1971/2010	–*	.015	–*
Mauritania	1960	2002	2006	0	0,100	0
Nigeria	1960	1957	1957	36,220	36,220	37,200
São Tomé e Príncipe	1975	2003	2015 (est)	0*	0*	0*
Sudan	1956	1976	1976	6,615	5,000	6,700 (w/LNG)

* Neither Ghana nor São Tomé and Príncipe had measurable production in 2007.

an authoritarian country produces, the less likely it will make the journey to democracy."[33] As the rentier state argument posits, resource revenues free politicians from a need to tax.[34] Incumbents can use oil windfalls to support their coalitions and the armed forces, all the while ignoring demands for representative government and equitable development.[35] Citizens of petrostates thus suffer both lower rates of economic growth *and* authoritarian rule.[36]

This book shows that democratic processes are present in African petrostates' trade unions, voluntary associations, and political parties. Although many governments hold pluralist elections in which citizens may vote for a party of their choice, the contributions of Levitsky and Way, among others, show that these elections indicate competitive authoritarianism and partial democracy.[37] Still, many Africans enjoy far more fundamental liberties and legitimate rule, and, perhaps most importantly, their politicians operate under norms of horizontal accountability.[38] Diverse political arrangements allow states to make transitions to democracy and mediate social conflicts.

When referring to democracy, this study means competitive pluralist politics and the concomitant representation that politicians provide their constituents. Competitive elections are crucial elements of democracy; "the reins of government should be handed to those who command more support than do any of the competing individuals or teams."[39] In a competitive electoral system, multiple political parties are free to compete for office and elected officials are the choice of citizens casting their ballots. In this perspective, democracy and development parallel each other.

Countervailing pressures come from powerful individuals who establish clientelist networks. In African petrostates, networks became the foundations on which patrons built political machines to compete in elections. Political machines were products of history that emerged from conditions of uncertainty prevalent throughout Africa at the close of the twentieth century. After the 1990s, elections became increasingly common in Africa and so too did political

Hinder Democracy?" *World Politics* 53 (April 2001): 325–361; idem, *The Oil Curse: How Petroleum Wealth Shapes the Development of Nations* (Princeton: Princeton University Press, 2012), 63–109; Kevin K. Tsui, "More Oil, Less Democracy: Evidence from Worldwide Crude Discoveries," *The Economic Journal* 121, 551 (March 2011): 89–115.

[33] Ross, *The Oil Curse*, 65–66.

[34] Hazem Beblawi, "The Rentier State in the Arab World," In *Nation State and Integration in the Arab World*, Vol. II: *The Rentier State*, eds. Hazem Beblawi and Giacomo Luciani Beckenham (Kent, United Kingdom: Croom Helm Ltd., 1987).

[35] Michael Herb, "No Representation Without Taxation: Rents, Development, and Democracy," *Comparative Politics* 37, 3 (April 2005): 297.

[36] Ross, "Does Oil Hinder Democracy?" 328.

[37] Steven Levitsky and Lucan A. Way, *Competitive Authoritarianism: Hybrid Regimes after the Cold War* (New York: Cambridge University Press 2010).

[38] Guillermo O'Donnell, "Delegative Democracy," *Journal of Democracy* 5, 1 (January 1994): 61.

[39] Joseph A. Schumpeter, *Capitalism, Socialism, and Democracy* (London: George Allen & Unwin Ltd., 1943), 273.

machines. Although a groundswell of demand for free elections prompted change in state after state, leaders of opposition movements competed against autocrats in elections they could never win.[40] Despite the ultimate futility of their campaigns, regime opponents used political machines and patronage systems to demand voice and a share in the distribution of benefits.

Patronage systems that operate in African petrostates resemble others historically present elsewhere. In the classic model of a patronage system, a politician hires individuals who work for his organization and return to him a portion of their salaries.[41] The politician is the boss; he hires patrons who in turn engage clients. A client must bring the patron income. If he fails to do so, the patron either fires him or the "boss" fires the patron.[42] Political machines depend on networks that provide the patrons employees and clients to do their bidding. As African petrostates have developed, political machines, both for incumbent parties and their challengers, operate according to the exigencies of patronage networks. Patronage networks necessarily blend elements of older, historic relations with new political organizations.

Clientelist networks provide recruits for political machines. At the top, political machines attract elite actors who compete for wealth created by natural resource extraction and use their positions to exclude their rivals. During periods of price upswings, efforts to open political space encounter little opposition. However, during price downswings, elite actors retrench and use political machines to eliminate real and perceived threats to their positions. Tornell and Lane's influential concept of "the voracity effect" shows how during price downswings, individuals at the center of politics exclude rivals from resource windfalls and thereby capture a share of scarce fiscal revenues by closing political space.[43]

A crucial characteristic of a political machine is that it "sustains its members through the distribution of material incentives (patronage) rather than non-material incentives (appeals to principle, the fun of the game, sociability, etc.)."[44] This book shows how political machines have influenced politics in oil-producing countries that are simultaneously experiencing increases in earnings, rising capital stocks, rapid population growth, and urbanization. Political machines proliferate in cities and towns around patrons who distribute material benefits to their clients.[45] These organizations build on legacies that find their origins in colonial administrations and even precolonial African societies.

[40] Levitsky and Way, *Competitive Authoritarianism*, 17.
[41] Ronald N. Johnson and Gary D. Liebcap, "Patronage to Merit and Control of the Federal Government Labor Force," *Explorations in Economic History* 31, 1 (1994): 92.
[42] Joseph D. Reid Jr. and Michael M. Kurth, "Public Employees in Political Firms: Part A. The Patronage Era," *Public Choice* 59, 3 (December 1988): 254.
[43] Aaron Tornell and Philip R. Lane, "The Voracity Effect," *The American Economic Review* 89, 1 (March 1999): 42.
[44] James Q. Wilson, "The Economy of Patronage," *Journal of Political Economy* 69, 4 (August 1961): 370.
[45] Michael Johnston, "Patrons and Clients, Jobs and Machines: A Case Study of the Uses of Patronage," *The American Political Science Review* 73, 2 (June 1979): 385.

Conditions in African petrostates when they begin to export oil and receive revenues have varied widely, as the cases of Chad and Ghana aptly demonstrate. These differences are crucial in any explanation of outcomes or subsequent conditions in these countries. It is therefore necessary to pause and consider the variable extent to which African petrostates have experienced democracy and economic development. This reconsideration of outcomes explains Haber and Monaldo's finding that "to the degree that we detect any statistically significant relationships, they point to a resource blessing: increases in natural resource income are associated with increases in democracy."[46] Oil production provides revenues that political leaders may use for a variety of expenditures. As the political arena opens, people who have benefited from hydrocarbon revenues have incentives to mobilize political organizations to protect their interests and prolong their status. As citizens organize, the number of political associations grows and pluralism emerges in African petrostates.

This study proposes that the freedoms that accompany democracy have contributed to sustainable economic growth in African petrostates.[47] This perspective agrees with the proposition that "political liberties and democratic rights are among the 'constituent components' of development."[48] Oil revenues bring wealth to a society; they contribute to economic growth that spurs demand for political liberties, choices, and democratic rights. Increasing choices and expressions of political freedom are evident in the organizational response implicit in pluralist democracy and development. However, development is more than just economic growth that may favor only a small subset of the population.

Oil and Development

As a mineral, albeit nonrenewable, oil is fungible and may be transformed into *resource rents*, meaning any surplus value left over after reimbursement of all

[46] Stephen Haber and Victor Menaldo, "Do Natural Resources Fuel Authoritarianism? A Reappraisal of the Resource Curse," *The American Political Science Review* 105, 1 (February 2011): 3.

[47] A substantial literature in the social sciences debates whether democracy is necessarily a precondition of development or the inverse. See the seminal study by Seymour Martin Lipset, "Some Social Requisites of Democracy: Economic Development and Political Legitimacy," *The American Political Science Review* 53, 1 (March 1959); idem, "The Social Requisites of Democracy Revisited: 1993 Presidential Address," *American Sociological Review* 59, 1 (February 1994): 1–22; Larry Diamond, "Economic Development and Democracy Reconsidered," American Behavioral Scientist 35, 4/5 (March/June 1992): 450–499; Robert J. Barro, "Determinants of Democracy," *Journal of Political Economy* 107, 6 Part 2 (December 1999): S158-S183; idem, "Democracy and Growth, *The Journal of Economic Growth* 1 (March 1996): 1–27; Edward Glaeser, Rafael La Porta, Florencio Lopez-De Silanes, and Andrei Shleifer, "Do Institutions Cause Growth?" *Journal of Economic Growth* 9 (2004): 271.

[48] Amartya Sen, *The Idea of Justice* (Cambridge: The Belknap Press of Harvard University Press, 2009), 347.

necessary costs of extraction including a reasonable return on investment.[49] Oil is found in subterranean "reservoirs"; firms extract the hydrocarbons from "reserves" or the portions of reservoirs that may be produced with available technology at reasonable costs.[50] States typically extend ownership rights over the subterranean reservoirs. They then lease the rights to extract the oil to international companies that pay rents in the form of bonuses, royalties, taxes, and local fees and licenses.

Shortly after a government of an impoverished, agrarian country learns it possesses hydrocarbon reserves, it begins to receive revenues that continue until the oil companies deplete the reserves. Because the oil reserves – and revenues – eventually dry up, how well the state manages the revenues from the beginning is crucial to its developmental trajectory. However, the state's capacity to manage revenues is a function of its level of development at the time that international companies begin paying royalties and other revenues. Among the poorest African countries, oil revenues represent a logarithmic increase in government receipts; they clog a system incapable of efficiently and wisely investing such resources. It opens the door to dramatic mismanagement. Hence, revenue management is key to understanding a natural resource's impact on the political economy. If politicians manage oil windfalls efficiently, the economy grows; payments for resource extraction smooth expenditures, and political leaders can set aside a percentage of the windfall earnings for future generations. If, on the other hand, the task exceeds policymakers' abilities, the economy is vulnerable to a range of adverse economic outcomes. Price volatility exposes the economy to Dutch disease effects.[51] In many states, political leaders are likely to divert revenues to satisfy its supporting coalitions or reinforce authoritarian rule. Outcomes, whether optimal or inefficient, are variable and reflect circumstances in the country when it becomes a petrostate.

This book proposes that oil helps impoverished states grow economically. However, it is critical to emphasize that this trajectory is hardly linear and reverses are always possible. Economic growth or decline is not inevitable in petrostates. Change caused by oil exportation occurs on several levels. First, oil revenues fund public investments and overt displays of increased wealth such as military spending. Other subtle changes take shape over time. These include

[49] Philip Daniel, Brenton Goldsworthy, Wojciech Maliszewski, Diego Mesa Puyo, and Alistair Watson, "Evaluating Fiscal Regimes for Resource Projects: An Example from Oil Development," in *The Taxation of Petroleum and Minerals: Principals, Problems and Practice*, eds. Philip Daniel, Michael Keen, and Charles McPherson (New York: Taylor, Francis and Routledge, 2010), 191.
[50] Vaclav Smil, *Energy at the Crossroads: Global Perspectives and Uncertainties* (Cambridge, MA: MIT Press 2003), 181.
[51] This condition occurs when a booming sector attracts capital from a non-booming manufacturing sector. The non-booming sector then declines. A downward shift in the formerly booming sector price causes a decline across the economy. The classic statement is from W. Max Corden and Peter Neary, "Booming Sector and De-Industrialisation in a Small Open Economy," *The Economic Journal* 92, 3688 (December 1982): 825–848.

educational investments that bring a return after years, better health care, and advances in state construction leading to better public-sector service delivery. It is these subtle changes that perhaps have the greatest impact on African petrostates, especially in those countries that were poor agrarian economies or those mired in civil war.

As such, this book disagrees with a substantial literature that argues the economies of countries with abundant natural resources necessarily perform worse than countries without abundant endowments.[52] A second variant of this literature argues that natural resources are a trap and hydrocarbons, in particular, are nothing less than a curse.[53] Advocates of this perspective highlight the problem of politicians, who upon the receipt of resource revenues squander the wealth.[54] Finally, Sachs and Warner famously show how abundant natural resources correlate with dismal economic policy outcomes.[55] In effect, there is little the leadership of a new petrostate can do to avoid a fall into what Auty and Pontara call the staple trap.[56]

Unlike Auty's staple trap model, this book argues that natural resource production is not a trap, but rather an opportunity. This suggestion is not so simple as to argue that the discovery of hydrocarbons means that a state may soon enjoy development and democracy. Whereas the staple trap model presents data that show how abundant natural resources encourage rent seeking and lower rates of the capital accumulation necessary for sustainable economic growth, this book shows that changes occur on multiple levels and at different times in these societies.[57] The staple trap model holds that because oil production is both capital and technology intensive, political leaders have incentives

[52] Richard M. Auty, "Introduction and Overview," in *Resource Abundance and Economic Development* (New York: Oxford University Press, 2001b), 3; Michael L. Ross, "The Political Economy of the Resource Curse," *World Politics* 51, 2 (January 1999): 297–322; Jeffrey D. Sachs and Andrew M. Warner, "Natural Resource Abundance and Economic Growth," Center for International Development and Harvard Institute for International Development (November 1997).

[53] Paul Collier, *The Bottom Billion: Why the Poorest Countries Are Failing and What Can Be Done about It* (New York: Oxford University Press, 2007), 38–52; An early example of this perspective is Alan Gelb et al., *Oil Windfalls: Blessing or Curse?* (New York: Oxford University Press for the World Bank, 1998).

[54] Richard M. Auty, *Patterns of Development: Resource, Policy and Economic Growth* (New York: Edward Arnold, 1995), 19.

[55] Sachs and. Warner, "Natural Resource Abundance and Economic Growth," Center for International Development and Harvard Institute for International Development (November 1997); idem, "Natural Resource Abundance and Economic Growth," National Bureau of Economic Research Working Paper No. 5398 (1999); idem, "The Curse of Natural Resources" *European Economic Review* 45 (2001): 835–836.

[56] Richard Auty and Nicola Pontara, "A Dual-Track Strategy for Managing Mauritania's Projected Oil Rent," *Development Policy Review* 26, 1 (January 2008): 59–77.

[57] Auty and Pontara, "A Dual-Track Strategy," 59. See as well, Richard M. Auty and Alan Gelb, "Political Economy of Resource Abundant States," in *Resource Abundance and Economic Development*, ed. R. M. Auty (New York: Oxford University Press, 2001), 126–144.

to concentrate capital and expertise in one sector. These acts leave the economy vulnerable to the distortions associated with the Dutch disease.[58] However, the staple trap model ignores backward and forward linkages from local firms that service the industry, manage finances, and technological innovations that increase knowledge among a petrostate's citizens.[59] Auty and Pontara's model implies that once caught in the staple trap, citizens fall under persistent authoritarian rule. Worse, this perspective suggests these outcomes are inevitable; once a country discovers oil, the all-too-human tendencies toward greed and the accumulation of power bring dictatorship and poverty. This book contests such determinism.

If oil has any economic or political impact in Africa, it creates institutional conditions that are conducive to democracy and development. In this respect, this book follows a growing body of work that takes exception to the resource-curse literature's compelling picture of an ostensibly stable equilibrium.[60] It is counterintuitive that the discovery and exploitation of oil should necessarily have a negative impact on a country's political and economic performance. Oil is a mineral the export of which earns money. The central contentions of this book are first that African petrostates benefit from hydrocarbon production. To assert that a country would be better off without ever having discovered oil is to suggest that subsistence agriculture is preferable to rent-based economies. Such an assertion ignores the fact that without oil, many African petrostates would be agrarian, subsistence economies that depend on international donors for a substantial portion of their fiscal revenues. The question, therefore, is to what extent and under what circumstances do oil rents tend to cause poor economic performance and neopatrimonial, authoritarian rule, and under what conditions do they allow a country to flourish?

Second, oil can do nothing to determine a country's developmental trajectory. It is a state's leaders who manage the funds that are products of

---

[58] Auty and Pontara, "A Dual-Track Strategy," 60; Benn Eifert, Alan Gelb, and Nils Borje Tallroth, "Natural Resource Endowments, the State and Development Strategy," in *Fiscal Policy and Implementation in Oil-Producing Countries*, eds. Jeffrey Davis, Rolando Ossowski, and Annalisa Fedelino (Washington, DC: The International Monetary Fund, 2003), 83.

[59] The linkages concept is from Albert O. Hirschman, *The Strategy of Economic Development* (New Haven: Yale University Press, 1959), 90–107.

[60] Michael Alexeev and Robert Conrad, "The Elusive Curse of Oil," *The Review of Economics and Statistics* 91, 3 (August 2009): 586–598; Graham A. Davis, "Learning to Love the Dutch Disease: Evidence from the Mineral Economies," *World Development* 23, 10 (October 1995): 1765–1779; Thad Dunning, *Crude Democracy: Natural Resource Wealth and Political Regimes* (New York: Cambridge University Press, 2008); Haber and Menaldo, "Do Natural Resources Fuel Authoritarianism?"; Michael Herb, "No Representation without Taxation? Rents, Development, and Democracy," *Comparative Politics* 37, 3 (April 2005): 297–316; Daniel Lederman and William F. Maloney, eds., *Natural Resources: Neither Curse nor Destiny* (Stanford: Stanford University Press and the World Bank, 2007); James A. Robinson, Ragnar Torvik, and Thierry Verdier, "Political Foundations of the Resource Curse." *Journal of Development Economics* 79 (April 2006): 447–468.

oil development for good or bad outcomes. To assert that an impoverished country that discovers hydrocarbons is worse off than a country without natural resources is naïve. As Ghana and Chad demonstrate, ultimately it is the policymakers who decide how to use oil windfalls. Certainly, the sums of money oil companies pay in bonuses, royalties, and taxes vastly surpass pre-oil fiscal revenues. However, the increase in fiscal revenues has ripple effects that extend far beyond the oil sector. To conflate the impact of hydrocarbons into statistically convenient categories that demonstrate low growth and mismanagement misses the subtle social changes that accompany increased economic activities among non-oil producers.

Third, it is impossible to understand how political leaders respond to resource windfalls without first considering who these people are and the conditions in which they lived before oil was discovered. Preexisting conditions determine how politicians respond to new fiscal revenue streams. In an emerging producer, a frequent problem is that very few people in the entire country possess the skills to negotiate contracts, regulate private firms, and manage oil accounts. Political leaders have to engage industry specialists who can evaluate bids for licenses and contracts. They need geologists and engineers to assess proposed recovery rates and metering. They have to hire financial specialists to manage revenues. Finally, they need competent civil servants to work in ministries. Because people with these skills are largely absent, politicians have to choose whether or not to import people with skills to perform these tasks.

Fourth, petrostates go through phases of production from the time oil companies determine the presence of reserves to their final depletion. The oil sector's "proximate environment" at the time of discovery has an impact on what Porter terms the value chain, or activities that

can be divided broadly into those involved in the ongoing production, marketing, delivery, and servicing of the product (primary activities) and those providing purchase inputs, technology, human resources, or overall infrastructure functions to support the other activities (support activities). Every activity employs purchased goods, human resources, some combination of technologies, and draws on firm infrastructure such as general management and finance.[61]

Where the value chain describes processes in oil production, the phase of production indicates the political environment in the African petrostate. It is the political environment that shapes policy responses to hydrocarbon extraction.

Finally, the resource-curse literature is wrong in its suggestion that presidents cannot resist the temptation to plunder, govern through violence, and concentrate power in their executive offices. The problem with this formulation is its assumption that citizens passively accept nepotism, clientelism, corruption, and routine violence. Such a depiction is implausible; it imagines that

---

[61] Michael E. Porter, *The Competitive Advantage of Nations* (New York: The Free Press, 1990), 40.

people are complacent under an extreme dictatorship that endures for as long as the oil lasts. African petrostates change; these changes are a function of linkages that become salient at the onset of oil production. The increases in disposable capital influence shifts in population and the distributional policies the petrostate enacts as it matures in its phase of production.

Critical Actors and the Phase of Production

The foremost set of actors includes the president and his clan. In Angola, for example, an oligarchy has dominated the political economy since the civil war. Former military officers who came to office following a civil war or coup d'État control other countries. Many are tyrants who centralize decision making and monopolize economic opportunities. These despots have wives, children, siblings, and cousins. As their children mature, they appoint them to the key offices of state. The effect has been that in Congo, Equatorial Guinea, and Gabon, dynastic succession is a key element of clan politics.[62] Clan-based rule signifies the intervention of the president's relatives, often his children, who influence decisions about the contractual arrangements with oil companies, uses of oil revenues, appointments to key political offices, and who enters politics.

In African petrostates, clans dominate networks that have decided who benefits from resource wealth. Collins defines a *clan* as "an informal organization comprising a network of people linked by kin and fictive kin identities."[63] *Clan politics* refers to networks of individuals that capture the state's key entry points and exclude others from politics. It is paradoxical that many children of elite politicians receive their educations in Europe and North America and have been exposed to egalitarian ideas and democratic government.[64] These individuals often oppose, sometimes with violence, any efforts to democratize the petrostate. Indeed, Congolese President Denis Sassou Nguesso's strategies were to create interfamilial links with other Central African leaders. For example, his deceased daughter Edith Nguesso-Bongo was the wife of the late Omar Bongo Ondimba, president of Gabon. Her children, and Sassou's grandchildren, are prominent among Gabon's political elite. Another daughter, Sandrine Nguesso, is married to Joseph Kabila, president of Democratic Republic of Congo, and a third daughter, Claudia Lemboumba-Nguesso, is the wife of Martin Lembouma, an elite member of Gabon's oligarchy. In many respects, these people are representative of a nascent African petro-aristocracy.

[62] Jason Brownlee, "Hereditary Succession in Modern Autocracies," *World Politics* 59, 4 (July 2007): 610.

[63] Kathleen Collins, *Clan Politics and Regime Transition in Central Asia* (New York: Cambridge University Press, 2006), 25.

[64] For example, Gabonese President Omar Bongo Ondimba's daughter and later chief of staff, Pascaline Bongo Ondimba, received her undergraduate degree from the University of Southern California prior to attending the ultra-elite École Nationale d'Administration in France.

none

A second critical set of actors includes the employees of oil companies that explore, extract, and export crude oil from Africa. It is crucial to recognize the diversity of international corporations and state-owned oil companies that operate in this dynamic and rapidly changing market. Standard Oil with its multidivisional and vertically integrated corporate structure established the first business model that firms operating in Africa replicated. Before 1973, the so-called seven sisters formed a cartel of North American and European oil companies that absolutely dominated the international petroleum market.[65] Understanding the history of this cartel and how events forced its dissolution is indispensable for any explanation of events in African petrostates. The cartel so dominated oil production that African politicians lacked autonomy to contemplate reforms without first seeking advice from whichever oil company was active in the country.

Collusive relations were especially evident in the former French colonies. The French state-owned oil company Elf Aquitaine (now called Total) hired executives in France who were products of elite graduate schools, had close ties to national politicians, and developed personal relationships with African presidents.[66] In the early twenty-first century, the entry of Chinese national oil companies changed the international oil market and displaced North American and European supermajors.[67] However, the Asian scramble for Africa's oil has been far less aggressive than the behavior of U.S. and European oil companies after 1974.[68]

Individuals in the non-oil sector represent the final set of actors that both respond to policies and seek to influence policymakers' choices. Often, studies of oil-producing states either ignore or present as an undifferentiated "elite" the people who operate in various corporate groups that seek resource rents.[69] Some of these actors operate as gatekeepers for companies seeking contracts, or regime cronies who form a nucleus that influences policies. Cronies may be merchants, trade unionists, attorneys, journalists, students, and youth leaders; they participate in diverse networks and corporate social groups. At times, their actions legitimate the regimes that dominate different societies. Key to

---

[65] This cartel included BP, Gulf, Texaco, Royal Dutch Shell, Standard Oil of New Jersey, Standard Oil of California, Standard Oil of New York, and loosely, Elf-Aquitaine; they controlled 85 percent of the world's oil. Daniel Yergin, *The Prize: The Epic Quest for Oil, Money, and Power* (New York: The Free Press, 1991).

[66] Karl Laske, *Ils se Croyaient Intouchables* (Paris: Éditions Albin Michel, 2000), 280.

[67] Ian Taylor, "China's Oil Diplomacy in Africa," *International Affairs* 82, 5 (September 2006): 943.

[68] Alex Vines, Lillian Wong, Markus Weimer, and Indira Campos, *The Thirst for Africa's Oil: Asian National Oil Companies in Nigeria and Angola* (London: A Chatham House Report, August 2009): 25.

[69] See Ricky Lam and Leonard Wantchekon, "Dictatorships as Political Dutch Disease." Economic Growth Center Discussion Paper 795. New Haven: Yale University (January 1999). 3; Jensen and Wantchekon, "Resource Wealth and Political Regimes in Africa," 816; Dunning, *Crude Democracy*, 31.

changes among African petrostates is the emergence of a nascent middle class. As petrostates receive substantial revenues over lengthy periods, politicians need to establish agencies and recruit civil servants. A growing number of civil servants, professionals, and salaried workers is indicative of an emerging salaried middle class. These individuals resist extreme authoritarianism because in dictatorships the security of their property and opportunities is problematic. They see themselves as both privileged and worthy of status. However, at other times, these same supporters challenge dictators and demand more inclusive political opportunities. A churning thus occurs as these three sets of actors interact in Africa's petrostates.

The environment in which these actors compete and collude reflects each African petrostate's phase of production and the conditions present when the government receives resource windfalls. If the state has an established bureaucracy, it is better prepared to manage the hydrocarbon sector. The inverse holds as well; if the state lacks offices and procedures, it has to construct them and certain inefficiencies or bottlenecks are inevitable. Among contemporary African petrostates, only Angola, Gabon, and Nigeria entered independence with functioning oil sectors.

The *phase of production* refers to a temporal consideration of whether petrostates are emerging, mature, or declining producers. An *emerging producer* is a petrostate that has only just discovered oil and must therefore create the bureaucracy to supervise the sector and manage revenues. *Mature producers* are petrostates that have been producing oil for extended periods, but most importantly, their reserves are large enough to ensure that production will continue for decades. *Declining producers* are petrostates that have dwindling reserves and must make a transition to a non–rent-based economy. Behaviors consistent with a petrostate's phase of production reflect historical relations that precede hydrocarbon extraction and the inflows of resource rents.

In the immediate period after an oil company discovers petroleum reserves, policymakers have to establish a variety of agencies to manage the industry. An almost immediate task is to set up a licensing board to take bids for exploration and exploitation contracts. This task means that the state needs to have an agency with engineers and business actors who possess the technical expertise to negotiate contracts with oil companies. To complement the contract specialists, the state requires accountants, engineers, and auditors who have sufficient training to supervise compliance with contractual obligations. In most emerging producers, these skills are scarce.

Politicians and civil servants in emerging producers are at a decided disadvantage in their negotiations with oil companies whose highly trained executives are aware of both the substantial risks and potential profits. To manage revenues, presidents and ministers need to authorize accounts to receive revenues at the central bank and decide who has access to the funds. States in emerging producers tend to be small and composed of individuals who belong to the governing clique. Indeed, although the economics of oil production are entirely new to leaders of an emerging producer, arrangements often reflect pre-oil competition among social groups.

At a minimum, policymakers in mature producers have built the bureaucracy to manage the extractive industry sector. They have opened accounts in numerous banks that receive payments. In some countries, multiple banks receive payments contributing to higher transaction costs when the banks transfer revenues to the central bank. In other countries, accounts are in offshore facilities into which oil companies deposit royalties, taxes, and bonuses. Withdrawal rights extend to selected ministers, the president, and sometimes his children and clansmen. Political arrangements among coalition supporters build predictability about the distributions of rents. Meanwhile, in mature and declining producers, relations with petroleum companies are between seasoned politicians and oil executives; these people have interacted for years. Non–oil-sector actors have either achieved some arrangement with the political leadership for contracts and other benefits or they operate in their own niches. Political parties are active in elections, albeit fraught with violence and fraud, or competitive authoritarian voting that predetermines the outcomes at the polls.

Declining producers face multiple political and economic challenges. Politically, governing coalitions support a president who is often an authoritarian ruler. Among declining African petrostates, the president dominates the offices of state, especially those connected to the oil sector. Relations between the ruling clan and oil companies are close and personal. In Congo, the president solicited oil-backed loans that oil companies gladly gave him because they received oil at a negotiated price, usually below market value.[70] These oil-backed loans gave the president money up-front; he then rewarded his cronies and non–oil-sector supporters with public-sector contracts and opportunities.[71] Arrangements between the regime and non–oil-sector actors involved linked strategies of co-option and violent repression. Years of oil revenues have transformed the economies of these poor states; development is evident in the availability of choices to go to hospitals for health care, attend universities, and send children to primary and secondary schools. However, income distribution is often skewed; the presidents create opportunities to reward supporting coalitions that have absorbed new members who are the children of clients.

PROPOSITIONS

As petrostates progress through different phases of production, oil wealth spills over into the larger economy. A regime headed by a predatory tyrant

---

[70] Global Witness, *The Riddle of the Sphinx: Where Has Congo's Oil Money Gone?"* (London: Global Witness Ltd., December 2005), 3.

[71] John F. Clark, "The Neo-Colonial Context of the Democratic Experiment of Congo-Brazzaville," *African Affairs* 101 (April 2002): 171–192.

has difficulty absorbing all the revenues that oil extraction generates. As more revenues enter the economy, the GDP increases, the average annual per capita income also rises, and unanticipated outcomes transpire. These unanticipated outcomes, as discussed, include incremental changes that are consequences of improved health care, better education, urbanization, and demographic growth. With a larger population that has more education and better health, demands for reforms are likely. Political organizations emerge to cater to a new generation's demands.

Clientelist networks coalesce and compete for riches and opportunities created by oil windfalls. Although it is tempting to dismiss such clientelist networks as vestiges of gerontocracies, it is equally plausible that they are elements of nascent political machines. Neopatrimonial authority is dominant in many political machines that are formative political parties operating in competitive authoritarian environments. The political machines constitute the primary components of a democratic shift that has been occurring in fits and starts among African petrostates since 1990, when reform movements in Benin and Zambia spearheaded democratic shifts in Africa. The transitions toward more democratic institutions in African petrostates reflected historic relations among social groups that had taken shape well before independence and the onset of oil production.

The following paragraphs present several propositions to assess the impact of oil production in Africa. These propositions appear prima facie to be hypotheses that the book explores. However, as the chapters in this book suggest, reality is never as neat as to comply universally with hypothetical propositions. The first proposition is that historic relations account for embedded clientelism in African political systems. This proposal emerges from the book's fundamental argument that preconditions are causative in how complex relationships shape outcomes in contemporary petrostates. The second proposition purports that countries experiencing chronic violence continue to suffer social unrest even with the added benefit of oil revenues. This proposition largely aligns with Reno's observation that warfare in Africa has undergone a fundamental shift from struggles to govern a nation state, as in wars of independence, to internal conflicts over control of capital cities and an ability to distribute wealth.[72] Violence is directed internally at competing groups with the aim of controlling states without any particular ideological inclination beyond seizure of political rule and the consequential benefits. Again, this proposition argues that the conflicts in African petrostates build on preexisting conditions, and oil is but an intermediate variable.

The third and final proposition is normative: although corruption should decrease in petrostates, that outcome is contrary to what has happened in the short term. First, it is necessary to adapt the World Bank definition of

---

[72] William Reno, *Warfare in Independent Africa* (New York: Cambridge University Press, 2011), 1–4.

corruption – the abuse of public position for private gain – to suggest that it is behavior that involves the abuse of position for private gain.[73] The essence of this approach is that individuals in both the state and private sector may take advantage of opportunities their positions offer to make illegitimate profits. Having stated that corruption involves an abuse of position for private gain, it is helpful to consider that different types of venality include petty, grand, and systemic corruption.[74] Beyond these distinctions, politicians have incentives to manipulate laws and procedures to facilitate systematic corruption so that their access to revenues from hydrocarbon production and exports remains unimpeded.[75] Such systems are among the most difficult to reform.

Normative analysis would suggest that the increase in revenues should enable political leaders to build a bureaucracy to regulate the oil sector and include agencies of accountability. However, Transparency International's Corruption Perception Index contradicts this normative proposition. With the notable exceptions of Gabon and Ghana, most African petrostates are among the most corrupt countries in the world. What this proposition suggests is that if the agencies to control malfeasance are absent at the onset of oil production, they are all the more difficult to construct. Multiple processes are occurring in tandem; as petrostates develop and become more representative, incentives intensify to build the agencies to control corruption. However, if the state's starting point is rudimentary, meaning the existing bureaucracy lacks basic agencies to reduce malfeasance, it is unlikely given the myriad demands for revenues that political leaders will choose to build agencies of accountability. The state will continue to pay a reputational price for its history of systemic corruption.[76] One need only consider the reputational costs that Nigeria continues to pay despite its government's attempts to reduce corruption through audits and participation in the Extractive Industries Transparency Initiative and an effective anticorruption commission.

Proposition I: History Embeds Behavior in African Petrostates

To understand outcomes in contemporary petrostates, it is necessary to trace continuities and discontinuities from their pre-oil histories. It is difficult to

---

[73] The World Bank, *Helping Countries Combat Corruption: The Role of the World Bank* (Washington, DC: the World Bank, September 1997). This definition encompasses individuals who work in corporations or private companies and engage in corrupt behavior (e.g., insider information brokering) and public servants.

[74] See Susan Rose-Ackerman, *Corruption and Government: Causes, Consequences, and Reform* (New York: Cambridge University Press, 1999) esp., 27 and ch. 6.

[75] John Joseph Wallis, "The Concept of Systematic Corruption in American History," in *Corruption and Reform: Lessons from American Economic History*, eds. Edward L. Glaeser and Claudia Goldin (Chicago: University of Chicago Press, 2006), 23–62.

[76] Jean Tirole, "Persistence of Corruption," Institute for Policy Reform Working Paper 152 (October 1992).

explain how leaders respond to the extractive industries without a sense of the historic relationships among diverse social groups, their interests, and histories. In each state, contemporary social groups animate political economic interactions according to historic relations that predate oil production. By analyzing the petrostate's history it is possible to assess the relative influence of different groups and map their influence in state construction. If a state has few functioning ministries to manage the resource revenues, then funds enter what is little more than a black hole; presidents and their cronies have extraordinary discretion to use the revenues as they desire. This proposition therefore points to the importance of understanding the extent of state construction before oil production commences as a means to trace how the sector shapes subsequent development.

This book proposes that clientelism is both a social and economic response to changes in African societies. Clientelism informs group behavior that reproduces relations of the proverbial "big men" or those patrons who dispense favors and opportunities to their "small boys," or their underlings who serve as foot soldiers and menial help.[77] These networks are present in practically every petrostate; their members generate profits for patrons who control access to key decision makers. In various countries these big men, or godfathers in Nigeria, support the political machines that politicians organize to compete in elections. The political machines comply with formal rules enshrined in articles governing political party behavior, constitutional term limits, and electoral processes.[78] Patrons use political machines to compete in elections; even if they lose, their influence increases with each election. Clientelist networks are therefore building blocks of machine politics in African petrostates.

In authoritarian African petrostates, numerous presidents have over time relaxed bans on rival political parties; they permit labor organizations, and the publication of independent journals and newspapers. Active political organizations are often expressions of patrons who maintain their clientelist networks and party machines. Clientelism is a short-term manifestation of the reinforcement of informal institutions by which patrons accumulate considerable political influence. The clientelist networks are constituent elements of party machines that extend the patrons' influence and access to wealth. Clientelist networks animate relations in party machines and nascent pluralist democracy in African petrostates. Patrons of these networks come from specific regions and ethnic groups; they recruit and retain clients according to ethnic origins and clan affiliations. History, whether real or contrived, forms the bonds that reinforce clientelist relations and the hierarchic composition of political machines.

[77] Jean-François Bayart, *L'Etat en Afrique: La Politique du Ventre* (Paris: Libraries Arthème Fayard, 1989), 268.
[78] Daniel N. Posner and Daniel J. Young, "The Institutionalization of Political Power in Africa," *Journal of Democracy* 18, 3 (July 2007): 127.

The patrons' objectives include the control of political positions that enable them to seize resource rents. However, as a petrostate shifts from being an emerging to a mature producer, spillover effects include a bureaucracy and the entrenchment of elite clientelist networks. When the patrons of these clientelist networks gain political office, they may earn substantial wealth by operating as brokers or gatekeepers. These *brokers* "sell" information and facilitate contracts in exchange for commissions.[79] *Gatekeepers* control access to chief executives, officers of domestic national oil companies, ministers, and presidents.[80] Brokers and gatekeepers control valuable information about the availability of key decision makers or investment opportunities that they then exchange with international companies. Brokers and gatekeepers are generally patrons of clientelist networks that operate as interest groups; they lobby to control areas of economic activity such as contracts to construct oil facilities.[81] The issue is the extent to which the clientelist networks form political machines and nascent interest groups that in turn animate pluralist politics in these oil-exporting states.

Through an analysis of a petrostate's history it is possible to explain the arrangements and compromises reached among elite political actors to understand why certain outcomes occur in different contexts. Before the onset of oil production, leaders of clientelist networks had mobilized supporters for specific political goals. These goals shifted after the discovery of oil and receipt of the first payments of natural resource revenues. In a number of petrostates, competition among political elites was a destabilizing factor that provoked coups, civil wars, or violence. The proposition is that the histories of Africa's petrostates account for responses to oil production. In Ghana, for instance, voters approved the 1992 constitutional referendum that defined republican political institutions.[82] When Kufuor announced the oil discoveries in 2007 – production would begin in 2010 – these democratic institutions had been in place for more than fifteen years. Ghana had the agencies and institutions that augured well for the state's ability to manage the nascent oil sector.

Whereas Ghana's state operated through institutions of democracy, Angolan institutions reflected that it was at war from independence in 1975 to 2002. Angola's tragic history from the time of Portugal's second colonization to its postwar reconstruction sheds light on practices of exclusion that embedded violence in social relations.[83] More than twenty-seven years of civil war embedded

79 Steffen Hertog, *Princes, Brokers, and Bureaucrats: Oil and the State in Saudi Arabia* (Ithaca and New York: Cornell University Press, 2010a), 26.

80 Mamadi Corra and David Willer, "The Gatekeeper," *Sociological Theory* 20, 2 (July 2002): 180.

81 Michael Cowen and Liisa Laakso, "An Overview of Election Studies," *The Journal of Modern African Studies* 35, 4 (December 1997): 73.

82 Emmanuel Gyimah-Boadi, "Ghana's Uncertain Political Opening," *Journal of Democracy* 5, 2 (April 1994): 76.

83 Kristin Reed, *Crude Existence: Environment and the Politics of Oil in Northern Angola* (Berkeley and Los Angeles: University of California Press, 2009), 6–7.

an oligarchy in the state that controlled Angola's oil sector. Informal rules distributed benefits and influence to the oligarchs, who denied the Angolan citizens any voice in the distribution of resource rents.[84] In 2012, ten years after the war's end, presidential elections reelected the governing party and deepened the oligarchs' enduring control. As these cases show, it is necessary to situate development in a context of continuities to understand the trajectories of African petrostates.

Proposition II: States with Histories of Routine Violence Before the Onset of Oil Production Will Continue to Have High Levels of Social Unrest Afterward

This proposition holds that in societies with histories of violence, political actors see violence as a valid strategy to achieve particular goals. In every colony, to varying degrees, coercion was an element of political domination. Where colonial states widely resorted to physical coercion, people in the postcolonial states forgave violence as routine behavior. In effect, the banality of violence in some societies inured authorities to the harm they inflicted on their citizens. Worse, in states that had experienced civil wars, violence became a governing strategy, especially during significant political events such as elections, census taking, or voter registration.

Violence is behavior that shapes political outcomes, and in this specific sense, it is also a political strategy. The conceptual differences between civil conflicts, ethnic violence, coups, and full-blown civil war are ambiguous; attempts to differentiate among these events obscure the impact of violence on common citizens.[85] Kalyvas highlights a need to distinguish the organizations, groups, or individuals that are engaging in organized brutality.[86] First, bloodshed that occurs during a civil war has lasting effects. In Angola, international intervention prolonged the civil war for decades; citizens' wariness of authorities persisted long after the 2002 cessation of hostilities and was starkly evident in the 2012 elections.[87] Repressive policies, summary executions, and routine human rights abuses under Portuguese colonialism preceded the twenty-seven-year civil war and account for a weariness that had set in among the Angolan people.[88]

---

[84] Ricardo Soares de Oliveira, "Business Success, Angola-Style: Postcolonial Politics and the Rise of Sonangol," *The Journal of Modern African Studies* 45, 4 (2007a): 595–619; see as well, idem, *Oil and Politics in the Gulf of Guinea* (New York: Columbia University Press, 2007b).

[85] Christopher Blattman and Edward Miguel, "Civil War," *The Journal of Economic Literature* 48, 1 (March 2010): 31.

[86] Stathis N. Kalyvas, *The Logic of Violence in Civil War* (New York: Cambridge University Press, 2006), 10.

[87] Reed, *Crude Existence*, 54.

[88] Amnesty International, *Above the Law: Police Accountability in Angola*, AFR 12/005/2007. New York: Amnesty International (September 2007).

Second, in societies with lengthy histories of civil bloodshed, violence may occur when organized groups feel threatened and find no means to represent their interests. Into these circumstances step what Bates called "specialists in violence" who use their access to arms and subordinates to cause states to collapse.[89] Falola relates that when the Christian Kataf in Kaduna State, Nigeria, felt threatened by their Muslim neighbors, the Kataf engaged in preemptive violence.[90] Wilkinson finds that ethnic violence in India may be a *planned* strategy by which political leaders try to ensure electoral success.[91] This violence in India resembles events during Nigeria's 2007 elections when patrons of political machines engaged unemployed youth to beat and kill their rivals' supporters.[92] Although the 2011 elections were notable for relatively less brutality, the extreme violence that godfathers incited had become shockingly banal in Nigerian society.[93] These examples put in context the hypothesis that violence has become a routine element of life in some African petrostates and draws its impetus from historical experiences.

Proposition III: Levels of Corruption Diminish as a Petrostate Shifts from Being an Emerging to a Mature Producer.

In principle, secure presidents should receive greater payoffs by stabilizing property rights and enacting democratic reforms than they might expect from acts that repress their people and allow officials to engage in systemic corruption.[94] This normative depiction of politicians' motives would suggest that they have reason to build a bureaucracy to manage oil revenues for future generations. By permitting systemic corruption, political authorities reduce their legitimacy and undermine their ability to enjoy long-term rule. International oil companies that bargain for contracts along with other African presidents of oil-exporting states socialize politicians of emerging producers. They persuade leaders of emerging petrostates to adopt guarantees for private property in the oil sector, respect for contracts, and predictable regulatory procedures.

[89] Robert H. Bates, *When Things Fell Apart: State Failure in Late-Century Africa* (New York: Cambridge University Press, 2008) 16.

[90] Toyin Falola, *Violence in Nigeria: The Crisis of Religious Politics and Secular Ideologies* (Rochester: University of Rochester Press, 2001) 214.

[91] Steven I. Wilkinson, *Votes and Violence: Electoral Competition and Ethnic Riots in India* (New York: Cambridge University Press, 2004), 1.

[92] Human Rights Watch, *Criminal Politics: Violence, and "Godfathers" and Corruption in Nigeria*, 19, no. 16(A) (New York: Human Rights Watch, October 2007).

[93] European Union, Election Observation Mission, "Nigeria: Final Report: General Elections" (April 2011).

[94] Rose-Ackerman, *Corruption and Government*; see as well, Paul Collier and Jan Willem Gunning, "Sacrificing the Future: Intertemporal Strategies and Their Implications for Growth," in *The Political Economy of Economic Growth in Africa: 1960–2000*, vol. 1, eds. Benno J. Ndulu, Stephen A. O'Connell, Robert H. Bates, Paul Collier, and Chukwuma C. Soludo (New York: Cambridge University Press, 2008), 220.

If property rights are ambiguous, then the levels of risk are unacceptable and oil companies will avoid or postpone investments. By the same token, if contracts lack stability, investors will shun high-risk markets. Finally, when regulatory procedures are unpredictable, international firms factor the degree of uncertainty into their contracts. When all three variables lack reliability, investors will expect to encounter corruption in their interactions with the state. In sum, inefficiency in a petrostate's public sector manifests itself not just in high levels of corruption, but in lower earnings from hydrocarbon extraction.

Presidents of emerging petrostates learn quickly from their counterparts in other countries. The avenues of instruction vary. For instance, many francophone Central African presidents joined Masonic lodges in Paris.[95] Their French Masonic brethren socialized them on the norms of doing business with French companies, negotiating contracts, bonuses, royalties, and tax payments. Other avenues of learning are evident in efforts of African presidents to socialize their colleagues. Equatorial Guinea's Theodore Obiang Nguema famously visited with the Gabonese doyen Omar Bongo Ondimba, who played an informal role in Equatorial Guinea's integration into the Communauté Économique et Monétaire de l'Afrique Centrale (Central African Economic and Monetary Community) and its adoption of the franc CFA as its currency.[96] As Obiang had further interactions with other African presidents, the former army chief of staff abandoned khaki uniforms for tailored suits and a presidential demeanor.

Authoritarian rulers also learned strategies to commandeer oil windfalls for their private advantage from each other. For example, given the similarities in particular corrupt practices, it might be reasonable to conclude that their elders taught them to include provisions in contracts that ensured payments into offshore accounts. The absence of bureaucratic controls presented opportunities for a president to protect his access to oil revenues. Such a degree of sophistication was not present in emerging producers that still lacked savoir faire in their relations with international oil companies. The phase of production thus influenced political choices evident in a leaders' tolerance for corruption in the state.

As the 2011 figures displayed in Table 1.2 demonstrate, corruption is pernicious in African petrostates. Angola, Chad, Congo, Equatorial Guinea, Mauritania, Nigeria, and Sudan are solidly in the bottom quartile with the world's most corrupt states. In Angola, Chad, and Sudan, post-conflict states, the impact of war accounts for the partial construction of the states. In other petrostates, extreme authoritarian rulers seize rewards to distribute to their

---

[95] According to Antoine Glaser, the presidents of Central African Republic, Chad, Congo, and Gabon are active in freemasonry and have interactions in Parisian lodges, most notably the Grand Loge National de France (GLNF). See Antoine Glaser, "Un Système du Gouvernement Parallèle," *Le Nouvel Observateur* (27 Janvier à 2 Février 2011): 26.
[96] See among other articles, François Soudan, "Le Mystérieux M. Obiang," *Jeune Afrique* (9 Octobre 2006).

TABLE 1.2 *Transparency International Corruption Perception Index – 2012*

Country	TI – CPI Index (N = 176)
Ghana	64
Gabon	102
São Tomé and Príncipe	72
Cameroon	144
Mauritania	123
Nigeria	139
Congo	144
Angola	157
Chad	165
Equatorial Guinea	163
Sudan	173

Source: Retrieved from http://www.transparency.org.

supporters. Other dysfunctional aspects aside, the most corrupt states confront increasing intolerance among international organizations. This intolerance influenced investment decisions by European and North American corporations and has opened investment opportunities for Asian national oil companies that eschew condemnations of malfeasance in the interest of securing contracts for the oil their booming economies demand.

As political leaders of emerging producers receive more revenues, all else being equal, they should have incentives to reduce looting. Olson's famous formulation holds that with the passage of time, tyrants have economic reason to shift from being roving to stationary bandits.[97] Collier and Gunning use Olson's concept to illustrate the crucial point that looting is hardly a viable long-term strategy.[98] It is therefore possible to hypothesize that as petrostates receive oil windfalls, their leaders should decide to constrain officials who might be intent on looting. In so doing, the leaders create the conditions for greater economic growth. Although evidence suggests that autocrats of many African petrostates have ceased rapacious looting, according to Transparency International, many of these states remain among the most corrupt in the world. Still, even in the petrostates that were among the poorest (e.g., Chad), increased levels of democracy present elements of hope.

However, politicians face two conflicting goals: first, they need oil revenues to fund government expenditures. Second, they need revenues to pay for support they expect from members of the ruling coalition. To optimize the process,

[97] The concept of roving versus stationary bandits comes from Mancur Olson Jr., "Dictatorship, Democracy, and Development," *The American Political Science Review* 87, 3 (September 1993): 567–576.
[98] Collier and Gunning, "Sacrificing the Future," 214.

policymakers must have a banking system to receive payments, and they need a petroleum or mining ministry. If the political leaders chose to negotiate production-sharing contracts (PSCs), they need to establish a domestic national oil company. However, many emerging producers lack both the personnel and the educational facilities to train employees to work in the oil sector. Because they do not have adequately skilled civil servants to manage fiscal revenues from signature bonuses, royalties, and taxes, corruption is all but inevitable. The critical normative challenge is to revise methods of conducting business to shift norms away from behavior that endorses corruption.

In numerous African petrostates, authorities manipulate laws, rules, and methods of conducting official business to implant what Wallis termed "systematic corruption."[99] *Systematic corruption* involves the manipulation of the political system; it is the starting point for many African petrostates. Presidents that came from impoverished backgrounds and seized power via violent means, meaning a coup or military conquest, have short time horizons for their longevity in office. The fact that they came to office through violence erodes their security and therefore they have incentives to plunder to get what they can while they can. In African petrostates, predatory coalitions may include members of the president's clan or cronies who share a desire to deny others any wealth from oil. In petrostates, the receipt of resource rents enables authoritarian leaders to extend their rule because they have the means to purchase military ordnance to combat their rivals and control groups in society.

Regardless of how the leaders come to office, payments for oil quickly surpass an emerging producers' absorptive capacity and create irresistible temptations for even the most altruistic leaders.[100] The availability of funds encourages individuals to try to get access to the money whether through insider contracts or graft. As Auty has observed, politicians have to insulate the windfalls from predatory coalitions in the state.[101] This objective may run counter to a need to reward supporters, and the only available source of money is from oil earnings. Hence, the president uses corruption as a governing strategy despite the fact that the behavior destabilizes economic institutions and correlates with lower rates of economic growth.[102] It would seem axiomatic that presidents

[99] Wallis, "The Concept of Systematic Corruption in American History."

[100] *Absorptive capacity* refers to the bureaucracy's ability to absorb additional fiscal revenues without inefficiencies in public expenditures. François Bourguignon and Mark Sundberg, "Absorptive Capacity and Achieving the MDGs," UNU-WIDER Research paper No. 2006/47 (Helsinki, Finland: United Nations University-World Institute for Development Economics Research, 2006): 1.

[101] Richard Auty, "The Political State and the Management of Mineral Rents in Capital Surplus Economies: Botswana and Saudi Arabia," *Resources Policy* 27, 2 (June 2001c): 80.

[102] Stephen Knack and Philip E. Keefer, "Institutions and Economic Performance: Cross Country Test with Alternative Institutional Measures," *Economics and Politics* 7 (November 1995): 208.

of emerging producers have incentives to reduce the most blatant forms of corruption as the petrostate matures.

Because petrostates are selling a product on the international market, methods of doing business necessarily reflect norms in the global economy. In the immediate postcolonial period, representatives of oil companies developed personal ties with African presidents. As senior executives at France's Elf Aquitaine understood, personal relationships were absolutely crucial to foster sustainable business relations in Africa.[103] By 2000, a growing intolerance toward bribery in international business was evident in the incarceration of Elf Aquitaine's former chief executive officer and several senior officers.[104] In the United States, the venerable Riggs Bank closed after allegations surfaced that its senior executives had facilitated money laundering for Chile's Augusto Pinochet and Equatorial Guinea's Obiang Nguema.[105] Other examples include the successful Foreign Corrupt Practices Act (FCPA) prosecutions of individuals implicated in bribing Nigerian officials to secure an $8 billion contract to build a pipeline from the Bonny Island liquid natural gas terminal.[106] Finally, the Dodd-Frank Act of 2010 applies the FCPA inclusion criteria for companies and requires that international corporations make a public disclosure of payments to foreign governments. These laws have imposed norms of transparency in natural resource extraction that constrain corporate behavior in Africa.

Although it may be in the leader's interests to reduce corruption, if war breaks out or a significant opposition organizes against the regime, presidents adopt strategies to ensure regime survival. These measures include a distribution of public contracts to cronies, strategic appointments to offices that have access to rents, or outright payments to powerful rivals. Leaders are purposive; they agree to particular arrangements according to their calculations of risks and benefits. Every leader learns that his regime must comply with norms that the international oil market defines. Companies bid for mining leases; when doing so, they calculate and factor the risks of corruption into their bids. The effect is that when negotiating contracts in corrupt markets, "intangible costs" are factored into contractual bids before signing the contract.[107]

103 Antoine Glaser and Stephen Smith, *Ces Messieurs Afrique 2: Des Réseaux aux Lobbies* (Paris: Calmann-Levy, 1997), 96.

104 John R. Heilbrunn, "Oil and Water? Elite Politicians and Corruption in France," *Comparative Politics* 37, 3 (April 2005): 277–292.

105 Several high level Riggs Bank executives were indicted after release of the United States Senate Minority Staff of the Permanent Subcommittee on Investigations, *Money Laundering and Foreign Corruption: Enforcement and Effectiveness of the Patriot Act: Case Study Involving Riggs Bank* (Washington, DC: United States Senate Permanent Subcommittee on Investigations, July 15, 2004).

106 Barbara Crutchfield George and Kathleen A. Lacey, "Investigation of Halliburton Co./TSKJ's Nigerian Business Practices: A Model for Analysis of the Current Anti-Corruption Environment on Foreign Corrupt Practices Act Enforcement," *The Journal of Criminal Law and Criminology* 96, 2 (Winter 2006): 503–525.

107 Daniel Johnston, *International Petroleum Fiscal Systems and Production Sharing Contracts* (Tulsa, Oklahoma: PennWell Publishing Company, 1994), 58–59.

Presidents of mature producers understand these costs and have incentives to reduce inefficient and corrupt behavior. One question is why Ghana has been able to avoid the substantial levels of corruption suffered by people in other petrostates. The answer this book proposes is that it is the histories of these countries that account for their behavior after the discovery of hydrocarbons. Ghana was already a functioning democracy at that time and had in place several agencies to discourage and prosecute corruption.

ORGANIZATION OF THE BOOK

The book takes a thematic approach to explain democratic and developmental outcomes among Africa's oil producers. Following this introduction, Chapter 2 presents a historical analysis of conditions in these states before they began exporting hydrocarbons. It concentrates on colonialism and its impact on the postcolonial state. Historical factors are critical for understanding conditions that are present in a country when oil companies discover oil. A given petrostates' response to oil production is a function of their colonial experiences. Variable levels of colonial investments shaped the extent of bureaucratic development in countries that later became petrostates. In the poorest colonies, postindependence state construction posed a serious challenge because the wide configuration of agencies and ministerial controls were absent.

Chapter 3 proposes that the given state's relationship with oil companies stems largely from its history, levels of bureaucratic construction, and changes as the country goes through its phases of production. The business side of this extraordinarily dynamic international market includes private companies, large international corporations, and companies wholly owned by sovereign governments. African bureaucracies in what had been agrarian economies lacked the technical expertise to understand contractual nuances and the complexities of managing multiple revenue streams from bonus payments, royalties, and taxes.[108] Relationships between oil companies and the state reflect historical arrangements. When an impoverished producer first interacts with the sophisticated executives who work for international companies, it is unlikely that contracts will be favorable to the petrostate. Hence, the value chain involves, on the one hand, political authorities who regulate licenses and contracts; on the other, the companies that extract and market the oil. These companies have changed over the years from the vertically integrated corporations that dominated world markets until the 1973 oil crisis to the new national

---

[108] Thomas Baunsgaard, "A Primer on Mineral Taxation," IMF Working Paper WP/01/139 (Washington, DC: The International Monetary Fund, September 2001); Johnston, *International Petroleum Fiscal Systems*; Carole Nakhle, "Petroleum Fiscal Regimes: Evolution and Challenges," in eds. Philip Daniel, Michael Keen and Charles McPherson, *The Taxation of Petroleum and Minerals: Principles, Problems and Practice* (New York: Routledge, 2010), 89–121.

oil companies wholly owned by sovereign governments. An understanding of these changes is essential to an analysis of contemporary developments among Africa's petrostates.

Chapter 4 analyzes how the phase of production – whether a petrostate is an emerging, mature, or declining producer – influences the impact of resource rents on a country's development. This chapter sets forth a framework in which it is possible to situate the activities of oil companies and political actors according to the length of time hydrocarbon extraction has occurred in a given country. To an important degree, a state's capacity to manage resource revenues is a function of the phase of production, and their levels of development when oil was discovered had an impact on revenue management. Indeed, although the economics of oil production are entirely new to leaders of an emerging producer, arrangements often reflect pre-oil competition among social groups. Although with time petrostates established the organizations by which they could manage extraction, exportation of oil, and complex revenue streams, if at their starting point the state was deeply underdeveloped, it was unlikely agencies of horizontal accountability were present to prevent malfeasance and inefficient management. These deficiencies highlight the importance of understanding the level of state construction that preceded the discovery of hydrocarbons.

Chapters 5 and 6 discuss the core themes of democracy and development in African petrostates. Chapter 5 considers the relationship of resource revenues and development in African petrostates. It examines the problem of corruption in emerging, mature, and declining producers. To do so, it discusses allegations of corruption in Kosmos's failed sale of its rights to Ghana's Jubilee Field to ExxonMobil. With the entry of the Ghanaian Serious Fraud Office (replaced in 2010 by the Economic and Organized Crime Office), a remarkable degree of accountability came to bear on this controversy. As Chapter 5 shows, this accountability contrasts strikingly with the clan-based rule in Equatorial Guinea where the president and his clan dominate the oil sector. Finally, the chapter turns to malfeasance and state capture in Congo, where the system of rule has empowered members of the president's immediate family as well as his cronies.

Chapter 6 presents an analysis of the emergence of political machines that animate electoral competition in a growing number of African petrostates. Nigeria and Gabon illustrate the interactions of democratic elections, corruption, and machine politics. It shows how partial state construction under colonial rule prompted social actors to establish clientelist networks that served as the foundations on which patrons built political machines. This chapter explores relationships of corruption and partial state construction, political machines, and democracy in African petrostates.

Finally, the Conclusion discusses the policy implications of development and democracy in African petrostates. It argues that the picture is far more complex than deterministic depictions of development in oil-exporting economies. Across the African continent, population growth has put pressures on political leaders who must accommodate competing demands from new generations. These demands impel presidents to relax the authoritarian structures of rule and permit greater political participation. Meanwhile, oil revenues contribute to a general improvement of living conditions for the citizens. These events have major policy implications for how these states may develop after they extinguish their oil reserves. The conclusion discusses the central argument that conditions in Africa's petrostates have improved as a result of oil production. Economically, the countries are better off with the oil than they were without it. Politically, spillover effects from lengthy periods of receiving oil rents have empowered segments of the younger generations who demand political voice. The discovery and production of oil is a positive event in the long run.

CONCLUSION

This book presents a theory of democracy and development in Africa's petrostates. To develop this theory, the book employs a methodological approach that draws on historical and archival research, an intensive study of newspapers, journals, Internet sources, and selective fieldwork.[109] First, a review of historical literature includes material from archival research and a close reading of secondary literature. Second, analysis of international and local newspaper accounts provides information on contemporary developments. Third, the book draws upon a broad literature that includes work in economics and political science, country reports, and working papers published by the International Monetary Fund and the World Bank, and a variety of reports from nongovernmental organizations such as Amnesty International, Human Rights Watch, and the International Crisis Group. Fieldwork in various African countries, some petrostates and some non-oil producers, complements the review of secondary literature, newspaper research, and deep experience as a development practitioner and student of African political economy.

African petrostates are better off with oil than they would have been had oil companies never discovered the oil and gas. Payments for hydrocarbons influence outcomes, but the mineral in and of itself has no causal impact on policies in African petrostates. It is necessary to several questions about the political economic context into which oil windfalls enter. First, what did these countries look like when they received the first payments for oil exports? What was the institutional structure in these states when oil revenues became available for political leaders to seize, spend, and distribute? What was the extent of development in the new petrostate's bureaucracy, judiciary, and executive branch? These questions highlight the importance of domestic responses to resource rents and the impact of corruption on these societies.

[109] The book places a pedagogical emphasis on inference that it draws from Gary King, Robert Keohane, and Sidney Verba, *Designing Social Inquiry: Scientific Inference in Qualitative Research* (Princeton: Princeton University Press, 1994).

Second, how do various social groups articulate and mediate conflicting interests? The incentives for individuals to join clientelist networks illustrate one aspect of how people organize to gain particular goals. Then, the question arises as to what extent do groups engage in violence to seek their aims. The use of violence by political machines bears many similarities to a history of machine politics elsewhere in the world. This shift in African politics suggests growing pluralism on the continent that reflects the growing elements of democracy in these societies.

A final set of problems involves the various actors in the oil sector. State actors include the president, his ministers, the director general of the central bank, heads of agencies, and clients of these various patrons. The companies extracting oil are critical actors in the country that collaborate to greater or lesser degrees with the president and his associates. Finally, individuals in the non-oil sector are part of the equation for how hydrocarbon production and its consequential windfalls affect a petrostate. Questions include how these different actors respond to the opening of an oil sector. A related question is what influences international companies' behavior in specific countries? How do domestic coalitions respond to the insertion of new international investors and the availability of resource rents? Finally, what are the distributional choices that leaders make, and how do they influence non-oil sector actors?

The developmental trajectory of countries changes after international companies discover oil and when bonuses, royalties, and taxes begin to influence political and economic development. Relative to other economic activities such as cultivation of timber, cocoa, coffee, cotton, and primary commodities, oil has unique characteristics. First, oil is a nonrenewable natural resource. Second, oil extraction is capital intensive and demands significant technological expertise in which international companies have a comparative advantage. Third, onshore and offshore production can have terrifically destructive effects on the environment to which relatively impoverished African states have limited capacity to respond. Finally, the signing of production contracts calls for auctions of offshore mining leases, and loose management of revenue streams in the value chain present lucrative opportunities for corrupt officials. The combination of these elements contributes to a structure that changes rapidly when oil production begins and the country receives substantial payments.

Improved economic circumstances, greater economic choices, and representative democracy may seem unlikely outcomes in African petrostates. Many rulers of African petrostates were former military men who reproduced authoritarian hierarchies in the governments. However, a countervailing pattern was also evident in the regular elections and political organizations active in the civil societies. In response to what appears to be contradictory patterns, this book adopts an interpretive methodology. It cautions overreliance on self-reported data. The countries on which the book concentrates its analysis were among the poorest in the world at the time oil was discovered. Resource rents transformed agrarian, often subsistence economies into rentier states that receive their fiscal revenues from the sale of oil. Accordingly, the chapters follow a thematic approach to show that the effect of oil was not uniformly negative. In conclusion, it is necessary to refine approaches to countries with abundant natural resources to account for elements of democracy and indicators of development.

2

Historic Paths: Colonialism and Its Legacies

INTRODUCTION

Through a consideration of historic patterns, it is possible to detect the antecedents that account for continuities in how African petrostates conduct their business. Any explanation of current outcomes in African petrostates calls for an analysis of continuities from pre-oil periods to the present. This chapter contends that the behavior and political practices in contemporary African petrostates originated in colonial rule. To frame the discussion, the chapter employs a methodology drawn from comparative historical analysis to observe how sequential events led to specific "causal configurations" in contemporary African petrostates.[1] This discussion of colonialism examines how colonial institutions shaped state construction in Africa; it untangles the origins of contemporary political economic arrangements.

This chapter relates the ways in which decisions taken by colonial authorities contributed to inequalities and authoritarian rule after independence. It follows an increasing number of observers who have noted the colonial origins of inequalities and authoritarianism in contemporary Africa.[2] First, the analysis follows van de Walle's criticism of arguments that cite as primary causes of inequalities in African societies such variables as low levels of economic development, asymmetrical distributions of land, or variable degrees of integration into the global economy; it builds on his suggestion that colonial practices are the origins of contemporary outcomes.[3] In their analysis of the origins

---

[1] James Mahoney and Dietrich Rueschemeyer, "Comparative Historical Analysis: Achievements and Agendas," in *Comparative Historical Analysis in the Social Sciences*, eds. James Mahoney and Dietrich Rueschemeyer (New York: Cambridge University Press, 2008), 11–13.

[2] Daron Acemoglu and James A. Robinson, *Why Nations Fail: The Origins of Power, Prosperity, and Poverty* (New York: Crown Publishing, 2012), 335–344.

[3] Nicolas van de Walle, "The Institutional Origins of Inequality in Sub-Saharan Africa," *The Annual Review of Political Science* 12 (2009): 312–314.

of democracy and dictatorship, Acemoglu and Robinson have presented a second explanation of how embedded inequalities have a negative impact on democracy and development.[4] These analyses tend to use broad generalizations that are problematic in their failure to consider specificity of particular cases. For instance, whereas van de Walle's analysis of stunted class formation under colonialism includes variables of partial state construction, the extractive nature of colonial administrations, meagre social sector investments, and relatively high levels of corruption, it tends to gloss over important differences among colonial regimes and within each colony.[5] For one, he fails to consider how behavior adopted by colonial officials served as a model for African leaders who, after independence, reproduced the culture of impunity and imposed authoritarian rule. This chapter corrects the problem of over-generalization by focusing on the differences between British, French, and Portuguese colonialism.

HISTORICAL PATHS

My argument builds on and complements the research of many others who have studied Africa's colonial and postcolonial states.[6] The analysis agrees with Young's insight that "the patterns of the past remain embedded in the present."[7] These patterns are most evident in the partial sovereignty by which European powers imperfectly dominated the territories they had colonized. It follows from this analysis that European colonial administrators governed through many of the same practices as precolonial kings who controlled individuals and expended little energy or resources to control a strictly delineated territory.[8] My contention is that continuities are more evident in African petrostates than discontinuities. Colonial administrations grafted European political institutions

---

[4] Daron Acemoglu and James A Robinson, *Economic Origins of Dictatorship and Democracy* (New York: Cambridge University Press, 2006), 63–64.

[5] Van de Walle, "The Institutional Origins of Inequality in Sub-Saharan Africa," 315–319.

[6] The African colonial state is a subject on which many have written, notably Jean-François Bayart, *L'État en Afrique: La Politique du Ventre* (Paris: Fayard, 1989); Catherine Boone, *Political Topographies of the African State: Territorial Authority and Institutional Choice* (New York: Cambridge University Press, 2003); Frederick Cooper, *Colonialism in Question: Theory, Knowledge, History* (Berkeley and Los Angeles: University of California Press, 2005); Toyin Falola, *Colonialism and Violence in Nigeria* (Bloomington and Indianapolis: Indiana University Press, 2009); Jeffrey Herbst, *States and Power in Africa: Comparative Lessons in Authority and Control* (Princeton: Princeton University Press, 2000); Mahmood Mamdani, *Citizen and Subject: Contemporary Africa and the Legacy of Late Colonialism* (Princeton: Princeton University Press, 1996); Christine Messiant, *1961. L'Angola Colonial, Histoire et Société: Les Prémisses du Mouvement Nationaliste* (Bâle, Switzerland: P. Schlettwein Publishing, 2006); Nicolas van de Walle, *African Economies and the Politics of Permanent Crisis, 1979–1999* (New York: Cambridge University Press, 2001); and Crawford Young, *The African Colonial State in Comparative Perspective* (New Haven: Yale University Press, 1994).

[7] Young, *The African Colonial State in Comparative Perspective*, 296.

[8] Herbst, *States and Power in Africa*, 64.

onto the precolonial African systems. The European colonial state included a bureaucracy with quasi-meritocratic recruitment and partially sovereign regulatory agencies that maintained control through both the threat and routine use of violence. These institutional legacies influenced subsequent behavior that shaped politics in the African postcolonial state.

Coercion was critical to suppress dissent among colonial subjects. In postindependence Africa, coercion is evident in routine violence that is critical to the maintenance of rule for many presidents. These leaders learned from European colonial powers that imposed tax structures and administrations on their colonies without any consideration that there would be a postcolonial period. For example, they established offices to oblige their subjects to buy seeds and tools for agrarian production and other offices to which farmers sold their production for set prices. However, they failed to train managers, accountants, or auditors to oversee the balance sheet of fiscal revenues and expenditures.

The process of decolonization was brutal, slow, sloppy, and venal. Employment in impoverished African states attracted both the ambitious and corrupt; talented entrepreneurs preferred to avoid the state's attention and many fled the continent.[9] The cumulative effect was a bifurcation between a partially constructed state and a dynamic private sector. In many circumstances, actors in this dynamic private sector disengaged from the formal economy and sought their fortunes in a booming, untaxed informal sector.[10] This bifurcation contributed to chronic fiscal crises that drove many independence-era presidents to visit their former colonial masters "hat in hand" as they beseeched them for financial assistance.

Institutional change in African petrostates reflected patterns of behavior ingrained in each country's history.[11] For example, colonial administrators enjoyed a sense that they could do whatever they liked because lax or nonexistent controls facilitated a culture of impunity. This behavior embedded inequalities in colonial society that would in turn influence postcolonial institutions.[12] Postcolonial officials replicated their predecessors' culture of impunity

---

[9] Boone, *Political Topographies of the African State*, 208.

[10] Victor Azarya and Naomi Chazan, "Disengagement from the State in Africa: Reflections on the Experience of Guinea and Ghana," *Comparative Studies in Society and History*, 29, 1 (January 1987): 106–131.

[11] This point owes much to the historical emphasis found in Avner Greif, *Institutions and the Path to the Modern Economy: Lessons from Medieval Trade* (New York: Cambridge University Press, 2006), 14.

[12] The impact of inequalities and the emergence of authoritarianism in postcolonial development is a critical contribution of Stanley L. Engerman and Kenneth L. Sokoloff, "Factor Endowments, Inequality, and Paths of Development among New World Economies," *Economia* 3 (Fall 2002): 64. See as well Kenneth L. Sokoloff and Stanley L. Engerman, "History Lessons, Institutions, Factor Endowments, and Paths of Development in the New World" *Journal of Economic Perspectives* 14, 3 (Summer 2000): 217–232. Their perspective follows the work of Douglass C. North, *Institutions, Institutional Change and Economic Performance* (New York: Cambridge University Press, 1990).

and belief in personal entitlement. The culture of impunity that began among colonial authorities carried over into postcolonial administrations, contributing to heightened levels of corruption and disastrously inefficient bureaucracies.

The colonial state created profound inequalities between its agents and the people they governed.[13] European colonial authorities enjoyed a social status so far above their African subjects that they could rule without accountability for their abusive actions or crimes. From the inhumane forced labor practices of the Portuguese to the horrific atrocities visited on hapless Africans in the Belgian Congo, brutality was constant in colonial states. The constancy of violence and a pervasive culture of impunity embedded dysfunctional institutions in countless African societies. Postcolonial leaders reproduced many of the worst colonial practices in the societies over which they held sway.

Inequalities were persistent and pervasive in the countries that became African petrostates. Engerman and Sokoloff have argued that

in societies that began with extreme inequality, the elites were both inclined and able to establish a basic legal framework that ensured them a disproportionate share of political power and to use that influence to establish rules, laws, and other government policies that gave them greater access to economic opportunities than the rest of the population, thereby contributing to the persistence of the high degree of inequality.[14]

Extractive practices and exclusivity were consistent with the forms of rule that colonialism implanted in many African states. Historical patterns of inequalities and elite privilege were therefore evident in the paths taken by leaders of contemporary African petrostates.

A comparison of Portuguese, British, and French colonialism shows that the African colonial state was never a single model. Instead, considerable variation was evident among the different colonial administrations and forms of government that European powers transferred to Africa. Internal variation was also evident within colonies. For instance, extracting taxes was a common goal for all the colonies. Officials' assessments of potential tax revenues therefore determined the practices of the colonial state's representatives who differentiated between regions that possessed natural resources, commercial holdings, or agricultural potential and those regions with few ostensible endowments. Second, tax payments were higher among urban populations that paid their taxes in cash. Folks who lived in rural Africa paid a head tax and fulfilled obligations required under the widely despised forced labor commitments. Whereas the colonial state was a constant presence in African cities, in the hinterland, a visit from a delegation of highly guarded officials was a rare occurrence and often ended with the seizure of able-bodied men as forced laborers to work on colonial projects.[15]

[13] Bayart, *L'État en Afrique*, 87.
[14] Engerman and Sokoloff, "Factor Endowments, Inequality, and Paths of Development among New World Economies," 64.
[15] This general discussion of tax policy is on the basis of archival research on French-speaking Africa and the imposition of colonial development policies (*mise-en-valeur*), work on British

The stark fiscal realities of colonial rule compelled European administrators to make harsh choices. A certain percentage of expenditures had to pay security and administrative costs. What remained was not enough to develop the multiple organizations that would provide public sector services on a wide scale. Hence, at independence, African leaders inherited partial bureaucracies that could neither formulate economic policies nor resist the demands of key constituencies. Colonial administrators focused on economic extraction as their fundamental responsibility and ignored the needs of African societies. Whereas the delivery of health care, education, and social services were concerns of nineteenth-century European governments, colonial administrations in Africa invested in the social sector only as far as such investments might promise a return. After World War I, austerity policies limited European leaders' prerogatives to invest in the colonies. Hence, at independence, Africa's states were strikingly small and delivered few if any services to their citizens.

THE COLONIAL STATE

In the late nineteenth century, European powers invaded and conquered a hodgepodge of centralized kingdoms, city-states, dispersed realms, and acephalous communities. Once the colonial conquests ended, the Europeans imposed administrations that levied colonial taxes on the subjugated population. Although new boundaries, territorial names, and rulers emerged at the onset of colonial rule, the people acquired neither a national identity nor legal rights. Young correctly rejects the official claims of statehood; European colonial administrations governed through force and not legitimate consent.[16] As Herbst emphasizes, the Europeans were ambivalent about ruling rural Africa and failed to extend their rule beyond colonial cities.[17] They contrived a partial administration complete with new categories for local leaders (notables) and designated as "evolved" the educated minority that served as interpreters for the newly arrived European settlers.[18] Meanwhile, the Africans lived in complex societies with multiple interlinked practices, religions, and norms. As a result, colonial settlers were often aloof and oblivious to the people with whom they were living.

Because the colonial state was a creation of military conquest, it lacked legitimacy and, outside of policies that favored urban developments, enforced little sovereignty. Subjects paid taxes and received little in return. Few colonial states possessed an effective bureaucracy; only the executive branch, in the person of the governor, had any real power. Courts operated through a dual

taxation schemes, and a close reading of the works on Portuguese colonial fiscal regimes that included horrific forced labor practices, described further.
[16] Young, *The African Colonial State in Comparative Perspective*, 43.
[17] Herbst, *States and Power in Africa*, 67.
[18] Frederick Cooper, *Colonialism in Question*, 175.

legal system, one system for Europeans and another for Africans.[19] A paltry number of trained Africans staffed bureaucracies that supposedly administered the colonies; their functional purpose was to assist European officials in maintaining control over the territory. Even in French and British colonies, where, after World War II, the Africans received the right to vote for representatives in constituent assemblies, authorities failed to define formal political institutions. Colonial authorities announced the rules that governed candidate selection and party formation and the Africans complied. It was to these hollow administrations that the French and British transferred responsibilities at independence.

The idea that colonialism was a "civilizing mission" had lost its luster by the turn of the twentieth century; European politicians grasped the harsh fiscal realities of paying for their empires. Conklin relates how French Governor General Ernest Roume recognized the limited commitment of colonial subjects who had only become "French" in the preceding two decades; he objected to "a vision of progress that equated economic development, and more specifically the construction of railroads" with civilization.[20] Such a vision entailed, in a practical sense, the collection of taxes to pay for the railroad and conscription of forced laborers to complete its construction. Colonialism established an economy, but failed to implant capitalism.[21] Indeed, the process whereby Europe acquired its colonies was an onerous form of coercive diplomacy wherein a forceful annexation of a territory followed minor, oftentimes contrived diplomatic disputes.[22] Although the Europeans had gone to Africa to eliminate competition with African kings and merchants, they soon found their colonies an expensive encumbrance.

Colonial lobbies, active in Germany, the United Kingdom, and France, convinced reluctant governments to commit funds, send troops, and, eventually, colonize Africa. The French Colonial Lobby emerged from the 1889 Congrès Colonial International under the leadership of none other than Eugene Etienne, Jules Ferry, and Léon Gambetta.[23] It represented merchants who wanted nothing less than to drive their African competitors out of business. After military conquests, commercial houses despoiled their competitors; firms such as John Holt, Lever Brothers, the Compagnie Française de l'Afrique de l'Ouest (CFAO), and Société Commerciale de l'Ouest Africaine (SCOA) remained active in Africa for as long as the markets were profitable, and withdrew as soon as

[19] Susan Rose-Ackerman, "Establishing the Rule of Law," in *When States Fail: Causes and Consequences*, Robert I. Rotberg, ed. (Princeton: Princeton University Press, 2004), 182–221.

[20] Alice Conklin, *A Mission to Civilize: The Republican Idea of Empire in France and West Africa* (Stanford: Stanford University Press, 1997), 71.

[21] Richard Sandbrook, *The Politics of Africa's Economic Stagnation* (New York: Cambridge University Press, 1985), 42.

[22] Jeffry A. Frieden, "International Investment and Colonial Control: A New Interpretation," *International Organization* 48, 4 (Autumn 1994): 559.

[23] Stuart Michael Persell, *The French Colonial Lobby 1889–1938* (Stanford: Hoover Institution Press, 1983), 8.

profits declined.[24] In many African colonies, especially in those territories with little ostensible promise, European administrations made few investments, and extraction was the primary goal.[25] Indeed, administrations in remote or land-locked colonies were desperate for revenues that were not forthcoming, and the original populations that inhabited Chad, Gabon, Mauritania, São Tomé and Príncipe, and Equatorial Guinea suffered as a result.

Stripped of its ideological underpinnings, colonialism was a military conquest from which selected economic actors in Europe drew direct benefit. Because the goal was to benefit European trading houses or provide material inputs for metropolitan industries (e.g., cotton), colonial administrators were indifferent about developing the territories they governed. In those regions endowed with resources that European interest groups deemed attractive, investments were relatively high, especially in the urban sectors, railroads, and roads for commercial transport. For rural areas that appeared devoid of potential for agricultural production (cocoa, cotton, or coffee) or natural resources (hard rock minerals or gemstones), colonial administrations limited their investments. Indeed, differences between European undertakings in attractive regions and those without perceived value attest to an official apathy toward injecting capital investments into colonial territories with little ostensible wealth.

Having conquered much of Africa, the Europeans built cities in which they could place administrators who were responsible for tax collection and managing labor requirements for colonial projects. However, when rural Africans migrated to the cities, European authorities saw them as uncivilized peasants with little or nothing to contribute.[26] Whereas the colonial state actually governed urban Africans, in rural villages, elders and chiefs controlled people through the religious strictures of ancestral worship and the younger generations' fears of exclusion. Dual authority emerged in African societies; although people obeyed the laws of the colonial state, they also submitted to traditional authority.[27] This particular duality continued long after independence, and in contemporary African petrostates, "big men" dominate clientelist networks they use to capture and distribute wealth in arrangements reminiscent of colonial Africa.

The impact of European rule on different African societies varied according to the potential for settlement or lucrative investments. Whereas landlocked

[24] Catherine Coquery-Vidrovitch, "L'Impact des Intérêts Coloniaux: S.C.O.A. et C.F.A.O dans l'Ouest Africain, 1910–1965," *The Journal of African History* 16, 4 (October 1975): 595–621.

[25] Daron Acemoglu, Simon Johnson, and James A. Robinson, "Reversal of Fortune: Geography and Institutions in the Making of the Modern World Income Distribution," *The Quarterly Journal of Economics* 117, 4 (November 2002): 1235.

[26] Catherine Coquery-Vidrovitch, "La Ville Coloniale « Lieu de Colonisation » et Métissage Culturel," *Afrique Contemporaine* 4 (1993): 20.

[27] Richard L. Sklar, "The African Frontier for Political Science," in *Africa and the Disciplines: The Contribution of Research on Africa to the Social Sciences and Humanities*, eds. Robert H. Bates, V.Y. Mudimbe, and Jean O'Barr (Chicago: University of Chicago Press, 1993), 87.

territories with pastoralist inhabitants received few investments, coastal regions capable of agricultural production were attractive. Acemoglu and his collaborators have suggested that the Europeans chose to settle or establish skeletal commercial outposts according to the prevalence of potentially fatal maladies.[28] This argument presents a feasible explanation for why the vast expanses of Chad, Sudan, Mauritania, and the forests of Central Africa received so few investments. Colonial ministries encountered difficulty in recruiting staff to work in the administrations located in remote colonies. Indeed, an appointment with the colonial ministry was inferior to more prestigious posts with the ministry of finance, foreign affairs, or even the interior. If the colonial ministry lacked prestige, a posting in a far-flung office aggravated the perceived insult.

The French Colonial Ministry tended to attract either people from overseas departments or the least talented French nationals. Among these appointments, better-connected people went to Abidjan, Dakar, Douala, Libreville, and Brazzaville; the less fortunate went to posts such as Fort Archambault, Bangui, Parakou, Port-Gentil, or any of a variety of rural assignments. Many French administrators harbored resentment over stalled careers; they treated the unfortunate colleague who had sympathies for the Africans with contempt. For example, in 1939, a French colonial administrator named Pazat, serving in the Oubangui Colony (Central African Republic), attempted to win salary increases for African chiefs who were earning less than his chauffeur. In confidential reports, his colleagues recommended that other administrators avoid the "unstable" Pazat.[29] Officials would have passed similar behavioral norms from one cohort of colonial authorities to the next with an outcome that French colonial officials' behavior vacillated between coercion and selective kindness. Such practices deepened misunderstandings and inequalities among Africans who differentiated among themselves according to social categories that French colonial personnel defined.

For talented individuals from overseas territories, such as governor-general of French Africa Félix Éboué, the Colonial Ministry was a way to gain entry into the most prestigious ranks of the French state. Éboué, once a former colonial subject, became a French citizen and successful civil servant. He wrote that each African subject has "mores, laws, and a fatherland (*patrié*) which are not ours. We cannot bring him happiness according to the principles of the French Revolution, which is our revolution, nor by introducing the Napoleonic Code, which is our book of statutes, nor by placing our officials in place of

---

[28] Daron Acemoglu, Simon Johnson, and James A. Robinson, "The Colonial Origins of Comparative Development: An Empirical Investigation," *The American Economic Review* 91, 5 (December 2001): 1370.

[29] Lettre Confidentiel, No 104 du 13 Avril 1939, "A/S d'un Secours Hiérarchique contre M. Pazat et Administrateur Adjoint Formulé par M. de Saint Félix Gouverneur de l'Oubangui," ANSOM, AEF 4 (3) D51.

his chiefs."[30] Éboué's wisdom reflected a growing awareness among postwar colonial administrators that eventually they would have to grant the Africans self-rule. His perceptions influenced the modalities of decolonization that began after the Second World War.

Decolonization and the Origins of Preexisting Conditions in African States

Decolonization left a void in African bureaucracies; European civil servants vacated their posts and many of the positions remained unfilled. Although African civil servants were supposed to assume responsibilities for the positions that colonial administrators had previously occupied, gaps in their educations left many unable to perform the tasks. A second issue was that many of the new bureaucrats behaved according to the norms of their supervisors. As the previous discussion implies, many European colonial administrators' competence was questionable. Worse, in many cases, European officials failed to transfer norms of probity and due diligence to their successors. This failure to train African civil servants found expression in dysfunctional behaviors that included absenteeism and solicitation of bribes. As independence approached, competition increased among different political parties and, in colonies such as Nigeria, political leaders accused one or the other party's leaders of having engaged in fraud, bribery, and graft.[31] There were few exceptions to this pattern of recrimination and defense; acrimony impeded cooperation in the soon-to-be independent state.

Political rivalries among African politicians occurred as a backdrop to the economic realities that constrained policymaking and any aspirations for development European administrators might have entertained after World War II. In a number of colonies, the administrations worked to protect access to resources, real and anticipated, after decolonization. Hence, the experiences of different decolonizing states were attributable to a variety of contractual arrangements signed prior to independence. Contracts for production rights remained in force after independence, a reminder that economic motives were the basis for colonialism. Consequently, decolonization varied from colony to colony in terms of administrative decisions and contractual rights.

Many contemporary petrostates gained independence, but their governments lacked civil servants trained to manage even a minimal state much less the multiple revenue streams in royalties, taxes, and bonuses from oil production. The dearth of trained civil servants stemmed from conscious colonial policies; in French Africa, officials resisted any efforts to train people to manage

---

[30] Félix Éboué, *La nouvelle politique indigene pour l'Afrique Équatoriale française* (Paris: 1945), quoted in Franz Ansprenger, *The Dissolution of the Colonial Empires* (New York: Routlege, 1989), 152.
[31] Robert Tignor, "Political Corruption in Nigeria Before Independence," *The Journal of Modern African Studies* 31, 2 (June 1993): 176.

the commanding heights of the colonial state. It was even worse in Portuguese Africa where colonial authorities abused and terrorized the populations. As a result, the postcolonial state was simply incapable of performing the tasks required to manage an extractive industries sector.

The Europeans imposed a minimal state to rule Africa that Herbst called "administration on the cheap"; colonialism satisfied commercial objectives, but provided few public services.[32] Colonial officials imposed austerity measures and failed to train people to work in the state. Hence, the states were without individuals able to make difficult decisions about expenditures, protections for private property, mediation of social conflicts, or negotiations among diverse interests. After independence, they left a cadre that lacked the training to respond to the challenges of an increasingly global economy. Indeed, as van de Walle has observed, "at independence, most countries could count only a handful of native college graduates. The colonial administration was almost entirely in the hands of Europeans with Africans holding at most clerical posts."[33] Fiscal shortages rapidly overwhelmed the paltry numbers of African leaders who might have hoped to construct an effective, European-type nation-state. Their lack of fiscal revenues became poignantly evident by the late twentieth century, as postindependence presidents were incapable of governing and "specialists in violence" used authoritarian regimes to plunder partially constructed states across the continent.[34]

Taxes and State Construction

Taxation was a vexing problem for African colonial states. To administer their new subjects, colonial states required a bureaucracy and agencies to collect taxes. As stated, European authorities chose to govern the vast and sparsely inhabited territories by controlling people rather than economic activities.[35] Europeans reconfigured governing practices as they built an administrative apparatus that depended on coercion. From the African population they recruited a new elite cadre distinct from precolonial elite who had surrounded the kings and chiefs. As Young notes, "The colonial state in Africa lasted in most instances less than a century – a mere instant in historical time. Yet it totally reordered political space, social hierarchies and cleavages, and modes of economic production."[36]

The African colonial state divided society between the cities and countryside; in each, change occurred along a spatial axis endogenously.[37] In effect, agrarian producers experienced a developmental trajectory that differed qualitatively

[32] Herbst, *States and Power in Africa*, 73.
[33] Van de Walle, *African Economies and the Politics of Permanent Crisis*, 129.
[34] Robert H. Bates, *When Things Fell Apart: State Failure in Late Century Africa* (New York: Cambridge University Press, 2008), 16.
[35] Herbst, *States and Power in Africa*, 64.
[36] Young, *The African Colonial State in Comparative Perspective*, 9.
[37] Boone, *Political Topographies of the African State*, 2.

from their urban compatriots that engaged in commerce and small-scale manufacturing. This pattern of endogenous change within differentiated sectors persisted after independence. A critical element of continuity was present in the division between the formal sector petroleum industry and the agrarian sector. For agrarian producers, the elements of change stemmed from climate and shifts in exchange rates that affected prices for inputs and export crops; for the oil sector, resource rents motivated actors to solicit foreign investments and create clientelist networks. In many circumstances, the networks reproduced pre-independence relations with European commercial interests long present on the African continent.

The particular organization by which states extracted fiscal revenues emerged from colonial arrangements for infrastructure and administration. From the first years of colonial rule, officials required African subjects to pay taxes. Shortly after conquering substantial swaths of Western and Central Africa, the French announced to their new subjects that they had to reimburse France all expenses incurred in the military campaigns.[38] In communities unable to muster the cash to pay their new tax obligations, rulers had to assemble laborers who worked under the corvée or forced labor laws. Although precolonial kings had routinely collected duties from merchants crossing their realms, the colonial head tax and forced labor practices were quite foreign. Forced labor provided colonial authorities a pool of workers who could work on railroad and road construction, urban development, and other projects. This labor source enabled the administrations to establish outposts for European trading companies. It is understandable that the Africans widely despised the forced labor requirements colonial officials imposed on their communities.

Forced labor was a norm widely practiced in every European colony, albeit with notable variations. For example, Clarence-Smith relates that in Spanish Guinea, the inhabitants of Fernando Poo (present-day Bioko) that owned more than a hectare of land were exempt from forced labor requirements because their production enabled them to meet their tax obligations.[39] In Nigeria, colonial authorities required that Africans pay their taxes in cash; this requirement forced a percentage of the population into wage labor, especially in the mining areas of the country.[40] Angola's people had enjoyed relative autonomy until the late 1890s, when the Portuguese imposed their second colonialism and passed laws that required anyone who could not demonstrate independent taxable wealth to work for an unspecified period to develop the colony.[41] Those Africans deemed to owe taxes, the Portuguese called *contratos*, or contracted

---

[38] Young, *The African Colonial State in Comparative Perspective*, 45.

[39] W.G. Clarence-Smith, "African and European Cocoa Producers on Fernando Poo, 1880s to 1910s," *The Journal of African History* 35, 2 (1994): 189.

[40] William Freund, "Theft and Social Protest among the Tin Miners of Northern Nigeria," in *Banditry, Rebellion, and Social Protest in Africa*, ed. Donald Crummey (Portsmouth, NH: Heinemann Educational Books Inc., 1986), 52.

[41] Messiant, *1961, L'Angola Colonial, Histoire et Société*, 76–77.

workers; many worked in horrific conditions where a number died. What these various experiences demonstrate is how the need to pay for colonial invest-ments drove European administrations to adopt policies that intensified hostil-ity both to colonial rule and later the independent state.

Investments in infrastructure including schools, health clinics, railroads, roads, and ports required revenues that colonial authorities raised through taxation and loans. As governments typically issued bonds to finance public projects, they punished tax evasion severely by extended periods of forced labor or even mili-tary interventions. For example, when southern Angola's Cokwe people refused to pay taxes, the Portuguese militarily crushed their resistance.[42] Coercive prac-tices were common among colonial customs officials, especially along contested borders such as the mandated territories in Cameroon and Togo, where controls tended to be lax.[43] Independent African governments reproduced these practices because import duties and excise taxes were critical sources of fiscal revenues for states that lacked an active manufacturing sector or abundant natural resources. Among the petrostates, oil rents provided the majority of fiscal revenues and, accordingly, the political elite turned a blind eye to widespread corruption among customs officers, police, and other civil servants.

Throughout the colonial period, tax collection was a delicate process. Announcements of new tax levies provoked strikes and demonstrations as African merchants blocked the streets in Nigeria, Cameroon, Congo, Dahomey, Togo, and numerous other colonies. In 1933, riots in French Togo erupted after the administration announced major tax increases. A colonial newspaper in the Gold Coast Colony exclaimed, "There is going to be a revolution in Togo!"[44] This headline came after three days of protests; colonial troops from Abidjan killed at least 15 people and jailed 500.[45] Reports from administrators suggest that French authorities in Lomé feared the inhabitants of Togo were going to chase them from the territory. In São Tomé and Príncipe, a number of small shareholders called *forros* protested the 1953 decision to increase their taxes. Portuguese colonial authorities violently responded in an event known as the Batepá massacre, which became a symbol of Portuguese repression and contrib-uted to a radicalization of the Saotomean elite.[46] Throughout Africa, protestors'

[42] W.G. Clarence-Smith, *Slaves, Peasants and Capitalists in Southern Angola 1840–1926* (New York: Cambridge University Press, 1979), 95.
[43] Piet Konings, "The Anglophone Cameroon Nigeria Boundary: Opportunities and Conflicts," *African Affairs* 104, 415 (April 2005): 285.
[44] Société de Nations, Territoire Français sous Mandat de Togo, "Renseignements Reçu du Dahomey et Télégrammes Échangés aux Gouverneur de Cette Colonie, " Affaires Politiques et Administratives (APA), Direction des Affaires Politiques et Administrative: Troubles de 1933, Rapports Divers sur les Évènements, Correspondances, Extraits d'Articles de Presse, etc. 1933, Correspondances No. 138, Carton No. 1, Dossier No. 1, ANT.
[45] "Extraits de Presse sur les Troubles de Lomé 1933, APA, No. 1," Carton 1, Dossier No. 1, ANT.
[46] Gerhard Seibert, *Comrades, Clients and Cousins: Colonialism, Socialism and Democratization in São Tomé and Príncipe* (Boston: Koninklijke Brill, 2006), 59–88.

frustration stemmed from a refusal by colonial authorities to grant them any representation; tax revolts continued well after the Second World War.

Tax collection was a fundamental challenge for colonial and postcolonial states even in those territories with substantial resources. In countries with agricultural resources, colonial administrations established marketing boards and distribution centers to tax agrarian producers. This pattern continued after independence; politicians who needed to extract fiscal revenues from agrarian producers made concessions to rural elites to realize that goal. In Senegal, Côte d'Ivoire, and Ghana, Boone shows how national elites expanded political space to accommodate rural leaders and absorb them into party structures.[47] National politicians co-opted local political leaders to control agrarian production and, through the continued operation of commodity-marketing boards, they ensured predictable revenue streams from agriculture. However, in Chad, Mauritania, Southern Sudan, São Tomé and Príncipe, and other poor countries the agrarian base was weak. Except for forced labor requirements, colonial authorities ignored farmers, small-scale merchants, and fishermen who lived in these countries. A consequence of this benign neglect was the urban bias and political distortions that Bates so powerfully characterized in his seminal analyses of rural policies in independent Africa.[48] This ambivalence toward the poorest populations continued after independence and the discovery and beginning of hydrocarbon production, even for those people who lived in the oil-producing regions. The sentiment was that they contributed few fiscal revenues to the government, and politicians could ignore any complaints about the practices of international oil companies. As a consequence, no agencies monitored the oil companies' practices, and in many regions a progressive degradation of living conditions occurred, most egregiously in places such as the Niger Delta.[49]

Taxation, although a necessity for any state, led to colonial practices of routine violence or simply the threat of violence. During the interwar period in Angola, the Salazar administration imposed a reinvigorated colonialism. Portuguese Governor José Norton de Matos imposed severe austerity measures and rescinded the privileges *assimilado* and *mestiço* populations had gained during the nineteenth century.[50] The perceived injustices of these policies encouraged Angolan students to join the Angolan liberation movement. Some, such as Agostinho Neto when he was a medical student in Portugal,

---

[47] Boone, *Political Topographies of the African State*, 328.

[48] Robert H. Bates, *Markets and States in Tropical Africa* (Berkeley and Los Angeles: University of California Press, 1981).

[49] See the now more than twenty studies published under Michael Watts's direction in the Niger Delta Economies of Violence Working Papers Series, Institute of International Studies, University of California, Berkeley (multiple dates).

[50] David Birmingham, *Empire in Africa: Angola and Its Neighbors* (Athens, Ohio: Ohio University Press, 2006), 67.

became luminaries of the nascent Angolan liberation movement.[51] Neto had received his early education from Protestant missionaries in Angola; he then went to Lisbon where he met soon-to-be leaders of Lusophone Africa's anticolonial movement including Vasco Cabral and Amílcar Cabral, among others. They despised the capricious manner with which the Portuguese administrators levied taxes and forced Africans to work on roads, railroads, and other infrastructure projects.

Angola was relatively wealthy compared to Chad, southern Sudan, and eastern Mauritania where tax collection was sporadic and a dangerous enterprise for colonial authorities. Chadian sultans, for instance, violently resisted colonialism; France defeated them one by one during the early twentieth century and established a system of ostensibly subservient chieftaincies.[52] This subservience was illusory. In 1921, colonial authorities in Niger complained that northern Chadian chiefs were raiding neighboring villages in remote areas. The raiding parties would seize men in Niger and then turn their captives over to colonial authorities in Chad to fill forced labor quotas.[53] An understandable nervousness is apparent in these reports; the French had no idea how to negotiate with the warlike sultans. It was easier to ignore them, remain in Fort Lamy (N'Djamena), and work with the southern people they collectively called the Sara. To the French, the Sara seemed receptive to Christianity, responded well to French language and education, and provided leaders such as François Tombalbaye, Chad's first president. However, by ignoring the warlike north, France embedded inequalities in Chadian society that contributed to authoritarian rule and civil war after independence.

French Colonialism

French colonialism in Africa began in the mid-1860s when French merchants built a settlement on the island of Gorée off the Senegalese coast. The implantation of colonialism occurred gradually over decades. First, French missionaries had been active along the coast converting local populations to Christianity. Second, a population of repatriated slaves called Brazilians established trading houses during the 1830s that competed with European companies. The Brazilians were shrewd businessmen who amassed considerable fortunes during the slave trade before the 1851 British blockade. For example, Domingo

[51] See the fascinating interview with the Movimento Popular de Libertação de Angola (MPLA's) former minister of foreign affairs. Mário de Andrade, "Sur la Première Generation de MPLA: 1948–1960, Entretiens avec Christine Messiant (1982)," *Lusotopie* (1999): 193.

[52] Bernard Lanne, *Histoire Politique du Tchad de 1945 à 1958: Administration, Partis, Élections* (Paris: Éditions Karthala, 1998), 14–15.

[53] Rapport de la Colonie du Tchad, 2eme Trimestre 1921. Situation Politique (ANF 200 MI 2134, 6G4). On the raids, Capitaine de Girval, Représentant de Circonscription de Borku-Ennendi, Colonie du Tchad. "Rapport à M. le Gouverneur de l'Afrique Équatoriale Française" 21 Mars 1921, ANF, GG14 200, MI 2134.

Martinez was a prominent entrepreneur in the precolonial Danhomé Kingdom; he became wealthy selling slaves and later palm products. However, his success competing against the French trading house Régis and Fabre would be his undoing. Reportedly, Martinez's wealth evoked the Danhoméan king's jealousy; the king granted the French company Régis and Fabre a major concession for palm plantations that Martinez had wanted. An infuriated Martinez reportedly died of apoplexy, and the king's vassal, the viceroy of Ouidah, confiscated his wealth.[54] This meddling of a French trading house in a kingdom's internal affairs became a pattern replicated in other territories; it was the prelude to colonialism.

Eventually, French trading houses tired of competition with African merchants and unpredictable kings; they lobbied their government to send troops to protect their investments. The impetus to intervene in Africa caused a rancorous debate among French politicians in the Third Republic. On the one side, Georges Clemenceau argued that colonial expansion would be an unnecessary fiscal burden. On the other, Jules Ferry, in his influential 1890 book *Le Tonkin et la Mère Patrie*, asserted that France needed colonies to counter rising protectionism in Europe.[55] Ferry was an able spokesman for the Colonial Lobby whose members coveted overseas possessions for raw materials and markets. By 1900, the Colonial Lobby had won the policy debate, and France established colonies in Southeast Asia, the Maghreb, and West and Equatorial Africa.

After the First World War, the Colonial Lobby continued to pressure the ever-reluctant Clemenceau and his Colonial Minister Henri Simon to finance infrastructure projects in French overseas territories.[56] Given the war's costs and a perception that a colonial empire would drain resources from a depleted economy, Clemenceau and his coalition opposed investments in the colonies. His coalition lost both this policy debate and the 1921 elections. France retained her colonies despite a diminishing capacity to pay the costs of their administrations. Within fifteen years, fiscal constraints would force French politicians to rethink colonial policy. This policy shift meant that France would reduce its colonial investments to pay only for extractive purposes.

Taxes and Economic Policies in French Africa

Long-standing advocates of colonial expansion argued that France should develop (*mise-en-valeur*) her overseas territories by enlisting the participation of indigenous populations. In 1921, the Minister of Colonies Albert Sarraut dictated that colonial possessions must contribute to France's economic recovery

---

[54] David A. Ross, "The Career of Domingo Martinez in the Bight of Benin 1833–1864," *Journal of African History* 6, 1 (March 1965): 84.

[55] Jean-Marie Mayeur and Madeleine Rebérioux, *The Third Republic from its Origins to the Great War 1871–1914*, trans. J.R. Foster (New York: Cambridge University Press, 1987), 94.

[56] C.M. Andrew and A.S. Kanya-Forstner, "The French Colonial Party and French Colonial War Aims 1914–1918," *The Historical Journal* 17, 1 (March 1974): 88.

and finance their own administrative costs.[57] Sarraut dismissed the *mission civilatriçe* and proposed instead to transform the colonies into economically viable territories in association with France.[58] First, Sarraut's *politique d'association* would train a local elite cadre to administer the colonies and work for French firms. France would promote self-government for the colonies, reduce administrative costs, and continue to extract as much as possible. Second, the proposed changes responded to fears in France of Bolshevism and its growing influence in international politics.[59] For territories that the French perceived to have little economic value, such as Chad and Mauritania, authorities favored populations in colonial capitals and ignored the rest. Inequalities that became entrenched in different territories would influence postcolonial developments for decades.

During the interwar period, development meant that through the right policy mix even impoverished colonial territories could pay for themselves. To prepare the colonies for this goal, the French invested in schools to offer selected Africans French language instruction.[60] To their dismay, colonial authorities observed that the Africans did not care about learning French. In 1925, the governor of French Equatorial Africa, Robert Antonetti, questioned education expenditures; he complained that African students had acquired only minimal skills, most could not read or write, and could only speak a few words to impress others.[61] His observations led others in the French colonial ministry to question the efficacy of appropriations to educate Africans.

Throughout French Africa, a small number of European administrators resided in colonial outposts sometimes protected by an armed military presence. Their mandate was to collect taxes and duties to defray the costs of administration. The experience, however, could be terrifying. Indeed, "Practitioners of British and French colonialism were well aware, often to the point of obsession, of just how meekly they had penetrated the vast parts of Africa they had suddenly committed themselves to ruling."[62] Consider the story of a French administrator named Caït, who, in February 1905, the Colonial Ministry posted to Sakété, a rural village in the Dahomey Colony. Caït's orders were to establish a customs post and collect duties from merchants traveling between

[57] Albert Sarraut, *La Politique d'Association* (Paris: Payot, 1921).
[58] Catherine Coquery-Vidrovitch, "Colonisation ou Impérialisme: La Politique Africaine de la France Entre les Deux Guerres," *Le Mouvement Social* 107 (April–June 1979): 51.
[59] Martin Thomas, "Albert Sarraut, French Colonial Development, and the Communist Threat, 1919–1930," *The Journal of Modern History* 77 (December 2005): 918.
[60] Conklin, *A Mission to Civilize*, 80–81.
[61] Gouvernement Général de l'Afrique Equatoriale Française, Enseignement Instructions Relation a l'Application de la Circulaire du 8 Mai 1925 du M. le Gouverneur Général R. Antonetti Réorganisant l'Enseignement en Afrique Equatoriale Française. Programme, Directions, Pédagogiques, Examens (Brazzaville: Imprimerie de Gouvernement Général, 1925) (Paris: Centre de Documentation Française, 8° Br 6421, Inv.37 839).
[62] Herbst, *States and Power in Africa*, 81.

periodic markets in the Dahomey Colony and Nigeria. From the beginning, the people of Sakété rejected the French administrator and his wife who, uninvited, had settled in their village. During a ceremony to commemorate the last king's death, the drums, dancing, and representations of fetishes frightened Caït, who ordered a detachment of gendarmes to disperse the ceremony. The people of Sakété saw the orders as sacrilegious and marched in protest to the administrator's house. When they arrived, a terrified Madame Caït shot several demonstrators. The village exploded; rioters burned the colonial buildings and chased Caït and his wife from the town. Shortly thereafter, troops returned, arrested several of the rioters, and reinstalled Caït in office.[63] An uneasy peace followed.

Such "misunderstandings" as occurred in Sakété were indicative of the serious gulf between African subjects and colonial officials who tried to impose discipline on the lands under their command. During the 1920s, French administrators in marginal colonies received few appropriations, and the Ministry instructed them to impose strict fiscal austerity. In Chad, for example, the French trading companies that depended on forced labor avoided investing outside of Fort Lamy and Fort-Archambault.[64] First, their decisions reflected an assessment that Chad promised little return on investment. Second, as previously emphasized, the violent nature of northern populations terrified French administrators. For the local population, interactions with colonial officials brought little benefit because the administrations had little to no money. Third, France imposed monetary reforms to mitigate the negative effects of the First World War that aggravated domestic tensions and inequalities among indigenous populations.

Monetary reforms imposed after World War I caused social unrest. For example, during the early 1920s, French administrators decided to mint coins to circulate in the colonies. The inflow of coins had an inflationary impact, as paper currency was simultaneously in circulation. Paris issued blanket orders to colonial administrators that they must reduce the rate of inflation. Gaston Fourn, Governor of the Dahomey Colony, complained, "The quantity of paper money on the market is greater than normal needs and coin is leaving the territory."[65] He increased the head tax from two-and-a-quarter francs per person to fifteen francs for each man, ten for each woman, and five per child, and with a proviso that Africans had to pay half their taxes in coins. Fourn equated complaints about the taxes as resistance "to submit to our administrative rules and confirms that the campaign undertaken by certain elements called *évolués* that has continued for several years can bring nothing but problems."[66] His strategy

---

[63] Drawn from the archival reports in Colonie du Dahomey, "Rapport Politique de 1er Trimestre 1905," ANF, 200 MI 1637.

[64] Lanne, *Histoire Politique du Tchad de 1945 à 1958*, 27–28.

[65] Colonie du Dahomey, "Rapport Politique Trimestriels 1921," Première Trimestre, ANF, 2G21-16, 200 MI 1695.

[66] Colonie du Dahomey, "Rapport Politique Trimestriels 1922," Troisième Trimestre, ANF, 2G22-17, 200 MI 1698.

backfired; African merchants hoarded the coins from their colony and debased coins from other colonies; inflation continued to rise and the gap between the colonial state and its subjects widened.

Social Cleavages and Class Formation in French Africa

French administrators separated the Africans into legal categories that included a small number of citizens (*citoyens*) and evolved (*évolués*), and a large number of common Africans (*indigènes*). After 1947, the Colonial Ministry added a fourth category for evolved officials (*évolué notables*). These ranks determined individual rights and socioeconomic rank; common Africans had few privileges or rights. Africans with French citizenship or evolved status were a tiny minority. Bernault reports that, between 1941 and 1946, only 136 Gabonese and 283 Congolese had acquired the status of *évolués*.[67] The practice to limit entry into the elite was a conscious policy choice by colonial authorities whose reports demonstrate a paternalist attitude toward their evolved subjects and disdain for the rest.

From colonial reports it is evident that French authorities felt even if information about Europe was scarce, their innate superiority should spark curiosity among the Africans. When this curiosity was not forthcoming, colonial administrators expressed dismay. For example, in 1939, one official in the Department of N'Gonnie (Gabon Colony) complained that the people knew "nothing of events in Europe and thought of little more than stomachs, their little meetings, and were incapable of reflection."[68] He advocated a reduction in social sector expenditures because it was futile to fund education. As a consequence of such attitudes, the numbers of educated Africans remained few. Herein lies an explanation for the fact that when France granted its colonies independence in 1960, 72,500 French civil servants were working in colonial bureaucracies.[69] When these bureaucrats returned to France, there was no one to replace them. The prejudicial behaviors that had permeated colonial society formed legacies that had destructive effects on the postcolonial states.

Disparities in education funding deepened inequalities between the Europeans and Africans. Nowhere were these inequalities more apparent that in legal proceedings that favored French companies over all others. Even those Africans who possessed language skills and an understanding of colonial law were defenseless in commercial disputes with European merchants. In 1887, France introduced the *indigénant*, a legal system that gave administrators discretion over how they might choose to enforce colonial laws.[70] The indigénant allowed

---

[67] Florence Bernault, *Démocraties Ambiguës en Afrique Centrale: Congo-Brazzaville, Gabon 1940–1965* (Paris: Éditions Karthala, 1996), 90.

[68] Territoire de Gabon, Département de la N'Gonnie, Rapport Politique, 2ème Semestre, 1939. ANSOM, AEF 4(1) D47.

[69] Van de Walle, *African Economies and the Politics of Permanent Crisis*, 129.

[70] Richard Roberts and Kristin Mann, "Law in Colonial Africa," in *Law in Colonial Africa*, eds. Richard Roberts and Kristin Mann (Portsmouth, New Hampshire: Heinneman Educational Books, Inc., 1991), 17.

French firms to seize African assets with little cause. A poignant illustration occurred in 1928–1929 in Congo when Jean Weber, the French manager for the Compagnie Forestière Sangha-Oubanui (CFSO), used the judicial system to eliminate an African competitor. Weber's rival was a Senegalese merchant named Pathé Cissé, who Weber had repeatedly tried to force out of business. To that end, he tirelessly lobbied French administrators in Brazzaville to charge Cissé with illegally purchasing rubber and ivory. In 1929, colonial authorities seized Cissé's assets along with those of other Haoussa merchants they expelled from French Equatorial Africa (Afrique Équatoriale Française – AEF).[71] The CFSO subsequently consolidated its forestry holdings in Congo, at least momentarily free from African competitors. Not a single African entrepreneur could have seen what happened to Cissé and thought they might receive fair treatment in any conflict with a French firm. Such patterns of abusive behavior became a norm that colonial authorities reproduced in other territories.

Political Events and the Colonial State

Before the Second World War, colonial administrators could at their discretion forbid or allow meetings of African voluntary associations. Although French law extended rights of association to French labor and social groups in 1901, no such laws governed organizations in French overseas territories. Officials would promptly arrest any nationalist leaders who dared to challenge their authority. France incrementally relaxed the prohibitions on associational activity when the Popular Front government (1934–1938) legalized African trade syndicates in 1937 with a proviso that members must possess the same levels of education and fluency in French required for status as évolué.[72] However, very few people were able to acquire this status despite fifteen years of the politique d'association. This failure had lasting ramifications for state capacity, which remained strikingly low after independence.

Even under the Popular Front government, colonial administrators who had been conservative appointees were suspicious of trade unions. For instance, a "secret bulletin" in early 1936 raised an alarmist warning: "The communists obey directives from the Cominterm and continue to support nationalist movements among the colonized people."[73] In Africa during the late 1930s, trade unions and political parties enjoyed legal protections on a conditional basis. Indeed, when a series of strikes paralyzed Congo's forestry sector in July 1946, French administrators expressed consternation over workers who protested low wages and a lack of official engagement with the local people's needs.[74]

---

[71] Various reports, M. Laperge, Inspecteur des Colonies, Missions d'Inspection des Colonies 1928–1929, ANSOM, AEF (3) D6.

[72] Georges Lefranc, *Histoire du Front Populaire (1934–1938)* (Paris: Payot, 1965), 306.

[73] "Bulletin Colonial No 1 Janvier 1936," ANSOM, AEF 1 B474 (20 Février 1936).

[74] Colonie du Congo, Département de Konilou, "Rapport Politique" (Année 1946), ANSOM, AEF 4 (2) D79, 1946–47.

Such actions gave French officials impetus to reject applications for self-help groups called *amicales*, trade unions, and other associations given their suspicions of African intentions.

Because urban populations were relatively small, it was easy for the French to control African nationalist leaders. In 1940, the population of Brazzaville was approximately 25,000 inhabitants and Libreville had only 6,200 people.[75] Chad's Fort Lamy, a remote outpost, had a tiny population of primarily Sara people who supported the few politically active individuals in the colony.[76] These relatively small populations made the establishment of political organizations in the AEF – for example, trade unions, amicales, or friendship societies and newspapers – understandably difficult during the interwar period. For instance, when a small group in Libreville petitioned colonial authorities for authorization to establish the Association de Berceau Gabonais, a family planning association, to distribute food aid and financial assistance to needy families, the administration rejected the application, stating, "Present law does not permit such an organization."[77] Because the number of people who participated in the association was so small, the rejection indicated perhaps how tenuously the French felt they held power in Gabon.

Even though French politicians had determined after the Second World War that maintaining their empire was fiscally untenable, proponents of colonialism clung to the notion that France's colonies "belonged to the same *patrie*, and the *patrie* was a big family."[78] But for the overwhelming majority of Africans, the colonial state was an oppressive and violent organization. If elite Africans expressed nationalist sentiments, French administrators clamped down without hesitation. When the Gabonese nationalist leader Léon M'ba publically criticized colonialism, authorities in Libreville arrested him on charges of sedition and sent him into exile in the Oubangui Colony. While in exile, M'ba established links with the Freemasons in Gabon and used informal relationships to regain the confidence of French colonial officials.[79] After the war, M'ba used this confidence to convince French administrators to allow him to convene the "Congrès Fang" on February 26–28, 1947. This decision was curious because colonial officials reported on the conference that the Fang "are entirely against us, but give us their support out of fear. Practically the entire Fang nation obeys Léon M'ba who orchestrates their movements … and, in the name of Fang population, the chiefs elected M'ba their Paramount Chief."[80] By receiving the

[75] Bernault, *Démocraties Ambiguës en Afrique Centrale*, 56.
[76] Sam C. Nolutshungu, *Limits of Anarchy: Intervention and State Formation in Chad* (Charlottesville: University of Virginia Press, 1996), 39.
[77] Territoire du Gabon, Directeur des Affaires Politique, No 611, "Association de 'Berceau Gabonais,'" (13 Octobre 1939) ANSOM, AEF (1) D51.
[78] Conklin, *A Mission to Civilize*, 136.
[79] Bernault, *Démocraties Ambiguës en Afrique Centrale*, 219.
[80] Territoire du Gabon, Rapport Politique – Année 1947, Chefferie – Faits Importants – Assemblées de Chefs. ANSOM AEF 4 (1) D55; see as well the excellent analysis by Bernault, *Démocraties Ambiguës en Afrique Centrale*, 220–221.

nomination and title of chef supérieur at the 1947 Congress, M'ba had devised a strategy to position himself as the legitimate leader to govern Gabon after independence.

Postwar colonial administrators found it increasingly difficult to repress nationalist leaders who challenged their authority. Sending nationalist leaders into exile ceased to be an option. In Chad, for instance, regional politicians emerged to compete in elections when the French granted the Chadians freedom to form political parties.[81] In response to these freedoms, the number of registered voters increased from 308,000 in 1952 to approximately 1,200,000 in 1957.[82] These new voters divided their support between François Tombalbaye and his rival Toura Gaba; later, elite Chadians supported Tombalbaye in his struggle for power against the ambitious Gabriel Lisette.[83] The Chadian experience shows how African politicians had quickly grasped the need to act collectively if they expected to be effective competitors.

Whereas African politicians made significant progress toward political autonomy, indigenous business interests did not enjoy the same degree of autonomy. Even in the waning days of colonialism, administrators continued to sign contracts with French mining companies exploring for minerals. During the 1950s, reports from the *Direction des Mines et de la Géologie* describe the efforts of French firms to locate resources and obtain production licenses throughout the AEF. From a review of licenses granted, evidently colonial administrators made the acquisition of mining licenses easy for French companies systematically denying African entrepreneurs similar licenses. In 1952, for example, the *Direction des Mines* awarded two different licenses ("Type A" for diamonds and gemstones, "Type B" for gold and precious metals) to French mining companies that would retain their validity after independence.[84] Economic opportunities reserved for European firms during late colonialism ensured that French mining interests remained active in Chad, the Central African Republic, Congo, and Gabon after 1960. Such arrangements favored African political winners who benefited from their ties to French investors and the French state, and penalized entrepreneurs who were outsiders.

Portuguese Colonialism

The seafaring Portuguese established overseas settlements in Africa, Brazil, Timor, and Goa on the Indian subcontinent during the fifteenth century.

---

[81] Nolutshungu, *Limits of Anarchy*, 31.

[82] Elikia M'Bokolo, "French Colonial Policy in Equatorial West Africa in the 1940s and 1950s," in *The Transfer of Power in Africa: Decolonization, 1940–1960*, eds. Prosser Gifford and Wm. Roger Louis (New Haven: Yale University Press, 1982), 201.

[83] Nolutshungu, *Limits of* Anarchy, 34.

[84] Direction des Mines et de la Géologie, Conseil du Gouvernement, Affaire No 3I. (20 Juin 1952) ANSOM, AEF (7) D45. Records of multiple licenses granted under this order are present in ANSOM archival boxes from the Direction des Mines et de la Géologie from 1952 to independence.

Although from the fifteenth to nineteenth centuries the Portuguese had limited influence in their African colonies, the overseas possessions were still a source of national pride. In the nineteenth century, Portugal's monarchy reasserted sovereignty over its colonies and encouraged Portuguese companies to invest in mining and plantation farming. In Mozambique, for example, three Portuguese firms – Zambesia, Luabo, and Boror – established copra, sisal, and later sugar plantations that employed African laborers.[85] Other investors in Mozambique included the British entrepreneur J.P. Hornung, who owned the Sena Sugar Company that was a major player in the sugar boom that occurred during the early twentieth century.[86] Although the Portuguese labor laws in Mozambique dictated that all African subjects had a legal obligation to work, some flexibility was evident in exceptions to that blanket requirement.[87] By contrast, the labor laws enacted for Angola and São Tomé and Príncipe were notoriously inhumane and contributed to the emergence of a revolutionary intelligentsia in both colonies. Thus, whereas the colonial authorities in Mozambique attracted investments, Portuguese officials in colonial Angola encouraged settlers to establish plantations but metropolitan mining companies began producing diamonds. The policies pointedly excluded African entrepreneurs.

After the Second World War, nationalist movements attracted a revolutionary intelligentsia across Lusophone Africa. Their leaders, however, encountered violent resistance from Portuguese colonial authorities. At the very time the British and French colonial officials were organizing elections so that Africans could vote for representatives in constituent assemblies, Portuguese authorities were reinforcing authoritarian rule with all its instruments of terror and coercion. In colonial Angola, the Salazar government launched a terror campaign during which Portuguese agents arrested and probably killed any Angolans who expressed nationalist sentiments.[88] Those who escaped assassination fled into exile and conducted their campaigns from Congo-Brazzaville, Congo-Leopoldville, Northern Rhodesia, and Europe. The outcome was that colonial Angola developed a "highly centralized administrative system and a repressive political climate" that served as a model for the post-conflict state.[89] This response to nationalist movements in Angola, Guinea Bissau, and São Tomé and Príncipe had a determinant impact on postcolonial institutional development.

As part of their campaign to suppress nationalist movements, Portuguese officials in Angola opposed social-sector investments and firmly rejected

[85] Leroy Vail and Landeg White, *Capitalism and Colonialism in Mozambique* (Minneapolis: University of Minnesota Press, 1980), 120–121.
[86] Malyn Newitt, *A History of Mozambique* (Bloomington: Indiana University Press, 1995), 408–414.
[87] Vail and White, *Capitalism and Colonialism in Mozambique*, 135.
[88] John Marcum, The Angolan Revolution. vol. II. *Exile Politics and Guerilla Warfare (1962–1976)* (Cambridge, MA: MIT Press, 1978), 2.
[89] Tony Hodges, *Angola: Anatomy of an Oil State*. Second edition (Bloomington and Indianapolis: Indiana University Press, 2004), 48

any interventions by other European colonial powers or international organizations.[90] Authorities in Lisbon steadfastly refused to make educational investments that might have enabled individuals in its colonies to construct postcolonial states. Inequalities in Portuguese colonial societies radicalized a nationalist intelligentsia that emerged in Angola, Guinea-Bissau, Mozambique, and São Tomé and Príncipe. Because officials in the Portuguese government refused to consider even moderate political movements in its African colonies, without exception, every Lusophone African colony had a "revolutionary" independence movement. Indeed, colonial administration in Lusophone Africa was notable for its extractive policies and extraordinarily oppressive rule.

Social Class Formation in Angola

Although the Portuguese first settled in Angola during the sixteenth century, it was not until the nineteenth century that Lisbon recolonized the territory in a process called the second colonialism. In 1822, Brazil gained independence from Portugal and shortly thereafter the monarchy began its practice of expatriating convicts they called *degredados* to Angola.[91] This settler population increased as a result of the monarchy's conscious policy decision and, eventually, more than 200,000 Portuguese in the colony enjoyed a status and lifestyle they could never have expected in Portugal.[92] The settlers were overwhelmingly men who worked as farm managers and civil servants in urban administrations. These people occupied positions for which they had neither education nor training; in Portugal most had been little more than peasants.[93] To stabilize this settler population, the Lisbon government encouraged the men to take African wives and practice "Lusotropicalism," a conscious effort at social engineering noteworthy for its "policy of miscegenation" that was nothing less than forced marriages of African women to Portuguese degredados.[94] Still, a clear social hierarchy developed between the various categories of people who settled in Angola.

Distinctions among the inhabitants of Portuguese colonial Africa resembled the system in the French colonies with their four classifications of évolués notables, évolués, and indigénes. This social hierarchy reinforced the domination of Angolan society by Portuguese colonial settlers who were the administrators, security personnel (police, customs, and military), civil servants, as well as a large number of merchants, plantation owners, and managers. Below the white Portuguese were Angolans called assimilados and the mestiços, who

[90] David Birmingham, *Empire in Africa: Angola and Its Neighbors* (Athens, Ohio: Ohio University Press, 2006), 85.

[91] Gerald J. Bender, *Angola under the Portuguese: The Myth and the Reality* (Berkeley and Los Angeles: University of California Press, 1978), 23.

[92] Birmingham, *Empire in Africa*, 84.

[93] Messiant, 1961. *L'Angola Colonial, Histoire et Société*, 55.

[94] Bender, *Angola under the Portuguese*, 3–18.

Portuguese administrators collectively categorized as *civilizados*.[95] In Angola, the number of civilizados was relatively small; the majority of Africans lived under a social hierarchy that differentiated among the free laborers or urban salaried labor, *volontarios* or itinerant workers, *semi-volontarios*, and contratos who were forced labor conscripts supposedly on contract for one year, or as long as eighteen months if they worked for Diamang, the state-owned diamond producer.[96] It was not until 1961 that Portuguese authorities officially ended the widely detested forced labor system and introduced other forms of taxation.[97] Until that time, volontarios and semi-volontarios lived in precarious circumstances; on the whim of a Portuguese settler, administrator, or security officer, an Angolan was vulnerable to seizure and forced labor. Even worse, the individual might be sent to the cocoa plantations on São Tomé and Príncipe from which, in all probability, he would never return.[98]

Before Portugal imposed its second colonialism, Angola was home to a thriving Creole community of former slaves who had settled in Luanda, Benguela, Moçâmedes, and other towns along the coast.[99] Portuguese administrators ascribed the names Kimbari or Mbari for this mestiço and assimilado population. These people were remarkable because their primary language was Portuguese and they had assimilated many Portuguese cultural traditions.[100] Under the second colonization, Portuguese settlers competed with the Kimbari, who lived along the coast. Around 1840, during the early years of Portugal's second colonization, the Kimbari built the coastal town of Moçâmedes, where they set up trading outposts.[101] A vibrant Creole society emerged in Moçâmedes and other coastal settlements. Prominent families participated in influential Protestant and Catholic congregations, and their children would receive their educations in Portugal.[102] It was the Kimbari descendants who organized and animated the Movimento Popular de Libertação de Angola – MPLA – during the years of anticolonial activity and the civil war.

Portugal's second colonization intentionally suppressed the Kimbari people. After imposition of the second colonization, the urban Kimbari had established several associations in Luanda and Benguela, notably the Anangola and Liga Nacional Africana, which represented their corporate interests.[103] However, in

---

[95] Messiant, *1961. L'Angola Colonial, Histoire et Société*, 69.
[96] Messiant, *1961. L'Angola Colonial, Histoire et Société*, 225–247.
[97] M. Anne Pitcher, *Transforming Mozambique: The Politics of Privatization, 1975–2000* (New York: Cambridge University Press, 2002), 31.
[98] Messiant, *1961. L'Angola Colonial, Histoire et Société*, 233.
[99] W.G. Clarence-Smith, "Review Essay: Class Structure and Class Struggles in Angola in the 1970s," *Journal of Southern African Studies* 7, 1 (October 1980): 118.
[100] Clarence-Smith, *Slaves, Peasants and Capitalists in Southern Angola 1840–1926*, 8.
[101] Clarence-Smith, *Slaves, Peasants and Capitalists in Southern Angola 1840–1926*, 14.
[102] Christine Messiant, "Protestantisme en situation coloniale: Quelles marges," *Lusotopie* (1998): 246.
[103] Messiant, *1961. L'Angola Colonial, Histoire et Société*, 341.

the early twentieth century, Portuguese administrators opposed their interests. For example, in 1912, Norton de Matos attempted to sever the social bonds between the urban Creole, Kimbari society in Luanda and Benguela, and metropolitan Portugal.[104] He contemptuously rejected their pretensions of civilization and refused to recognize any status differences between the Creole population and other African populations that inhabited the colonial territory.[105] Norton de Matos increased taxes and ordered administrators to conscript Kimbari men as well as women into forced labor gangs.[106] These policies horrified the refined Creole dignitaries and contributed to the rise of an intelligentsia whose members grew more receptive to revolutionary rhetoric as Portuguese colonialism became progressively more repressive. Hence, processes of class formation evident in Kimbari identity encountered direct resistance from the Norton de Matos administration.

Portuguese leaders felt that Angola, Mozambique, Guinea-Bissau, and São Tomé and Príncipe should be agrarian societies that would feed the metropole. In keeping with this policy direction, Norton de Matos reduced the already meager funding for education and relegated African education to Catholic and Protestant missions.[107] For the Creole population, education retained a value, and they paid for their children to attend mission schools. As a consequence, the proportion of African students studying in Angola dropped. For example, in one Luanda secondary school, 5 percent of the children were black Africans, 39 percent mulatto, and 65 percent Portuguese.[108] The effect of this policy was a highly stratified society with a large illiterate population. Missions became the recruiting grounds for anticolonial militants. Otherwise, Portuguese settlers dominated economic activities in Angola; at independence, trained, literate personnel were rare, and scarcely 1 percent of the population had received exposure to European education.[109]

In the mining sector, Angolan labor organizers attempted to establish trade union syndicates. However, in general, organized labor confronted a hostile state under Portugal's second colonialism. First, until the abolishment of slavery in 1911, most of proletarian labor (i.e., workers separated from the means of production) had taken the form of forced labor for which owners had to make nominal payments.[110] Considerable variation was present between colonies. For example, in Mozambique, forced labor officially ended in 1878. After Portuguese authorities signed the Witwatersrand Native Labor Association agreement that provided laborers for South African mines, firms had to enter

---

[104] Birmingham, *Empire in Africa*, 9.
[105] Bender relates how even though Norton de Matos opposed the policy of miscegenation, he felt the Africans to be inferior to Portuguese settlers. *Angola under the Portuguese*, 206.
[106] Birmingham, *Empire in Africa*, 67.
[107] Messiant, 1961. *L'Angola Colonial, Histoire et Société*, 94.
[108] Birmingham, *Empire in Africa*, 85–86.
[109] Marcum, *The Angolan Revolution*, Vol. II, 1.
[110] Clarence-Smith, *Slaves, Peasants and Capitalists in Southern Angola 1840–1926*, 30.

contractual negotiations with workers instead of the former practices of forced labor.[111] By contrast, in Angola, forced labor persisted well into the final years of Portuguese colonialism.

Angola's Republican Constitution of 1911 stipulated that Africans had to work, but limited their obligations to two years.[112] These policies were a revision of the 1876 law that stipulated laborers would be "contracted" to work on settler plantations, the diamond mines, or for the most unlucky, the perennially labor-short cocoa plantations in São Tomé and Príncipe. Because Portuguese colonial administrators banned trade unions in Lusophone Africa, it was only in the early 1960s, under pressure from the United Nations's (UN) International Labor Office, the Organization of African Unity, and various governments, that Portugal granted its workers some measure of liberties enjoyed by other peoples in Africa.[113] Still, organized labor in wartime Angola had not attained the influence that might have been expected of the MPLA government with its professed adherence to Marxism Leninism.

Political Events and the Colonial State in Angola

During most of its history, Portugal was a monarchy. In October 1910, the Portuguese Republican Party under Afonso Costa established Portugal's First Republic, thereby ending monarchic rule. The First Republic ushered in a lengthy period of turbulence; Costa was an indecisive ruler who governed through patrimonial networks.[114] The period of 1915 to 1926 in Portugal was politically unstable. Political actors criticized Costa's sympathies for Germany at the onset of World War I; they worried that if Portugal sided with Germany and the Axis lost the war, the country would lose its colonial empire.[115] In January 1915, the military removed Costa from office. Three years later, in December 1917, Sidónio Pais established a short-lived populist dictatorship that ended when an opponent assassinated him. Portugal thereafter lurched from regime to regime until 1933, when Antonio Salazar took power and established the fascist "New State" (*Estado Novo*) that reinforced Portuguese colonialism in Africa. Angola's experiences as a colony under fascist Portugal contributed legacies of authoritarian rule that continued through the civil war and its post-conflict reconstruction.

Administrators serving in Salazar's New State transferred fiscal austerity policies from Portugal to the colonies. The overriding goal was to ensure that

---

[111] Newitt, *A History of Mozambique*, 492.
[112] Bender, *Angola under the Portuguese*, 141.
[113] Marcum, *The Angolan Revolution*, vol. II, 104.
[114] Manuel Baiôa, Paulo Jorge Fernandes, and Filipe Ribeiro de Meneses, "The Political History of Twentieth-Century Portugal," *E-Journal of Portuguese History* 1, 2 (Winter 2003): 4. Retrieved from http://www.brown.edu/Departments/Portuguese_Brazilian_Studies/ejph/html/issue2/html (accessed 14 July 2007).
[115] António Costa Pinto, "'Chaos' and 'Order': Preto, Salazar and Charismatic Appeal in Inter-War Portugal," *Totalitarian Movements and Political Religions* 7, 2 (June 2006): 204.

the colonies provided a profit and protected the supremacy of white settlers.[116] These goals of fiscal austerity and profit maximization shaped administrative priorities; the colonial state violently repressed dissent and imposed rigid labor requirements on African populations. Hence, at the time when other European powers were facilitating the transfer of rule to African-led governments, Portugal was fighting nationalist movements through assassination and a marginalization of rural populations.[117] Demands for independence were nothing less than treason, as the colonies were part of Portugal.

Angola's nationalist movements united briefly under Holden Roberto, who gained some repute when he lobbied the UN to stop labor abuses in Angola. Officials at the UN responded to his entreaties by submitting a request to the Portuguese government to investigate conditions in the colony; the Portuguese refused, stating that Angola was a part of Portugal and not a colony.[118] Roberto then approached the United States, Great Britain, and African leaders at the Organization for African Unity to request financial and diplomatic support. However, external powers would not contribute meaningful sums until the 1960s, which left exiled Angolan political activists dependent on their ethnic bases for support.[119] Roberto received support from his Kongo base; the mestiço, Kimbari, and Mbundu populations provided funding for Agostinho Neto, and the large Ovimbundu group divided its support between the two. By 1960, when much of Africa gained independence, the ethnic and social cleavages that would animate the combatants in Angola's civil war had already emerged. Moreover, the depth of inequalities in Angola proved a source of jealousy and sparked the authoritarian response of the Kimbari elite that dominated the MPLA government.

São Tomé and Príncipe
São Tomé and Príncipe are two islands in the Gulf of Guinea that served as way stations for Portuguese slave traders. Some traders settled on the islands; they established sugar plantations that required a constant replenishment of labor.[120] To ensure population growth, Portugal's monarch encouraged settlers to marry slave women and, by decree in 1515, manumitted these women and their children, thus creating a Creole population that took the name of forros.[121] The forros spoke Portuguese as their native language, practiced Catholicism, and reflected many of the cultural traits of Portugal.[122]

[116] Messiant, 1961. *L'Angola Colonial, Histoire et Société*, 124.
[117] Chabal, "Lusophone Africa," 31.
[118] Birmingham, *Empire in Africa*, 83.
[119] Marcum, *The Angolan Revolution*, vol. II., 241.
[120] Seibert, *Comrades, Clients and Cousins*, 22.
[121] Seibert, *Comrades, Clients and Cousins*, 28.
[122] Malyn Newitt, "São Tomé and Príncipe: Decolonization and its Legacy, 1974–90," in *The Last Empire: Thirty Years of Portuguese Decolonization*, eds. Stewart Lloyd-Jones and Antonio Costa Pinto (Portland, OR: Intellent Books, 2003), 38.

This population resembled the Kimbari people in Angola that developed an oligarchic class structure wherein some forros developed plantations and others a system of small-scale private holdings that produced cocoa for exportation. The forros acquired autonomy and a class identity. Thus, when Portugal sent settlers to Africa during the second colonization period, conflicts were almost inevitable. Like Norton de Matos, the Portuguese administrators who arrived in São Tomé and Príncipe in the nineteenth century rejected the forros' claims of civilization and Portuguese identity.

The Portuguese who settled on São Tomé and Príncipe during the sixteenth century engaged primarily in sugar production. As they found in Brazil, the labor requirements of sugar plantations compelled plantation owners to get slaves from Angola. The *Angolares*, as the Portuguese called this population, worked on the sugar plantations. After 1530, however, slave rebellions erupted with some regularity so as to disrupt sugar production. In 1585, for instance, a runaway slave named Amador organized an uprising that assembled more than 2,000 angolares. They seized the island of São Tomé and set up their own kingdom.[123] It was not until 1596 that the Portuguese captured Amador, who they hanged and left on display as a warning to other slaves.[124] Amador thus became a symbol of resistance to colonialism and injustice among the people of São Tomé and Príncipe. His revolt, however, convinced many Portuguese plantation owners to move their operations to Brazil; São Tomé and Príncipe fell into a lengthy period of low economic activity until the introduction of cocoa and the reimposition of colonialism in the early nineteenth century.

Cocoa production in Africa increased markedly during the nineteenth century. Portuguese colonial authorities introduced cocoa to São Tomé and Príncipe in 1822. São Tomé and Príncipe's competitors were the European and African farmers in Southwestern Nigeria, Southern Gold Coast Colony, and Côte d'Ivoire who had planted cocoa to meet a growing worldwide demand for chocolate. Cocoa cultivation, although profitable, is also highly labor intensive; it enjoys no economies of scale. Plantation owners therefore needed a constant influx of workers to pick the cocoa pods and prepare them for export to Europe. Accordingly, the Portuguese resumed their former practice of seizing workers in Angola and shipping them against their will to São Tomé and Príncipe. Officially sanctioned raiding parties would regularly scour the Angolan countryside and capture any Africans they encountered, bind them, put them on ships for São Tomé and Príncipe, and then consign them to colonial cocoa plantations. The conditions under which these people worked were atrocious.

Angolans, understandably, lived in fear of being kidnapped, although few would have known the horrific fate of those captured as "contract workers"

[123] L.M. Denny and Donald I. Ray, "São Tomé and Príncipe," in *Mozambique, São Tomé and Príncipe: Politics, Economics and Society*, ed. Bogdan Szajkowski (New York: Pinter Publishers, 1989), 132.
[124] Seibert, *Comrades, Clients and Cousins*, 36.

on cocoa plantations in São Tomé and Príncipe.[125] People declared as contratos and transported to São Tomé and Príncipe lived in the worst possible conditions. During the 1880s, cocoa production increased as plantation owners responded to demand from the British company Cadbury Chocolates that by 1886 was purchasing a substantial quantity of cocoa from São Tomé and Príncipe.[126] In 1905, Henry W. Nevinson published a series of articles that appeared in *Harpers Monthly Magazine* that exposed inhumane labor practices in São Tomé and Príncipe.[127] These articles described how Portuguese raiders would capture people in Angola, march them to the coast in shackles, and then put them on a transport ship to São Tomé. Subsequent articles described how plantation owners kept contracted workers in appalling conditions that were far worse than those of slaves; slaves were investments that plantation owners protected by feeding, clothing, and keeping healthy.[128] Contratos cost plantation owners nothing; they were forced laborers who, should they fall ill and die, represented no financial loss; a farmer could rely on a replacement furnished by the administration.[129]

Nevinson's stories shocked Cadbury's Quaker owners, who canceled all contracts for cocoa from São Tomé and Príncipe and shifted their purchases to the Gold Coast Colony. Shortly after Nevinson published his articles, corporate shareholders of other European chocolate manufacturers boycotted cocoa from São Tomé and Príncipe.[130] Firms thereafter signed contracts for cocoa grown in the Gold Coast Colony; cocoa production in São Tomé and Príncipe declined markedly in the late nineteenth century. Portugal's inhumane labor practices had two unanticipated consequences: first, São Tomé and Príncipe entered an extended period of economic decline that only eased after the discovery of oil in the early twenty-first century; and second, the Gold Coast Colony (Ghana) became one of the world's leading cocoa producers.

British Colonialism

In many respects, British coercive administrative practices resembled the colonial policies of France and Portugal. First, the primary motive for British

[125] David Birmingham, "Angola," in *A History of Postcolonial Lusophone Africa*, Chabal et al. (Bloomington and Indianapolis: Indiana University Press, 2002), 139.

[126] Lowell J. Satre, *Chocolate on Trial: Slavery, Politics, and the Ethics of Business* (Athens, OH: Ohio University Press, 2005), 42.

[127] Henry W. Nevinson, "The New Slave Trade," *Harpers Monthly Magazine* 111, 663–667 (1905).

[128] Nevinson, "The Slave Trade of To-Day," part VI. "The Slaves at Sea," *Harpers Monthly Magazine* 111, 668 (1905): 237–246.

[129] Gerhardt Seibert, "Le Massacre de Février 1953 à São Tomé: Raison d'Être du Nationalisme Santoméen" *Lusotopie* (1997): 175.

[130] The companies included Cadbury Brothers, Fry and Sons, Rowntree and Company, and the German firm Stollwerck. Seibert, "Le Massacre de Février 1953 à São Tomé," 174. For an account of this process, see Satre, *Chocolate on Trial*.

colonialism was to protect commercial trading houses that wanted to dominate African markets. Military conquests that preceded the establishment of colonies often followed contrived conflicts between African kings and British merchants. Once they had conquered the territories, the British established administrations and levied taxes to fund colonial investments. The British had few pretensions of civilizing their subjects or integrating the colonies into metropolitan Britain. Instead, the British saw their colonies as commercial endeavors; indeed, between 1900 and 1930, Great Britain supplied 75 percent of her West African colonies' imports and bought 50 percent of their exports.[131] Successive governments granted trading companies considerable leverage and enacted policies to manage the productive sectors in their colonies. For example, the creation of farmers' unions and cooperatives in the Gold Coast Colony, particularly in the cocoa belt, rewarded selected producers who prospered in the colonial economy.[132]

The Gold Coast Colony was among the first Crown colonies in Africa. In February 1874, disagreements over trade accords resulted in the king, called the Asantehene, ordering the incarceration of several British merchants. Major General Sir Garnet Wolseley issued an ultimatum for their release, and when the time passed, he invaded Kumasi and forced the Asantehene to give the British exclusive rights to trade with the Asante kingdom.[133] The real attraction of Asante was the extraordinary gold reserves under the Asantehene's control. In July 1874, the British established the Gold Coast Colony and began to extract wealth from their new possession.

The Gold Coast Colony mined gold and cultivated cocoa for an expanding world market. In 1921, the British began to administer the cocoa-rich western region of German Togoland, called the Volta Region, under a League of Nations mandate. In the Volta region, the British worked diligently to integrate the population into the Gold Coast Colony.[134] Accordingly, administrators encouraged cocoa production in the forest zones where there is sufficient rainfall to support cocoa cultivation. British colonial officials invested in road construction on the basis of the Asante road system. First, this renovation of the Asante roads made it more profitable to ship cocoa via the Gold Coast Colony than through Lomé in French Togo. Second, British administrators required truck drivers transporting cocoa to pay for a card that they would

[131] A.G. Hopkins, *Economic History of West Africa* (New York: Columbia University Press, 1973), 174.

[132] Boone, *Political Topographies of the African State*, 158.

[133] Ivar Wilks, *Asante in the Nineteenth Century: The Structure and Evolution of a Political Order* (New York: Cambridge University Press, 1975), 240. See as well, David Kimble, *A Political History of Ghana: The Rise of Gold Coast Nationalism 1850–1928* (New York: Oxford University Press, 1963), 271–272.

[134] These observations are from British Government, *Report on the British Mandated Sphere of Togoland*, Presented to Parliament by Command of His Majesty (London: His Majesty's Stationary Office, multiple years).

have stamped by officials at "Preventive Service Stations"; the stations were situated at regular intervals along the road to the port at Tema.[135] This requirement meant that even trucks heading to French Togo had to drive west into the Gold Coast Colony to get a stamp before they could turn east toward Lomé. Third, in 1934, the British established several cocoa producers' cooperation societies and marketing boards. The producers' cooperatives distributed fertilizer, tools, and seeds; the marketing boards purchased farmers' cocoa at the port. These boards endured well after independence, and Kwame Nkrumah, Ghana's first president, used them to reward cronies and extend his influence into the rural sector.[136]

By contrast, the legacies of colonial administration are strikingly apparent in British Bechuanaland (Botswana). First, the colony included a responsible executive, a functioning legislature, a cabinet, and a civil service; it was a state capable of developing legislative priorities, passing laws, and implementing rules and norms.[137] Botswana's postcolonial state included a representative government composed of effective offices, agencies of horizontal accountability, and competent personnel. More importantly, the state protected the institutions of private property and engaged in policies that were widely inclusive.[138] When diamonds were discovered, Botswana's state had the bureaucratic structures to manage a significant extractive industries sector. Botswana's experiences demonstrated the attributes of a positive historical development in good administrative practices that endured after independence.

Botswana, a country with abundant natural resources, is an excellent example of how colonial practices influenced postcolonial realities. Colonial officials in Bechuanaland worked to create a sustainable civil service, stabilize property rights, and safeguard private property. This policy stance had a long-term positive impact on the Southern African colony. British administrators were careful to instill norms of due diligence and probity in Bechuanaland. As a result, Botswana's postindependence government defined institutions to "protect the property rights of actual and potential investors, provide political stability, and ensure that the political elites are constrained by the political system and the participation of a broad cross-section of the society."[139] These policies influenced politicians' decisions to require that mining companies pay a modest royalty and specified that the government would also have partial ownership of every mine.[140]

[135] British Government, *Report on the British Mandated Sphere of Togoland for 1929*, Presented to Parliament by Command of His Majesty (London: His Majesty's Stationary Office, 1929), 22.
[136] Boone, *Political Topographies of the African State*, 167.
[137] J. Clark Leith, *Why Botswana Prospered* (Montreal: McGill-Queen's University Press, 2005), 30–31.
[138] Daron Acemoglu, Simon Johnson, and James A. Robinson, "An African Success Story: Botswana," in *In Search of Prosperity: Analytic Narratives of Economic Growth*, ed. Dani Rodrik (Princeton: Princeton University Press, 2003), 80–119.
[139] Acemoglu, Johnson, and Robinson, "An African Success Story: Botswana," 84.
[140] Leith, *Why Botswana Prospered*, 61.

Botswana inherited a bureaucracy of trained civil servants who worked according to norms of due diligence and accountability. When the DeBeers mining company discovered diamonds in 1967, a year after independence, Botswana's government had a bureaucracy able to manage windfalls without major economic disruptions or Dutch disease effects. Civil servants reinforced a strategy to use revenues for development purposes and maintain high levels of government spending relative to Gross Domestic Product (GDP).[141] This strategy depended on the government's ability to strike bargains with diverse social groups and prevented a politicization of natural resource production. Botswana's political leaders isolated the earnings the state received from mining from fiscal expenditures, thereby offsetting inflationary pressures and enabling the government to smooth budgetary shortfalls during periods of price volatility for diamonds.[142] As a result, Botswana's government delivered high rates of economic growth to its citizens and enjoyed political legitimacy. Such a successful record provided a beacon for former British colonies with abundant natural resources. The question is why this level of success failed to occur in other former British colonies.

A failure to reach sustainable social bargains among former colonial elites had a significant impact on postcolonial arrangements in Anglophone African petrostates. For example, Nigeria's military dictators were indifferent to any need for consensus among their citizens. As a consequence, the state had shallow legitimacy; most Nigerians saw it as weak and controlled by group interests. After the fall of Nigeria's Second Republic in 1983, each successive military administration fleeced the government, thereby undermining any sense of legitimacy. General Ibrahim Babangida showed an uncanny knack for making crucial social bargains that solidified and prolonged his tenure in office.[143] His regime, although dysfunctional, rewarded various networks headed by former politicians of the First and Second Republics – "Old Brigades and money bags."[144] The bargains Babangida made with older networks reinforced prebendal politics and protected the clientelist systems that patrons had established in Nigeria's Second Republic.[145] As I will discuss in Chapter 6, these clientelist systems are the foundations of political machines that lent such turbulence to Nigeria's development in the twenty-first century. Distributional patterns represented important continuities in Nigeria that persisted after colonial rule.

[141] Dani Rodrik, *One Economics Many Recipes: Globalization, Institutions, and Economic Growth* (Princeton: Princeton University Press, 2007), 39.
[142] Leith, *Why Botswana Prospered*, 84.
[143] Peter M. Lewis, "From Prebendalism to Predation: The Political Economy of Decline in Nigeria," *The Journal of Modern African Studies* 34, 1 (March 1996): 87–88.
[144] William Reno, "Old Brigades, Money Bags, New Breeds, and the Ironies of Reform in Nigeria," *Canadian Journal of African Studies* 27, 1 (April 1993), 67.
[145] Richard Joseph, *Democracy and Prebendal Politics in Nigeria: The Rise and Fall of the Second Republic* (New York: Cambridge University Press, 1987), 58–59.

Social Class Formation in British Africa: Nigeria

Among the challenges confounding British policy outcomes in Africa was the sheer size of the empire's colonial holdings on the continent. British territories were vast logistical nightmares for administrations. The impetus for the colonial empire came from the trading houses that searched for precious metals, agricultural opportunities, and trade. In the mid-nineteenth century, the British established the Lagos Protectorate to control commercial maritime routes off the West African coast.[146] When the British consul, Campbell, arrived in Lagos in 1853, he complained about a large population engaged in lively commerce that competed against the British trading companies.[147] This competition could not endure when British houses entered the markets. For instance, British firms operating along the Niger River systematically displaced precolonial African firms that had dominated the trade. Consider King Ockiya of Nembe's impassioned 1877 plea to British administrators in Lagos:

> Many years ago we used to make our living by selling slaves to Europeans which was stopped by your Government and a Treaty made between you and our country.... Some years ago the White men began trading on the Niger with the intention of opening up this river, this did us no harm ... but lately within the last six years they have begun putting trading Stations at our places and consequences [sic] they have stopped our trade completely. .... This means starvation to my people as well as Natives under my rule I have about 8,000 people and there are another 8,000 in the lower part of the Niger suffering with me.[148]

His pleas went unanswered, and the Royal Niger Company continued to build outposts north of Ilorin.[149] It was an inexorable process; by 1900, the Royal Niger Company had established a monopoly in Southern Nigeria that forced most African exporters out of business.[150] In time, a class of merchants would recognize their mutual goals; they organized as middlemen to compete against British firms operating on the Niger River.

British trading houses dominated retail outlets and the purchase of raw materials. Between 1900 and 1920, the Royal Niger Company lobbied to obtain a charter that gave the company a monopoly over commerce on the Niger River; it expanded its trading posts in the Nigerian interior from forty-two to

---

[146] Robert Smith, *The Lagos Consulate 1851–1861* (Berkeley and Los Angeles: University of California Press, 1979).

[147] Jean Herskovitts Kopytoff, *A Preface to Modern Nigeria: The "Sierra Leonians" in Yoruba, 1830–1890* (Madison: The University of Wisconsin Press, 1965), 86.

[148] "King Ockiya and Chiefs of Brass (Nembe) to Lord Derby: Niger Trade, 21 February 1877," in *British Policy towards West Africa: Selected Documents 1875–1914 with Statistical Appendices 1800–1914*, ed. C.W. Newbury (London: Oxford at the Clarendon Press, 1971), 95.

[149] Margery Perham and Mary Bull, eds., *Frederick Lugard, The Diaries of Lord Lugard*, vol. 4, *Nigeria, 1894–5 and 1898*, (Evanston, IL: Northwestern University Press, 1963), 26–39.

[150] Tom Forrest, *The Advance of African Capital: The Growth of Nigerian Private Enterprise* (Charlottesville: University Press of Virginia, 1994), 13.

fifty-four.[151] This arrangement excluded African merchants from the lucrative river trade. More pertinently, by granting rights to corporations registered in London, British merchants could ignore complaints from African competitors unable to represent themselves in British courts; by 1914, the competitive position of African businessmen had substantially deteriorated.[152] Whereas Nigerian trading companies that might have wanted to compete with British houses lost market share, African firms emerged as middlemen to take advantage of commercial opportunities in the river trade where they did not compete with the British.[153] Contracts with these middlemen displaced older trading arrangements by which chiefs profited from commerce on the Niger River. This shift, in turn, had an impact on political bargains that dated to precolonial Nigeria.

Colonial administrators paid considerable attention to their need to extract revenues from agrarian production, especially through the cultivation of palm oil, rubber, and cocoa. Palm oil production increased in value significantly during the nineteenth century. Companies such as Great Britain's Palmolive and the French firm Régis & Fabre established outposts along the West African coast to purchase palm oil for the growing European market in soaps and detergents. Meanwhile, other British, French, and German companies looked for profitable tropical commodities. For example, in the late nineteenth century, a brief boom occurred in Nigeria when wild rubber production jumped from 56 pounds in 1893 to 5,867 in 1894; 5,069,577 pounds in 1895; and then peaked in 1896 at 6,484,363.[154] What ended the rubber boom in 1897 was the shift of production to Brazil and Liberia; Nigerian farmers turned to planting cocoa. Devastating losses exposed farmers to the volatilities present in international markets; such lessons would be relearned during postindependence oil booms and busts.

Political Events and British Colonialism in Nigeria
Colonial administration in Nigeria presented a complex set of problems because of the incremental fashion in which the British colonized the territory. First, the British converted the Lagos protectorate into a crown colony before colonizing the rest of Nigeria. Second, the British governed Nigeria through a system of rule that Lugard devised to "retain native authority" and "work through and by the native emirs. At the same time it is feasible by degree to bring them gradually into approximation with our ideas of justice and humanity."[155] Lugard

[151] Colin Newbury, "Trade and Technology in West Africa: The Case of the Niger Company, 1900–1920," *The Journal of African History* 19, 4 (October 1978): 551–575.
[152] A.G. Hopkins, "Economic Aspects of Political Movements in Nigeria and in the Gold Coast 1918–1939," *The Journal of African History* 7, 1 (January 1966): 134.
[153] Forrest, *The Advance of African Capital*, 17.
[154] Sara S. Berry, *Cocoa, Custom, and Socioeconomic Change in Rural Western Nigeria* (New York: Oxford University Press, 1975), 29.
[155] Lord Fredrick Lugard, quoted in Margery Perham, *Lugard: The Maker of Modern Nigeria: The Years of Authority 1898–1945* (Hamden, CT: Archon Books, 1968), 140.

devised this system of so-called indirect rule as a means to include northern Nigerian authorities in the legislative administration of the crown colony; colonialism in Southern Nigeria was far more ubiquitous.[156] The British system of native administration effectively "left intact the essential institutions of traditional government in the emirates for the time when Northern Nigeria confronted a fundamentally new objective of colonial rule – namely to introduce and develop democratically representative institutions of government" as political norms.[157] The effect of indirect rule in Northern Nigeria was to empower the four most important chiefs – the Sultan of Sokoto, Emir of Kano, Emir of Katsina, and Aku Uka of Wukari – and grant them the status of ministers without portfolio.[158]

Difficult choices confronted the British regarding how they would administer the territories under their control, especially in more desolate settings that reflected shortages both in fiscal revenues and competent personnel.[159] By granting territorial leaders a degree of autonomy, the British established circumstances wherein leaders were able to protect their discretionary prerogatives. The Nigeria colony comprised three administrative units: Lagos, Northern Provinces, Southern Provinces, and, after 1922, the addition of the Cameroons Mandate. In 1939, the British expanded the colony to five units: Lagos, Northern Region, Western Region, Eastern Region, and provisional Cameroons Trust Territory. A slow process of including Nigerian dignitaries in the administration occurred after World War II.

Participation in the governing structures meant nothing less than control over patronage positions and state largess. First, political elites used their positions to allocate jobs, money, and access to public contracts to their clients.[160] Nigeria's 1957 constitution established rules that favored the North and denied the divided Southern peoples outlets to articulate their political aspirations. Second, substantial differences emerged in social sector expenditures between cities where the colonial state was more effective at influencing social groups and rural communities that received limited appropriations. This favoritism of urban populations persisted well after oil became the major source of fiscal revenues and agrarian production was of marginal importance to the state.

[156] James S. Coleman, *Nigeria: Background to Nationalism* (Berkeley and Los Angeles: University of California Press, 1958), 46; Peter M. Lewis, *Growing Apart: Oil, Politics, and Economic Change in Indonesia and Nigeria* (Ann Arbor: University of Michigan Press, 2007), 126.
[157] C.S. Whitaker, *The Politics of Tradition, Continuity and Change in Northern Nigeria 1946–1966* (Princeton: Princeton University Press, 1970), 28.
[158] Richard L. Sklar, *Nigerian Political Parties: Power in an Emergent African Nation* (Princeton: Princeton University Press, 1963), 443.
[159] Cooper, *Colonialism in Question*, 166–167.
[160] Lewis, *Growing Apart*, 130.

Nigeria as an Emerging Petrostate

Explorations for hydrocarbons began in Nigeria in 1907 when John Simon Bergheim set up the Nigerian Bitumen Corporation to drill wells near Lagos.[161] Initial drillings were unsuccessful; still, in 1914, shortly before the outbreak of World War I, British authorities passed the Colonial Mineral Ordinance that restricted leases and licenses to British companies and subjects. Postwar reconstruction and the Great Depression postponed further developments until 1937, when Shell merged with British Petroleum (BP) and obtained a grant for exclusive exploration and mining rights in all of Nigeria. Initial explorations were unproductive. Shell-BP turned their attentions to the Middle East and Central Asia, where they were far more successful. However, by the 1950s companies were again exploring for oil in Nigeria.

During the late colonial period, geologists ascertained that Nigeria's coastal region probably contained significant petroleum reserves. However, it was not until 1956 when drilling near a village called Olibori in the Niger Delta basin found what appeared to be a significant hydrocarbon reservoir.[162] Shell-BP announced the find, and by the time exports began from installations in Port Harcourt, a large number of oil companies had obtained exploration leases.[163] More announcements of significant reserves followed; many of these companies partnered with Shell-BP.[164] BP and Shell split in 1975 with a proviso that Shell would retain the investments in Nigeria. Shell currently manages these holdings through two firms, the Shell Companies in Nigeria and Shell Petroleum Development Company of Nigeria Limited. These companies have operated with a sometimes-breathtaking contempt for people living in the Niger Delta.

Nigeria is a country with many contradictions. Although it began to receive substantial oil revenues in 1960, the watershed year was 1974, when world oil prices quadrupled. Since then, successive military and civilian governments have squandered the earnings and created legacies of corruption. The effects of billions of dollars in oil wealth lost to corruption have left common Nigerians apathetic as they go through their daily struggles simply to find enough to eat.[165] However, its economy is extraordinarily dynamic as evident from numerous Nigerians who are clever business actors operating worldwide. It is a country with contrasting, and even contradictory, levels of performance and inequality. These contradictions reflect legacies of colonial rule that made

[161] Jedrzej George Frynas, *Oil in Nigeria: Conflict and Litigation between Oil Companies and Village Communities* (Piscataway, NJ: Transaction Publishers, 2000) 9.
[162] Sarah Ahmad Khan, *Nigeria: The Political Economy of Oil* (Oxford: Oxford University Press, 1994), 39.
[163] Scott R. Pearson, *Petroleum and the Nigerian Economy* (Stanford: Stanford University Press, 1970), 15.
[164] Khan, *Nigeria*, 16.
[165] Wale Adebanwi and Ebenezer Obadare, "When Corruption Fights Back: Democracy and Elite Interest in Nigeria's Anti-Corruption War," *The Journal of Modern African Studies* 49, 1 (June 2011): 190.

accommodations for a highly diverse population. In the late twentieth century, routine violence and inequalities posed significant challenges for Nigeria's future development.

CONCLUSION

This chapter has examined the different colonial experiences among Africa's petrostates. It sets a backdrop for the book's larger argument that it is the circumstances when oil is discovered that shapes a state's management of natural resource wealth. Institutions established during colonial rule formed models that shaped postcolonial states. These institutions represent more continuity than discontinuity. Indeed, the practices that European colonial powers used to administer their particular colonies had enduring legacies. In effect, the chapter agrees that colonialism was little more than an extractive system established to enrich European capitalism.[166] In remote or difficult territories, the Europeans left skeletal administrations that operated through extractive practices. For instance, for French administrators a posting to the Chad or Oubangui-Chari colonies was tantamount to exile. How the Europeans governed their colonies, or ignored them, was crucial to postcolonial state construction and the state's subsequent capacity to interact with oil companies and manage revenues.

This chapter has described inequalities that colonialism embedded in African societies. These inequalities influenced outcomes and petrostates' subsequent political economic development. The extent of exclusivity influenced whether political leaders adopted authoritarian politics or more democratic processes. In marginal territories, colonial authorities favored one population over another, leading to inequalities, exclusion, and extractive economic systems. Hence, these states were without traditions of transparent government, and their leaders never accepted norms that politicians should be accountable for their actions. Instead, policymakers of contemporary African petrostates replicated the authoritarian norms that had shaped colonial rule.

Colonialism introduced firms and contractual relations that postcolonial governments reproduced. As we discuss in greater depth in Chapter 3, European and North American oil companies were active in Africa to satisfy the domestic economies' demands for hydrocarbons. Although it might be tempting to see the oil companies as agencies of restraint on African petrostates, that is not the case.[167] Whereas the discovery of oil prompted critical changes that persisted through the phases of production, the oil companies were participants in

---

[166] Jacques Marseille, *Empire Colonial et Capitalisme Français: Histoire d'un Divorce* (Paris: Éditions Albin Michel, 1984), 25.

[167] Paul Collier, "Learning from Failure: The International Finance Institutions as Agencies of Restraint in Africa," in *The Self-Restraining State: Power and Accountability in New Democracies*, eds. Andreas Schedler, Larry Diamond, and Marc Plattner. (Boulder: Lynne Rienner Publishers, Inc., 1999), 313–330.

the sector and had moderate influence. Chapter 3 turns to the influence of oil companies that entered African countries with specific goals to extract hydro-carbons and return a profit for their shareholders.

African petrostates have relations with oil companies that reflect their colonial experiences. During the 1960s, European and North American international oil companies dominated African markets. By 2010, the markets had changed as evident from the entry of national oil companies from Brazil, India, China, and other rapidly growing economies. African leaders' responses reflected colonial and postcolonial contractual relations and relative differences in ownership of oil reservoirs. As argued in Chapter 3, the entry of national oil companies is a shift in relations that has long-term implications for development and democratization of Africa's petrostates.

3

Oil Companies: Corporate Strategies and Profits

INTRODUCTION

Chapter 2 analyzed the different colonial experiences of the countries that became oil-exporting states in the late twentieth century. It showed how colonialism shaped political and economic institutions in these countries. Colonial rule defined a number of economic and political institutions that influenced postindependence development throughout Africa. Chapter 2's goal was to depict the conditions present at the time hydrocarbons were discovered in these countries. It demonstrated how various arrangements evident in political factions and economic institutions reflected historical bargains and experiences independent of oil extraction or the receipt of payments for hydrocarbon extraction.

In this environment, different political and economic organizations operated according to the goals of their respective executives. The oil companies were key among these organizations. Some enjoyed close relations with presidents and their ministers that emerged from colonial arrangements between administrators and the emerging elite African politicians. Others developed relations with state leaders after independence; the strength of their relationships built on repeated interactions and negotiations. Whatever the nature of their interactions, the oil companies' executives had a decisive influence in shaping the industries that animated each country's oil sector. These relations were outcomes of history and the conditions that were present in the country at the time oil companies discovered hydrocarbon reserves.

This chapter examines the role of private-sector actors that entered African markets via different companies. It shows how they responded to international market shifts and reacted to increasing competition among a variety of companies. The chapter takes a historical approach to provide a sense of how this extraordinarily dynamic market has changed worldwide and in Africa. The reason to consider the oil companies is that they figure prominently among private-sector actors that shaped development and democracy in African petrostates. When they enter an economy to commence extractive operations, their activities have direct consequences on the subsequent developments in the new oil exporter. However, the firms respond to conditions they encounter in those states in how they negotiate contracts, build installations, and develop continuing relations with the country's leaders. Consequently, it is essential to situate democracy and development in these African states in a context of different actors that necessarily includes the oil companies.

Standard Oil Corporation is the classic business model that other oil companies replicated. It was the first international oil company and operated as a multidivisional, vertically integrated corporation with offices around the world. Standard Oil Corporation informed the business organization other companies adopted whether they were from Asia or even the new African firms such as Angola's Sonangol. Hence, a historical discussion enriches an explanation of shifts in Africa as it transited from the twentieth to the twenty-first centuries. Equally important are the revenue management systems in each petrostate. The second part of this chapter reviews the different tax instruments by which states that administer mineral exports accumulate resource rents. In this fashion, the chapter provides a sense of the challenges that new producers face when they begin to receive windfalls from hydrocarbon extraction. The argument is that particular management strategies that states undertake reflect the institutional conditions present in the country before the discovery of oil.

OIL COMPANIES AND CHANGING STRATEGIES
IN A HISTORICAL PERSPECTIVE

This chapter presents stylized facts about the role of oil companies in Africa. First, it notes how conditions in a given country at the time oil companies discover hydrocarbon reserves affect that state's participation in this highly dynamic market. These conditions have a direct impact on which oil companies are active in the market, the firms' contractual expectations, and, most importantly, how the government manages resource revenues. In countries where metropolitan oil companies found hydrocarbon reserves either before or shortly after independence, the influence of the former colonial master was paramount. Moreover, after the 1974 oil crisis, profound changes restructured who were the principal actors in the international market and the nature of contractual relations. I examine how different types of contracts require both the oil companies and governments adopt new approaches to this shifting sector. The oil companies' impact on any petrostate's policy choices was most evident in those countries where colonial bonds were slowest to loosen.

We pay close attention to the corporate and increasingly national companies that animate the hydrocarbon sector in Africa. This perspective allows us to evaluate how historical continuities and discontinuities are manifest in development challenges and contractual arrangements in diverse petrostates. A considerable transformation is evident in the entry of Asian and Latin American companies that have introduced new business practices in the conduct of explorations, drilling, pumping, and marketing oil. New contractual arrangements are no less important for these assessments of how new actors are paying the governments of African petrostates.

The oil industry is a dynamic productive sector that has experienced technological revolutions in its ability to extract crude from subterranean reserves found under extraordinary ocean depths. Other changes include new rules that constrain the companies' abilities to pay bribes to foreign governments as a strategy to secure contracts. Indeed, the U.S. Dodd-Frank Act, passed in 2010, requires companies that conduct business in the extractive industries to report what they pay foreign governments in Central Africa to the United States' Securities and Exchange Commission.[1] Third, sovereign states wholly own many of the companies from Latin America and Asia. However, the essential nature of the industry – meaning, exploration, discovery, extraction, and closure – remains the same. Hence, this chapter presents a context by which we may comprehend the diversity of actors and their goals in this vibrant industry.

This chapter discusses the companies that are crucial actors in Africa's oil-exporting states. These firms influence political leaders, interact with local populations, import technologies, and transfer institutions of capitalism to these countries. In some cases, the oil companies are the perpetrators of egregious abuses such as the environmental disasters in the Niger Delta.[2] Other cases include blatant corruption in which oil companies pay bribes to political leaders or ignore the outright theft of funds by presidents and their families.[3] With the possible exception of Shankleman's monograph on oil and business, the political economy of how diverse corporations collude with government leaders and cooperate and compete with each other is an area of inquiry that analysts

---

[1] Senate and House of Representatives of the United States of America, "Dodd-Frank Wall Street Reform and Consumer Protection Act," HR 4173 (January 5, 2010).

[2] See the shocking report, United Nations Environmental Programme, *Environmental Assessment of Ogoniland* (New York: UNEP, 2011). Niger Delta Economies of Violence Working Paper Series (Berkeley: Institute of International Studies, various dates). Retrieved from http://oldweb. geog.berkeley.edu/ProjectsResources/ND%20Website/NigerDelta/pubs.html.

[3] In Nigeria, the U.S. Department of Justice (DOJ) has alleged that executives at KBR, a subsidiary of the Halliburton Corporation, paid substantial bribes to government officials to secure contracts to build three liquid natural gas (LNG) "trains" to liquefy natural gas so that it might be transported for commercial distribution. Simon Romero and Craig S. Smith, "Halliburton Severs Link with 2 Over Nigeria Inquiry," *The New York Times* (June 19, 2004). In 2009, Halliburton agreed to pay $382 million of $402 million in criminal fines in eight installments over the next two years to resolve the DOJ investigation. Rigzone, "KBR Pleads Guilty in Bonny Island Bribes Case," retrieved from http://www.rigzone.com/news/article.asp?a_id=72822 (accessed 12 February 2009).

of democracy and development in resource-abundant countries have ignored.[4]
This chapter fills that gap in the literature and generates several hypotheses to
account for the influence of corporations on development and democracy in
African petrostates.

An analysis of the history of oil companies demonstrates how different
firms have adapted to political economic change in African petrostates. First,
the chapter assesses the nature of oil corporations to highlight the productive
organization that endured from the nineteenth century. Second, the chapter
shows how oil executives fostered collaborative relationships with presidents
that built on historic contacts between European and North American companies and African politicians. Among the French colonies, for example, a
close personal relationship between the presidents of Cameroon, Gabon, and
Congo with André Tarallo, Elf's "Monsieur l'Afrique," was evident in the gifts
the presidents gave the French oil executive.[5] In return, he ensured that payments went directly into their personal accounts in France, Switzerland, and
Luxembourg.[6] For Elf, these close relations meant the state-owned company
received favorable contracts to extract oil in Africa.[7] These relations reflected
the French government's attitude that access to oil was a matter of national
security.

The uncertainties generated by the 1973 oil embargo prompted European
and North American oil corporations to explore for reserves and compete for
market share in Africa. Oil corporations negotiated with African leaders for
contracts that were often informal "gentlemen's agreements" that sought to
exclude competitors from specific markets.[8] These agreements resembled the
"most-favored nation" that preceded colonial conquests in their stated exclusivity. Markets changed, national governments passed laws to regulate international oil companies, and by 2010, shares of these corporations were trading in
stock markets worldwide including Accra, Lagos, and Johannesburg. Oil executives, regardless of personal goals, answered ultimately to their shareholders.[9]

Although these corporations have close, often personal relations with
African leaders, their organizations reflect the history of oil corporations.

[4] Jill Shankleman, *Oil, Profits, and Peace: Does Business Have a Role in Peacemaking?* (Washington, DC: United States Institute of Peace Press, 2006).

[5] Stephen Smith and Antoine Glaser, *Ces Messieurs Afrique: Le Paris-Village du continent noir* (Paris: Calman Lévy, 1992), 64–82.

[6] Karl Laske, "L'ex-Monsieur l'Afrique d'Elf entendu," *Libération* (5 Avril 2000).

[7] De Gaulle's Africa advisor, Jacques Foccart, repeatedly emphasized that access to oil was a matter of national security. See *Foccart Parle: Entretiens avec Philippe Gaillard* (Paris: Fayard 1995).

[8] For a lengthy treatment of the collusive relations between the French oil company Elf Aquitaine and various African presidents, see François-Xavier Verschave, *Noire Silence: Qui Arrêtera la Françafrique?* (Paris: Éditions les Arènes, 2000), esp. 419–421.

[9] The corporation emerged as an economic organization in the sixteenth century when the English monarch granted charters of incorporation to horizontally integrated trading companies. Ron Harris, *Industrializing English Law: Entrepreneurship and Business Organization, 1720–1844* (New York: Cambridge University Press, 2000), 18–19.

North American and European oil corporations began as vertically integrated, multidivisional firms that explored for reserves, drilled wells, shipped crude to refineries, and sold gasoline in trademark service stations. Different companies operating in Africa adopted strategies that reflected their risk assessments. As the history of each petrostate influenced its response to oil revenues, so the history of each corporation shaped its operations in Africa. In 2012, the oil corporation that negotiated exclusive contracts with African governments was an organization of the past; times had changed.

This chapter analyzes the different oil companies active in Africa. It considers how this dynamic sector developed since independence when large oil corporations from North America and Europe dominated production. Most notably, in the late twentieth century, companies from Asia and Latin America entered the African market, where they competed in all the major petrostates for valuable contracts. Unlike European and North American corporations whose single purpose is to make profits for their shareholders, Asian and Latin American governments own and finance these companies to meet their surging economies' energy demands. Their entry into Africa has altered market conditions, and in some countries these national oil companies have displaced European and North American corporations.

Competition for oil has increased worldwide because of the emergence of Asian and Latin American economies. With increased competition, governments might, in theory, have reason to encourage their state-owned companies to bribe foreign officials to secure contracts. However, the international community has grown increasingly intolerant of corruption. Oil companies must comply with the 1977 U.S. FCPA (that bans U.S. corporations or foreign companies whose securities are listed on U.S. markets from bribing foreign leaders).[10] Although Cragg and Wolf are critical of the FCPA's effectiveness, their criticism misses the crucial shift in norms evident in the numerous anti-corruption initiatives in international organizations.[11] In 1997, members of the Organization for Economic Cooperation and Development (OECD) signed a convention based largely on the FCPA.[12] Finally, a vast majority of the world's governments endorsed the 2006 United Nations Convention Against

---

[10] Martin T. Biegelman and Daniel R. Biegelman, *Foreign Corrupt Practices Act Compliance Guidebook* (Hoboken, NJ: John Wiley and Sons Inc., 2010). For example, in 2006, the Norwegian national oil company, Statoil ASA, headquartered in Norway and listed on the New York Stock Exchange, agreed to pay a $10.5 million penalty for bribing an Iranian official so that Statoil might develop portions of the South Pars field and gain access to Iranian oil and gas projects. See U.S. Dept. of Justice, "U.S. Resolves Probe Against Oil Company that Bribed Iranian Official" (October 13, 2006). Retrieved from http://www.usdoj.gov/opa/pr/2006/October/06_crm_700.html (accessed 11 October 2009).

[11] Wesley Cragg and William Wolf, "The US Foreign Corrupt Practices Act: A Study of Its Effectiveness," *Business and Society Review* 107, 1 (2002): 98–144.

[12] OECD, *Convention on Combating Bribery of Foreign Public Officials in International Business Transactions and Related Documents* (Paris: OECD, 2011).

Corruption that imposes new constraints on governments and private-sector actors.

An unfortunate aspect of fierce competition is that it creates opportunities for corruption, especially in states that have variable levels of bureaucratic development. In Africa, business transactions occur in countries with marginally constructed states, which translates to few bureaucratic controls over the public sector. Before the FCPA led to an expansion of rules to govern companies that did business in the United States, or the OECD anti-bribery convention, oil executives routinely bribed African officials to secure contracts. The critical factor in whether the officials were receptive to bribes was first the level of bureaucratic development that shaped their calculation of being caught.

Economic, political, and social circumstances at the time companies discovered hydrocarbon reserves mattered. If the African country were an impoverished agrarian economy, its politicians would have found the sums offered by oil companies to be dazzling. If, however, the country had experience in the extractive industries, some bureaucratic development would be in place. If the country had an authoritarian regime, its ruling coalitions would have every incentive to shrink the regime to limit information and access to oil revenues. These developmental factors might influence a civil servant's motives to engage in being a gatekeeper and illegally stealing money from the state. They would make an assessment of the probability of getting caught and punished and act accordingly. Unfortunately, many African states are unable to manage their personnel whose behaviors reflect cognitive patterns that recall the dismally low levels of state construction. In such circumstances, a culture of impunity leaves officials free to demand and accept bribes as they wish.

Two crucial changes occurred in Africa's hydrocarbon sector during the early twenty-first century. First, African private corporations and domestic national oil companies emerged to compete with international and national oil companies. Individuals who had worked for international oil corporations established firms that bid against Asian, European, Latin American, and North American companies. A second important shift was manifest in the widespread adoption of PSCs. These contracts require that governments establish oil companies to participate in production. The most successful of these state-owned oil companies is Angola's Sonangol, which since 1976 has participated in Angola's oil production.[13] In 2009, Sonangol made its first foray into other African markets, notably Guinea, where, in partnership with Chinese oil companies, it has submitted bids to develop offshore reserves.[14]

---

[13] See the seminal article by Ricardo Soares de Oliveira, "Business Success, Angola-Style: Postcolonial Politics and the Rise and Rise of Sonangol," *The Journal of Modern African Studies* 45, 4 (2007): 595–619.

[14] In October 2009, China and Sonangol together approached the Guinean government to offer services to develop potential oil reserves. See Tom Burgis and William Wallis, "China in Push for Resources in Guinea," *The Financial Times* (October 11 2009).

African companies adopted the organizational structures of the European and North American firms that dominated the world oil market until 1973. In the following paragraphs, the chapter first discusses the history of large vertically integrated oil corporations in the international petroleum market. Second, it describes types of companies that comprise the international oil corporations, national oil companies, and domestic national oil companies. In the final section, the chapter analyzes contractual arrangements that determine how windfalls flow into petrostates and the dynamics of revenue management. The intent of this chapter is to further the thematic argument of this book that only through a historic understanding of the political economy of Africa's petrostates, and the diverse actors operating in their societies, is it possible to understand elements of development and democracy. It therefore shows that oil companies are key actors in African petrostates; their representatives collaborate with political leaders and seek to fulfill the profit imperative for their shareholders. These relations are indicative of historical continuities that may influence how Africa's oil sector develops in the future.

THE HISTORY OF OIL COMPANIES

The history of international oil companies began when a small number of entrepreneurs established firms to market kerosene and oil as an industrial lubricant. By the mid-twentieth century, a few companies had established a cartel; its members shared information, controlled prices, and prevented opportunism and cheating with a credible threat of ostracism.[15] These companies dominated the production value chain; they controlled upstream processes including the exploration and production of crude oil as well as downstream operations that included methods of payments, the location of refineries, and sale of the product in brand name service stations.[16] This vertically integrated corporation responded to competition among companies from different countries and the surge in demand for gasoline that popular marketing of the automobile created. Today, a multitude of highly differentiated firms operate worldwide; these range from large international oil corporations to small oil companies that operate in high-risk environments. The particular characteristics of the contemporary oil market evolved from a monopolistic corporate model spearheaded by Standard Oil Company.

Standard Oil

The story of Standard Oil is the tale of how John D. Rockefeller established international subsidiaries, divisions for production, refining, and sales, and

[15] D.K. Osborne, "Cartel Problems," *The American Economic Review* 66, 5 (December 1976): 835.

[16] Michael E. Porter, *Competitive Advantage: Creating and Sustaining Superior Performance* (New York: The Free Press, 1985), 36.

then dominated the oil market worldwide. Standard Oil started as a business that sold a high-demand product on the international market. Its development into a vertically integrated corporation was incremental and progressed in response to market exigencies. The business model became one that different oil companies adopted as they entered a ruthlessly competitive market. Today, the Chinese national oil companies, Indian oil firms, Brazil's Petrobras, African oil companies, and traditional international oil companies all adopted some variant of the Standard Oil business model.

The business model was clear and on the basis of what would be depicted as a prototypical corporation. A crucial characteristic of the "modern corporation" is a separation of ownership and control in which the corporation's shareholders (owners) delegate responsibility to professional managers (controllers) who have an explicit mandate to increase profits.[17] These modern corporations adopted a structure that included multiple divisions and a managerial hierarchy.[18] This delegation of responsibility to corporate managers creates a professional class that works in a context of environmental, biological, physical, social, and moral influences.[19] Other firms imitated Rockefeller's business model; even after its dissolution in 1911, Standard Oil and its numerous divisions participated in a cartel of British and American corporations that produced most of the world's oil.

Rockefeller created the Standard Oil Company in the 1860s; by 1900, Standard Oil was a giant that dominated the American hydrocarbon sector. The story begins in 1862 when the young Rockefeller invested $4,000 in an Ohio oil refinery and began exporting kerosene to distributors around the world.[20] He had recognized that urban growth would increase demand for artificial lighting and kerosene was an inexpensive alternative to tallow and whale oil.[21] Rockefeller's refinery grew to be one of the largest in the world. In 1870, with four partners, he established the Standard Oil Company that eventually became the Standard Oil Trust.[22]

Rockefeller and his partners first had to overcome transportation problems; they needed to move large quantities of kerosene from refineries in Cleveland to ports and other American cities. Tarbel's explanation for Rockefeller's success was that he manipulated and coerced the railroads to get a lower price

[17] Adolf A. Berle and Gardiner C. Means, *The Modern Corporation and Private Property* Tenth printing. (New Brunswick, NJ: Transaction Publishers, 2009), 5.
[18] Alfred D. Chandler, *The Visible Hand: The Managerial Revolution in American Business* (Cambridge: Harvard University Press, 1977), 1.
[19] Chester Barnard, *The Functions of the Executive* (Cambridge: Harvard University Press, 1938/1968), 285.
[20] Ron Chernow, *Titan: The Life of John D. Rockefeller* (New York: Vintage Books, 2004).
[21] David S. Landes, *Dynasties: Fortunes and Misfortunes of the World's Great Family Businesses* (New York: Viking Penguin, 2006), 220.
[22] Daniel Yergin, *The Prize: The Epic Quest for Oil, Money, and Power* (New York: The Free Press, 1991), 35–55.

to transport the refined oil to ports.[23] Granitz and Klein have reexamined this argument; they propose that Rockefeller cooperated with railroad baron Cornelius Vanderbilt to divide up their respective cartels.[24] This cooperation enabled the Standard Oil Company to lower unit production costs. As Chandler has shown, Rockefeller succeeded in cutting unit costs from 2.5 cents in 1880 to .45 cents in 1885.[25] These reductions enabled Standard Oil to cut prices, supporting McGee's famous argument that Rockefeller engaged in predatory cost cutting in refining, not transportation, and he was thereby able to drive competitors from business.[26] Indeed, once he had resolved the transportation problem, Rockefeller increased his shipments to markets in Europe and Asia. In the early 1880s, the firm exported 69 percent of its kerosene overseas; of this, 70 percent went to Europe and approximately 22 percent to Asia.[27]

European demand for kerosene surpassed that of the United States. Thus, Rockefeller set up divisions for marketing in Europe and Asia and transformed Standard Oil into a multidivisional international corporation.[28] At first, he avoided the production side of oil – Rockefeller felt that oil fields were simply too large and production too risky to merit investment.[29] However, the extraordinary demand for oil products convinced him to invest in production, marketing, and management; he established subsidiary corporations for each phase of the value chain – meaning downstream exploration and production, and upstream refining and marketing.[30] Rockefeller presciently recognized that the oil industry was ideal for a corporate strategy of vertical integration. Standard Oil thus became the largest oil company in the world, with a presence from exploration and production to the sale of a finished product. However, after Tarbell published *The History of the Standard Oil Company* in the early twentieth century, the trust became the symbol of ruthless monopolistic capitalism.[31] In 1911, the Supreme Court ruled in favor of the dissolution of the Standard Oil Trust, arguing that by imposing unreasonable restraints on trade,

---

[23] Ida M. Tarbell, *The History of the Standard Oil Company*, vol. I (New York: Cosimo Classics, 2009), 38–69.

[24] Elizabeth Granitz and Benjamin Klein, "Monopolization by 'Raising Rivals' Costs': The Standard Oil Case," *The Journal of Law and Economics* 39, 1 (April 1996): 3.

[25] Alfred D. Chandler, "Organization Capabilities and the Economic History of the Industrial Enterprise," *Journal of Economic Perspectives* 6, 3 (Summer 1992): 82.

[26] John S. McGee, "Predatory Price Cutting: The Standard Oil (N.J.) Case," *The Journal of Law and Economics* 1, (October 1958): 144.

[27] Alfred D. Chandler, *Scale and Scope: The Dynamics of Industrial Capitalism* (Cambridge: Harvard University Press, 1990), 92.

[28] Mira Wilkins, "Multinational Enterprise to 1930: Discontinuities and Continuities," in *Leviathans: Multinational Corporations and the New Global History*, eds. Alfred D. Chandler, Jr. and Bruce Mazlish (New York: Cambridge University Press, 2005), 61; on the multidivisional corporation, see Chandler, *The Visible Hand*, 423.

[29] Tarbell, *The History of the Standard Oil Company*, vol. II, 156.

[30] Chandler, *Scale and Scope*, 92.

[31] Tarbell, *The History of the Standard Oil Company*, 2 volumes.

it had violated the Sherman Anti-Trust Act. A consequence of this ruling was that the oil sector shifted from monopoly to oligopoly.[32]

European Oil Companies and Africa

The Europeans reacted with alarm to Rockefeller's monopoly. At first, European oil companies responded to Standard Oil's challenge in the early twentieth century by citing the threat of foreign monopolies. Entrepreneurs such as William D'Arcy, Marcus Samuel, John Fisher, and Calouste Gulbenkian travelled to European capitals where they presented an image of Standard Oil as an evil monopoly that would impose unfair prices on Europe's citizens.[33] D'Arcy received encouragement from the British government to explore in Great Britain's colonial possessions; by 1910, his Shell-BP was well on the way to becoming one of the world's largest oil corporations.

European governments resisted involving the state in the creation of oil companies. Great Britain's parliament rebuffed attempts by Marcus Samuel, the Chief Executive Officer of Shell Transport and Trading Company, to solicit greater government involvement even though he offered the Admiralty a "controlling voice" in his oil company.[34] In France, Georges Clemenceau famously dismissed any urgency about energy needs with his witticism, "When I want some oil, I'll find it at my grocer's."[35] Despite such opposition, others prevailed. On the eve of World War I, automobiles were touring French roads and their drivers needed gasoline. This increased demand for gasoline alarmed French politicians who saw dependence on foreign corporations as a threat. An urgent clamor erupted to find oil, build refineries, and create national companies that would ensure a stable supply of gasoline.[36] Indeed, by 1914, large multidivisional oil corporations had emerged in practically every European country.[37]

The automobile and demand for gasoline that it created was by itself insufficient to convince French leaders that they needed to secure access to oil. This goal only became a national priority after the First World War when aircraft, trucks, personnel carriers, and to a lesser extent tanks, became indispensable to the war effort. Clemenceau reversed his opposition and publicly recognized that France's war effort depended on the internal combustion engine. Between 1914 and 1918, French imports of oil quadrupled from 276,000 to 1 million tons, most of which came from the Western hemisphere.[38] Because the Germans

[32] Joseph A. Pratt, "The Petroleum Industry in Transition: Antitrust and the Decline of Monopoly Control in Oil, *The Journal of Economic History* 40, 4 (December 1980): 818.

[33] Gregory P. Nowell, *Mercantile States and the World Oil Cartel, 1900–1939* (Ithaca: Cornell University Press, 1994), 49.

[34] G. Gareth Jones, "The British Government and the Oil Companies 1912–1924: The Search for an Oil Policy," *The Historical Journal* 20, 3 (September 1977): 647.

[35] Yergin, *The Prize*, 189.

[36] François Roche, *TotalFinaElf: Une Major Française* (Paris: Éditions le Cherche Midi, 2003).

[37] Chandler, *Strategy and Structure*, 163.

[38] W.G. Jensen, "The Importance of Energy in the First and Second World Wars," *The Historical Journal* 11, 3 (September 1968): 543.

had successfully occupied the Pas-de-Calais region where the French mined most of their coal, railroads were unavailable for transport.[39] The French had to move goods, men, and military supplies by truck, which deepened a dependence on the United States for oil. A frightening vulnerability became clear in 1917 when Clemenceau discovered that gasoline stocks were so low that France would be unable to move troops and supplies to the front; he turned to American President Woodrow Wilson for help.[40] Wilson authorized transfer of the needed oil, and French troops fought on.

French politicians recognized that without independent access to oil, France would be vulnerable after the war's end. The perception that oil shortages posed a national security threat convinced Clemenceau that the country needed a concrete energy policy.[41] Thus, in July 1917, he organized the Commissariat Général des Pétroles to coordinate exploration and manage the domestic distribution of oil.[42] However, it was not until 1924 that the Millerand government formed a partnership with private investors to establish the Compagnie Française des Pétroles (CFP).[43] By 1927, France completed its organization of the oil sector; the CFP explored and produced crude and the Compagnie Française de Raffinage refined the crude into gasoline.[44] The National Assembly awarded these companies legal status in March 1928.[45] Although there were no oil reservoirs in metropolitan France, the CFP was a major step in French efforts to secure oil supplies.

The scramble for African oil had a tentative start in the 1920s. Along with his multiple investments in Persia, D'Arcy secured an exclusive contract for Shell-BP to explore for oil in Nigeria.[46] Meanwhile, in 1934, the French Syndicat d'Études et de Recherches Pétrolières (SERP) explored in the Gabon Colony.[47] Its efforts were unsuccessful; the SERP drilled several dry onshore wells during the mid-1930s. These efforts slowed during the Great Depression. Automobile sales dropped worldwide, and oil executives felt little urgency to expand their explorations in difficult economic times.[48] In 1939, however, Nazi

---

[39] Jensen, "The Importance of Energy in the First and Second World Wars," 539.

[40] Roche, *TotalFinaElf*, 21.

[41] Nowell, *Mercantile States and the World Oil Cartel*, 116.

[42] Eric D.K. Melby, *Oil and the International System: The Case of France, 1918–1969* (New York: Arno Press, 1981), 10.

[43] Nowell, *Mercantile States and the World Oil Cartel*, 141.

[44] Philippe Bernard and Henri Dubief, *The Decline of the French Republic 1914–1938*, Anthony Foster, trans. (New York: Cambridge University Press 1985), 138–139.

[45] Melby, *Oil and the International System*, 101.

[46] Sarah Ahmad Khan, *Nigeria: The Political Economy of Oil* (Oxford: Oxford University Press, 1994), 19; Scott R. Pearson, *Petroleum and the Nigerian Economy* (Stanford: Stanford University Press, 1970), 15.

[47] Gilbert Rutman et al., *Elf Aquitaine des origines à 1989* (Paris: Fayard, 1998), 56.

[48] In the United States, new automobile registrations declined between 1929 and 1930 by 20 percent, with a concomitant drop in the sale of gasoline. See Christina D. Romer, "The Great Crash and the Onset of the Great Depression, *The Quarterly Journal of Economics* 105, 3 (August 1990): 607.

Germany's *Blitzkrieg* cruelly proved that motorized military units were the new technology as armies of the Third Reich occupied Western Europe in a matter of days.

The Second World War demonstrated to all that national security depended on access to energy supplies. After liberation in 1944, the French government founded the Institut Français de Pétrole and, in November 1945, the Bureau de Recherche Pétrolière received a mandate to explore for oil in all of France's overseas possessions.[49] The CFP explored for oil in Algeria, Chad, Gabon, and Congo. In the late 1950s, the company made its first significant discoveries. Executives at CFP succeeded in securing exclusive contractual rights over blocks in Gabon and Algeria. These contracts were instrumental in achieving French oil security, even after independence when widespread nationalizations gained momentum in the Middle East and North Africa in 1973.

During the 1970s, a number of African states nationalized companies in the extractive industries. These acts were something of a culmination of events that began as African states gained independence from France, Great Britain, and later, Portugal. The behavior of European and North American international oil companies presented African leaders with viable business models. When the major oil-producing Middle Eastern kingdoms nationalized firms operating in their countries, many African leaders jumped at the opportunity to get control of domestic resources. The Nigerian National Petroleum Company, the Sociedade Nacional de Combustíveis de Angola (Sonangol), and other domestic national oil companies took their cues from what had occurred in the Middle East and North Africa. In practice, the African state-owned oil companies became desirable appointments for regime cronies and members of the ruling families. Indeed, political elites would later seek positions in these companies to capture revenues and use them for their personal enrichment.[50]

The 1973 Oil Embargo

In October 1973, the Organization of Petroleum Exporting Countries (OPEC) announced an oil embargo against the United States and Europe in retaliation for their support of Israel during the Yom Kippur War. Leaders of Middle Eastern oil states demanded a renegotiation of contractual arrangements. Particularly, nationalist leaders asked why European and North American companies should have preferential access to their oil reserves. However, with supplies threatened, oil executives recognized they needed to diversify their sources of oil, and companies increased explorations in a newly assertive Africa. By 1974, Nigeria's membership in OPEC showed the extent to which the influence of colonial arrangements had diminished. Although Elf and Shell

---

[49] Roche et al., *TotalFinaElf*, 39.

[50] Reportedly, members of Angola's elite political class and management of Sonangol have been implicated in schemes to gain profits from the oil company. See "Angola: Marques takes them on," *Africa Confidential* 53, 2 (20 January 2012).

continued to enjoy advantages in their relationships with various presidents, Africa's leaders exercised greater discretion in how they managed the hydrocarbon sector.

The 1973 Oil Embargo introduced the nationally owned oil company that would negotiate as an equal with foreign companies. This cognitive shift represented an important modification in officials' thinking. First, political leaders in the oil-producing states would declare any extractive industries national assets. Second, the 1973 events presented an opportunity for political leaders to take policy actions ostensibly on behalf of their people. It was a win-win situation for the people with official duties. However, the human capital shortages manifest in the lack of skilled civil servants to manage oil revenues and work in the oil industry left the countries dependent on oil companies for technical expertise and accounting insights.[51] The oil companies in 1974 provided African governments with qualified personnel to manage hydrocarbon extraction and revenue management, at least in principle, until the state built its domestic capacity.

Global oil production involved multiple companies in upstream and downstream productive processes.[52] Before 1973, it was an oligopolistic market that included seven large, vertically integrated corporations called the "seven sisters"; along with the CFP, these companies dominated production and marketing.[53] Then, in 1970, the leaders of Middle Eastern and North African governments demanded a greater role in the dispensation of contracts and ownership of production facilities. These producers declared that they would begin to phase in incremental nationalizations of their extractive industries.

Incremental nationalizations were consistent with national governments' claims that they had an inherent right to control production of natural resources within their borders. In early 1973, leaders of Saudi Arabia and Abu Dhabi signed the Participation Agreement with international oil companies; by this agreement, they began a process of taking control of exploration and production in their borders.[54] The Participation Agreement was a phased nationalization; oil companies would transfer 25 percent of their operations to the host governments' companies in 1973 and 5 percent each year thereafter until they had transferred 51 percent.[55] Whereas Saudi leaders adopted an incremental

---

[51] Goldsmith shows convincingly that the critical problem confronting Africa's civil services is not that they are overstaffed; rather, the skill set is deficient and they are seriously understaffed. See Arthur A. Goldsmith, "Africa's Overgrown State Reconsidered: Bureaucracy and Economic Growth," *World Politics* 51, 4 (July 1999): 520–546.

[52] Shankleman, *Oil, Profits, and Peace*, 30.

[53] Daniel Yergin attributes this name to the Italian oilman, Enrico Mattei, who created Azienda Generale Italiana Petroli and its later conglomerate corporation, Ente Nazionale Idocarburi. The seven sisters included Exxon, Mobil, Chevron, Texaco, Gulf, British Petroleum, and Royal Dutch Shell. See *The Prize*, 501–505.

[54] Valérie Marcel with John V. Mitchell, *Oil Titans: National Oil Companies in the Middle East* (Washington: Brookings Institution Press, 2006), 28–29.

[55] Marcel, *Oil Titans*, 29.

nationalization strategy with a generous compensation package for the seven sisters and CFP, Algerian policymakers immediately seized 51 percent of French holdings.[56] The Saudis had feared that the international oil cartel might retaliate and exclude them from world markets. They therefore articulated an incremental strategy to create national oil companies that would operate the wells, transport and store the crude oil, and manage the downstream marketing of their refined product. The agreement appeared to be an orderly transition from the European and North American domination of Middle Eastern and North African oil production to sovereign ownership by national governments.

The Yom Kippur War and Participation Agreement fundamentally changed the international oil market. First, the conflict between Israel and the Arab states affected contractual agreements between the international oil companies and members of newly established OPEC, which imposed an embargo on oil exports to the West. The embargo empowered OPEC; representatives of oil-exporting countries began negotiating with the seven sisters and their governments as equals. Second, as a consequence of the Participation Agreement, Middle Eastern and North African governments established national oil companies to manage their upstream production. By the close of the twentieth century, these national oil companies controlled 90 percent of the world's oil; five of them accounted for 25 percent of the world's production and possessed half of its reserves.[57] For North American and European oil companies, a ground shift had occurred; they could no longer expect to enter countries and extract hydrocarbons at will. Leaders of Africa's petrostates might have been able to use the threat of nationalization as a bargaining strategy in contract negotiations; however, African politicians recognized a necessity for assurances of their governments' respect for property rights.

Despite Saudi efforts to assuage concerns over supply through an incremental transfer of ownership, the nationalizations destabilized a delicate balance between supply and demand; European companies perceived that their once-predictable supply of oil was at risk.[58] The 1973 Arab-Israeli War and oil embargo thus had a profound impact on perceptions of market stability. First, oil companies' assessments of risk shifted into nonquantifiable uncertainty when the Arab embargo blocked shipments to Europe and North America without specifying an end. Second, North American and European international corporations, the seven sisters, lost their unrestricted access to Middle Eastern oil reserves as a result of the war. These events and the consequential perceptions that access to hydrocarbons was hardly secure reinforced a sense that the companies had to find other sources of oil. Africa therefore drew the attention of international oil companies that had to decide whether to accept significant risks and enter markets such as Nigeria, Angola, Sudan, Congo,

[56] Yergin, *The Prize*, 584.
[57] Marcel, *Oil Titans*, 1.
[58] Yergin, *The Prize*, 619.

and Gabon that possessed proven reserves. Compounding these calculations during the mid-1970s was an increasing number of coups and civil wars that influenced the international firms' willingness to invest in an ostensibly unstable African oil market.

THE ACTORS: INTERNATIONAL, NATIONAL, AND DOMESTIC NATIONAL OIL COMPANIES

Three types of oil companies are active in Africa. Their organizations reflect the continuing influence of Standard Oil's business model. International oil companies (IOCs) include large vertically integrated corporations that extract oil from reserves in numerous countries. Traditionally, these highly capitalized corporations have headquarters and shareholders in Europe and North America. However, in the twenty-first century, African entrepreneurs with lengthy experience working for IOCs have started firms that compete for contracts in the most lucrative markets. Second, national oil companies (NOCs) are firms established and majority owned by sovereign governments. Finally, domestic national oil companies (DNOCs) operate in their home countries; they are nominal partners with IOCs and NOCs in joint ventures and production-sharing contracts. DNOCs often lack capital, and their symbolic participation is a means by which governments try to collect more resource rents. In total, these three categories of oil companies employ thousands of people in Africa and share in the bounty of the continent's crude oil.

International Oil Companies

IOCs have been active in Africa for decades. During the early twentieth century, a small number of Anglo-American IOCs dominated oil production and operated as a cartel. For decades, these companies controlled the "aboveground resources"; they provided capital, technological expertise, and deep knowledge and experience in markets and market development.[59] In 1973, the Participation Agreement began a process that ended the Anglo-American IOCs' monopoly over world petroleum reserves. Indeed, influence shifted to NOCs that took over IOCs' assets.[60] The new actors that control a third of the world's oil and gas supplies include Saudi Arabia's Aramco, Russia's Gazprom, the Chinese National Petroleum Company, National Iranian Oil Company, Venezuela's Petróleos de Venezuela, S.A., the Brazilian company Petrobras, and Malaysia's Petronas; these companies invest in aboveground resources and dominate international markets. In mature African producers, such as Angola,

---

[59] Tom Nicholls, "NOCs 1 – IOCs 0" *Petroleum Economist* 72, 4 (01 April 2005): 4–9.
[60] Carola Hoyos, "The New Seven Sisters: Oil and Gas Giants Dwarf Western Rivals," *The Financial Times* (11 March 2007).

Sonangol participates in oil production and enjoys a strong reputation for efficiency.[61]

International oil companies operating in Africa range from the supermajors to majors, the still smaller independents, and finally the lean frontier specialists that operate in emerging producers. ExxonMobil, BP, Royal Dutch Shell, Total, ChevronTexaco, and ConocoPhillips are large, vertically integrated corporations that fall under the category of *supermajor*. The supermajors pump crude oil that they refine into finished products to sell on consumer markets. They often share production contracts with a number of *majors* that include Unocal and Occidental Petroleum. Differences between the majors and supermajors are evident in refining capacity, size, and marketing of consumer products. The *independents* are smaller than the majors and include Marathon, Amerada Hess, and Addax. The smallest IOCs are the *frontier specialists* or *wildcatters* that engage in deep-sea drilling, other technologically difficult operations, and risky markets. Frontier specialists accept high risk-to-investment ratios that might discourage larger firms; supermajors and majors tend to enter markets where frontier specialists have incurred the costs of exploration that entail the risk of dry wells in addition to significant profits when they hit pay dirt. All these IOCs compete against each other as well as African, Asian, and Latin American NOCs.

By 2000, a series of mergers created five "super supermajors". For instance, Exxon, already the world's largest oil company, merged with Mobil to become ExxonMobil. Relative to worldwide IOCs, the "so-called Big-Five (BP, Chevron, ConocoPhillips Company, ExxonMobil, and Royal Dutch Shell) had $120.8 billion in profits in 2006 from 9.7 million barrels per day (bpd) of oil production. By contrast, the next 20 largest American oil firms had $31.2 billion in profits from 2.1 million bpd in oil production."[62] Despite their extraordinary size, the supermajors control a relatively modest percentage of the world's oil reserves.[63] Quite possibly, the consolidations reflected IOC executives' awareness that Saudi Arabia's Aramco and Russia's Gazprom dwarf the supermajors; ExxonMobil's 11.2 billion barrels of reserves are not even 5 percent of Aramco's holdings, and its 66,907 billion cubic feet of natural gas reserves are insignificant compared to Gazprom's 1,000,000 billion cubic feet.[64] Mergers may have enabled the supermajors to reduce information costs, opportunism, and risk and to compete with NOCs, but only as minor players.

International oil companies confront several dilemmas in their competition with NOCs. The first dilemma is evident in local populations that tire

---

[61] Sonangol was a product of war and the Angolan state's driving need for revenues to carry on the conflict. See Soares de Oliveira, "Business Success, Angola-Style."

[62] Amy Myers Jaffe and Ronald Soligo, "The International Oil Companies" (Houston: The James A. Baker III Institute for Public Policy of Rice University, 2007), 2.

[63] Hoyos, "The New Seven Sisters."

[64] Carola Hoyos, "National Oil Companies: Majors Have a Tough Job," *The Financial Times* (29 May 2006).

of environmental damages resulting from petroleum production. Shell Oil's environmental negligence in the Niger Delta has been a costly reminder that local conditions do matter. The 2011 United Nations Environment Programme (UNEP) report presents evidence of Shell's blatant disregard for the human costs of bungled production in the Niger Delta.[65] Such management failures and unconscionable negligence incur substantial reputational costs and lead to boycotts and shareholder dissatisfaction. A second dilemma is corruption and demands from in-country counterparts for clandestine payments. For many executives at the supermajors and majors, Statoil's conviction for FCPA violations is a poignant lesson.[66] In its efforts to gain entry into the Iranian market, Statoil paid officials bribes in violation of international statutes. By the same token, Elf Aquitaine's former CEO, Loïk Le Floch Prigent, learned that complicity with corrupt leaders imposes significant costs when those ties violate national laws.[67]

When oil prices are high, opportunities for substantial profits motivate some IOCs to ignore possible reputational risks. Marathon Oil, an American independent, holds highly profitable production-sharing contracts (PSCs) in Equatorial Guinea that reportedly guarantee the rights to exploit new liquid natural gas fields at favorable terms.[68] Conceivably, the reason Marathon won such contracts was the company's alleged willingness to deposit funds in accounts held by members of President Obiang-Nguema's family in the now-defunct Riggs Bank.[69] By distributing mosquito nets to the poor on Bioko Island, Marathon has tried to counter the perception that it cares little for the common people while doing business with a ruthless dictator. Such corporate social-responsibility investments are good public relations programs, but failed to shield Marathon from the U.S. Senate Subcommittee investigation and a public relations disaster stemming from the Riggs Bank money-laundering case. Conceivably, rampant corruption may weaken other IOCs' resolve to invest in Africa; however, should they leave, they are painfully aware that new competitors from Asia and Africa will immediately take over their contracts.

National Oil Companies

Sovereign governments finance and own NOCs either in their entirety or majority. The most famous NOCs are Sonatrach (Algeria), the Abu Dhabi National

---

[65] UNEP, *Environmental Assessment of Ogoniland*.

[66] U.S. Dept. of Justice, "U.S. Resolves Probe Against Oil Company that Bribed Iranian Official."

[67] Karl Laske, *Ils se Croyaient Intouchables* (Paris: Éditions Albin Michel, 2000); Jacques Follorou, "Loïk Le Floch-Prigent et la Fable du Trésor Ivoirien," *Le Monde* (28 Septembre 2012); John R. Heilbrunn, "Oil and Water? Elite Politicians and Corruption in France," *Comparative Politics* 37, 3 (April 2005): 277–292.

[68] Martin Quinlan, "Equatorial Guinea: developing high margin LNG," *Petroleum Economist* (May 2005).

[69] United States Senate Subcommittee, *Money Laundering and Foreign Corruption*.

Oil Company (United Arab Emirates), the National Iranian Oil Company, the Kuwait Petroleum Company, and Saudi Aramco. These companies have tentatively entered international markets, but because their domestic reserves are so large, they are profitable working in their national boundaries. Saudi Aramco, for instance, controls approximately 20 percent of the world's proven oil reserves; it has the capacity to produce 12.5 million barrels a day.[70] In some countries, the NOCs refine their oil for export and domestic consumption. In other countries, the NOCs ship their crude to refineries located elsewhere; they then import gasoline and other refined products for domestic consumption.[71] This decision to export oil and import refined products is a strategy among some Middle Eastern NOCs that limited their investments to the domestic market.

Numerous governments created NOCs to compete in international markets. These companies include Brazil's Petrobras, India Offshore Oil Corporation, Indian Oil and Natural Gas Company, the Korean National Oil Company, Japan Oil, Gas, and Metals, Japan's Inpex Holdings, Malaysia's Petronas, Norway's Statoil, and China's numerous NOCs, the largest of which include Sinopec, the Chinese National Offshore Oil Company (CNOOC), and the China National Petroleum Corporation and its subsidiary PetroChina. Among the most influential of China's NOCs is the CNOOC, which operates like a multinational corporation.[72] Of the Asian NOCs, Malaysia's Petronas was among the first to begin operations in Africa, Latin America, and Central Asia.[73] Petronas is indicative of Asian NOCs in Africa, where it is a full equity partner with ExxonMobil and ChevronTexaco in Chad and holds percentages of offshore blocks in Angola and Equatorial Guinea.

By 2000, a number of NOCs were competing with the international oil companies for contracts in African petrostates. The stunning entry of Asian firms as major players in the international oil sector shows the extent to which competition has changed. In 2005, "half of the biggest 50 oil companies are fully or majority state-owned. Ranked by oil reserves, nine out of the top 10 are NOCs."[74] An expansion of Asian NOCs into markets that North American and European IOCs had dominated was a reflection of their governments' increasing wealth and technological expertise. For example, China's energy needs prompted the Beijing government to adopt a two-tiered strategy: first, they used their substantial foreign reserves to lend governments money in exchange for oil. In March 2009, Chinese NOCs won contracts in Angola, Uganda, Ghana, Nigeria, Equatorial Guinea, and even Sudan, whose leader,

---

[70] Daniel Yergin, *The Quest: Energy, Security, and the Remaking of the Modern World* (New York: The Penguin Press, 2011), 287.

[71] Marcel, *Oil Titans*, 200.

[72] Chris Alden, *China in Africa* (New York: Zed Books, 2007), 39.

[73] Alex Forbes, "Scramble for Assets Goes Global," *Petroleum Economist* 75, 2 (February 2008).

[74] Nicholls, "NOCs 1 – IOCs 0,"

Omar Bashir, the International Court of Justice indicted for crimes against humanity. Other Chinese NOCs have offered cash-strapped governments oil-backed loans; in 2009, Sinopec offered a $25 billion loan to two Russian producers for 300,000 barrels a day and Brazil's Petrobras $10 billion in exchange for 160,000 barrels a day.[75] In September 2009, CNOOC made an offer to provide the Nigerian government $30.00–$50.00 billion or $50.00–$83.33 a barrel for 6 billion barrels of oil.[76] If CNOOC had succeeded in convincing Nigeria's leaders to sign the loan agreement, it would have locked the price per barrel and alleviated issues of market volatility. Although China's reasons were obvious, the rewards for Nigeria were less clear, especially if the price per barrel of Brent grade oil exceeded $100.00.

A second strategy included the acquisition of IOCs either in their entirety or a percentage share. Whereas notions of market capitalism would suggest that these efforts should be straightforward transactions, politics enters negotiations over the purchase of large, well-known oil companies. In June 2005, CNOOC offered $18.5 billion to acquire the U.S. oil company Unocal. CNOOC had arranged a $7 billion interest-free loan from its state-owned parent, the China National Offshore Oil, and the Industrial and Commercial Bank of China.[77] As details of the negotiations became public, Chevron complained to the U.S. Congress, which prompted Congressional hearings and protectionist sentiments. In early August, executives with CNOOC announced they were withdrawing their bid with an explanation that "this political environment has made it very difficult for us to accurately assess our chance of success, creating a level of uncertainty that presents an unacceptable risk to our ability to secure this transaction."[78]

The failure of CNOOC to take over Unocal served as a lesson to Chinese NOCs; Sinopec kept a veil of secrecy over its ultimately successful bid to purchase the Canadian corporation Addax Petroleum for $7.24 billion.[79] In July 2012, CNOOC discretely acquired Canada's Nexen Corporation for $18.2 billion, the largest acquisition of a foreign company.[80] As Table 3.1 below suggests, between 2005 and 2009, the Chinese NOCs discretely purchased international companies to ensure the country's skyrocketing economy the energy it needs to continue growing. The Chinese NOCs have adopted a business

[75] Geoff Dyer and Kate Mackenzie, "Chinese Groups Court West for Partnerships," *The Financial Times* (April 19, 2009).
[76] Tom Burgis, "China Seeks Big Stake in Nigerian Oil," *The Financial Times* (September 28, 2009).
[77] James Politi, "CNOOC Funding for Unocal Scrutinised," *The Financial Times* (29 June 2005).
[78] Statement issued by CNOOC in Hong Kong announcing their withdrawal from negotiations. Quoted in David Barboza, Andrew Ross Sorkin, Steve Lohr, "China's Oil Set Back: The Overview; Chinese Company Drops Bid to Buy U.S. Oil Concern," *The New York Times* (August 3, 2005)
[79] "China's Unswerving Appetite for Energy," *Petroleum Economist* 76, 8 (August 2009).
[80] Leslie Hook, Anousha Sakoui, and Stephanie Kirchgaessner, "Cnooc Heeds Lessons of Failed Unocal Bid," *The Financial Times* (July 24, 2012).

TABLE 3.1 *Selected Chinese Cross-Border Oil and Gas Acquisitions*

Date	Target	Deal Value ($bn)
2005	PetroKazakhstan (Kazakhstan)	4.2
2006	Akpo offshore oil and gas field in Nigeria	2.7
2006	Udmurtneft (Russia, 99.49 percent)	3.7
2006	Kazakh Oil and Gas Assets (Kazakhstan)	1.9
2008	Total (France, 1.6 percent)	2.9
2008	BP (UK, 1 percent)	2.0
2008	Awilco Offshore (Norway)	4.3
2008	Tanganyika Oil (Canada)	2.0
2009	Singapore Petroleum (Singapore)	2.4
2009	Addax Petroleum (Switzerland)	8.9
2012	Devon Energy – Shale gas assets	2.2
2012	BHP Billiton – percentage shares of Woodside Petroleum Inc.	1.6
2013	Nexen Inc.	15.1

Source: Diverse articles in print media. See Julie Jiang and Jonathan Sinton, *Overseas Investments by Chinese National Oil Companies: Assessing the Drivers and Impacts* (Paris: OECD/International Energy Agency, 2011).

model pioneered by Standard Oil in their aggressive strategy of acquisitions and mergers. A significant difference however is that China's NOCs may borrow interest-free loans directly from the state. As a consequence, the Chinese NOCs have a considerable freedom in their acquisition strategies.

Many IOCs perceive risk in Africa to be high; as a consequence, European and North American firms avoid partnerships with African state-owned companies. African governments have attempted in vain to reverse the perception that risk is high because of corruption. For example, many international oil companies believe that participation with the Nigerian National Petroleum Company is a high-risk investment; they see markets in Nigeria as unstable, the government permits systemic corruption, and inflated local costs mean that the IOC will need to import goods to make up for shortages in local markets.[81] These problems are also present in other African petrostates. The consequence was to create opportunities for Chinese NOCs who adhere to China's official policy that eschews condemnation of corrupt or brutal governments.

Domestic National Oil Companies

Over the last decade, African petrostates have increasingly replaced joint ventures and concessions with PSCs. However, PSCs require governments to launch state-owned companies to fulfill their contractual obligations.[82]

[81] Martin Quinlan, "Nigeria: Looking for Explorers," *Petroleum Economist* (May 2005).
[82] Ernest E. Smith and John S. Dzienkowski, "A Fifty-Year Perspective on World Petroleum Arrangements, *Texas International Law Journal* 24, 1 (1989): 37.

Decisions to adopt PSCs demonstrate two critical developments. First, this shift in contractual arrangements confirms the highly dynamic nature of oil production in Africa. Changes in ownership structures, in turn, increased demand for particular managerial technologies.[83] African states' ownership of the oil reservoirs is a legacy of colonial laws that define subterranean mineral reserves as the people's property.[84]

When the African petrostates auction reserves, they enter into contract negotiations to determine supervisory responsibilities and production partnership with DNOCs. PSCs contain specific formulas to divide oil between DNOCs and their partners, whether IOCs or NOCs. In all probability, African petrostates established DNOCs to capture a greater portion of the wealth generated from oil production. Given the African petrostates' relative youth and the short time in which they have been producing oil, it is impressive how many DNOCs, as well as privately owned domestic companies, participate in production. By 2009, Angola, Cameroon, Congo, Equatorial Guinea, Gabon, Ghana, Mauritania, Nigeria, and Sudan had all established oil companies to meet contractual obligations in PSCs.[85] However, inefficiency was common among some DNOCs that lacked necessary skills to engage actively in upstream oil production. As a result, leaders of African governments contracted with experts to work in DNOCs and operate with international oil firms.

Constraints on DNOCs are a function of a producer's phase of production. For emerging producers, the costs of upstream investments are high and returns do not begin until the wells are in full production. Still, oil revenues represent a significant multiplication of pre-oil fiscal receipts, especially among the poorest African countries. They therefore encounter serious challenges in the organization of DNOCs and the management of resource windfalls because in general they lack trained individuals. For mature producers, the DNOC permits states to capture a larger share of the resource rents.[86] Oftentimes, however, the institutions that control dysfunctional behavior are poorly defined or not operational, as occurred in Nigeria when the state fell under the sway of generals who used their positions to plunder the wealth from oil production. Among declining producers, DNOCs established practices that were in place for lengthy periods. Politicians such as Omar Bongo Ondimba and Denis Sassou Nguesso used the company as a source of finance by which they distributed

[83] Pauline Jones Luong and Erika Weinthal, *Oil is Not a Curse: Ownership Structure and Institutions in Soviet Successor States* (New York: Cambridge University Press, 2010), 7.
[84] Gilbert Stone, "The Mining Laws of the West African Colonies and Protectorates," *Journal of Comparative and International Law* 2, 3 (1920): 259–266.
[85] Menachem Katz, Ulrich Bartsch, Harinder Malothra, and Milan Cuc, *Lifting the Oil Curse: Improving Petroleum Revenue Management in Sub-Saharan Africa* (Washington, DC: The International Monetary Fund, 2004), 58–59.
[86] Charles McPherson, "National Oil Companies," in *Fiscal Policy Formulation and Implementation in Oil-Producing Countries*, eds. J.M. Davies, R. Ossowski, and A. Fedelino (Washington, DC: The International Monetary Fund, 2003), 184.

rents to coalition supporters, thereby protecting their positions in office. The DNOC became part of an apparatus by which the presidents maintained control over resource revenues.

Leaders of African petrostates have incentives to create DNOCs to exert greater control over revenue streams. Politicians viewed oil revenues "as financing; specifically, a portfolio transaction that converts oil assets into financial assets."[87] This perspective meant that policymakers failed to see revenues as future wealth, but instead as money available for consumption. Consider the strategies undertaken by the wartime Angolan government. In 1975, just before independence, soon-to-be President Agostinho Neto convened the National Commission for the Restructuring of the Petroleum Sector. He wanted to reassure Gulf Oil and other companies operating in the Cabinda enclave that his government was indeed *the* government of Angola. Neto recognized that his political survival depended on his ability to honor the contracts the IOC had signed with the Portuguese government; oil revenues had contributed approximately $450 million to Portuguese fiscal revenues in 1974.[88] He therefore enlisted help from key political advisors – Percy Freudenthal, Morais Guerra, Desiderio Costa, and several others – to establish a DNOC; in June 1976, Sonangol began operations under Freudenthal's stewardship as "the Angolan oil concessionaire, sector regulator, and tax gathering agent" that would manage the oil sector.[89] Freudenthal and his colleagues organized Sonangol as Angola's DNOC, which operated first as a concessionaire and later as a full partner with IOCs operating in the country.[90]

After the Angolan civil war ended in 2002, a transparent accounting of revenues proved problematic for Sonangol.[91] Because oil revenues had been indispensible to the MPLA government's war effort, Angola's political leaders developed a clandestine system of transfers both of oil and money to arms dealers. Although Sonangol represented an island of competence in Angola's civil war economy, it operated in a nontransparent fashion.[92] For instance, the DNOC had rights to retain up to 10 percent of its revenues to cover operating expenses. However, auditors found that Sonangol routinely kept the entire 10 percent and "currently all bonuses, whether signature, exploration, commercial discovery or production bonuses are paid directly to Sonangol.... The Tax Directorate of the Ministry of Finance does not record bonus payments

[87] Steven Barnett and Rolando Ossowski, "Operational Aspects of Fiscal Policy in Oil-Producing Countries," IMF Working Paper WP/02/177 (October 2002): 5.

[88] John Marcum, *The Angolan Revolution. Vol. II: Exile Politics and Guerrilla Warfare (1962– 1976)* (Cambridge, MA: MIT Press, 1978), 253.

[89] Soares de Oliveira, "Business Success, Angola-Style," 598–600.

[90] Alec Russell, "Angola Offers Timeframe for Sonangol Shake-Up," *The Financial Times* (October 11, 2007).

[91] Francisco Carneiro, *Angola: Oil, Broad-Based Growth, and Equity* (Washington, DC: The World Bank, 2007).

[92] Soares de Oliveira, "Business Success, Angola-Style," 600.

in its aggregation of annual tax receipts."[93] However, since the end of Angola's civil war in 2002, the government promulgated reforms to improve revenue management and end Sonangol's discretionary use of oil revenues.[94] Despite efforts to reduce, at a minimum, the perception of corruption, three regime insiders, including Sonangol's former CEO Manuel Vicente, have been implicated in an insider-trading scheme that allegedly netted each millions.[95]

FISCAL REGIMES IN AFRICAN PETROSTATES

A petroleum fiscal regime has two objectives: for the state, it provides wealth accruing from hydrocarbon extraction; for the oil company, its goal is the optimal recovery of oil to ensure a profit.[96] Certain principles inform the majority of the world's fiscal regimes that govern mining and hydrocarbon production. First, subterranean resources are the property of the state.[97] This principle is a constitutional provision. Second, the government must ensure that its fiscal regime is perceived to be fair for both its citizens and the companies extracting the oil. Third, fiscal regimes are unique to each state; the mix of royalties, taxes, bonuses, and other fees is a product of negotiations. The fiscal regime depends largely on the petrostate's phase of production. Even with ownership falling to the state, two distinct contractual systems organize hydrocarbon production in the world: the concessionary scheme and the contractual system.[98] Whereas the concessionary scheme, common in the United States and United Kingdom, assigns ownership rights to the concessionaire, the contractual system is the rule in Africa and other developing countries. However, it is crucial to recognize that contractual systems vary among countries in terms of the royalty payments, taxes, and bonuses.

African governments receive compensation for hydrocarbon extraction through joint ventures (JVs), service contracts, or PSCs. In Nigeria, for instance, the majority of contracts are JVs with some PSCs. The Nigerian National Petroleum Company (NNPC) and IOCs share production costs. They sell oil on international and domestic markets and pay royalties – an average 20 percent depending on the field – a Petroleum Profit Tax of 85 percent on JVs and

[93] KPMG for the Ministry of Finance, *Assessment of Angolan Petroleum Sector* – Final Report vol. 1b – *Executive Summary* (Luanda: Ministry of Finance, Republic of Angola, 5 May 2004), 16.

[94] Carneiro, *Angola: Oil, Broad-Based Growth, and Equity*, 39–65.

[95] Tom Burgis, "U.S. to Probe Cobalt Oil Links in Angola," *The Financial Times* (February 21, 2012); see, as well, *Africa Confidential*, "Angola: Marques Takes Them On," 53, 2 (20 January 2012).

[96] Carole Nakhle, "Petroleum Fiscal Regimes: Evolution and Challenges," in *The Taxation of Petroleum and Minerals: Principles, Problems, and Practices*, eds. Philip Daniel, Michael Keen, and Charles McPherson (New York: Routledge, 2010), 89.

[97] Denis Guirauden, "Legal, Fiscal and Contractual Framework," in *Oil and Gas Exploration and Production: Reserves, Costs, and Contracts*, ed. Jean-Pierre Favennec, trans. Jonathan Pearse (Paris: Editions Technip, 2004), 179.

[98] Nakhle, "Petroleum Fiscal Regimes," 93.

Service Contracts, and 50 percent on PSCs.[99] These royalties, taxes, bonuses, and fees are typical of revenue management schemes in African petrostates, especially for governments that receive a majority of their fiscal revenues from oil earnings.

In some cases, concessions coexist with JVs or PSCs. These arrangements are reflections of past negotiations between oil companies and African leaders. Corporate executives had a single purpose: they wanted to increase profits for their shareholders and extract oil for the least amount of money. The contracts they negotiated specified the sums that their companies would pay in royalties, taxes, bonuses, and fees. In general, corporate executives tried to bargain for neutral tax instruments that would have a minimal impact on investment decisions, meaning that the company would make profits despite the taxes.[100] Because oil companies may anticipate some tax obligation regardless of price volatility or unanticipated production problems, they have an incentive to use hedging strategies to offset losses from unsuccessful drilling, poor quality crude, or political instability that causes lapses in production.[101] Although oil companies must cushion their operations from adverse events, they pay royalties and taxes in addition to corporate social-responsibility investments.

Whereas corporations have to make profits for their shareholders, African leaders have a political imperative to get the maximum rent for the oil. Their optimal strategy is to set the overall tax rate as high as possible, usually between 25 and 35 percent.[102] If a government exceeds this threshold, it risks pushing oil companies out of the country. These conflicting goals cause a tension between states and companies. To alleviate that tension, governments use nontax instruments such as local content provisions in any PSC that requires oil companies to make investments in infrastructure and training of personnel. Most bids for contracts are negotiated in auctions and include local content provisions.

Hydrocarbon production is capital intensive and requires advanced technological knowledge. Because many African petrostates were agrarian economies before companies discovered oil, they were incapable of providing expertise and inputs on a scale to meet the demand from the nascent oil industry. Oil companies therefore imported engineers or people with relevant expertise

---

[99] Federal Government of Nigeria, Ministry of Finance, Budget Office of the Federation, "2013 Fiscal Year: Understanding Budget 2013" (Abuja: 2013) retrieved from http://www.budgetof-fice.gov.ng/bof_2013-update/Understanding%20the%202013%20Budget.pdf.

[100] Philip Daniel, Brenton Goldsworthy, Wojciech Maliszewski, Diego Mesa Puyo, Alistair Watson, "Evaluating Fiscal Regimes for Resource Projects: An Example from Oil Development," in *The Taxation of Petroleum and Minerals: Principles, Problems, and Practices*, eds. Philip Daniel, Michael Keen, and Charles McPherson (New York: Taylor, Francis and Routledge, 2010), 190.

[101] Denis Frestad, "Corporate Hedging under a Resource Rent Tax Regime," *Energy Economics* 32 (March 2010): 459.

[102] Nakhle, "Petroleum Fiscal Regimes," 96.

to manage the extractive industries.[103] The lack of expertise is no less a problem in revenue management. Whereas an African petrostate may have competent ministers or directors of DNOCs, few have sufficient numbers of chartered accountants to manage multiple and complex revenue streams. For instance, a majority of the African petrostates has signed the Extractive Industries Transparency Initiative (EITI). Many have hired external auditors and accountants to check over their books. However, compliance with the EITI can be a serious challenge, as Nigeria's 2006 audit demonstrates; the government was unable to account for millions of dollars because of possible underpayments for royalties, failure to pay taxes, and the absence of recorded payments by the Central Bank of Nigeria.[104] Similarly, when Ghana's Chamber of Mines tried to reconcile reported income from gold mining companies with audits of government receipts conducted by the Ghana EITI, it found significant discrepancies.[105] In many petrostates, information about contracts between oil companies and governments as well as payments is unavailable.

Contracts and tax regimes vary from country to country but have tended to follow historical patterns. First, the concessionary regime involves payments for oil according to a set formula agreed upon by the oil companies and the government. Second, PSCs include the DNOC as a production partner that assumes a percentage share of the total production less cost of oil. The PSC has assumed increasing importance in Africa. Finally, a number of oil companies sign risk service contracts (RSCs) with governments that set production conditions. Within these three contractual categories variations exist. However, in Africa, regardless of whether the agreements are concessionary regimes, JVs with oil mining leases (OMLs), PSCs, or RSCs, the oil company must provide a majority of start-up financing and operational costs. Then, it pays royalties, taxes, and bonuses that determine the fiscal impact of oil production. Most importantly, it is the oil company that assumes the burden of any risk.

Contractual Arrangements

Oil companies entered agreements to manage payments according to one of four contractual regimes that were common in Africa in the late twentieth

---

[103] Jones Luong and Weinthal, *Oil is Not a Curse*, 183.

[104] Hart Group, *Nigeria Extractive Industries Transparency Initiative: Final Report* (London: Hart Group, 2006), 5. What this report indicates is a problematic practice where payments enter the national banking system through local banks. The local banks may hold onto the funds for a period before transferring the revenues to the central bank. As a consequence, audits and accounting for payments at any one point in time is difficult and prone to inaccuracies. See International Monetary Fund, *Nigeria: Financial Sector Assessment Program, Crisis Management and Crisis Preparedness Frameworks*, Technical Note, IMF Country Report 13/143 (May 2013), 7.

[105] Ian Gary, *Ghana's Big Test: Oil's Challenge to Democratic Development* (Baltimore: Oxfam America, February 2009), 9.

century. Concessions were the first regime; they were carryovers from the colonial period when administrators granted European mining companies ownership rights of minerals. The mining company would acquire proprietary rights over the minerals; in exchange it would pay the colonial power a royalty on production.[106] Concessionary agreements granted the company exclusive rights to a block for a fixed period of time either for the minerals in a specified area or the entirety of the territory.[107] Crucially, the colonial administration ceded its property rights over the minerals at either the well or the mine. The mining company then took all responsibility for the value chain.

After independence, concessions continued as the principal contractual arrangement, oftentimes grandfathered from colonial rule. In a concession, the government grants an oil company exclusive ownership rights; the firm then accepts all risks to explore, develop reserves, pump oil, and distribute the petroleum product.[108] In a concessionary system, the oil company makes royalty payments to the government; it then deducts costs of exploration, construction, and production (called cost oil); finally, remaining revenues (profit oil) constitute taxable income that the government may divide between provincial and national taxes.[109] In some cases, governments levy income taxes on profit oil. Firms pay taxes, royalties, and fees to local banks that transfer the funds to the central bank, and eventually, the revenues flow into the national treasury; governments have no reason to establish state-owned companies. Concessionary systems continue to operate among mature and declining producers such as Congo, Gabon, and in some Nigerian fields.

The JV was a second contractual system common in African petrostates that were producing oil in the 1980s. "'Joint ventures' are business agreements whereby two or more owners create a *separate entity*" in a specific economic sector, in this case oil, but "do *not* involve shared equity."[110] The JV is a partnership, a "joint subsidiary" of two organizations for a specific productive goal.[111] In an ideal type example, the JV means that the contractor and government share costs and risks.[112] National oil companies that participate in JVs are responsible for their share of production and have to contribute "cash calls" on a regular basis. However, in Africa, the limited capacity of petrostates to share costs meant the oil company assumed the risk for exploration and construction of facilities. In return, the company could anticipate a higher

---

[106] Daniel Johnston, *International Petroleum Fiscal Systems and Production Sharing Contracts* (Tulsa: PennWell Publishing Company, 1994), 29.
[107] Nakhle, "Petroleum Fiscal Regimes," 94.
[108] Guirauden, "Legal, Fiscal and Contractual Framework," 174.
[109] Johnston, *International Petroleum Fiscal Systems*, 31.
[110] Kathryn Rudie-Harrigan, "Joint Ventures and Competitive Strategy," *Strategic Management Journal* 9, 2 (March–April 1988): 142 (emphasis in original).
[111] Jeffrey Pfeffer and Philip Nowak, "Joint Ventures and Interorganizational Interdependence," *Administrative Science Quarterly* 21, 3 (September 1976): 399.
[112] Johnston, *International Petroleum Fiscal Systems*, 105.

percentage of the profit. This particular contractual arrangement would entail greater government participation in the production process.

PSCs structure contractual relations between oil companies and African petrostates. Like the concessionary system, contractors first pay royalties, then they recover cost oil, and on the remaining profit oil the government levies taxes.[113] In a PSC, "the state retains ownership of the resource and appoints the investor as 'contractor' to assist the government in developing the resource. Payment for the contractor is a share of production, and the government will not reimburse the contractors for exploration if hydrocarbon deposits do not justify development."[114] The structure of a PSC resembles that of agricultural sharecropping, in which land belongs to a landlord and the sharecropper receives a percentage of the production.[115] In a PSC, the contractor provides capital, equipment, and technical expertise; all equipment then reverts to the petrostate as its property.[116] The PSC generally operates according to specific rules that are legally binding agreements excepting a force majeure. These practices contribute to the revenues that a government receives.[117]

PSCs are long-term arrangements between a government and foreign contractor, generally an IOC.[118] Most observers agree that the first PSC was negotiated between the Indonesian DNOC Permina and the Independent Indonesian American Petroleum Company in the 1960s.[119] The crucial element of a PSC is that the contractor assumes all financial risk, but when explorations are successful, they receive a guaranteed return equivalent to around 40 percent of the crude oil produced annually. Contracts stipulate that companies may recover cost oil for that amount of oil to reimburse expenses incurred for exploration and construction of facilities. If costs exceed 40 percent of crude oil, the outstanding balance is rolled over to the next year. The remaining 60 percent is then divided between the contractor and DNOC at 35/65 percent, respectively.[120]

As a rule, governments auction PSCs. First, oil companies bid in international auctions for the OML. Second, the governments declare a minimum amount each contractor must pay in a signature bonus. Third, the governments require that successful bids include local content provisions, meaning investments in infrastructure, hiring local firms, and construction of schools and health clinics. Fourth, the bid must contain a letter of guarantee for the signature bonus. Finally, a government panel evaluates the bids and awards the contracts according to signature bonuses, local content, and technical considerations. Although a

[113] Johnston, *International Petroleum Fiscal Systems*, 42.
[114] Katz et al., *Lifting the Oil Curse*, 48.
[115] Johnston, *International Petroleum Fiscal Systems*, 22.
[116] Robert Fabrikant, "Production Sharing Contracts in the Indonesia Petroleum Industry," *Harvard International Law Journal* 2 (Spring 1975): 312.
[117] Johnston, *International Petroleum Fiscal Systems*, 35.
[118] Baunsgaard, "A Primer on Mineral Taxation," 12.
[119] Fabrikant, "Production Sharing Contracts," 334.
[120] Fabrikant, "Production Sharing Contracts," 312.

TABLE 3.2 *Signature Bonuses – 2005 – Joint Development Zone*

Signature Bonuses	Block 2	Block 3	Block 4	Block 5	Block 6
Total (million US$)	$71	$40	$90	$37	$45
Nigeria (60%)	$42.6	$24	$54	$22.2	$27
São Tomé and Príncipe (40%)	$28.4	$16	$36	$14.8	$18

Source: Retrieved from Oil and Gas Journal (http://www.ogj.com (accessed on 06/13/2005)).

single contractor wins the OML, the lead company has an incentive to distribute risk by soliciting participation from other companies in exchange for a percentage of the oil. A large offshore block may include a lead contractor who holds the OML and receives the highest percentage of oil produced; its partners are other IOCs and the DNOC. Once the contractor receives the award, the company must pay the signature bonus, usually within thirty days.

In theory, the signature bonus enters the government's treasury upon signing the PSC. The bonuses are one-time upstream payments an IOC makes at the beginning of the oil production stream. Because signature bonuses are typically millions of dollars, they discourage undercapitalized firms from making frivolous bids.[121] Signature bonuses are attractive to politicians, who see them as windfalls rather than de facto loans that contractors amortize over the life of a well. The upstream nature of signature bonuses fits nicely into the myopic needs of political leaders who need funds to distribute to cronies and supporters. Table 3.2 indicates the impact of signature bonuses on São Tomé and Príncipe. In the early twenty-first century, Nigeria and São Tomé and Príncipe established a Joint Development Authority to create the Joint Development Zone in oil fields that overlapped each country's territorial waters. Although the 40/60 percent division of oil favored Nigeria, the signature bonuses São Tomé and Príncipe received were substantial; in 2005, São Tomé and Príncipe and its 157,000 inhabitants received signature bonuses totaling $113.2 million in an economy that had a total Gross National Income of only $48 million in 2003![122] Some observers criticized awards to Nigerian companies that had little or no experience in deep-sea production and insubstantial capital assets. Still, the bonuses paid to the São Tomé and Príncipe government created fears that the sums exceeded its absorptive capacity.[123] An ability or inability to absorb substantial revenues without leakage because of inefficiencies and corruption is a potential challenge to emerging producers such as São Tomé and Príncipe.

[121] Baunsgaard, "A Primer on Mineral Taxation." IMF Working Paper WP/01/139. Washington, DC: The International Monetary Fund (September), 12.
[122] The World Bank, *World Development Indicators 2005* (Washington, DC: The World Bank, 2005), 22, 41.
[123] "Exploration and Production, Nigeria – São Tomé and Príncipe: Second Round Awarded," *Petroleum Economist* (July 2005).

The third common contractual arrangement is the RSC. In this arrangement, the contractor is responsible for all costs that accompany exploration and development of the well. The government allows recovery of these costs when the exploration is successful. After the contractor recovers costs associated with exploration and well development, the government pays the contractor a fee that is a percentage of remaining revenues. This fee is taxable income. The oil produced belongs in its entirety to the government. As Johnston notes, service fee contracts are common in countries that are oil importers.[124]

As more African governments recruit trained engineers in country, policymakers have incentives to use RSCs. Like the concessionary system and PSC, the RSC requires that the contractor finance all expenses associated with exploration and production. The issue of entitlement distinguishes the RSC from the two other forms of contracting; instead of granting the contractor rights to a percentage of the oil, the government pays the contractor a fee instead.[125] This "minute" difference does not affect the arithmetic that is almost identical to the PSC.[126] The RSC is a fee-based contract that makes cash payments that the government taxes. As in a PSC, the contractor in an RSC pays first a signature bonus at the signing of the contract. Then, if its explorations are successful, the contractor pays a discovery bonus. In some cases, a contractor pays a production bonus once production reaches a predetermined benchmark; however, most contractors prefer to pay taxes that more accurately reflect market prices for the oil they pump.[127]

For oil companies, any contract carries risks. First, the question of ownership of minerals is really a minor difference between a concessional or contractual system; whereas a concessional system transfers ownership of the mineral at the well, a contractual system transfers ownership at the point of exportation. Second, regardless of the particular arrangements, contractors assume an agency role vis-à-vis the government. This agency role means that for a limited period of time the government delegates managerial responsibilities to a company that must then report to government ministers or other authorities. Third, the oil company bears all financial risks for exploration, production, and marketing of the mineral. For instance, perhaps as many as nine out of ten exploration licenses fail to find commercially viable reserves, and the contractor bears all risks of a dry well.[128] Thus, an oil company must factor the costs of

[124] Johnston, *International Petroleum Fiscal Systems*, 87.

[125] David Johnston, "How to Evaluate the Fiscal Terms of Oil Contracts," in *Escaping the Resource Curse*, eds. Macartan Humphreys, Jeffrey D. Sachs, and Joseph E. Stiglitz (New York: Columbia University Press, 2007), 62.

[126] Johnston, *International Petroleum Fiscal Systems*, 88.

[127] Jenik Radon, "The ABCs of Petroleum Contracts: License-Concession Agreements, Joint Ventures, and Production-Sharing Agreements," in *Covering Oil: A Reporter's Guide to Energy and Development*, eds. Svetlana Tsalik and Anya Schiffrin (New York: Open Society Institute, 2005), 70.

[128] Radon, "The ABCs of Petroleum Contracts," 62.

drilling dry wells and other exploration expenses into any agreement it reaches
with the government. The type of agreement is of secondary importance to the
details contained in any concession or contract regime.[129]

REVENUE MANAGEMENT: LAWS, TAX CODES, AND CONTRACTS

As previously stated, many petrostates inherited mining tax laws from colonial
administrations. These tax codes define the respective responsibilities of lease-
holders (oil companies) regarding operations of wells, payment of taxes and
royalties, and relations with local communities. Efficient revenue management
is a significant challenge for African petrostates. Although the governments
have a menu of practices from which they may select a management strategy, the lack of trained civil servants makes revenue management problematic.
This section considers different types of revenue management regimes in Africa.
In African petrostates, leaders choose practices that correspond to political exigencies and their perceived security in office.

Perhaps the oldest and most common tax is a severance tax, also called
a royalty tax that governments assess on gross output or revenue. In Mali,
Africa's third largest gold producer, the government assesses three types of
taxes, royalties, and corporate income taxes, and because the Malian state is an
equity shareholder in the mines, it receives dividend payments. In petrostates,
the oil company pays a royalty that is a negotiated percentage of the price per
barrel from the onset of production. In some circumstances, the royalty may be
as low as 5 percent; in others it may be as high as 20 percent. Considerations
of the oil's quality, cost in extraction (e.g., water depth), and difficulties in
transport are factors in the determination of royalty amounts. After the initial
royalty payments, oil companies evaluate the expenses they incurred in exploration and construction of production facilities. In compensation, they receive
reimbursement in cost oil. Then, the contractor receives profit oil on which
the government assesses various taxes. Table 3.3 displays the different fiscal
regimes in selected African petrostates. Whereas Angola and Chad use concessions as their primary fiscal arrangement, ownership rules correspond to the
other states in that minerals belong to the governments.

Direct and Indirect Taxation

African petrostates negotiate various tax instruments with oil companies that
specify amounts of signature bonuses, royalties, corporate taxes, progressive
profit taxes, income taxes, and fees. These instruments operate in the same
country regarding fields that come on line at different times, leading to multiple revenue streams that are difficult for even a highly trained administrative
cadre to manage. After receipt of an accounting for cost oil, the government

[129] Johnston, "How to Evaluate the Fiscal Terms of Oil Contracts," 55.

TABLE 3.3 *Petroleum Laws and Codes in Selected African Petrostates*

Country – Law	Ownership provisions	Administrative reporting path	Licenses	Fiscal provision
Angola: Constitution Art. 12.1	All minerals belong to the government of Angola	Sonangol/CBA -» Min. Petro -» Pres dos Santos	Concessions, JVs, PSCs	Royalties – corporate taxes – DNOC participation
Chad: Loi N° 011/PR/1995 du juin 1995	All minerals belong to the government of Chad	IOC consortium -» Min. Petro -» Pres Idriss Déby	Concessions	Royalties – corporate taxes as assessed by local and national authorities
Congo: Loi N° 24-94 du 23 août 1994	All minerals belong to the government of Congo	SNPC -» Min. chargé des Hydrocarbures -» Pres Denis Sassou-Nguesso	JVs, PSCs	Royalties – corporate taxes – DNOC participation (heavy external debt on the basis of oil-backed loans)
Gabon: Loi N° 14/82 du 24 janvier 1983	All minerals belong to the government of Gabon	SNPG -» Min. Petro -» Pres Ali Bongo	JVs, PSCs	Royalties – corporate taxes – DNOC participation
Ghana: 2011 Petroleum Revenue Management Law (Act 851)	All minerals belong to the government of Ghana	GNPC -» Min. Petro -» Pres John Dramani Mahama	JVs; majority are PSCs	Royalties – corporate taxes – DNOC participation
Nigeria: Constitution of 1999	All minerals belong to the government of Nigeria	NNPC -» Min. Petro Diezani Alison-Maduike -» Pres Goodluck Jonathan	JVs, PSCs	Royalties – corporate taxes – DNOC participation (derivation scheme distributes 13% of revenues generated by oil production in each state

assesses income taxes, progressive profit taxes, and resource rent taxes on gross revenues.[130]

Indirect taxes include royalty payments that are a percentage of the price the company receives per barrel when production begins. Royalties are the traditional method by which oil companies pay governments for oil production.[131] Governments assess several types of royalty; some companies pay royalties for production volume and others pay a royalty on the value of production.[132] A challenge in a tax royalty system is to establish a method to ensure proper measurement of production so that payments reflect rates of extraction.[133] In countries where governments retain royalty tax instruments, officials may be doing so as a response to political pressures to show that the country is indeed benefiting from oil extraction.[134] Other indirect tax instruments include sales and excise taxes, value-added taxes, import and export duties, and property taxes. These instruments allow governments to receive taxes on the everyday business expenses that oil companies must incur.

Direct taxes are cash payments that oil companies make to governments according to the amount of oil pumped from a particular field.[135] Common among the direct tax instruments is the corporate income tax. The Resource Rent Tax (RRT) is a second instrument that links to an investment payback ratio. The RRT resembles the proportional income tax; however, it is only payable when earnings have attained a predetermined level or threshold rate of return.[136] However, officials in African petrostates have few incentives to use RRT because it subsidizes negative cash flows and taxes only positive flows at a proportional rate as a means to tax oil companies operating in the country. A third tax instrument is the Progressive Profit Tax (PPT), which adjusts to upward price volatility. The PPT ensures that a government receives increased revenues when profits for a given block rise. Other instruments include capital gains taxes, and local governments may require that companies pay a stamp tax for property sales.

Many oil companies operate multiple concessions at different stages of production. A strategy some use is to reduce their tax liability by deducting upstream

---

[130] Johnston, "How to Evaluate the Fiscal Terms of Oil Contracts," 59.

[131] James Otto, Craig Andrews, Fred Cawood, Michael Dogett, Pietro Guj, Frank Stermole, John Stermole, and John Tilton, *Mining Royalties: A Global Study of Their Impact on Investors, Government, and Civil Society* (Washington, DC: The World Bank, 2006), 41.

[132] Baunsgaard, "A Primer on Mineral Taxation," 10.

[133] Daniel, "Petroleum Revenue Management," 23.

[134] Otto et al., *Global Mining Taxation*, 53.

[135] James Otto, Maira Luisa Batarseh, and John Cordes, *Global Mining Taxation Comparative Study* (Golden, CO: Institute for Global Resources Policy and Management, The Colorado School of Mines, March 2000); Philip Daniel, "Petroleum Revenue Management: An Overview," Paper prepared for Workshop on Petroleum Revenue Management (Washington: The World Bank, October 23–24, 2002).

[136] Philip Daniel, "Evaluating State Participation in Mineral Projects: Equity, Infrastructure and Taxation," in *Taxation of Mineral Enterprises*, ed. James M. Otto. (Boston: Graham & Trotman/Martinus Nijhoff,1995), 177.

expenditures in a new block from the profits in an operating concession. Governments then "ring-fence" individual oil blocks to prevent this strategy.[137] Ring-fencing separates taxable projects so that a block with declining production cannot be used to reduce taxes on earnings from a block with high levels of productivity.[138] These virtual fences are outcomes of intensive negotiations between senior government officials and representatives of oil companies. Their use demonstrates the complexity of revenue management in petrostates.

The shift to PSCs opened up opportunities for grand corruption. First, governments auction the blocks and award offshore mining leases to the winner. The outcome of the bidding process depends on the contractors' submission of qualifying financial information, the amounts they agree to pay in signature bonuses, provisions to hire local firms, and plans to invest in community development. At each stage, opportunities arise for insider-information brokering, side payments to officials on the eligibility panel, and payoffs to local officials. Then, the arrangements for signature bonus payments need to ensure that the funds enter the petrostate's central bank, which drafts strict withdrawal rules. Otherwise, presidents and their cronies may divert the bonuses for personal or political purposes.

Dishonest behavior often follows the payment of signature bonuses. These one-time payments to governments occur at the signing of contracts. Unfortunately, when companies pay bonuses, money deposited in government accounts leaks when presidents seize funds for personal reasons. For instance, when Chad received its first bonus for the commencement of oil production in the Doba fields in 2001, President Déby diverted a substantial portion for military expenditures.[139] Initially, the World Bank declared that Chad was in violation of its agreements; however, it seems clear that Chad, as a sovereign state, could use the bonuses as the president so desired. The World Bank backpedaled and noted that Déby's use of the funds was not technically in violation of his agreements.[140] His use of the bonuses for short-term political purposes highlights the potential problems that confront emerging petrostates that have few agencies to manage resource revenues. In other petrostates, an egregious practice has been the transfer of large sums to the personal accounts of leaders who have accumulated fortunes.[141]

[137] Baunsgaard, "A Primer on Mineral Taxation," 7.
[138] Otto et al., *Global Mining Taxation*, 52.
[139] Babette Stern, "Le Tchad a Acheté des Armes avec l'Argent du Pétrole," *Le Monde* (22 Novembre 2000).
[140] Ian Gary and Nikki Reisch, *Chad's Oil: Miracle or Mirage: Following the Money in Africa's Newest Petrostate* (Baltimore: Catholic Relief Services, 2005), 42–44.
[141] In 2009, French prosecutors undertook multiple judicial actions to freeze the accounts of African leaders from Congo, Equatorial Guinea, and Gabon. Omar Bongo Ondimba had millions of Euros in accounts in numerous European banks. Prosecutors asserted that the sums in his accounts far exceeded any reasonable amounts he might have accumulated as the president of Gabon. See, "Les Comptes d'Omar Bongo Saisis à Paris," *SudOuest* (Bordeaux, 26 Février 2009). Also, BBC, "France halts African Leaders Case." Retrieved from www.bbc.co.uk (accessed 29 October 2009).

CONCLUSION

In this chapter, I have reviewed corporate histories, strategies, and how the international oil market adjusted from being dominated by a cartel of European and North American corporations to a fiercely competitive market that includes companies with diverse goals and strategies from around the world. This narrative bridges the historical discussion in Chapter 2 with the consideration of economic growth as it occurs through a petrostate's productive life that I call its phases of production. As I discuss in Chapter 4, the underlying circumstances of the phases of production influences the contractual arrangements oil companies signed with African governments.

I have noted how colonial business relations are present in these contractual arrangements and how they have developed. If European firms signed contracts during colonialism or the immediate postcolonial period, the contract reflected colonial legislation. From prior to independence oil extraction in Africa was hardly a lucrative activity; contracts were largely concessions in which European oil companies, often from the metropole, had property rights over the reserves they were exploiting. After 1974, oil companies commenced widespread explorations in Africa. The contractual arrangements adjusted, and joint venture contracts were common. Conditions in the particular petrostates at the time of discovery determined whether contracts were concessions, JVs, or for later producers, PSCs.

This chapter has shown that North American and European international oil companies provided business models for other firms in Africa. The multidivisional, vertically integrated corporation is present in the national oil companies that have become active on the continent. In contemporary Africa, Asian and Latin American national oil companies have had a fundamental impact on Africa's petrostates. In response to contractual changes, most notably the use of PSCs, African petrostates have established increasingly influential DNOCs, most notably Angola's Sonangol, which remains a key actor in domestic production and international exploration.

Other continuities are evident in European national oil companies, particularly Elf Aquitaine, which reproduced colonial relationships and bribed national leaders in French Africa. For example, a system pejoratively referred to as *françafrique* integrated francophone African petrostates into a system dominated by French economic interests.[142] These arrangements were evident when former colonies were what we refer to as emerging producers. Despite seemingly anachronistic relationships, the influence of former colonial powers through firms in the extractive industries endures as many of these states are cycling through their different phases of production.

---

[142] Verschave, *La Françafrique.*

4

Economic Growth and Phases of Production

INTRODUCTION

Chapter 3 discussed the interaction between diverse oil companies and African petrostates. The chapter explored how historic relations influenced the relations between oil companies and African politicians. In postcolonial Africa, oil companies fostered personal ties between national leaders and company executives resting on a business model built on Standard Oil's multidivisional firm. Contracts were concessions and the low cost per barrel gave the oil companies considerable leeway in their negotiations with postindependence presidents. The 1974 oil crisis changed these relations, and leaders of petrostates, particularly in Nigeria, reevaluated their contractual relations with IOCs. I noted how contracts have shifted from concessions to PSCs; NOCs and IOCs thereafter entered African markets with diverse goals. An NOC's goals include the acquisition of energy for the home economy; their motivations are to get contracts that ensure energy for extended periods at the most advantageous price. For IOCs, the goal is enhancing shareholder profit. These diverging goals characterize competitive relations in contemporary African markets today.

This chapter considers the relationship between the "phase of production" and the value chain in the oil sector.[1] Among the critical influences is the *value chain* or entire productive process from exploration and discovery to the marketing of refined petroleum products. When government officials learn that their country possesses hydrocarbon reserves, it is an *emerging* producer. After ten years, officials have learned how to negotiate with IOCs and the multitude of NOCs, and the country is a *mature* producer.[2] Some countries have

---

[1] The concept of a value chain in productive industries is from Michael E. Porter, *The Competitive Advantage of Nations* (New York: The Free Press, 1990), 29, 41.

[2] The classification of a mature oil field is a field that has been in a production period and approaching a decline in the volume it is capable of producing without technological applications.

large reserves and may therefore be mature producers for decades. Others have smaller reserves, and within several decades they are facing the prospect of the end of oil. These petrostates are *declining* producers. The manner in which different petrostates respond to these three phases of production is a consequence of their levels of development at the time of discovery.

This chapter returns to the book's central theme: the conditions present in a country at the time of hydrocarbon discoveries are critical influences in political and economic institutional outcomes. If the country is extraordinarily poor and lacks experience managing an extractive industry, it is at a disadvantage in its negotiations with IOCs and Asian NOCs. It might have only rudimentary offices in its bureaucracy and few instruments to administer its new productive sector. In such countries, the banking sector may be so enfeebled that political leaders negotiate payments into offshore accounts. Such accounts are unfortunately difficult to supervise. By the same token, if the country has experience with the extractive industries as a consequence of mineral assets, its ministry of mines has the minimal financial systems to receive funds from oil production. As emphasized throughout this book, the critical problem is the institutional and bureaucratic conditions at the time of discovery.

The Phase of Production

Hydrocarbon production goes through a cycle that begins with drilling, field development, production planning, and finishes with "tertiary recovery," during which time the well operator injects fluids to "wash out" any oil remaining in a reserve.[3] The value chain refers to processes that begin with the award of contracts, the regulation and monitoring of operations, collection of taxes and royalties, revenue distribution and management, and the implementation of policies and projects that might contribute to sustainable growth.[4] For the petrostate, revenues are crucial from the first payments to the final deposits in a central bank after depletion of the hydrocarbon reserves. African petrostates typically adopt growth strategies that use and depend on resource rents. The challenge that these states face as they go through a productive life cycle is how well they shift from "rent-driven" to "skill-driven growth," which determines their future development.[5]

See Tayfun Babadagli, "Development of Mature Oil Fields – A Review," *Journal of Petroleum Science and Engineering* 57 (2007): 222–223.

[3] E.J. Durrer and G.E. Slater, "Optimization of Petroleum and Natural Gas Production – A Survey," *Management Science* 24, 1 (September 1977): 35.

[4] Eleodoro Mayorga Alba, "Extractive Industries Value Chain," Extractive Industries for Development Series #3, Africa Region Working Paper Series #125 (Washington: The World Bank, March 2009); Verena Fritz, Kai Kaiser, and Brian Levy, *Problem Driven Governance and Political Economy Analysis: Good Practice Framework* (Washington: The World Bank, 2009), 68.

[5] Richard M. Auty, "Natural Resource Endowment, the State and Development Strategy," *Journal of International Development* 9, 4 (1997): 660.

The *phase of production* is analogous to a life cycle of oil production from the discovery of oil to the closure of wells and reversion to a non-oil economy. This term refers to a set of political circumstances that shape revenue management in the petrostate. The phase of production is thus a temporal measure of what a country experiences at the onset of production and as its hydrocarbon sector passes through its life cycle. It is critical to recognize that the phase of production influences the timing of when diverse groups seek democratic reforms and the developmental impact of hydrocarbon revenues.

Revenues are the tangible payments of the oil's value after the oil companies have recovered the costs of production plus returns to capital invested in exploration and development of a field.[6] Once a government begins to receive revenues from oil, the extent of state construction has a decisive influence on its ability to manage windfalls. *State construction* refers to the establishment of an effective bureaucracy that engages individuals with the necessary competence to manage fiscal revenues and expenditures that accrue from hydrocarbon production. Political leaders tend to have different responses to revenue management according to conditions in the country at the time of discovery. These conditions reflect the country's level of state construction as well as historical relations and accommodations reached among diverse groups in society.

Although it is tempting to offer an arbitrary temporal division for the phase of production, the movement between different phases of production depends on continuing discoveries and the state's initial level of institutional development. Most important is the absence of unanticipated change; otherwise stated, the presence of stability. Leaders of petrostates adopt different strategies that reflect the phase of production. When oil production begins, a country is an *emerging producer*. Oil companies discover petroleum reservoirs, determine the size of reserves, begin drilling in other sites around the original well, and set up installations to recover oil and natural gas.[7] Within a period after the initial discovery of oil, diverse petroleum companies enter the market to explore for other fields. New discoveries extend the productive life of a petrostate's reserves. Once international companies start to produce oil, their executives try to deepen their bonds to the emerging petrostate's political leaders. Within the emerging petrostate, brokers emerge to take advantage of ambiguous rules, regulations, and laws governing access to politicians.[8] Politicians in emerging producers must then identify and engage individuals who can define a regulatory framework for operations and revenue collection. The tasks are daunting and require organizational acumen and vision.

[6] Philip Daniel, "Evaluating State Participation in Mineral Projects: Equity, Infrastructure and Taxation," in *Taxation of Mineral Enterprises*, ed. James M. Otto (Boston: Graham & Trotman/ Martinus Nijhoff, 1995), 167.
[7] Durrer and Slater, "Optimization of Petroleum and Natural Gas Production," 40.
[8] Steffen Hertog, "The Sociology of the Gulf Rentier Systems: Societies of Intermediaries," *Comparative Studies in Society and History* 52, 2 (April 2010b): 288.

A *mature producer* has the organizational mechanisms to manage the revenues from numerous fields that stream into different accounts at the central bank and DNOC. A mature producer has defined procedures to manage and absorb oil revenues. This management hardly excludes rent seeking. Influential politicians in mature producers organize inefficient "distributional coalitions" to seek revenues that oil companies pay to the government.[9] Members of these distributional coalitions share a sense of identity that sets them apart from the larger population. Some may be state employees who take advantage of the opportunities presented by oil windfalls. Others may be non–oil-sector individuals who have considerable influence that allows them to gain government contracts and seek further sources of resource rents. The composition and characteristics of these coalitions varies among petrostates.

In Nigeria, competition among its heterogeneous population motivated political actors to make zero-sum calculations about corrupt behavior. At the level of state governments, politicians capture the state governments and use their positions to distribute revenues and contracts to constituents who are members of their clan and ethnic group. On May 24, 2013, the Nigerian Governors' Forum (NGF), a nonpartisan assembly of thirty-six governors, elected a chairman. Prior to this election, supporters of President Goodluck Jonathan had expelled Rivers State Governor Rotimi Amaechi from the governing party.[10] Despite the president's actions, the thirty-six governors voted and elected Amaechi. A controversy erupted when disgruntled governors rejected the vote and declared another governor chairman. This competition for leadership positions among the state governorships was fierce and reflected each state's share of oil revenues and access to special constituency funds. As long as Nigeria is a mature producer, the governors remain powerful and such conflicts are predictable.

A petrostate without new discoveries and with diminishing, indeed almost exhausted reserves is a *declining producer*. In declining producers, ruling coalitions have governed sometimes for generations. The children of former leaders are more numerous than their parents; they demand both opportunities and political power. As the hydrocarbons decrease, these children become more vocal in their demands for political voice and opportunities. An analogy to this point is Auty's observation that the political influence of agricultural producers increases "geometrically" in proportion to resource depletion.[11] Individuals denied the wealth and opportunities enjoyed by their parents have every reason to join movements and political parties that assemble those who profess a desire for free elections and representative democracy. They often join with the reformers in formerly authoritarian regimes to agitate for political change.[12]

[9] Mancur Olson Jr., *The Rise and Decline of Nations: Economic Growth, Stagflation, and Social Rigidities* (New Haven: Yale University Press, 1982), 43.

[10] Taiwo Amodu and Desmond Mgboh, "NGF chair: Jonathan, Amaechi in final showdown," *The Sun* (May 24, 2013).

[11] Auty, "Natural Resource Endowment, the State and Development Strategy," 654.

[12] Consider the example of the Gabonese politician Zacharie Myboto (discussed further in

Opponents to the status quo confront the presidents and their cronies with demands for political openness. The former winners then seek to maintain exclusivity for the regime. Conflicts erupt between different factions in a struggle over who controls outcomes.

During a period of declining production, oil exports contribute less and less to fiscal revenues. Political arrangements in declining producers are vulnerable; depletion of resources and therefore falling revenues gives political elites a reason to shrink the inner sanctums of the state and even reassert authoritarian rule. In an influential article, Tornell and Lane demonstrate that the "voracity effect" occurs when there are no institutional constraints on rulers' discretion to distribute natural resource windfalls.[13] The voracity effect contradicts the Dutch disease model that argues the booming sector expands to accommodate factor movement from the other tradeable sector.[14] Rather than adjust to the loss of factors in the non-tradeables sector, consistent with the Dutch disease, Tornell and Lane show formally how in resource-abundant states greed among social actors increases proportionally to an increase in the windfall. Their model explains behavior in which actors mobilized to seize windfalls during oil booms because they perceived revenues to be increasing, and amplified demands for their share.

The voracity effect is particularly useful for understanding the competition for natural resource windfalls in declining producers where revenues are falling at the very time that leaders must expand the recipients of wealth to ensure security for their coalition. Windfalls are ebbing, and the winners who had consumed resource rents from more lucrative days are reluctant to find other sources of income. Tornell and Lane note: "If the collapse of an autocracy relaxes restrictions on the behavior of the powerful groups in a society, democratization may actually intensify the redistribution struggle in these countries."[15] Their contribution is to stress that it might be an error to make overly optimistic predictions about states that have made short-term democratic reforms.

In Congo during the early 1990s, lower growth rates led to instability, and reformers succeeded in convincing President Sassou Nguesso to relax his autocratic regime and allow his opponents to organize free elections. It was a serious miscalculation; he lost in the election's first round. A new government came into office and Congo's newly elected National Assembly passed a series of acts that excluded his former cronies from preferential contracts and benefits.

Chapter 6), who established a party in part to support the aspirations of his daughter and grandchildren.

[13] Aaron Tornell and Philip R. Lane, "The Voracity Effect," *The American Economic Review* 89, 1 (March 1999): 23.

[14] Tornell and Lane, "The Voracity Effect," 24. On the Dutch disease, see W. Max Corden and J. Peter Neary, "Booming Sector and De-Industrialisation in a Small Booming Economy," *The Economic Journal* 92, 3688 (December 1982): 825–848.

[15] Tornell and Lane, "The Voracity Effect," 42.

They lobbied Sassou who bowed to their pressure; he launched a rebellion, defeated his rival, and reimposed authoritarian rule. At the time of reform, leaders enact redistributive policies and the state confronts its greatest challenges. People who had been the winners under authoritarian rule were losers under reforms that redistributed benefits to other groups. These new losers had every reason to mobilize against the reforming state.

In many respects, Congo flipped back to a set of circumstances that were indicative of an emerging producer. The offices that managed hydrocarbon revenues were rudimentary and under the executive's control. Centralized decision making in the presidency and clientelism informed the standards for inclusion. Corruption was widespread, and Sassou distributed contracts and economic opportunities as a strategy to bind cronies to his regime. In short, Congo affirms how the voracity effect demonstrates that linearity in the political and economic development of African petrostates is hardly a given. Congo's experiences echo a need for caution in assessing developmental trajectories among these African oil producers.

The Phase of Production and Revenue Management

Where a particular country falls in terms of its phase of production has implications for types of rule (e.g., democratic, benign personal rule, neopatrimonial, or autocratic) and its politicians' relations with foreign and domestic investors. When a poor emerging producer begins to export oil, its tax base is *regressive*, meaning an impoverished, usually agrarian population provides meagre taxes and receives few social sector services.[16] The reliance on extractive taxes causes policy shifts that are distinctive from other taxation regimes in non-resource exporting economies.[17] Oil production shifts the levy of taxes from the poor to the wealthy, namely the oil companies. Petrostates that receive a majority of their tax revenues from the wealthy have every incentive to protect the property rights in that sector. Because petrostates are taxing the oil companies, politicians protect investments in the oil sector and the mass of the population receives little to nothing. Simply stated, "If a state is not taxing a group for some reason (for example, because there is no profit in it), it has no incentive to cater to that group."[18] Hence, agrarian populations expect little from their governments in the form of employment-generating investments or improvements in social-sector expenditures because agriculture provides so few fiscal revenues for the state.

[16] Jeffrey F. Timmons, "The Fiscal Contract: States, Taxes, and Public Services," *World Politics* 57, 4 (July 2005): 531

[17] Deborah Bräutigam, "Contingent Capacity: Export Taxation and State-Building in Mauritius," in *Taxation and State Building in Developing Countries: Capacity and Consent*, eds. Deborah Bräutigam, Odd-Helge Fjeldstad, and Mick Moore (New York: Cambridge University Press, 2008), 137–138.

[18] Timmons, "The Fiscal Contract: States, Taxes, and Public Services," 532.

As petrostates shift from emerging to mature production, certain commonalities are evident. Three sets of actors gain influence. First, political actors include officials whether elected, appointed, or military officers who came to office via coup. Second, patrons dominate civil society organizations, informal voluntary associations, and religious congregations. Finally, economic actors include both foreign and domestic investors active in the oil and non-oil sectors. These three sets of actors intermingle, seek narrow goals, cooperate, compete, and compromise with one another; their interactions shape the subsequent development in the African petrostates. Whereas advocates of the staple trap model might depict these relations as static, we see that they are dynamic, and change is a constant element even when the president remains in office for lengthy periods.[19] Moreover, these interactions are products of historical processes.

This chapter shows that the phase of production influences the context in which politicians make crucial decisions that reflect assessments of the coalitions' members' needs. Emerging African petrostates change rapidly; as quickly as their economies are developing becuase of the receipt of resource rents, so, too, are their polities. Although authoritarian rulers dominated many of these states at the time they discovered hydrocarbon reserves, the influx of oil revenues stabilized their coalitions and regimes. Second, political authorities might resist changes, but stability leads to increasing populations and pressures that compel policy shifts. Hence, although these states might have been neopatrimonial dictatorships, oil brings political stability and subtle changes occur.

THE PHASES OF PRODUCTION AND ECONOMIC GROWTH

Chapter 2 considered myriad organizations that composed the colonial state. European colonial administrations invested in specific African territories in as much as they could expect a return on that investment. In territories that possessed ostensibly fewer endowments, the colonial state was small and staffed by few trained personnel. Relative inattention to far-flung regions resulted in asymmetrical state construction; some regions received a smaller administrative apparatus and fewer investments. As a consequence, variable levels of development were apparent in colonies such as Sudan where the current South Sudan (Juba) was decidedly less attractive for investments and postings than Khartoum. Prospects for returns on investments were critical variables of the bureaucracy that European authorities established in their respective colonies.

---

[19] Richard M. Auty and Alan H. Gelb, "Political Economy of Resource Abundant States," in *Resource Abundance and Economic Development*, ed. R. M. Auty (New York: Oxford University Press, 2001), 138–141. See as well, Richard Auty and Nicola Pontara, "A Dual-Track Strategy for Managing Mauritania's Projected Oil Rent," *Development Policy Review* 26, 1 (January 2008): 59–60.

After independence, African political leaders continued to govern with the ministries and agencies they inherited from the colonial state. Even in the cases of Angola, Nigeria, and Congo, three colonial territories that received substantial investments, state construction reflected the economic circumstances of their respective European administrations. Because Portugal was poor, Angola's colonial state construction was minimal and its postcolonial skeletal administration entered a civil war that lasted for twenty-seven years.

The relative wealth of the colonizer shaped how an African country fared after independence. With the exception of selected enclaves, most colonial investments were in infrastructure, railroads and roads, ports, mines, and colonial plantations. Significant differences were apparent among the colonial powers. In Angola during the nineteenth century, Africans who lived along the Luanda–Benguela corridor benefited from colonial investments, but charter companies in the interior of southern Angola enslaved people to work in copper and gold mines.[20] Portuguese colonial policy was to send settlers to develop commercial farms, diamond mines, or any other activities that would furnish revenues for the metropolitan economy. The settlers stripped Angola's Creole elite of any privileges they enjoyed and treated all Angolans as their source of labor.[21] Their circumstances were similar to those of indigenous people in Spanish Guinea; settlers seized land and exported cocoa from Fernando Po (present-day Bioko) and timber from the mainland to provide revenues for a minimal administration that provided few if any public services.[22] After World War I, both Angola and Spanish Guinea experienced a second colonization that changed distributions of wealth and opportunity among the colonies' inhabitants.

By contrast, France and Great Britain had more money for private or public investments in Africa. Even though they were comparatively wealthier economies, two world wars had depleted the British and French governments' discretionary funds, and many politicians saw the colonies as expensive luxuries. After World War I, France announced its *politique d'association* and calls for development, mise-en-valeur, that intended to reduce administrative expenditures in its colonies and make them support themselves. For Chad, Mauritania, Upper Volta, Niger, and other colonies with few investment opportunities, colonial officials lived in capital cities; they only traveled to the hinterlands to collect taxes or recruit forced labor. The British used their supposedly indirect rule to favor particular individuals with whom they entered into coalitions to ensure the stability of rule. After independence, privileged individuals governed through clientelist networks that controlled the distribution of prebends among

[20] W.G. Clarence-Smith, *Slaves, Peasants, and Capitalists in Southern Angola 1840–1926* (New York: Cambridge University Press, 1979), 19.
[21] Gerald J. Bender, *Angola under the Portuguese: The Myth and the Reality* (Berkeley and Los Angeles: University of California Press, 1978), 142.
[22] Alicia Campos, "The Decolonization of Equatorial Guinea: The Relevance of the International Factor," *The Journal of African History* 44 (March 2003): 95–96.

patrons clustered in various regions. Oil revenues thus had a transformative effect.

The difference between the African petrostates and predatory regimes is that the revenue streams from hydrocarbon production freed leaders from a requirement to tax or plunder their population. A relative abundance of wealth enabled political leaders to fund their coalition partners, placate restless citizens, and co-opt real and potential opponents. These distributional choices changed with the phase of production. Leaders of emerging petrostates receive windfalls that multiplied the fiscal revenues available far in excess of the pre-oil tax base. Theoretically, policymakers adjust, and as the states make a shift from emerging to mature producers, the increases in revenues should finance better public service. The staple trap model suggests "super rents" encourage government leaders to seize revenues at the expense of creating sustainable wealth.[23] As a consequence, for instance, during Nigeria's military regimes, the generals diverted expenditures toward the "military in government" and neopatrimonial purposes instead of investing in development projects that might have reduced poverty.[24] Development lagged as a result.

Phases of Production and Political Economic Choices

Political leaders in African petrostates make a number of policy choices that have an impact on the efficient management of oil revenues. These choices are a function of the petrostate's specific phase of production. Leaders of emerging producers sign contracts with various oil companies active in the country. The executives of these corporations have a mandate to negotiate contracts that create profits for their shareholders. Oil companies' representatives thus have strategies that vary according to their perceptions of the country's level of development and the sophistication of its leaders. When interacting with the poorest states, some executives may believe that no one really enforces compliance with contracts as long as they pay bonuses, royalties, taxes, and the occasional bribe. In poor states, this assessment may accurately appraise the state's capacity to regulate its oil sector. However, as I suggest about the Kosmos Controversy in Ghana (Chapter 5), underestimating the capabilities of African leaders is an error that oil executives make at their own risk.[25]

---

[23] Auty and Pontara, "A Dual-track Strategy for Managing Mauritania's Projected Oil Rent," 59; on super rents, see Mick Moore, "Between Coercion and Contract: Competing Narratives on Taxation and Governance," in *Taxation and State Building in Developing Countries: Capacity and Consent*, eds. Bräutigam et al., (New York: Cambridge University Press, 2008), 59–60.

[24] J. Bayo Adekanye, "The Military," in *Transition Without End: Nigerian Politics and Civil Society Under Babangida*, eds. Larry Diamond, Anthony Kirk-Greene, and Oyeleye Oyediran (Boulder: Lynne Rienner Publishers Inc., 1997), 66.

[25] Such an error allegedly occurred in 2009 when Kosmos Energy shared geophysical details of the Jubilee Fields with ExxonMobil in direct violation of contractual provisions signed with the Ghanaian National Petroleum Company.

Petroleum companies operate within constraints that reflect the political economic conditions in a given country at different phases of production. Market conditions determine efficient revenue management. These conditions include whether oil is onshore or offshore, the size of the state's bureaucracy, and its capacity to regulate its extractive industries. External conditions include the international market and the price per barrel at the time the oil is sold. This chapter contributes a consideration of how political economic conditions, determined by initial conditions and the phase of production, influence outcomes in the value chain. These conditions converge to shape the politicians' responses to developments in the extractive industries and their goals, such as effective appropriation of resource rents, distribution of rents, or outright theft of revenues.

The agreements that politicians make with oil companies are often outcomes that reflect the phase of production. A state's political leadership chooses to negotiate contracts according to its experience with negotiations and understanding of the intricacies of contracting in the extractive industries. These contracts reflect the policymakers' perceived benefit and strategies at different points in the value chain from upstream operations of exploration, discovery, and production to the downstream activities of the receipt of royalties, taxes, and fees.[26] In African petrostates, colonial and immediate postcolonial experiences determined the policymakers' demands in contract negotiations.

Historical experiences shape contemporary arrangements in different petrostates. For example, prior to independence, Spanish (Equatorial) Guinea was marginal to Spanish economic and political interests.[27] Because the colony provided Spain with limited revenues from cocoa and forestry, authorities in Madrid had either ignored or repressed its people. In October 1968, Spain handed power over to democratically elected Francisco Macias Nguema, who imposed a horrific regime that devastated the economy and drove a substantial percentage of the population into exile.[28] His rule embedded repressive political institutions that influenced the successor government. Hence, when oil production began in 1995, violence and repression were the norms that defined Equatorial Guinea's political institutions. The government negotiated contracts with oil companies that were famously disadvantageous to the country.[29] More importantly, proceeds from the country's hydrocarbons benefited a small population and excluded an overwhelming majority.

[26] Michael E. Porter, "Toward a Dynamic Theory of Strategy," *Strategic Management Journal* 12 (Winter 1991): 98.

[27] Campos, "The Decolonization of Equatorial Guinea," 108.

[28] Max Liniger-Goumaz, *Small Is Not Always Beautiful: The Story of Equatorial Guinea*, translated by John Wood. (Totowa, New Jersey: Barnes and Noble Books, 1989), 54–60.

[29] For several stories, see Justin Blum, "Equatorial Guinea, USA: US Oil Firms," *Washington Post* (September 9, 2004); Peter Maass, "A Touch of Crude," *Mother Jones* (January/February 2005).

The phase of production has an influence on bureaucratic organization in each petrostate. Within emerging African producers the levels of state construction varied widely; the state in Chad, Mauritania, São Tomé and Príncipe, and Equatorial Guinea had partial bureaucracies that provided their citizens minimal services. Their bureaucracies, like the poorest states in Africa, had a dearth of competent personnel, both in term of absolute numbers of civil servants and their educational preparation, which impeded management of the public sector and economic growth.[30] The absence of competent civil servants to manage oil revenues also imposed constraints on any ability to absorb oil windfalls. In Equatorial Guinea, perhaps the worst case, oil companies deposited bonuses, royalties, and taxes into accounts that the president controlled; the funds never entered the consolidate budget.[31] Without a competent staff to review contracts or manage oil revenues, leakage because of venality and incompetent personnel were sure to follow. However, as more money flows into their economies, Africa's emerging petrostates adopt better laws that enable benefits from oil production.

Bureaucratic efficiency, or the lack thereof, reflected conditions present in various states at the time of independence. Leaders of newly independent African states confronted several dilemmas. First, chronic fiscal shortages undermined any credibility these leaders may have wanted for in their policy pronouncements. Second, this lack of credible commitment denied politicians legitimacy. People avoided the independent state much as they had fled colonial rule. This lack of legitimacy, an unfortunate legacy of colonial rule, deepened the state's detachment from society. Third, many African governments were fiscally incapable of funding, much less staffing, effective ministerial offices. Their fiscal revenues were so low that they were dependent on international donors to fund their fundamental public services. Hence, when the hollow states in Chad, Mauritania, and even Gabon, began to export oil, they did not have ministries or agencies with competent personnel to manage the revenues.

In the poorest African states, political leaders campaigned in elections in which participation was highest in cities. They had few incentives to listen to social demands, much less represent people from ethnic groups apart from theirs. Economic conditions in many African states at independence were dismal, and politicians built coalitions of supporters in urban centers to ensure their security in office. Many came to office during civil wars, and oil revenues provided a critical means to maintain their rule. Angola's Neto, for instance, depended on oil rents to purchase military arms and sustain the MPLA and his political machine. Colonial relations conditioned his choices as he reinforced the positions of his fellow Kimbari who came from Luanda and Benguela.

[30] Arthur A. Goldsmith, "Africa's Overgrown State Reconsidered: Bureaucracy and Economic Growth," *World Politics* 51, 4 (July 1999): 522.
[31] Human Rights Watch, *Well-Oiled: Oil and Human Rights in Equatorial Guinea* (New York: Human Rights Watch, July 2009).

The dysfunctional configuration of power that emerged in Angola during its first postwar decade reflected the embeddedness of networks that had emerged during the liberation struggle and twenty-seven-year civil war.

Officials in African countries that receive revenues from oil exports often need to balance political demands from diverse groups with their public fiduciary responsibilities. These dual tasks were sometimes daunting, especially in countries with a high degree of ethnic and linguistic fractionalization.[32] Politicians reached out to leaders of social coalitions for support; in return, they distributed funds, privileges, and opportunities. For instance, after the contested 2007 elections, Nigeria's President Yar'Adua heard multiple demands from numerous constituencies. Unfortunately, hopes for probity faltered when reports emerged of the Peoples Democratic Party's (PDP) practices of keeping "PDP Youth" on the payroll and using them to foment violence against his rivals during the elections.[33] In 2011, the incumbent PDP paid diverse social groups with party funds so they would support its electoral campaign.[34] A similar pattern of domination and a scramble for campaign funds occurred in Angola as the dos Santos administration tried to ensure its position in office during the 2012 elections.[35] Nigerian and Angolan politicians divert oil revenues according to their assessments of need.

Emerging Producers

The numerous challenges inherent in managing oil revenues are hardly unique to African emerging producers. After Norway discovered oil in 1969, substantial windfalls contributed to inflation and an overvalued currency; groups mobilized to lobby Norway's leaders for a portion of the revenues.[36] In response, the Bank of Norway (Norges Bank) enacted policies to reverse inflationary pressures by depositing oil revenues into accounts isolated from the general budget, and they resisted efforts by interest groups to get a share.[37] In 1990, the Storting (Norway's parliament) passed Act No. 36 to set up a sovereign

---

[32] William Easterly and Ross Levine, "Africa's Growth Tragedy: Policies and Ethnic Divisions," *The Quarterly Journal of Economics* 112, 4 (November 1997): 1203–1250.

[33] Human Rights Watch, *Criminal Politics: Violence, and "Godfathers" and Corruption in Nigeria* 19, no. 16(A), (New York: Human Rights Watch, October 2007), 29.

[34] Guillaume Thiery, "Partis Politiques et Élections de 2011 au Nigeria: l'Action Congress of Nigeria en Champagne," *Afrique Contemporaine* 239 (2011): 97.

[35] Lydia Polgreen, "Change Unlikely from Angolan Election, but Discontent Simmers," *The New York Times* (August 31, 2012).

[36] E. Røed Larsen, "Are Rich Countries Immune to the Resource Curse: Evidence from Norway's Management of Its Oil Riches," *Resources Policy* 30 (2005): 76.

[37] Benn Eifert, Alan Gelb, and Nils Borje Tallroth. "Natural Resource Endowments, the State and Development Strategy," in *Fiscal Policy and Implementation in Oil-Producing Countries*, eds. Jeffrey Davis, Rolando Ossowski, and Annalisa Fedelino (Washington, DC: The International Monetary Fund, 2003), 92–98.

wealth fund in the Norges Bank.[38] By 2013, Norway's Government Pension Fund Global (GPFG) had grown into a multibillion-dollar powerhouse with major investments in markets worldwide. The Norwegian response demonstrates that even under significant pressures, emerging producers may avoid the pitfalls of the Dutch disease and other negative effects of substantial resource revenues.

Norway's GPFG is the prototypical sovereign wealth fund (SWF) that has become common in petrostates. These funds are a countercyclical policy response predicated on the permanent income hypothesis (PIH) that a percentage of resource rents should be set aside for expenditure smoothing and a second amount saved for future generations.[39] Because the PIH fails to take into account the circumstances in countries with endemic poverty and governance challenges, some question whether an SWF is feasible.[40] The alternative is to put revenues in income-generating investments that would serve the same function as an expenditure-smoothing investment. These investments, however, attract rent seeking and thereby pose their own difficulties in revenue management for emerging petrostates.

The initial year in emerging producers involves a socialization process; policymakers, especially autocratic rulers, learn how to behave in an international business environment. Officials who negotiate exploration and production contracts with oil companies sit across the table from highly trained engineers and business executives. Presidents and their ministers learn how to communicate with the oil executives and navigate in a new policy environment. Revenues that accrue from these contracts transform their states in both positive and negative ways. First, positive effects include the inevitable technology transfer from large, vertically integrated corporations to African leaders. Contract negotiations teach policymakers about the intricacies of international markets. Over time, any oil exporter experiences cyclical changes, and political leaders learn about price volatility. Third, politicians create an administrative apparatus to manage the oil sector. The administration includes a petroleum ministry with a minister and subordinates in different offices to manage revenues. If the contractual arrangements are PSCs, it is necessary to create a domestic national oil company. Policymakers then have to open accounts in the central bank and develop some expertise in accounting for oil revenues.

---

[38] The Norwegian Storting undated this act in 2005 with passage of the Government Pension Fund Act No 123 of 21 December 2005. Retrieved from http://www.nbim.no/en/About-us/governance-model/government-pension-fund-act/.

[39] Jeffrey Davis, Rolando Ossowski, James Daniel, and Steven Barnett, "Stabilization and Savings Funds for Nonrenewable Resources: Experience and Fiscal Policy Implications," Occasional Paper 205 (Washington, DC: International Monetary Fund, 2001), 8–9.

[40] Thomas Baunsgaard, Mauricio Villafuerte, Marcos Poplawski-Ribeiro, and Christine Richmond, "Fiscal Frameworks for Resource Rich Developing Countries," IMF Staff Discussion Note SDN/12/04 (May 16, 2012), 4.

For emerging African petrostates, like other mineral-exporting states around the world that had no experience with complex revenue management, the challenge was to isolate oil windfalls from special interests.[41] Norway's success is evident in policies that were successful in isolating revenues from political interests. Its historic democracy gave Norwegian citizens a belief that their representative government held their best interests. Accordingly, a number of emerging petrostates worldwide looked to Norway as a model they tried to emulate. Indeed, a variety of oil-exporting countries such as Timor Leste, Nigeria, and São Tomé and Príncipe have adopted the strict withdrawal rules and procedures employed by Norway's GPFG.

The principal challenge for emerging African oil exporters is that they have partial bureaucracies that were outcomes of meager colonial investments in education, health, and an administrative apparatus. Simply stated, the petrostates were without the strong, independent central bank, ministries, and audit agencies to oversee the bonuses and revenues oil companies paid when they began production. This lack of bureaucracy had a variable impact on political economic outcomes and shows how a petrostate's history influences the conditions present at the time of discovery. For instance, after independence, Equatorial Guinea's president imposed an authoritarian regime; he invested nothing in a civil service or administration and reportedly had educators executed.[42] In chronically impoverished Chad, its leaders never resolved the historic rivalries that had caused an intractable civil war to endure from the time of independence. São Tomé and Príncipe, an outlier among these cases, has remained under the rule of a small, cohesive oligarchy that depends on clan politics and a remarkable level of societal consensus.[43]

Other colonies, such as Congo, Nigeria, Angola, and the Gold Coast Colony (Ghana), had enjoyed colonial investments in their mining sectors. When they became oil exporters, their administrations included agencies to manage natural resources. The size of their bureaucracies varied. For example, when a consortium of firms discovered significant offshore reserves in Ghana, the state was a functioning democracy. Its administration included offices that managed revenues from gold mining, and Ghana had several agencies to deter corruption. Although, in 2012, Ghana's experience with significant oil revenues might seem early for predictions, its preconditions at the onset of production auger well for the future. Its democracy preceded the discovery of oil reserves. By contrast, Angola was a country at war; its central bank and various

---

[41] See the analysis on Trinidad and Tobago for an illustration of this point in a non-African case. Richard Auty and Alan Gelb, "Oil Windfalls in a Small Parliamentary Democracy: Their Impact on Trinidad and Tobago," *World Development* 14, 9 (September 1986): 1166.

[42] Human Rights Watch, *Well-Oiled*, 7.

[43] Gerhard Seibert, *Comrades, Clients and Cousins: Colonialism, Socialism and Democratization in São Tomé and Príncipe* (Boston: Koninklijke Brill NV, 2006), 522.

ministries had experiences receiving windfalls from hydrocarbons, but the primary incentive was to use the revenues for arms and state survival.

The presidents of Africa's emerging producers came from varied backgrounds. Some were self-anointed revolutionaries; others led opposition parties; and there were military officers. They were all patrons of clientelist networks. Oil production transformed their circumstances from a dependence on excise taxes from imports for their primary fiscal revenues to rent-driven growth. The early receipt of resource rents exceeded their bureaucracies' abilities to absorb the money, and many leaders in emerging African petrostates diverted funds for political purposes.[44] Others replicated the behavior of colonial authorities: they protected the property rights of taxpaying oil companies and treated non-taxpaying populations as irrelevant.

Several aspects of oil production are consistent in every petrostate and reflect how political authorities manage the value chain. In emerging producers, three key actors are influential. First, representatives from oil companies strike up relationships with sometimes-unsavory authoritarian leaders. These executives represent oil companies that want licenses to explore and, if their explorations are successful, they want long-term production contracts. At this point, oil executives enjoy a level of competence that far overshadows their African counterparts at the negotiating table.

A perverse convergence of goals is common at the point of discovery. Oil executives want the oil, and leaders of poor African states need money. A second set of actors is the leadership whose need for revenues leaves them as price takers. In countries under neopatrimonial leadership, the imperative for revenues shapes how policymakers negotiate with oil companies. As a consequence, bad contracts among emerging producers are common; for minimal bribes or signature bonuses deposited into accounts to which presidents enjoy withdrawal rights, companies receive tax breaks and lower royalty payments.[45] After payment of the bonus, oil companies invest in drilling for reservoirs, and if exploration is successful, developing the reserve; rent buildings for in-country corporate headquarters and hire engineers, construction specialists, and other technical staff. These developments occur at a dizzying pace in emerging producers. Executives with IOCs resist changes in the contractual arrangements as a strategy to protect their substantial initial investments.

[44] Chad's President Déby diverted bonuses for arms. His decision was striking given his contractual agreements with the World Bank and other investors in the Cameroon-Chad Pipeline. See Babette Stern, "Le Tchad a Acheté des Armes avec l'Argent du Pétrole." *Le Monde* (22 Novembre 2000).

[45] Gobind Nankani emphasizes the problem of the disadvantages Africans face in negotiations with executives from international oil companies. "Development Problems of Mineral Exporting Countries," World Bank Staff Working Paper No. 354 (1979). Paul Collier similarly discusses the problem of asymmetrical information in contract negotiations. *The Plundered Planet: Why We Must – and How We Can – Manage Nature for Global Prosperity* (New York: Oxford University Press, 2010), 70.

Third, individuals that are often the president's clansmen or close associates sell access to leaders, and for a facilitation fee help selected companies bid for contracts. *Brokers*, otherwise called middlemen, have access to information that they are able to sell to others who want it.[46] The concept of a middleman who facilitates transactions is hardly unknown among U.S. companies that must comply with the restrictions of the Foreign Corrupt Practices Act; they have clear reason to pay commissions to brokers for contract information. These brokers facilitate transactions between oil companies and political leaders; in this sense, they operate as gatekeepers and serve as intermediaries between oil companies and political authorities with discretion to grant contracts.

Although it is tempting to suggest that African petrostates should become more efficient in revenue management, different conditions present at their starting points influence the institutions and agencies that manage revenues. For Equatorial Guinea or Chad, for instance, oil revenues hardly influenced political arrangements that preexisted the onset of production. Conflicts and predatory rule were well ensconced before any oil company began to extract hydrocarbons. It is crucial to avoid deterministic reasoning for all petrostates. African petrostates develop according to historical trajectories that precede the onset of production. Oil is an intermediate variable; it influences but does not determine outcomes.

Economic Growth in Emerging Producers

In 1970, practically all the countries that in the future would become Africa's petrostates were poor. Development indicators for emerging producers displayed in Table 4.1 suggest that these countries have reaped substantial rewards from improved economic circumstances. For instance, in 1970, Mauritania's people, on average, earned $155 a year; the average income in Sudan was $141, and Ghana $241.[47] These relatively low levels of development would have influenced their ability to manage oil revenues and employ them for sustainable economic growth. In 1970, the first year for which there are reported statistics, Chad had an average per capita annual income of $125. It was among the poorest states in the world. Even though oil companies pumped oil from Chad's Doba Fields for almost a decade, by 2010, questions of how the bureaucracy could absorb and use revenues efficiently remained a question for officials at the IMF.[48] As Table 4.1 shows, Chad's rent-driven economy grew 15 percent in 2003. In 2012, the principal donor concern was helping Chad make a transition from rent-driven to skill-driven growth, especially in light of the country's high levels of poverty and lack of human capital.

[46] Hertog, "The Sociology of the Gulf Rentier Systems," 305.
[47] World Bank, *World Development Indicators 1970* (Washington, DC: The World Bank).
[48] IMF, "Chad: 2010 Article IV Consultation – Staff Report," IMF Country Report No 10/196 (Washington: The International Monetary Fund, July 2010), 6.

TABLE 4.1 *Emerging Producers*

Country	Start of production	Pop (M) (2012)	GDP $Bn (2012)	GDP% Growth (2012)	Per Cap GNI PPP $US (2012)	Pop (M) (2003)	GDP $Bn (2003)	GDP% Growth (2003)	Per Cap GNI PPP $US (2003)
Chad	2002	12.5	11.0	5.0	1,320	9.3	2.7	15	720
Ghana	2008	25.4	40.7	8	1,940	20.3	7.6	5	1,060
Mauritania	2006	3.8	4.2	8	2,520	2.96	2.8	6	1,680
São Tomé and Príncipe	2015 (anticipated)	188,098	264m	4.0	1,850	147,455	98m	7	1,280

Source: World Bank, World Development Indicators 2013.

Governments of emerging producers must cope with legacies of poverty and the legacies embedded by the inequalities of colonial rule. As emerging producers, Chad, Congo, and Mauritania were under authoritarian rulers. Presidents had discretion to use the oil rents as they chose without any agencies of accountability to impose controls. By contrast, São Tomé and Príncipe and Ghana have representative governments and democratic institutions of rule. These legacies are important for considering how oil-exporting states in Africa may respond to the inflows of revenues and social contradictions that may be consequences of shifts in capital endowments.

Ghana: A Democratic Emerging Producer

Ghana as an emerging producer presents numerous differences that are critical compared to other petrostates at similar times. Ghana is an outlier in Africa; its elected government rules through the political institutions of republican democracy.[49] Indeed, Ghana may present a case that falsifies blanket arguments that oil revenues cause policy distortions, including a lack of democracy, because of an erosion of social capital.[50] First, Ghana has been a democracy since 1992; it has held numerous elections that have resulted in several alternations of power. The extent of Ghanaian democracy makes it unique among the African states in general and most certainly among the petrostates. In 1991, military leader Jerry Rawlings scheduled a constitutional referendum and elections.[51] Rawlings won the 1992 presidential election and a second term in 1996. He came to office with remarkable legitimacy, which allowed him to use economic performance to his advantage and enact sweeping reforms.[52] Rawlings's decision to abide by the constitutional term limits followed by his acceptance of his rival's victory in the 2000 elections was a landmark. It demonstrated that "Africans' commitment to democracy can be refreshed by alternations in power by way of elections."[53] Ghana has since held elections in 2000, 2004, and 2008 that underline the new petrostate's commitment to democracy.

---

[49] Steven Levitsky and Lucan A. Way, *Competitive Authoritarianism: Hybrid Regimes after the Cold War* (New York: Cambridge University Press, 2010), 299–305.

[50] For a lengthy and excellent analysis of the role of social capital in Africa economic growth, see Paul Collier and Jan Willem Gunning, "Explaining African Economic Performance," *Journal of Economic Literature* 37 (March 1999): 64–111; also Michael Woolcock, Lant Pritchett, and Jonathan Isham, "The Social Foundations of Poor Economic Growth in Resource Rich Countries," in *Resource Abundance and Economic Development*, ed. R.M. Auty (New York: Oxford University Press, 2001).

[51] Jeffrey Herbst, "Ghana in Comparative Perspective," in *Economic Change and Political Liberalization in sub-Saharan Africa*, ed. Jennifer Widner (Baltimore: The Johns Hopkins University Press, 1994), 184.

[52] Jeremy Youde, "Economics and Government Popularity in Ghana," *Electoral Studies* 24, 1 (March 2005): 13.

[53] Michael Bratton, "The 'Alternation Effect' in Africa," *Journal of Democracy* 15, 4 (October 2004): 147.

Although Ghanaian elections have been free and with minimal levels of corruption or violence, a noisy democracy emerged in the country with some disquieting signals about the government's ability to manage resource revenues efficiently. First, Ghana's party system reflects the ethnoregional cleavages that were apparent during the late 1940s at the beginnings of decolonization.[54] This intervention of historic competition demonstrates the centrality of colonial developments in contemporary African petrostates. Second, neopatrimonialism persists in select ministries and agencies of state where particular leaders dominate staffing decisions and try to centralize political power under their networks in Accra and other urban centers.[55] Electoral abuses in the 2008 elections may have contributed to Ghanaians' block voting, a situation that sets "a dangerous time bomb of unresolved conflict which could detonate in future elections."[56] In this respect, Ghanaian parties continue to resemble the organizations established by nationalist leaders Nkrumah and Danquah who represented voting blocks in different regions of the country.[57] Block voting implies that networks impose rules at the polls; people cast votes according to instructions from patrons and calls into question the extent of freedom in its grassroots democracy.[58].

In spite of these problems, the extent of democracy and development sets Ghana apart from other African petrostates at the time they discovered oil. Oil adds another source of fiscal revenues to an economy that already receives important earnings from exports of cocoa, cotton, gold, and industrial diamonds. Normatively, with a democratic government in place, management of the oil sector should include transparent procedures for awarding contracts, public awareness about negotiations over the contents of various contractual arrangements, methods for payments of royalties and taxes, and accountability for misbehavior or incompetence. Ghana, however, faced significant challenges in the first years of oil exploration and early production. First, its government has resisted pressures to disclose in full the content of contracts, or declare what oil companies have paid in licensing fees, and what they may anticipate to receive in bonuses, royalties, and corporate income taxes.[59]

Although Ghana is in the early stages of defining the institutions that regulate production, disclosure of contracts, and audits of production and

---

[54] Minion K.C. Morrison, "Political Parties in Ghana through Four Republics" A Path to Democratic Consolidation," *Comparative Politics* 36, 4 (July 2004): 422.

[55] Kevin S. Fridy, "The Elephant, Umbrella, and Quarrelling Cocks: Disaggregating Partisanship in Ghana's Fourth Republic," *African Affairs* 106, 423 (April 2007): 281–305.

[56] Heinz Jockers, Dirk Kohnert, and Paul Nugent, "The successful Ghanaian election of 2008: a convenient myth?" *The Journal of Modern African Studies* 28, 1 (March 2010): 95.

[57] Jay Oelbaum, "Ethnicity Adjusted? Economic Reform, Elections, and Tribalism in Ghana's Fourth Republic," *Commonwealth and Comparative Politics* 42, 2 (July 2004): 244

[58] Jockers et al., "The Successful Ghana Election of 2008: A Convenient Myth?" 112.

[59] Ian Gary, *Ghana's Big Test: Oil Challenge to Democratic Development* (Boston: Oxfam America, February 2009), 30.

payments, the government has made progress in declarations of contracts and public records of the activities of international oil companies operating offshore fields. Second, Ghana has many accountability agencies in place, including the Economic and Organized Crime Office (formerly the Serious Fraud Office), a Commission on Human Rights and Administrative Justice, and an active Office of the Accountant General that performs the treasury control function. These agencies work to deter corruption especially in the regions outside the capital, Accra. Ghana's parliamentary Public Accounts Committee investigates incidents of corruption and like police officers in the Ministry of Interior it has a mandate to forward allegations of malfeasance to prosecutors.[60] These agencies work to prevent and investigate corruption. As Chapter 5 discusses further, scandals in the oil sector have been increasingly under the scrutiny of these agencies of accountability.

Mature Producers

Among mature producers, agreements between political leaders and oil companies have been in place for years. Politicians have established ministries, agencies, and sometimes a DNOC that negotiates with international oil companies and participates in the upstream production process. Oil companies' executives and officials in the petrostate share a familiarity that reduces negotiation and information costs for both parties; the country officials know how their partners in the oil companies think about contract negotiations.[61] Negotiations occur between colleagues who share training and experiences in the African oil sector. Upstream procedures inform how officials in ministerial offices receive and process applications for exploration and production licenses. If all were working as hoped, oil companies download templates from the Internet before they bid for contracts or make investments. In addition, presidents, ministers, and senior officials have established relationships with oil executives. These relationships shape business transactions. Unfortunately, this familiarity also produces opportunities for corruption and collusion among the actors.

Mature petrostates have built the bureaucracies to manage downstream transactions in the value chain. In theory, a central bank functions with efficiency and receives the royalty payments and taxes that it then transfers to a savings account or the consolidated budget as fiscal revenues. In practice, few African central banks have a staff competent enough to manage the windfalls

---

[60] These observations are the product of fifty interviews of public officials conducted in 2004. John R. Heilbrunn, "Ghana: Anti-Corruption Diagnostic," Report commissioned by GTZ (Accra: GTZ, October 2004).

[61] The testimonies made during the Elf trials between Elf's executives – including such individuals as André Tarallo, Alfred Sirven, Alain Guillon, Jean-Claude Vauchez, and Philippe Hustache – and African presidents and their families illustrate the types of relations that emerged in mature and declining African petrostates. See John R. Heilbrunn, "Oil and Water? Elite Politicians and Corruption in France," *Comparative Politics* 37, 3 (April 2005): 277–296.

efficiently. In Angola, for example, the Central Bank of Angola (BNA) depends on the state-owned oil company Sonangol to perform certain treasury-like functions; Sonangol subsidizes expenditures in the oil sector and has had chronic problems of unexplained discrepancies between declared payments and reported deposits.[62] Angola's domestic oil company is "the pivotal tool for the interests of the presidential clique known as the *Futungo de Belas* ... a nebulous group of unelected officials and businessmen" that clusters around President Jose Eduardo dos Santos.[63] Sonangol arrogates responsibilities that normally are in the domains of the Ministries of Finance and Petroleum.

A principal problem in mature producers is that multiple ministries and agencies simultaneously oversee revenue management and collection. To return to the example of Angola, its Ministry of Finance and National Tax Directorate (DNI) have a mandate to determine royalty and tax rates and collect estimated taxes on a monthly basis.[64] Meanwhile, Sonangol sets the prices for fiscal revenue collection on the basis of information provided by oil companies. Third, Sonangol is a concessionaire, but it takes responsibilities that otherwise would be under the DNI, the National Bank of Angola (BNA), and Ministries of Petroleum (MinPet) and Finance (MinFin).[65] Angola's exceptional traits stem from the fact that it only emerged from decades of civil war in 2002; the war delayed the construction of agencies that would otherwise have managed oil revenues. On one hand, Angola is a mature producer and this maturity influences how oil companies interact with the government. On the other, the Angolan state has many of the same problems that challenge emerging producers that have to build autonomous agencies to manage resource rents. It demonstrates how, when revenue management involves multiple corporate entities (in the Angola case, MinFin, MinPet, DNI, the BNA, and Sonangol), serious inefficiencies occur and officials have opportunities for corruption. The effect is a failure of the rule of law, inefficient revenue management, and low levels of development for Angola's citizens.

In mature producers, the rule of law is a crucial element of protecting the property rights that stabilize oil-sector transactions. In Nigeria, for instance, competition for mining leases is evident in bidding competition for rights to explore and develop blocks among different companies. Nigeria is notable for its highly complex society in which fierce electoral contests among its elite politicians has found expression in violence and entrenched corruption. These struggles have left economic growth and the expansion of political and social

[62] World Bank, *Angola: Public Expenditure Management and Financial Accountability*, Report No. 29036-AO (Washington, DC: The World Bank, February 16, 2005), 10–11.

[63] Ricardo Soares de Oliveira, "Business Success, Angola-Style: Postcolonial Politics and the Rise of Sonangol," *The Journal of Modern African Studies* 45, 4 (2007): 606.

[64] PREM 1, Africa Region, *Angola: Public Expenditure Management and Financial Accountability*, 21.

[65] Francisco Carneiro, *Angola: Oil, Broad-based Growth, and Equity* (Washington: the World Bank, 2007), 46.

opportunities as secondary objectives for Nigeria's elite patrons and politicians who, instead, fight for domination and the rewards of political offices. In a succession of presidential elections, the country hovered between anarchy and democracy.

In an influential paper, Sala-i-Martin and Subramanian observe that between 1965 and 2000, Nigerian leaders squandered the country's wealth, and constant efforts to get rich from the capture of oil revenues adversely altered their ability to govern.[66] In the next paragraph, we consider the 2005 bidding round for mining leases governing offshore and onshore oil blocks. This round indicates the difficulties that stem from Nigeria's turbulent history, in which leaders of ethnic groups, patrons, and oil companies fought and competed over who would dominate the economy. Initial publicity and calls for bids suggested that perhaps Nigeria would be able to manage the process in a transparent fashion that could reverse its reputation as one of the world's most corrupt countries. However, political interference in post-auction months showed that the sums exceeded the abilities of Nigeria's anticorruption champions to control; events in late 2005 and 2006 suggested that post-auction scandals were advance warning of the corruption evident in the Excess Crude Account (ECA) that lost $16 billion between 2007 and 2011. In response to the losses and uncertainties that have accompanied the ECA, the federal government of Nigeria passed the Nigeria Sovereign Investment Authority (Establishment) Act, 2011, to establish a sovereign wealth fund insulated from the political pressures that affect the ECA.[67]

The 2005 Auctions for Nigerian Production Sharing Contracts

In May 2005, Nigeria opened a bidding round for the offshore and onshore oil leases for seventy-five blocks. Events that followed illustrated the fragility of upstream resource management in the value chain of a mature producer. Rules for the round stipulated that contractors had to submit their bids no later than May 29, 2005. Every bid had to include a minimal $50 million signature bonus, projections of cost oil, specific plans for work commitment, and local content (the extent to which local firms would participate in the production process). A panel evaluated the bids on a 100-point basis: the promised signature bonus (40 points); the cost oil ceiling (20); local content – or corporate social responsibility investments (20); and the contractors had to guarantee a specific work commitment for local firms (20).[68] In addition to a signature bonus, authorities required competing firms to promise other inducements. Procedural rules for

---

[66] Xavier Sala-i-Martin and Arvind Subramanian, "Addressing the Natural Resource Curse: An Illustration from Nigeria" IMF Working Paper WP/03/139 (July 2003): 14.

[67] See Federal Government of Nigeria, "Nigeria Sovereign Investment Authority (Establishment) Act, 2011" (2011); Xan Rice, "Nigeria Plans Big Boost to Sovereign Fund," *The Financial Times* (October 3, 2012).

[68] Martin Quinlan, "Nigeria: Looking for Explorers," *Petroleum Economist* (May 2005).

the auction included sealed bids, public opening and disclosure of bidders, and transparency in the awarding of contracts.

This bidding round differed from other rounds in Nigeria for several reasons. First, the round attracted few supermajors; it elicited bids from a large number of smaller firms from Asia and Africa; and it was quite different from the discretionary awards of contracts that had been standard practice under military regimes.[69] The supermajors' disinterest allowed seventy-nine oil companies to submit bids for the blocks including national oil companies from India, South Korea, and China.[70] In addition, numerous Nigerian firms competed for contracts. The Nigerian government estimated that the seventy-five blocks would bring revenues of $3.75 billion in signature bonuses. In August, the panel announced awards of forty-four blocks that promised $2.63 billion to the Nigerian treasury.[71] Observers applauded the transparency of the bidding process that diverged from earlier rounds when military authorities awarded contracts "at ridiculously low fees to top government functionaries which they in turn sub-let to their cronies or to multinationals in which they have interests."[72] Despite national pride in the transparent bidding process, it was unclear how many firms that had won blocks could raise the capital to fulfill their commitments.

Once the panel announced the awards, winners had thirty days to pay the signature bonuses. Months passed, however, and the federal government gave the laggards until December 15, 2005, to pay the signature bonus. Despite the extension, by February 2006, the government had received bonuses for only twenty-five blocks; nineteen of the "winners" had failed to pay the signature bonuses. In response, the federal government offered the blocks again for auction, but with far less transparency than the May 2005 round.[73] In this competition, local and state politics entered the picture; deals and counter-deals involved patrons of networks that were operating at the pinnacles of national parties.[74] Neopatrimonial politics shaped the post-auction bidding competition in a sad foreshadowing of what would happen during the 2007 elections.

Political interference from politicians seeking campaign finance shaped the bidding competition in February 2006 to a far greater extent than in May 2005. In part, the interference was from chiefs and godfathers who were gathering campaign chests to pay patronage jobs and finance the cult groups that

[69] Dino Mahtani, "Oil development: New players struggle for funds," *The Financial Times* (May 15, 2006).
[70] Mike Odunyi, "Nigeria is Building a New Crop of Indigenous Operators," *Alexander's Gas and Oil Connection* 10, 14 (July 20, 2005).
[71] Mike Odunyi, "Oil Blocks Sale to Fetch N337 bn," *This Day* (Lagos) (5 September 2005).
[72] "Editorial," *Daily Champion* (Lagos) (5 September 2005).
[73] Dino Mahtani, "Doubts over Nigeria's Oil Block Awards," *Financial Times* (February 14, 2006).
[74] Vincent Nwanma, "Nigeria: 'Last-Minute' Offer of 45 Oil Blocks Draws Criticism," Rigzone. Retrieved from http://www.rigzone.com/news/article.asp?a_id=43514 accessed 5–04–2007.

were the enforcement sides of their networks.[75] Others were clamoring to increase tax rates for international investors that might win contracts. Just before the May round, the Nigerian Parliament debated increasing tax rates for production contracts from 50 to 85 percent, prompting a cautionary word from presidential oil advisor Edmund Daukoru that the parliament needed to avoid frightening international investors.[76] This clamor to increase tax rates inflamed a popular perception that international oil companies were unfairly profiting from Nigerian oil. It was in this churning political environment that the far more secretive auctions occurred in February 2006.

The 2006 competition for unallocated blocks attracted national oil companies that had recently entered African markets. For example, India's Oil and Natural Gas Company (ONGC) competed against the South Korean National Oil Company (KNOC) for deep-water Blocks 321 and 323; the tactics the two NOCs employed in this bidding competition was indicative of the unfolding scramble for Nigerian oil. The ONGC's bid included a $175 million signature bonus for Block 321 and $310 million for Block 323. At the same time, the KNOC submitted a bid with local content offers to construct two power plants, a 1,200-kilometer liquid natural gas pipeline, and a $90 million signature bonus for each block. KNOC won the auction. However, doubts about the bid evaluator's integrity emerged when it was revealed that the KNOC had no experience with deep-sea drilling.[77] Similar questions were raised about Nigerian firms that had little or no experience in offshore extraction, and many lacked the capital necessary to finance such operations.

Allegations of corruption in the bidding process were increasingly common in late 2006. In October, Nuhu Ribadu, then the director of Nigeria's Economic and Financial Crimes Commission, announced an investigation into questionable awards. When Addax Petroleum disclosed that it had agreed to pay $90 million to the Nigerian firm Starcrest for productive rights to a block, Ribadu wanted to understand how Starcrest acquired control of the block, as the firm had neither sufficient capital nor experience in deep-sea oil production.[78] Investigations revealed other possible cases of corruption where Nigerian companies won contracts and then allegedly tried to sell them to international oil companies for a fee.[79] When a number of companies failed

---

[75] Richard L. Sklar, Ebere Onwudiwe, and Darren Kew, "Nigeria: Completing Obasanjo's Legacy," *Journal of Democracy* 17, 3 (July 2006): 101; Pauline von Hellermann, "The chief, the youth, and the plantation: communal politics in southern Nigeria," *The Journal of Modern African Studies* 48, 2 (June 2010): 260.

[76] News Brief, "Nigeria," *Petroleum Economist* (May 2005).

[77] This paragraph draws from the report by Hector Igbikiowubo and Luka Binniyat, "South Korea Beats India to Nigeria's Blocks 321 and 323," *The Vanguard* (Lagos) (March 14, 2006). Retrieved from http://allafrica.com (accessed 14 March 2006).

[78] Dino Mahtani, "Nigeria Vows to Investigate $90 Million Oil Deal," *Financial Times* (October 31, 2006).

[79] Nwanma, "Nigeria: 'Last-Minute' Offer of 45 Oil Blocks Draws Criticism."

to pay the signature bonuses, the Nigerian government announced a second round of bidding, and that round created opportunities for corruption when politicians were seeking campaign finance. After such a positive round in 2005, it appeared as if business in Nigeria had returned to its informal rules and usual practices.

This discussion of the 2005 bidding round indicates the importance of transparency in oil sector transactions. However, the persistence of corruption and intergroup competition is evident from the questionable awards and entry of Nigerian firms with little or no experience in upstream processes of exploration and extraction. On one hand, this bidding round shows how fundamental changes in the activities of new actors find expression in new firms competing for contracts that only entered the international oil market in the early twenty-first century. On the other, continuities are clear in the degree of corruption and competition that animated the bids and later auctions.

Economic Growth in Mature Producers

Economic growth in mature producers reflects the revenues from oil exports. For example, the World Bank reported in 2008 that Angola had consistent economic growth at 15 percent. Development indicators for mature producers in Table 4.2 show extraordinary increases in wealth as measured by GDP. The most impressive performance has been in Equatorial Guinea, which has propelled the country into the ranks of middle-income countries. In 2008, Equatorial Guinea was a mature oil producer with a GDP of $18.5 billion and an average per capita gross national income (GNI) of $14,980, the highest in Africa. Its per capita GNI is higher than Estonia ($14,570), Hungary ($12,810), and Seychelles ($10,220). Considering that Equatorial Guinea's 1970 GDP was $66.3 million and its people lived on an average of $227 a year, the jump in the early twenty-first century is an extraordinary transformation. Even in 1985, a decade before the beginning of oil production and almost two decades after independence, Equatorial Guinea's GDP was only $75 million, and its average annual per capita income was $460. Although these data for 2008 are most impressive, they fail to show income distribution and the social impacts of the increased income from oil exports.

Perhaps a critical factor is the size of relative populations as well as the extent of state construction. Unlike emerging producers, a mature petrostate has had the opportunity to build ministries of petroleum, mines, or natural resources to manage production and revenue collection. The central banks have created accounts into which oil companies deposit royalties and taxes. Finally, political leaders are careful to ensure the property rights for companies in the oil sector because it contributes the lion's share of fiscal revenues. Mature producers therefore regulate the sector and distribute resource revenues to different recipients, albeit with varying degrees of efficiency.

The data in Table 4.2 show that Nigeria has enjoyed a more than 7 percent increase per year in its GDP during the twenty-first century's first

TABLE 4.2 *Mature Producers (Over Ten Years of Production)*

Country	Start of production	Pop (M) (2012)	GDP $Bn (2012)	GDP% Growth (2012)	Per Cap GNI PPP $US (2012)	Pop (M) (2003)	GDP $Bn (2003)	GDP% Growth (2003)	Per Cap GNI PPP $US (2003)
Angola	1968	20.8	114.2	7	5,490	15.4	14	3	2,250
Eq.Guinea	1995	736,296	17.6	2	18,880	568,552	2.95	14	7,770
Nigeria	1957	169.8	262.6	7	2,420	132.5	67.7	10	1,320
Sudan	1976	37.2	58.8	-10	2,030	29.97	17.65	7	1,290

Source: World Bank, World Development Indicators 2013.

decade. However, most Nigerians have not benefitted from these increases in aggregate wealth, which leaves open assertions that Nigeria's experiences confirm the resource curse predictions. Conversely, Nigeria is a case that argues for the primacy of politics and history in any assessment of its economic performance since independence. When the British colony declared independence on October 1, 1960, its GDP was $4.2 billion and it had a diversified economy of cocoa, mining, oil, and limited manufacturing.[80] A civil war led to a tenuous peace that embedded policy inefficiencies; after faltering attempts at civilian government, a series of military coups imposed brutal regimes and infamous levels of corruption. Over years, oil companies would pay billions to Nigerian military governments that through a combination of incompetence and venality failed to produce economic development. Corruption denied the state needed funds to pay for basic social-sector services. The "scams" that plagued Nigeria's economy were evident in such behaviors as over-invoicing contracts, requiring substantial commissions for standard contract negotiations, and the infamous "419" scams that attract greedy individuals with offers of millions from supposedly dead relatives whose bank accounts have been frozen.[81]

The Nigerian case demonstrates the costs of poor political decisions in a heterogeneous society fraught with competition and violence. During the oil boom of the late 2000s, a barrel of Brent grade oil sold for more than $100, and oil exporters received large windfalls. Table 4.2 shows that Nigeria's population increased from 132 million inhabitants in 2003 to almost 170 million in 2012. The average per capita income (PPP GNI) nearly doubled during the same period, and the Nigerian GDP increased at respectable growth rates of 10.6 percent in 2004, 5.4 percent in 2005, 6.2 percent in 2006, 6.4 percent in 2007, and 6.0 percent in 2008.[82] These increases in GDP occurred despite the reduced output that was a result of conflicts in the Niger Delta.

Consider the differences displayed in Table 4.3; in 2004, China had a percentage growth rate that was half a percent smaller than Nigeria's growth. However, because the Chinese state encouraged investments and capital formation, its economy was less vulnerable to price volatility in international markets. In many respects, Nigeria validates Knack and Keefer's argument that corruption and violent instability undermine property rights and economic efficiency.[83] Whereas Nigeria grew at respectable rates, it did not define the

[80] World Bank, World Development Indicators (Washington: The World Bank, 2012). Retrieved from http://data.worldbank.org/data-catalog/world-development-indicators.

[81] Daniel Jordan Smith, *A Culture of Corruption: Everyday Deception and Popular Discontent in Nigeria* (Princeton: Princeton University Press, 2007), 44.

[82] All the statistics come from World Bank, *World Development Indicators 2012* (Washington: The World Bank).

[83] Stephen Knack and Philip E. Keefer, "Institutions and Economic Performance: Cross Country Test with Alternative Institutional Measures," *Economics and Politics* 7 (1995): 207–227.

TABLE 4.3 *Nigeria and China Compared*

	2004	2005	2006	2007	2008	2011
Nigeria GDP	$88 bn	$112 bn	$147 bn	$166 bn	$207 bn	$236 bn
Nigeria GDP % growth	10.6	5.4	6.2	6.4	6.0	7.0
Nigeria population	137 m	140 m	143 m	147 m	151 m	163 m
China GDP	$1.9 tr	$2.2 tr	$2.7 tr	$3.4 tr	$4.3 tr	$7.3 tr.
China GDP % growth	10.1	10.4	11.6	13.0	9.0	9.0
China population	1,296 bn	1,304 bn	1,311 bn	1,318 bn	1,325 bn	1,344 bn

Source: World Bank, World Development Indicators various years.

institutions conducive to sustainable growth. By contract, China has guaranteed property rights and put in place growth-generating policies with demonstrable results.

Although Nigeria's growth rates have failed to follow China's extraordinary performance, they indicate an economy that is growing. It is implausible that its export earnings are having no impact on other sectors. Indeed, the IMF reported in 2011 that Nigeria's non-oil sector had been growing at "a robust" 9 percent that would probably continue over the next several years.[84] Unfortunately, oil composed 90 percent of the country's exports, leaving it vulnerable to price volatility, as occurred in 2009 when oil prices fell, foreign investors reduced their exposure, and non–oil-sector growth dropped to 4.5 percent.[85] Still, the very size of Nigeria's economy makes it an important player in the international oil market. According to the World Bank's World Development Indicators for 2008, Nigeria's $115 billion GDP was 2 billion dollars less than the combined GDPs of all the other African petrostates.[86] Nigeria's economy has grown, but with problems in distribution and sustainable capital formation. These problems stem largely from endemic corruption and conflicts in the Niger Delta and northern Nigeria that have historical antecedents and have exerted an extremely negative impact on the economy's growth and political stability.

[84] IMF, "Nigeria: 2011 Article IV Consultation – Staff Report," IMF Country Report 12/194 (July 2012): 4.

[85] IMF, "Nigeria: 2009 Article IV Consultation – Staff Report," IMF Country Report 09/315 (November 2009): 5.

[86] Nigeria in 2006 had a GDP in current USD $115,337,822,208 compared to USD $117,428,760,112 for combined GDPs for Angola, Chad, Congo, Equatorial Guinea, Gabon, Mauritania, São Tomé and Príncipe, and Sudan.

Declining Producers

Among declining African petrostates, business arrangements have been in place for lengthy periods. Domestic actors who participate directly in the oil sector are typically members of an elite inner circle composed of clansmen and those who have close connections to the president and his family. Most non-clansmen have risen to their positions as a consequence of historic relationships that often preceded oil production. Some work as managers of DNOCs, others are brokers who influence the choice of firms that participate in the oil sectors, and some find employment at the central bank or in ministries with access to resource rents. Distributional demands pass through their offices and encounter the ingrained attitudes and informal institutions that decide allocations of wealth to members of the oligarchy. Oil oligarchs have reason to exclude others from the benefits of rule for as long as possible.

Declining producers face formidable challenges that include transition from an economy dependent on oil rents to a state that receives its fiscal revenues from income, sales, value-added, and customs and excise taxes. Development indicators for declining producers in Table 4.4 show that the GDP in declining producers grew slowly. Data for declining petrostates indicate low levels of economic growth and capital accumulation combined with growing populations. These data suggest that declining producers face a potentially unstable adjustment as they move into a fiscal environment that does not include resource rents.

Economic Growth in Declining Producers

The case that best illustrates the transition through which declining producers must pass is Cameroon. Oil production in Cameroon began in 1976; it reached a peak in 1986 when Cameroon exported 66 million barrels.[87] Production fell approximately 40 percent between 1986 and 1996 and by another 10 percent to approximately 90,000 bpd in 2005.[88] Although Cameroon's oil reserves were smaller than the billions of barrels in Nigeria, the economic impact of oil exports was that its GNP growth rate increased 13 percent between 1977 and 1981 and 8 percent between 1982 and 1986.[89] However, the cycle of oil production was short, and Cameroon transited from an emerging to mature and then declining producer quickly.

The Cameroonian government coped with the possible dislocations from oil windfalls in an organized fashion. First, President Paul Biya established a domestic national oil company to partner in production with international

---

[87] Dhaneshwar Ghura, "Private Investment and Endogenous Growth: Evidence from Cameroon," IMF Working Paper WP/97/165 (December 1997): 6.

[88] Stéphane Cossé, "Strengthening Transparency in the Oil Sector in Cameroon: Why Does It Matter?" IMF Policy Discussion Paper PDP/06/2 (March 2006): 5.

[89] P. Hugon, "Sortir de la Recession et Preparer l'Après-Pétrole: Le Préalbre Politique: Le Cameroun dans L'Entre-Deux," *Politique Africaine* 62, (Juin 1996): 36.

TABLE 4.4 *Declining Producers (Depletion of Reserves Estimated within Ten Years)*

Country	Estimated end of production	Pop (M) (2012)	GDP $Bn (2012)	GDP% Growth (2012)	Per Cap GNI PPP $US (2012)	Pop (M) (2003)	GDP $Bn (2003)	GDP% Growth (2003)	Per Cap GNI PPP $US (2003)
Cameroon	2012	21.7	29.98	5	2,320	17.22	13.62	4	1,730
Congo	2016	4.34	13.68	4	3,510	3.36	3.5	1	2,210
Gabon	2020	1.63	18.66	6	14,290	1.32	6.05	2	10,780

Source: World Bank, World Development Indicators 2013.

oil companies. It delegated responsibilities for revenue management to specific ministerial offices. Finally, the government created a saving mechanism by which it used the wealth generated by oil exports to retire debt and raise producer prices for the agricultural sector.[90] At the onset of oil production, Cameroon was thereby able to minimize Dutch disease effects that plagued other countries.[91] In 1990, it appeared that Cameroon would exhaust its oil reserves by the century's end; political leaders reoriented the economy to agriculture, forestry, and commercial development. As Cameroon moved through its different phases of production, the state's role in diversifying the economy was far more effective than its capability to broaden its political space.

After independence, Cameroon and Nigeria disputed the other's sovereignty over the Bakassi Peninsula. The origins of this contested sovereignty date to settlements after World War I when the Allies divided German Kamerun into British and French territories; British colonial administrators governed Anglophone Cameroon, including the Bakassi Peninsula, as part of the Eastern Region of Nigeria.[92] Although the British had administered the mandated territory as an integral part of Southeast Nigeria, the treaty was clear that the peninsula belonged to Cameroon.[93] Litigation over interpretations of the Anglo-German Agreement of March 1913 and whether Cameroon or Nigeria would govern the Bakassi Peninsula ended in 2002.[94] In October 2002, the International Court of Justice granted Cameroon sovereignty over Bakassi, with its proven oil reserves of approximately 400 million barrels.[95] Cameroon's Société nationale de Hydrocarbures resumed production almost immediately; however, by 2010, the reserves were steadily declining.[96]

Congo: A Declining Mature Producer
Political leaders in declining producers face a precipitous drop in fiscal revenues and therefore their latitude to spend resource rents on coalition-building

---

[90] Shantayanan Devarajan and Jaime de Melo, "Adjustment with a Fixed Exchange Rate: Cameroon, Côte d'Ivoire, and Senegal," *The World Bank Economic Review* 1, 3 (June 1987): 455.

[91] Nancy Benjamin, Shantayanan Devarajan, and Robert Weiner, "The Dutch Disease in a Developing Country: Oil Reserves in Cameroon," *The Journal of Development Economics* 30, 1 (January 1989): 74.

[92] Piet Konings, "The Anglophone Cameroon-Nigeria Boundary: Opportunities and Conflicts," *African Affairs* 104, 415 (April 2005): 278.

[93] British administrators had used this particular pattern of integrating the territory under a League of Nations mandate in the territory in German Togoland, as well. They required farmers in the cocoa-rich region to transport their harvest into the Gold Coast Colony to obtain a fiscal stamp before shipping in Lomé, French Togo's port, or Tema in the Gold Coast Colony.

[94] Peter H. F. Bekker, "International Decisions: Land and Maritime Boundary between Cameroon and Nigeria (*Cameroon v. Nigeria*; Equatorial Guinea Intervening), *The American Journal of International Law* 97, 2 (April 2003): 391.

[95] Bekker, "Land and Maritime Boundary between Cameroon and Nigeria, 387.

[96] United States Geological Survey, "2008 Minerals Yearbook: Cameroon and Cape Verde" (Washington, DC: U.S. Department of the Interior, November 2009).

activities. As revenues decline, former winners are necessarily excluded from a diminishing pool of wealth. Although Total made several discoveries of offshore reserves in Congo's territorial waters in the early twenty-first century, these discoveries are expected to peak in 2012 and then decline steadily thereafter.[97] However, conflict, instability, and state seizure by the president's clan have been pathologies consistent with a declining producer under strict authoritarian rule.

In the early twenty-first century, Congo enjoyed modest economic growth because of production from several new fields. This growth was despite a brief but destructive civil war. The country's non-oil sector enjoyed accelerated growth in 2010 as demonstrated by improved performance of its timber, transport, and telecommunications sectors.[98] Other indicators improved, as well; the completion rate of primary school students was 53 percent in 2002, 77 percent in 2004, 67 percent in 2005, 73 percent in 2006, 70.5 percent in 2009, and 70.8 percent in 2010.[99] Most importantly, on March 9, 2006, Congo qualified for debt relief under the Heavily Indebted Poor Country program of the World Bank and IMF. This achievement enabled the Sassou government to consolidate its economic programs in the late 2000s.

An immediate criticism of these data is that they mask inequalities in the income distribution in these societies. Perhaps a better indicator is the income share held by the highest 20 percent of the population. For example, in Congo in 2005, the richest 20 percent of the population held 53.1 percent of wealth. Although this percentage might seem inconsequential in light of income inequalities in many advanced economies, the levels of poverty found in Congo are extreme; 22.8 percent of the population lived on less than $1.25 a day. Income inequalities are slightly less striking in Gabon, where in 2005 the top 20 percent of the population held less than half the country's wealth. These data suggest that political leaders had reached an agreement to distribute funds from oil revenues to a select few and ignore most of the population. Such a distribution of benefits and opportunities is unsustainable and reflects a progression of policy choices that have adverse effects on the economy.

Gabon: A Middle-Income Declining Producer

Gabon is a declining producer. Oil production began in 1957 when Elf Aquitaine discovered a heavy crude in onshore reserves near Port Gentil. Since that time, other deep-sea discoveries have extended the date when Gabon transits to a non-oil economy. In 2013, the IMF stated that oil revenues constituted

[97] IMF, "Republic of Congo: Fifth and Sixth Reviews under the Three-Year Arrangement under the Extended Credit Facility and Financing Assurances Review – Staff Report," IMF Country Report 11/255 (August 2011): 6.

[98] IMF, "Republic of Congo: Joint IMF/World Bank Debt Sustainability Analysis," (July 15, 2011), 2.

[99] All statistics are from the World Bank, *World Development Indicators*.

45 percent of Gabon's GDP and 55 percent of budgetary revenues in 2012.[100] The centrality of hydrocarbons for Gabon's economy was an element of the Plan Stratégique du Gabon Emergent, in which the Ali Bongo Ondimba government emphasizes a need to diversify the economy and how it uses the oil resources.[101] Nonetheless, when IOCs operating deep-sea wells have depleted its proven reserves, Gabon will depend on its manganese mines and forestry sector for its exports and foreign reserves.

Since the early 1970s, the World Bank classified Gabon as a middle-income economy, a classification that acknowledges its more than $14,000 per capita PPP income. Although Gabon has performed well, equitable income distribution has been a problem, and approximately one-third of the overall population lives in poverty, a rate that resembles conditions in countries with far less auspicious indicators.[102] IMF estimates are that Gabon's oil reserves may last another forty years.[103] Their depletion means that the government will be dependent on sales or value-added tax, taxes on forestry exports, and customs and excise taxes for its basic fiscal revenues. Gabon faces a decline from the relative wealth of a middle-income country to a country with meager agricultural and mining revenues. In this context, the government's capacity to accommodate younger generations whose members have moved into positions of responsibility may determine Gabon's future prosperity and political stability.

In 2009, President Ali Bongo Ondimba signaled to Gabon's oligarchs that he would continue the system of rule his father had established when he came to office in 1967. Omar Bongo extended the same contracts to Elf that his predecessor and mentor Léon M'ba had negotiated. Although he avoided taking the oil-backed loans his neighbor in Congo had assumed, the elder Bongo worked to bind Gabon's oligarchy to French oil executives by joining them in a web of crisscrossing allegiances.[104] He personally knew Elf's representatives, who, in turn, understood the procedures and methods for paying taxes and royalties and the key people with whom they had to bargain for contracts. However, mismanagement of oil revenues, endemic corruption, and an inequitable distribution of income contributed to a lack of improvement in social indicators since the 1970s.[105] Investments in urban centers and the demonstrations of

[100] The International Monetary Fund, "Gabon: 2012 Article IV Consultation, IMF Country Report 13/55 (March 2013), 4.

[101] République Gabonaise, *Plan Stratégique Gabon Emergent: Vision 2015 et Orientations Stratégiques 2011–2016* (Libreville: République Gabonaise, Juillet 2012), 105–107.

[102] The International Monetary Fund, "Gabon: 2012 Article IV Consultation," 23.

[103] Cheikh Gueye, "Gabon's Experience Managing Oil Wealth." In *Oil Wealth in Central Africa: Policies for Inclusive Growth*, eds. Bernardin Akitoby and Sharmini Coorey (Washington: The International Monetary Fund, 2012), 198; Ali Zafar, "What Happens When a Country Does Not Adjust to Terms of Trade Shocks? The Case of Oil-Rich Gabon," World Bank Policy Research Working Paper 3403 (September 2004), 5.

[104] Stephan Smith and Antoine Glaser, *Ces Messieurs Afrique: Des Réseaux aux Lobbies* (Paris: Calmann-Lévy, 1997), 193–195.

[105] Zafar, "What Happens When a Country Does Not Adjust," 1.

wealth in luxury hotels and restaurants animated economic life in Libreville and several other key cities. Meanwhile, Bongo and his oligarchs left the countryside much as it had been at independence. Chapter 6 explores in greater depth the Bongo clan's capture of the Gabonese state and how it imposed a clan-based political economic system on Gabon's people.

Since well before independence, Gabon was an exporter of *okoumé*, a tropical wood prized in Europe and Asia for flooring and furniture. Even during the boom years of oil production, logging was the largest private-sector employer. Colonial investments in timber had transformed the sector into a major economic activity; large concessions were granted to French firms and a substantial number of indigenous loggers. Since independence, the logging companies have received licenses from a marketing board, the Société Nationale des Bois du Gabon (SNBG) that grants joint venture contracts wherein the SNBG holds 51 percent and the forestry company 49 percent.[106]

In colonial Gabon, the timber sector was the largest source of revenues and employment despite administrators' debates about reducing production to protect French industries.[107] However, Gabonese nationalists have asserted that between 1927 and 1935, French firms received profits in excess of 2 billion francs.[108] Gabon's timber production is a significant export that has increased in importance since the early 1990s. For example, okoumé production, almost 1.2 million cubic meters in 1992, increased to approximately 2 million cubic meters in 1996.[109] Gabonese timber production experienced a drop in exports from 2.7 m³ in 1999 to 700,000 m³ in 2004, reportedly because of blatant inefficiencies and corruption in the SNBG.[110] In May 2004, under pressure from the IMF, the Gabonese government grudgingly agreed to privatize the SNBG.[111]

The elder Bongo quietly postponed the 2004 agreement by delegating a steering committee to study the procedure. In this fashion, he delayed making the difficult choices that accompanied the SNBG's privatization.[112] As Gabon makes a transition from a petrostate to a non-oil economy, it is probable that forestry will become an attractive investment for the Bongo clan and its cronies. Nevertheless, a dependence on forestry promises lower incomes and

---

[106] AFP, "Le Secteur du Bois, Stratégique pour l'Économie Gabonaise, en Plein Crise," *Le Monde* (21 Décembre 2004).

[107] République française, Ministère des Colonies, "Dépêches Ministérielles de l'Okoumé," No 5983, AEF 1B 473 (7 Décembre 1936).

[108] Martin Edzodzomo-Ela, *Mon Projet pour le Gabon: Comment Redresser un Pays Ruiné par Trois Décennies de Mauvaise Gestion* (Paris: Éditions Karthala, 2000), 181.

[109] IMF, "Gabon: Statistical Appendix," Country Report No. 99/12 (February 1999): 18.

[110] AFP, "Le Secteur du Bois, Stratégique pour l'Économie Gabonaise, en Plein Crise."

[111] AFP, "Pressé par le FMI, le Gabon Restructure sa Filière Bois (Papier d'Angle)," *Le Monde* (21 Décembre 2004).

[112] IMF, "Gabon: Staff Report for the 2005 Article IV Consultation for the Government of Gabon, Third Review under the Stand-By Arrangement, and Review of Financing Assurances" (March 16, 2005): 18–19.

a reduction in tax revenues. Gabon stands out as a state that must make a transition from petrostate status to an economy that earns its foreign reserves from commerce and financial and advisory services.

Unfortunately, Gabon is a declining oil producer. Its principal challenge is to attract investors in hard rock mining, notably manganese, and timber.[113] In June 2010, Ali Bongo personally met with Patrick Buffet, CEO of the French mining conglomerate Eramet, to negotiate a contract for mining manganese, in which the Gabonese government would hold 25–35 percent of the company in conjunction with Eramet's subsidiary Comilog.[114] These meetings reflect a continuation of past patterns in which the president negotiates contracts directly with international investors on the basis of personal relations. The contract may provide Gabon's government a source of revenues to distribute to members of the family. However, this contract represents a potential shift in priorities; the ruling family is reducing its dependence on oil revenues to seek other sources of wealth.

CONCLUSION

This chapter has traced the relationship between economic growth and the phases of production in African petrostates. It presents three phases of production to provide a temporal guide for understanding the impact of resource rents. First, when explorations yield discoveries of oil, the country becomes an emerging producer. A range of pressures comes to bear on policymakers in the petrostate as rent seeking animates different social groups. Second, as oil companies continue to produce oil, the petrostate becomes a mature producer. In these producers, brokers emerge to profit from economic activities in the oil sector. Finally, declining producers are those petrostates with diminished reserves. It is among declining producers that the pressures for reform may be greatest.

In each phase of production, upstream and downstream productive operations are critical elements in how policymakers respond to oil windfalls. First, most emerging producers did not have in place the offices to manage the new productive sector. Deposits of taxes and royalties enter the central bank, but in many petrostates ill-defined withdrawal rules allowed some presidents and their clansmen to divert revenues for their personal expenses. In Chad, São Tomé and Príncipe, and Ghana conflicts erupted when individuals perceived that the presidents excluded some people and favored others. Even before the state began to receive revenues from oil production, competition erupted over the distribution of benefits from the new productive sector.

Presidents of mature producers have learned the importance of protecting the property rights that govern oil-sector transactions because they pay

---

[113] Ludvig Söderling, "After the Oil: Challenges ahead in Gabon," *Journal of African Economies* 15, 1 (March 2006): 139.

[114] AFP, "Le Gabon Entrera au Capital d'Eramet," *Le Monde* (17 June 2010).

a majority of fiscal revenues. Agreements and contracts are already in place; leaders of mature producers maintain relations with oil companies; resource rents are a fact of fiscal stability. In some mature producers, the Dutch disease causes overvalued exchange rates and a decline of manufacturing and other productive sectors. As a consequence, Nigeria and Angola, two mature producers, are dependent on oil revenues for the overwhelming majority of their fiscal revenues. Although mature African petrostates are growing economically, low levels of non-oil capital accumulation present challenges. Still, considering where these states began, the wealth created by oil production has been significant and its impacts are going to influence development for some time, even after the oil is exhausted.

Declining producers confront serious challenges to their hopes of prosperity. The drop in revenues places clear pressures on declining producers to develop means to ensure some economic growth. Services related to oil production, commercial enterprises, and banking are some of the activities in which the declining producers may find a comparative advantage. However, these African petrostates confront issues of low levels of human development; the choices available to their citizens are few. Meanwhile, increasing populations put pressure on political authorities to extend freedoms and rights that they had previously denied. Countervailing pressures arise, and as Congo experienced during the 1990s, civil war is a possible outcome.

A socialization process occurs in which leaders of emerging producers recognize a need to present their countries as reasonable investment risks for international oil companies. To the extent they fail in this endeavor, international companies have incentives to add a premium during contract negotiations. Hence, leaders such as Obiang Nguema strive to present an image of their rule as a benign developmental state that distributes oil revenues for the betterment of their citizens. Second, a cadre of individuals gains experience in international business at the highest levels. In mature and declining producers, these professionals work in ministries of petroleum or the DNOCs. They represent an increase in human capital and are potential leaders of reforms in the petrostates. Chapter 5 discusses the role of clans, clients, and cronies in the consolidation of democratic impulses in African petrostates.

5

Resource Revenues, Corruption, and Contracts

INTRODUCTION

The preceding chapters examined the historical development in African petrostates, the structure of oil companies, and how the phase of hydrocarbon production illustrates long-term relationships and their impact on policy outcomes. The centrality of historic relationships informs decisions about the people petrostates' rulers include in the distribution of resource windfalls and those individuals and groups they exclude. Executives with oil companies take advantage of long-standing relationships to secure favorable contracts. However, Africa's oil market is highly dynamic, and as new actors have entered to compete for contracts, market relations and long-standing contractual arrangements between petrostates and formerly dominant oil companies have shifted to include Asian and South American firms. Finally, a country's phase of production is the context in which these actors intermingle; the phase of production influences how the political leadership chooses policies and therefore developmental outcomes.

This chapter builds on the analysis presented in Chapter 4, which explores the impact of a petrostate's phase of production on policy outcomes. It assesses how the economic, social, and political conditions at the time of discovery and start of production shape a leadership's reaction to resource windfalls. Among the poorest countries (e.g., Chad), the partially constructed bureaucracies lacked trained personnel to conceptualize budgets, enforce laws to control government spending, and manage oil windfalls; corrupt practices became a norm. Authorities could behave with impunity. In the worst cases (e.g., Equatorial Guinea, Congo), the presidents put in place a corrupt system that led to a capacity to divert government resources for their personal gain. Corruption was a consequence of few controls, a sense of entitlement, and a culture of impunity that is a legacy of the autocratic colonial state.

Historical Antecedents of Corruption

The origins of dishonest and opportunistic behavior are present in colonial history when officials had wide discretion to do whatever they liked. This discretion was an outcome of the gulf that existed between the European authorities and their colonial subjects. Tignor notes that British officials were convinced that the Emirs of Northern Nigeria were "inherently oppressive and venal."[1] A similar sentiment is evident from cables that French colonial administrators sent from Congo during the Second World War; they complained that the Lari people from the Pool District were both dishonest and without intelligence.[2] In spite of this distrust, postwar French and British officials sought to identify African elites to whom they hoped to hand over political power. For example, the British promoted the Northern Nigerian politician Abubakar Balewa. In his 1950 electoral campaign, Balewa declared his commitment to combat corruption in public administration.[3] Similarly, French officials permitted Léon M'ba in Gabon to hold the Congrès Fang, at which he declared his commitment to better administration.[4] Afterward, M'ba used French support and his popularity to isolate his rival Jean-Hilaire Aubame and consolidate power.

At independence, African leaders inherited partially constructed states that were without ministries, departments, and agencies with competent officials to manage fiscal revenues and the budget process. As decolonization gained momentum, African presidents tried to raise the fiscal revenues needed to operate their weak, impoverished states. Corruption and mismanagement were norms. As a result, the states failed to provide basic services for their citizens, who were suspicious of officials and their motives.

This chapter begins with a consideration of corruption as a political problem that has economic consequences. Intuitively, the extent of corruption would seem a consequence of state construction; the more bureaucratic development in a given state, the less venality among its public servants. From this depiction it would follow that impoverished countries that had received marginal colonial investments would suffer more graft and bribery as underpaid officials try to supplement their meager incomes. As the petrostate transits from being an emerging to a mature producer, this perspective suggests there should occur a reduction in the rates of corruption. However, this reduced rate of malfeasance is not what happened. The question therefore is what are the preconditions that favor corruption or probity?

[1] Robert Tignor, "Political Corruption in Nigeria before Independence," *The Journal of Modern African Studies* 31, 2 (June 1993): 177.
[2] République française, Ministère des Colonies, Département de Pool, Rapport Politique Année 1942, N°425, (Brazzaville, le 27 mars 1943) ANSOM 4(2) D75.
[3] Tignor, "Political Corruption in Nigeria before Independence," 197–198.
[4] République française, Ministère des Colonies, Territoire du Gabon, Rapport Politique, Année 1947, Chefferie – Faits Importants, Assemblées de Chefs. ANSOM, AEF 4 (1) D55.

By distinguishing among the three phases of production it is possible to see how corruption is a reflection of a particular country's circumstances at the time it discovers hydrocarbons and begins production. In many petrostates, however, corruption is persistent. This chapter teases out three possible explanations for persistent public dishonesty. First, historic continuities explain far more than any negative effects of oil production. Second, predatory rule is a function of a leader's sense of security in office; an insecure president has incentives to use corruption to extend the time horizon of his rule. With time and shifts into mature production, autocrats stabilize property rights in the economy's productive sector, and levels of malfeasance diminish. Third, the embeddedness of democratic institutions creates norms that condemn malfeasance among public authorities. This chapter's focus is exploring these three explanations.

Natural Resources and Development

The discovery of oil might prompt a petrostate's people to expect better governmental performance and social and political opportunities. In this book, the term "development" implies outcomes that include widespread economic and social improvements, or what Sen has brilliantly portrayed as a freedom to choose.[5] When companies announce a significant discovery, the countries undergo a series of transformative changes. First, the state receives a substantial increase in fiscal revenues. In every petrostate, economic indicators suggest impressive rates of growth. This growth, as measured by aggregate statistics, may be illusory; few emerging producers have the bureaucracy in place to employ new fiscal revenues for investments that result in greater employment opportunities, better educational possibilities, and an expansion of health care. A petrostate may grow economically, as occurred in Angola during the last decade, but its citizens received few if any benefits from that growth. Instead, an oligarchy captured state offices and denied the Angolan citizens basic freedoms, obfuscated property rights, and distributed wealth inequitably. In 2012, the dos Santos government established a sovereign wealth fund on the basis of Norway's fund and named Jose Filomeno dos Santos, the president's eldest son, as its director.[6] These choices attest to the extent to which Angola's political elite succumbed to the temptations of seizing resource rents in an environment of few controls.

However, it is important to recall that these countries are young states; their bureaucracies reflected a relative newness to the organizations that assumed responsibility for administration. Although it is possible to show one by one how Africa's petrostates are young states, the point is that the discovery of

[5] Amartya Sen, *Development as Freedom* (New York: Alfred Knopf, 1999).
[6] Andrew England and William Wallis, "Angola Sets Up Fund to Preserve Oil Riches," *The Financial Times* (October 17, 2012).

oil imposed requirements for politicians to create ministries and agencies to manage the windfalls, and domestic national oil companies to partner with international firms. Considerable variation is present among these states; for one, at the onset of production, Ghana possessed agencies that could receive and manage mineral revenues; Chad, by contrast, had no such offices. The Déby government lacked the personnel to decide how to save revenues or use those savings to smooth expenditures during periods of downward price volatility. Its agreements with the World Bank to create offshore accounts that could shelter resource revenues from political uses fell apart shortly after production began. Thereafter, earnings from oil sales failed to alleviate poverty or have a positive distributional impact among Chad's people. Hence, although aggregate statistics for Chad suggest impressive levels of economic growth, social-sector indicators are less glowing.

Oil windfalls encourage corruption, cronyism, and inefficient financial management. In African petrostates, authoritarian leaders suddenly awash in petrodollars wallowed in the culture of impunity that had been present during colonial rule. Their actions resembled the behavior of European administrators who would, at their discretion, manipulate contracts, forego fiscal management, and take advantage of their privileged positions to enrich themselves. After independence, this culture of impunity encouraged presidents to divert fiscal revenues in a manner consistent with the dysfunctional behaviors that Johnston calls market corruption and oligarch and clan corruption.[7] Presidents manipulated markets to bestow unmerited wealth on their cronies and clans. All could be confident they would never be held accountable even if the corruption undermined the country's economic stability. However, presidents grew to understand that if they destabilized property rights, it would cause greater price distortions, lower rates of economic growth, and increased levels of poverty.[8] However, they would never be held accountable for these outcomes. Still, it would be too strong to suggest, as some of the more fervent among the resource-curse advocates might assert, that Chad would be better off without the oil production.

THE CORRUPTION DILEMMA IN AFRICAN PETROSTATES

The starting point of oil production represents a benchmark to measure political economic change. This chapter asserts that some level of corruption in African petrostates is understandable when considering their economies before the discovery of hydrocarbons. Most were agrarian economies whose farmers

[7] Michael Johnston, *Syndromes of Corruption: Wealth, Power, and Democracy* (New York: Cambridge University Press, 2005), 42–48.
[8] Stephen Knack and Philip E. Keefer use econometric tools to show the relationship between weak property rights and corruption, see "Institutions and Economic Performance: Cross Country Test with Alternative Institutional Measures," *Economics and Politics* 7 (1995): 207–227.

paid little in taxes, a cold fact that left the administrations often unable to even pay their wage bill. Before they discovered oil, customs and excise taxes and international development assistance provided the lion's share of fiscal revenues. With the discovery of hydrocarbons, however, their fiscal positions shifted; they became rentier states, albeit vulnerable to oil-price volatility. Moreover, their leaders could ignore political opponents and divert revenues to their clans, military constituencies, and cronies. Corruption thrived through informal institutions; clansmen became regime cronies and brokers who could demand commissions, gifts, and other favors that oil companies would clandestinely provide.

Corruption had an adverse effect on African economies whether or not they were oil exporters. This point rejects popular notions that corruption could be a redistributive mechanism.[9] As the cases discussed demonstrate, African dictators refused to distribute resource rents outside their clientelist networks and clans. Worse, such stylized assumptions ignore the fact that corruption is far more distortionary than taxation and undermines efficient resource management.[10] Instead, historical influences shape how different leaders respond to pressures to distribute resource rents via corrupt mechanisms. Thus, any discussion of corruption and revenue management in African petrostates has to study how historical continuities are manifest in political economic outcomes.

Revenue Mismanagement and Corruption among Petrostates

An unfortunate legacy of colonialism was a failure on the part of European administrations to train civil servants in fiscal management; few people had the skills to manage resource rents. The consequence was a lack of competent civil servants and inefficient behavior, notably, corruption. First, African petrostates have underdeveloped bureaucracies that have no offices to account for oil revenues. Decades of fiscal poverty left these bureaucracies without technocrats who have the skills to manage revenues efficiently. A society-wide dearth of chartered accountants, trained economists, and public administration specialists leave the states unable to absorb the moneys, much less use the revenues efficiently. Many development specialists have observed this inability to absorb revenues in low-income countries; the states are unable to absorb substantial revenues whether provided by international donor agencies or a natural resource windfall.[11] Aghion et al. refer to "absorptive capacity" as the ability

[9] This notion of corruption as a positive behavior in African societies is key to Patrick Chabal and Jean-Pascal Daloz, *Africa Works: Disorder as a Political Instrument* (Bloomington: Indiana University Press, 1999), 99.

[10] The distortionary effect of corruption is crucial in Andrei Shleifer and Robert W. Vishny, "Corruption," *The Quarterly Journal of Economics* 108, 3 (August 1993): 600.

[11] Hollis B. Chenery and Nicholas G. Carter, "Foreign Assistance and Development Performance, 1960–1970," *The American Economic Review* 63, 2 (May 1973): 460. For a similar treatment of development effectiveness and absorptive capacity, see François Bourguignon and Mark

of an economy to absorb new technologies; absorptive capacity is a function of the variable levels of human capital in a given state.[12] Their perspective highlights the lack of competent personnel to manage multiple revenue streams common in many African petrostates.

Revenue management is a particularly nettlesome problem for Africa's oil producers because their states lack competent personnel. In his study of aid-dependent states, Svensson has termed this problem "a broken information (accountability) feedback loop"; it occurs when a government receives multiple revenue streams from diverse donors but cannot account for their uses.[13] The lack of information, or rather a means to aggregate information in a coherent and manageable format, is the problem. As discussed in Chapter 3, oil revenues come in multiple streams from declining reserves, ongoing production in mature fields, and new wells. Because petrostates receive multiple revenue streams at different times of the year, the "broken information feedback loop" explains the absence of accounting for the aggregate payments that oil companies make. Inefficient management of resource revenues creates opportunities for corruption that the absence of technocrats deepens. Conceivably, such inefficiencies change as petrostates receive oil windfalls and its leaders learn how to manage revenues.

The second problem a state encounters in absorptive capacity is evident in the lag time between the receipt of revenues and their distribution as budgetary revenues for fiscal expenditures. In many countries, oil companies make deposits into accounts with regional banks often that have a responsibility to transfer the funds to the central bank. Imperfect supervision of these accounts creates a lapse between the time of deposit and its transfer to the treasury. The issue is whether this lag time is willful (to allow graft) or the result of incompetence. When the lag is intentional, the bank gets to use the funds for its private purposes or others misappropriate the moneys for private purposes. The government may then acknowledge inefficiency or deny its occurrence.

Equatorial Guinea may be an example of a willful denial; its 2008 GDP was almost twenty-five times larger than the country's GDP in the early 1980s. In spite of this growth in GDP, Equatorial Guinea's social-sector indicators are consistent with low-income African economies.[14] In 2008, for example, the average Equatorial Guinean could expect to live to fifty years of age. This life expectancy is far below that of other countries with similar per capita GNIs; for instance, in Estonia and Hungary, two countries with similar income

Sundberg, "Absorptive Capacity and Achieving the MDGs" UNU-WIDER Research Paper No 2006/47 (May 2006).

[12] Philippe Aghion, Peter Howitt, and David Mayer-Foulkes, "The Effective of Financial Development on Convergence: Theory and Evidence," *The Quarterly Journal of Economics* 120, 1 (February 2005): 175.

[13] Jakob Svensson, "Absorption Capacity and Disbursement Constraints," in *Reinventing Foreign Aid*, ed. William Easterly (Cambridge, MA: MIT Press, 2008), 312.

[14] All statistics are from the World Bank, *World Development Indicators 2009*.

levels, citizens may expect to live well past seventy. Another measure is infant mortality; in Equatorial Guinea, on average, 89.5 infants per 1,000 will fail to survive. Hungary has an infant mortality rate of 5.4 per 1,000; in Estonia, it is 4.4, which compares favorably with the United Kingdom's 4.8. These statistics reveal that whereas Equatorial Guinea has grown dramatically in terms of income, its social-sector investments have lagged far behind. The benefits of increased wealth have accrued to a tiny percentage of the population.

Third, citizens of many petrostates suffer violence that impedes effective management of resource windfalls. Unfortunately, many petrostates have dual challenges of high levels of venality and routine violence. Whether discussing the Bonny Island Liquid Natural Gas train scandal in Nigeria or the capture of lucrative sectors in Angola by President Eduardo dos Santos and his family, staggering levels of corruption appear commonplace.[15] In Angola, violence has become such a regular experience for its citizens that it is chillingly banal.[16] Although Nigeria issued an amnesty program for militants in the Niger Delta, the persistence of oil theft has remained a challenge for the federal government that accounts for the diversion of large sums of money.[17]

Finally, in many petrostates, politicians negotiated illicit arrangements to facilitate corrupt payments to secret accounts that they and their families controlled. Two U.S. Senate Subcommittee reports on money laundering published during the mid-2000s indicated a high level of dishonesty on the part of U.S. banks and corporations that colluded with Equatorial Guinea's president. On the surface, it may appear that the oil revenues are simply too much for dishonest politicians to ignore. However, it is necessary to recall where these states started and consider the progress they have made since oil production began. Equatorial Guinea was an impoverished cocoa producer under Spanish domination until 1967. Although it is tempting to focus on each petrostate's failings, the accumulation of wealth in even the most corrupt and autocratic state creates a possibility of development and, over time, the enactment of political reforms.

Corruption as a Willful Act in African Petrostates

Corruption correlates with low levels of state construction; leaders can manipulate both formal and informal rules to seize resource rents and distribute them to members of supporting coalitions. In petrostate after petrostate, venal entrepreneurs manipulated the economy for political purposes; they actively

---

[15] On the Bonny Island LNG train scandal, indictment documents retrived from http://www.justice.gov/opa/pr/2010/June/10-crm-751.html. On corruption in Angola, see Henrique Almeida, "Angolan President's Family Taint Corruption Fight," *Reuters* (December 3, 2009).

[16] Amnesty International has released numerous reports on violence perpetrated by Angola's police since 2002 when the war ended.

[17] Xan Rice, "Nigeria Begins Amnesty for Niger Delta Militants," *The Guardian* (August 6, 2009).

sought political office to gain economic advantage. This point follows the classic argument that class formation in Africa occurred not through capital accumulation in economic life but rather through political control.[18] Political control implies that less-than-scrupulous officials can manipulate economic opportunities and accumulate significant wealth as a consequence of their positions. When corruption permeates all levels of the state, it is *systemic*. When the dishonesty is a result of willful political manipulation of the economy, it is *systematic*. Systematic corruption occurs when

a group of politicians deliberately creates rents by limiting entry into valuable economic activities, through grants of monopoly, restrictive corporate charters, tariffs, quotas, regulations, and the like. These rents bind the interests of the recipients to the politicians who create them. The purpose is to build a coalition that can dominate the government. Manipulating the economy for political ends is systematic corruption. Systematic corruption occurs when politics corrupts economics.[19]

Political elites in a number of petrostates have used systematic corruption to accumulate staggering stocks of wealth. Because these elite politicians allow actors at the lower echelons of the state to engage in venal behavior, the corruption is systemic; however, as it is evident that politicians use exclusive contracts, monopolies, and restrictions to reap substantial rewards, corruption in African petrostates is systemic and systematic.

Politicians in African petrostates that commenced production while the countries were at dismal levels of economic development were free from rules and agencies that could have constrained their corrupt behavior. Transparency International's Corruption Perception Index (displayed in Table 5.1), a survey of surveys, shows that corruption is perceived to be widespread in Africa's petrostates. Although it is tempting to suggest that high levels of corruption correlate with the phase of production (e.g., higher rates of perceived corruption among emerging producers), the rankings displayed suggest otherwise. Among the emerging producers, Chad has consistently high scores for perceived corruption. It is, ironically, among the mature and declining producers that the perceptions of corruption appear highest. Practices that political leaders embedded in the states over which they held sway contributed to persistent corruption and unstable rule.

Conceivably, oil revenues create opportunities that officials embed in states to ensure their economic prospects. This notion posits that in mature and declining producers, both systemic and systematic corruption are probable. When countries with extreme poverty begin to receive oil windfalls, leaders entrench inefficient practices to capture rents. They build on institutions that

---

[18] Richard L. Sklar, "The Nature of Class Domination in Africa." *The Journal of Modern African Studies* 14, 4 (December 1979): 536–537.

[19] John Joseph Wallis, "The Concept of Systematic Corruption in American History," in *Corruption and Reform: Lessons from American Economic History*, eds. Edward L. Glaeser and Claudia Goldin (Chicago: University of Chicago Press, 2006), 25.

TABLE 5.1 *Transparency International Corruption Perception Index*

Country	CPI Index N = 159 (2005)	CPI Index N = 163 (2006)	CPI Index N = 179 (2007)	CPI Index N = 180 (2008)	CPI Index N = 180 (2009)	CPI Index N = 178 (2010)	CPI Index N = 183 (2011)	CPI Index N = 176 (2012)
Emerging Producers								
Chad	159	157	172	173	175	171	168	165
Ghana	65	70	69	69	69	62	69	64
Mauritania	N/A	86	123	118	131	143	143	123
São Tomé and Príncipe	N/A	N/A	118	123	113	101	100	72
Mature Producers								
Angola	151	142	147	158	159	168	168	157
Eq. Guinea	153	154	168	172	164	168	172	163
Nigeria	154	146	147	122	134	134	143	139
South Africa	46	51	43	54	55	54	64	69
Sudan	149	159	172	175	176	172	177	173
Declining Producers								
Cameroon	138	138	138	141	144	146	134	144
Congo	132	143	150	161	160	154	154	
Gabon	91	90	84	97	102	110	100	102

Sources: TI, Corruption Perception Index 2005–2012. Retrieved from http://www.transparency.org.

were present in the country when hydrocarbon extraction began. Preexisting conditions facilitate high levels of corruption, and oil is an intermediate factor. A second issue is the degree of organization that politicians need to fight wars. In Angola and Sudan, two mature producers, decades of war left their leaders without a compelling reason to establish offices of state that would manage revenues effectively for developmental purposes. Their war economies required that political leaders ensure unrestrained access to funds to purchase arms and maintain the cohesiveness of supporting coalitions.[20] Whatever the hypothesis, it is evident from the table that perception of corruption is highest in fragile states and those engaged in conflict.

Corruption is a political problem with economic consequences. It is behavior that imposes reputational costs for African petrostates. In African petrostates, political regimes rest on an increasingly centralized executive branch that operates free from controls.[21] Politicians choose to allow graft, influence peddling, and extortion in spite of the reputational costs that corrupt transactions impose on the economy. First, these political choices have much to do with the exigencies of keeping power. A permissive attitude toward dishonesty allows individuals to gather rents and enrich themselves. In this manner, they provide the regime needed support and malfeasance becomes an element of keeping political power. Second, when we review the backgrounds of leaders in countries that were among the world's poorest economies when they discovered oil, it is apparent that political leaders had narrow constituencies and little understanding of managing an economy. Politicians just did not know the costs that their behavior imposed on their economies. As a result, corruption continued unabated in the poorest states that had the least-developed bureaucracies. It was the way business was conducted.

As Table 5.1 suggests, African petrostates are among the most corrupt in the world. Transparency International has ranked Chad, Nigeria, Angola, Mauritania, Sudan, Congo, and Equatorial Guinea among countries that are systematically corrupt. The impact of such perceptions is that foreign investors factor corruption expenses into any contracts they negotiate with the country. Hence, as addressed in Chapter 3, contractual negotiations include those costs in the bids. Once dishonesty becomes a behavioral norm, officials and business actors form a perverse but stable relationship. Worse, embedded corruption reduces revenues for the state and deepens poverty. In the most fragile states, corruption and routine violence persist and weaken political institutions. In Chad, President Déby took power over a state that had been in chronic war. When oil companies paid his government bonuses at the onset of oil production, Déby diverted the funds to purchase military ordnance and ensure

---

[20] Richard Cockett, *Sudan: Darfur and the Failure of an African State* (New Haven: Yale University Press, 2010), 263.
[21] Nicolas van de Walle, "Presidentialism and Clientelism in Africa's Emerging Party Systems," *The Journal of Modern African Studies* 41, 2 (June 2003): 297–321.

his position in office.[22] Selected clansmen and cronies were winners in this diversion of funds. Losers included Tom and Timane Erdimi, Déby's nephews, who worked respectively as director of the national cotton company and coordinator of the oil and pipeline project. When they perceived that their uncle had excluded them from the benefits of oil production, they left the government, took up arms, and joined a crowd of insurgents that wanted to overthrow the government.[23] In the ensuing years, rebel troops twice entered the capital N'Djamena, effectively destabilizing the state and offsetting benefits from oil exports. Déby surrounded himself with the most loyal cronies and clansmen as a strategy to keep tight control over revenues and bonuses. In all three of these cases, political leaders centralized power in the face of state fragility.

Brokers and Gatekeepers: Informality and Corruption

When African petrostates first received oil revenues, people who had strong connections to the regime emerged to facilitate transactions and control resource rents. These individuals were brokers or gatekeepers (I use these terms interchangeably) who responded to investors' demands for information and contract facilitation.[24] *Gatekeepers* function both as middlemen who control access to key decision makers and information about contracts, licenses, and investment opportunities.[25] Many gatekeepers deny access to firms or individuals they deem to be unreliable or unable to pay the required fees. For example, Pascaline Bongo, Gabonese President Omar Bongo's first-born daughter, was the ultimate gatekeeper; anyone who wanted access to the president had to go through her. She and her siblings decided who entered the Gabonese market and who gained access to the rents available from its hydrocarbon sector.

Brokers in Africa typically established patronage systems that distributed benefits to their clients. These systems use historical relationships to establish networks that structure their ability to control information and access to contracts.[26] In networks, the brokers serve as informal middlemen who introduce clients to political leaders. *Middlemen* set up networks to procure illicit benefits for their clients that include access to contracts, real estate, jobs, credit, and other benefits for which they receive substantial commissions. For example,

[22] Babette Stern, "Le Tchad a Acheté des Armes avec l'Argent du Pêtrole," *Le Monde* (22 Novembre 2000).

[23] Han van Djik, "Briefing: Political Deadlock in Chad," *African Affairs* 106, 425 (October 2007): 701.

[24] Steffen Hertog, *Princes, Brokers, and Bureaucrats: Oil and the State in Saudi Arabia* (Ithaca and London: Cornell University Press, 2010a), 26.

[25] Mamadi Corra and David Willer, "The Gatekeeper," *Sociological Theory* 20, 2 (July 2002): 18.

[26] This pattern of using historical relationships to control access to influential positions is consistent with experiences in other regions. For example, see Luis Roniger, "Caciquismo and Coronelismo: Contextual Dimensions of Patron Brokerage in Mexico and Brazil," *Latin American Research Review* 22, 2 (1987): 71.

in India, Khanna and Johnston found that middlemen dominated government relations, and in return they received corrupt payment from economic actors who wanted access to contracts.[27] In petrostates, the brokers create a "product" in the form of access they can sell to oil companies that want to enter and operate in a particular market. The brokers operate through informal networks that monopolize the information marketplace and create rents as the brokers' principal sources of wealth.

In African petrostates, brokers decide who learns of bidding competition, licenses, and the types of contracts that are available for specific reserves. In his analysis of Saudi Arabia, Hertog notes how brokers fashion informal arrangements that compose "segmented networks."[28] These networks closely resemble patronage networks in African petrostates where key members of the presidents' clan or close associates serve as gatekeepers and transfer corrupt rewards to members of clientelist networks. As we see in the next section, in Ghana brokers were able to capitalize on their possession of inside information. Brokers identify entry points where companies and individuals can pay "fees" to get contracts and influence civil servants in decision-making positions. For payments, they navigate ministries to facilitate contract negotiations for oil companies. In effect, formal practices in a bureaucracy operate alongside informal arrangements. These arrangements in turn build on relationships among individuals that predate the discovery of oil. The origins of these arrangements date to relations their clans developed with colonial authorities. Hence, conditions in African petrostates are indicative of greater continuities than discontinuities.

CORRUPTION IN GHANA, EQUATORIAL GUINEA, AND CONGO

This chapter considers the problem of corruption as it occurs in countries at different phases of production. For an emerging producer, the chapter considers allegations of malfeasance in Ghana and how they have influenced development in that country. From a perspective of 2014, it may seem too early to assess the impact of oil on this young, emerging producer. However, for several reasons Ghana is an excellent case for considering the impact of hydrocarbon production. First, unlike other emerging producers, Ghana's government operates through the institutions of republican democracy. These institutions have brought norms of transparency and accountability that other petrostates have only glimpsed in their political organizations. Second, the actions of national and international oil companies indicate how the oil market in Africa is changing and adjusting to competition among diverse firms. Third, because of its extensive gold and diamond mines, the Ghanaian

---

[27] Jyoti Khanna and Michael Johnston, "India's Middlemen: Connecting by Corrupting," *Crime, Law, and Social Change* 48, 3–5 (December 2007): 152.
[28] Hertog, *Princes, Brokers, and Bureaucrats*, 22.

government had experience managing resource revenues. Ghana demonstrates how a country's starting point is crucial for understanding its developmental trajectory after the discovery of significant hydrocarbon reserves. Its legal obligations and ability to impose a regulatory structure on a nascent oil sector would soon be tested.

For a mature producer, the chapter analyzes questions of state capture and corruption in Equatorial Guinea. Before the small state became independent in 1968, Spain's colonial administration managed an extractive agricultural sector mainly producing cocoa and timber. Colonial administration had been highly authoritarian, and inequalities were rife among the population. Even after independence, extreme autocracy resulted in a small, ineffective state. It lacked the agencies necessary to administer oil revenues after Equatorial Guinea became an important producer in the 1990s. Consequently, the clan has diverted hundreds of millions into personal accounts.

Finally, the chapter examines events in Congo as a declining producer. In Congo, the president and his supporting oligarchs had opened accounts into which oil companies deposited royalties and taxes. The president, his children, and a number of cronies had exclusive withdrawal rights. They accumulated fabulous riches and Congo's people received the scraps; most languished in poverty. Worse, the methods Denis Sassou Nguesso allegedly used to launder ill-gotten gains served as lessons for other African leaders who also set up accounts into which oil companies deposited money. As a result, Transparency International litigated in French courts to freeze the funds until the political leaders demonstrate that they received the money legally.

Although these cases illustrate the question of venality in various petrostates at different phases of production, it is necessary to consider their particularities. Ghana is an emerging producer; it is also a democracy with agencies of restraint in three different anticorruption bodies. The contrast with Equatorial Guinea can hardly be greater. An autocratic clan has controlled Equatorial Guinea since its independence in 1967. Finally, the political systems that have dominated Congo since independence include a Marxist-Leninist regime, a brief period of a weak republican democracy, and a clan-based dictatorship. The chapter suggests that despite high levels of corruption and other inefficiencies, African petrostates have implemented elements of democracy in their political systems since the discovery of oil that build on relations that precede oil production; these democratic elements represent continuities from colonialism and even before.

ALLEGED CORRUPTION AND BROKERS IN AN EMERGING PRODUCER: GHANA

It might seem too early to judge whether Ghana might avoid the economic dislocations that have accompanied hydrocarbon production in other countries. However, van Wijnbergen's concept of "learning by doing" suggests that firms and states benefit from the experiences of others.[29] In this regard, Ghana presents an ideal case to assess the impact of oil revenues on an emerging producer. With a benchmark date of 2007, it is possible to track how the oil sector influences one of Africa's democratic governments. In 2010, according to its scores that rank countries from 1 (free) to 7 (not free), Freedom House accorded Ghana a score of "1" for civil liberties and "2" for political rights, indicating that the Ghanaians enjoy a "free" status.[30] Freedom House categorizes as free only Benin, Botswana, Cape Verde, Ghana, Mali, São Tomé and Príncipe, and South Africa for all of sub-Saharan Africa. In many respects, these political indicators support arguments that repeated elections constitute "self-fulfilling behavior" that reinforces norms of democracy.[31] The Ghanaian Parliament passed the 2011 petroleum revenue management law (Act 851) that requires the government deposit revenues into a future-generation oil fund called the Petroleum Revenue Fund. Act 851 provides for transparency and accountability as operational norms in oil-sector management.

Before 2007, Ghana had already been an economic success story; its economy averaged approximately 5 percent growth over the last decade, an achievement that reduced poverty from 52 percent in 1992 to 28.5 percent in 2006.[32] In reward for its economic management, the IMF and International Development Association of the World Bank determined in 2004 that Ghana had met all the conditions to advance under the Highly Indebted Poor Country initiative from the Decision Point to the Completion Point and receive debt relief.[33] Its impressive political economic performance complements and even provides credence to the sustainability of Ghanaian democracy.

Ghana's democracy is not, however, without ambiguities. Jockers et al. dispute suggestions that the 2008 presidential elections were entirely free; they note incidents of electoral fraud and block voting, and assert that politicians' behavior posed "a destabilizing factor" in Ghana's future democracy.[34] Conceivably, Ghana represents a state that is only on the cusp of experiencing the distortions that will test the government's ability to manage resource rents over an extended period. The potentially corrupting effects of oil windfalls give pause and might suggest that as the potential winnings of holding office increase so do politicians' incentives to engage in graft and electoral fraud.

[29] Sweder van Wijnbergen, "The 'Dutch Disease': A Disease after All?" *The Economic Journal* 94 (March 1984): 41.
[30] Retrieved from http://www.freedomhouse.org.
[31] Staffan Lindberg, *Democracy and Elections in Africa* (Baltimore: The Johns Hopkins University Press, 2006), 115.
[32] Jihad Dagher, Jan Gottschalk, and Rafael Portillo, "Oil Windfalls in Ghana: A DSGE Approach," IMF Working Paper WP/10/116 (May 2010): 6.
[33] International Monetary Fund, "Ghana Enhanced Initiative for Highly Indebted Poor Countries – Completion Point Document," IMF Country Report No. 04/209 (July 2004).
[34] Heinz Jockers, Dirk Kohnert, and Paul Nugent, "The Successful Ghana Election of 2008: A Convenient Myth," *The Journal of Modern African Studies* 48, 1 (March 2010): 111–112.

However, the passage of Law 851 and Ghana's experiences with the extractive industries augur well for the future.

Whereas in many African oil states significant discoveries create conditions that include the Dutch disease and rent seeking by politicians, Ghana appears to be an exception. First, its government has a supreme audit agency and offices for public financial management. These agencies are without question among the most difficult for a democratic government to construct because they can only conduct forensic audits when ministries and government offices provide them the data. In many African states, data collection about fiscal expenditures lags behind the creation of either internal or external audit agencies.[35] However, in addition to its audit agency, the Ghanaian government has a number of functioning agencies with mandates to investigate allegations of malfeasance. Since 1992, the government has made considerable progress integrating civil-society oversight of corruption in its public sector into both the popular consciousness and official practice. A vocal media buttresses the oversight provided by various civil-society organizations. The effect of these agencies has reinforced norms of due diligence and probity in the public sector.

The Kosmos Energy controversy in Ghana demonstrates how political and economic conditions present at the time of discovery have an impact on subsequent development. This controversy began in July 2007 when a consortium of international oil companies drilled successfully for oil in the West Cape area approximately 60 kilometers offshore of Takoradi-Sekondji. As expressed previously, the discovery of reserves of sweet light crude oil in the West Cape area of Ghana's territorial waters represented a major boon for the West African state.[36] Having coined the discovery the Jubilee Field, the Kufuor government celebrated Ghana's new status as one of Africa's emerging petrostates. Within a short time, further explorations continued to find other reservoirs that had considerable promise.

An issue for Ghana's political leadership is how to blunt the demands for a redistribution of resource revenues to supporting coalitions. The relative success of its anticorruption agencies is evident in Ghana's rank among the least corrupt countries in the Transparency International's Corruption Perception Index. However, with entry into the "club" of oil exporters, pressures on political leaders to manipulate contract negotiations and distribute resource

---

[35] While conducting field research in Ghana, the auditor-general expressed his frustrations with deficiencies of staff and convincing officials in line ministries to provide data in a timely fashion. As a result, forensic audits were often late in being deposited with the Public Accounts Committee of the Ghanaian Parliament. In Nigeria, the auditor-general echoed these very complaints. Worse, as a state-government auditor general in Nigeria put it, "We can bark, but we cannot bite."

[36] Republic of Ghana, Management of Ghana National Petroleum Corporation (GNPC), "Status Report on the Jubilee Field Oil and Gas Development (Tano Deepwater and West Cape Three Points)." Retrieved from www.gnpcghana.com/ (accessed July 30, 2010.)

rents to supporters were almost inevitable.[37] Policymakers in petrostates have conflicting incentives; on one hand they want to capture and distribute money to political supporters. On the other, they establish saving accounts for future generations, develop methods to respond to revenue uncertainty because of price volatility, and invest in employment-generating projects.[38] It is remarkable the extent to which Ghana's political leaders employed considerable fiscal discipline to counter an appreciation of the currency consistent with the Dutch disease effects.[39] Indeed, for an emerging producer, Ghana has avoided the most negative impacts of substantial oil revenues.

The Kosmos Controversy: The Actors

Three actors are critical in this controversy. First, the GNPC represents the Ghanaian government and by extension the people of Ghana. Second, Kosmos Energy, a small U.S. firm from Texas, began operations in Ghana in 2003. Third, the EO Group became a central actor in how the controversy unfolded. The controversy tangentially involved Tullow, Anadarko, and Sabre Oil, the consortium's other members. How these actors negotiated among each other and then reached a resolution is instructive for considering Ghana's probable trajectory as a petrostate. The paragraphs below present the goals of each actor.

In 1983, the ruling military government passed the Provisional National Defense Council Law 64 (PNDCL 64) to establish a national oil company, the Ghana National Petroleum Corporation (GNPC).[40] This law followed the American firm, Signal Oil and Gas's, discovery and depletion of the Saltpond Field during the 1970s. Signal Oil operated Saltpond as a concession. Flt. Lt. Jerry J. Rawlings, head of the PNDC, recognized that Ghana might have other offshore reserves and saw the utility of a Ghanaian DNOC that could manage oil production. Most importantly for subsequent outcomes, PNDCL 64 requires that geological information be classified as secret, proprietary information and the property of the Ghanaian government. In subsequent negotiations with oil companies, the Ghanaian government included this provision in all its contracts. The GNPC's managers were therefore key actors in the contract negotiations for the West Cape blocks, including the Jubilee Field.

---

[37] Richard M. Auty and Alan Gelb, "Political Economy of Resource Abundant States," in *Resource Abundance and Economic Development*, ed. R.M. Auty (New York: Oxford University Press, 2001), 133–134.
[38] Benn Eifert, Alan Gelb, and Nils Borje Tallroth, "Natural Resource Endowments, the State and Development Strategy," in *Fiscal Policy and Implementation in Oil-Producing Countries*, eds., Jeffrey Davis, Rolando Ossowski, and Annalisa Fedelino (Washington, DC: The International Monetary Fund, 2003), 83.
[39] Dagher et al., "Oil Windfalls in Ghana," 5.
[40] Government of Ghana, Provisional National Defense Council Law 64: Ghana National Petroleum Corporation Act, 1983.

The second key actor in this controversy was Kosmos Energy, a small firm that specialized in exploration and production in West Africa. When Kosmos Energy put together a business plan to explore in Ghana, it borrowed funds from two private equity firms, namely Blackstone Group and Warburg Pincus. These loans enabled Kosmos Energy to join a consortium with Tullow Ghana Limited, Anadarko WCTP Company, Sabre Oil, the EO Group, and the GNPC. In late 2006, the consortium began drilling for oil in Ghana's deep-water off-shore shelves. In June 2007, Tullow announced that the consortium had dis-covered reserves estimated to hold 600 million barrels that could produce up to 60,000 barrels a day. Subsequently, the consortium revised its estimates upward to 1.8 billion barrels.[41] What for Kosmos Energy had begun as a risky gamble became a huge success.

A third critical actor was the EO Group. This firm, founded in 2002, belonged to Dr. Kwame Bawuah Edusie and George Owusu. Having served as President Kufuor's ambassador to the United States, Edusie had connections he used to lobby U.S. companies such as Kosmos Energy to invest in Ghana. His partner, George Owusu, was a chemical engineer who had considerable experience in the U.S. oil industry. Edusie and Owusu used their contacts in the Kufuor gov-ernment to facilitate Kosmos's acquisition of licensing contracts. In compensa-tion, the EO Group received a 3.5 percent share in the as-yet-unproven Jubilee field; in 2010, that share was worth more than $200 million.[42] What changed was that Nana Akufo-Addo, the candidate for Kufuor's incumbent political party, the New Patriotic Party, lost the December 2008 presidential election to John Atta Mills and his National Democratic Congress.[43] In a negative light, it is possible to see that these cronies of the former administration were vulnera-ble to retaliation from the new government.

The Kosmos Controversy: Allegations

Most small firms such as Kosmos Energy lack the financial clout to develop their discoveries and maintain production. Hence, in a business strategy famil-iar to the international oil industry, Kosmos Energy tried to sell its 23.5 per-cent share of the Jubilee Field within two years of the discovery. A number of firms expressed interest and in 2009, ExxonMobil bid $4 billion to acquire Kosmos' share of the Jubilee field.[44] The controversy became political when the

---

[41] Martin Clark, "Ghana's Deep-Water Potential," *Petroleum Economist* (May 2008); *Petroleum Economist*, "Ghana: Jubilee Field Larger than Expected" (June 2008). See as well, Adu Koranteng, "Ghana to Discover More Oil and Gas," *The Statesman* (Accra) (April 9, 2009), retrieved from http://www.thestatesmanonline.com/ (accessed April 11, 2009).

[42] Wallis et al., "Corruption Probe into Oil Partners."

[43] Because of constitutional term limits, Kufuor was ineligible to run for office in December 2008. Cyril Kofie Dadieh, "The Presidential and Parliamentary Elections in Ghana, December 2008," *Electoral Studies* 28 (2009): 642–673.

[44] William Wallis, "Ghana Pledges Open Accounting as It Prepares for Oil Revenues," *The Financial Times* (December 4, 2009).

Ghanaian press reported that two former insiders of the Kufuor government stood to gain millions for facilitating the contracts.[45] Members of the newly elected Mills government alleged that the EO Group had engaged in insider information brokering; they expressed outrage at the profits Edusie and Owusu stood to gain for facilitating the contracts.[46] Such accusations prompted investigations into alleged corruption and calls to block the sale.

The GNPC accused Kosmos of having failed to inform it of plans to sell almost a quarter of a major national asset.[47] It alleged that Kosmos Energy had disclosed proprietary information about the field in its negotiations with ExxonMobil.[48] Officials at the GNPC cited both Article 23 of PNDCL 64 that prohibits any release of proprietary information and Article 16.4 of the contract that Kosmos Energy had signed with the consortium members that states unambiguously, "All data, information, and reports, including interpretation and analysis supplied by Contractors required or produced pursuant to this Agreement ... shall be treated as confidential and shall not be disclosed by any Party to any other person with the express written consent of the other Parties."[49] Kosmos Energy had disclosed proprietary information and failed to obtain the consortium members' consent; the GNPC declared them in violation of contract.

Officials in the Ghanaian government filed a lawsuit in which they alleged that Kosmos had failed to inform the GNPC of its negotiations with ExxonMobil.[50] ExxonMobil's $4 billion bid attracted international and domestic Ghanaian attention.[51] The Ghanaian Serious Fraud Office (SFO) opened an investigation into claims that Kosmos Energy had paid kickbacks to the EO Group.[52] Other investigations multiplied; in August 2010, the World Bank Group's International Finance Corporation and Multilateral Investment Guarantee Agency announced an inquiry that resulted in a temporary freeze of multilateral

[45] The Chronicle *(Accra)*, "Row Over Sale of Shares to Exxon: Kosmos Breaks Silence: 'We Broke no Laws'" (July 27, 2010). Retrieved from http://ghanaian-chronicle.com (accessed August 2, 2010).
[46] William Wallis and Martin Arnold, "'Sweat Equity' Probe Tests Ghana's Oil Jackpot," *The Financial Times* (January 7, 2010).
[47] Dr. Jemima Agyare, "Transparency, Accountability and Participation: A Formula to Enhance the Governance of Ghana's Petroleum Sector." *The Guardian* (Accra) (August 2, 2010). Retrieved from http://ghanaian-chronicle.com (accessed August 2, 2010).
[48] William Wallis, "Oil Riches to Test Trail-Blazer Ghana," *The Financial Times* (May 31, 2010); idem, "Oilfield Dispute Fires Up Ghana-US Match," *The Financial Times* (June 27, 2010).
[49] Republic of Ghana, Provisional National Defense Council Law 64: Ghana National Petroleum Corporation Act. Accra: Government Print Office (1983); idem, "Among the Republic of Ghana, Ghana National Petroleum Corporation, Kosmos Energy Ghana HC, and the EO Group in Respect of West Cape Three Points Block Offshore Ghana." (July 22, 2004). Accra: Government Print Office.
[50] Agyare, "Transparency, Accountability and Participation."
[51] William Wallis, "Ghana Seeks Way Out of Oil Dispute," *The Financial Times* (July 19, 2009).
[52] William Wallis, Martin Arnold, and Brooke Masters, "Corruption Probe into Oil Partners," *The Financial Times* (January 8, 2010).

development assistance.[53] Meanwhile, the United States Department of Justice began an independent investigation to determine whether Kosmos Energy had violated the Foreign Corrupt Practices Act. The Ghanaian press reported widely that the $4 billion sale price represented an eight-fold profit for Kosmos Energy.[54] When ExxonMobil attempted to close the deal, Joe Oteng-Adjei, the head of the GNPC, accused Owusu and Bawuah-Edusie of noncompetitive interference.[55] In this setting, it is hardly surprising that ExxonMobil decided to back out of the purchase. All might have seemed over in October 2010 when Kosmos's Chief Operating Officer Brian F. Maxted announced that ExxonMobil had withdrawn its $4 billion bid.[56] However, recriminations and investigations continued.

It is possible to see this investigation from several perspectives. First, quite probably Ghanaian politicians had failed to grasp the enormous profits the sale represented. From a popular perspective, it appeared as if an American oil company had come to an African market, hired a local firm to facilitate a contract, invested in the extractive industries, and three years later tried to take billions out of the country. Elected officials had a serious political problem of explaining to their constituents how a foreign company could reap such rewards. It was a political fiasco for Ghana's officials and a lightening rod for their opponents' criticisms.

A second perspective considered the case as business as usual in African petrostates. Officials from the former Kufuor administration made a lot of money facilitating contracts between the government and an American oil company. Owusu and Bawuah-Edusei had been cronies; they operated as brokers to facilitate a deal for Kosmos Energy for which they gained substantial compensation. To investigators in the Mills government, however, Owusu and Bawuah-Edusei's sizeable gain was only possible because of their contacts in the previous administration. Investigations in Ghana and the United States progressed until U.S. prosecutors determined that no indictable FCPA violations had occurred. Thereafter, investigations shifted back to Ghana's SFO, which subsequently found no wrongdoing despite appearances of insider brokering and malfeasance. Again, the appearance of unfair profits for an American oil company created a political dilemma for Ghana's politicians.

A third perspective questioned how Kosmos Energy could have acted with such arrogance given the provisions in the contracts it had signed. This perspective asked whether the firm's management believed that they could disclose information about the asset in direct violation of the contract, get the

53 William Wallis, "Review of Ghana's Oil Contract Holds Up Funding," *The Financial Times* (August 5, 2010).
54 Emmanuel K. Dogbevi, "Kosmos Energy under investigation for corruption in Ghana," *Ghana Business News* (January 8, 2010).
55 "Ghana: The Politics of No," *African Confidential* 51, 17 (August 27, 2010).
56 Rigzone, Kosmos Energy, "Kosmos Cancels ExxonMobil's $4B Deal for Ghana Assets." Retrieved from http://www.rigzone.com/news/article.asp?a id=97477 (accessed August 18, 2010).

money, exit the country before anyone would notice, and go on to the next exploration. Or, had their legal staff failed to inform them of potential liability? Kosmos Energy's accusations that GNPC officials only blocked the sale so they might resell it to Chinese national oil companies seemed plausible.[57] Indeed, within a few days of Maxted's October announcement, the GNPC, in collaboration with the CNOOC, submitted a bid of $5 billion to Kosmos Energy.[58] Kosmos Energy did not accept the bid.

Whatever the explanation, the botched sale informed Kosmos Energy and other IOCs operating in Ghana that market conditions in Africa were changing. Kosmos's management had failed to understand that Ghana was a republican democracy whose elected officials were accountable to their constituents. Executives at Kosmos apparently did not understand this critical element of Ghanaian development when they discovered the oil and seemed to believe they could do whatever they liked. Although Ghana's agencies of accountability were arguably inexperienced when they needed to audit complex contracts and hold IOCs accountable, the government's experience with the extractive industries helped it understand how to do business with Kosmos Energy. In short, Ghana in 2009 was far from a neopatrimonial state where international investors could seed some bribe money and operate with impunity.

The Kosmos Controversy: Resolution and Implications

International oil companies with lengthy experience in Africa have assumptions about the commitment of client governments to due diligence and financial probity. In some countries, a few strategic bribes would suffice to bend the rules. In other petrostates, a bribe or gift to a policymaker and sense of apology might have sufficed to end the controversy. However, Kosmos Energy's executives failed to perceive how Ghanaian politicians would react to the eight-fold profit they stood to gain by the sale. Incredulous reactions in the Ghanaian press suggested a perception that the extraordinary profit was at the expense of Ghana's citizens. As a consequence, Kosmos Energy and the EO Group became a symbol of corrupt and exploitative business practices.

Management at Kosmos Energy understood that it lacked the time to engage in protracted litigation. It needed to find some means to raise capital to service its debts to the Blackstone Group and Warburg Pincus and keep its wells operational. In March 2011, Kosmos filed a registration statement and prospectus with the United States Securities and Exchange Commission.[59] The prospectus noted that Kosmos Energy had identified forty-eight undrilled prospects within

[57] Wallis et al., "Corruption Probe into Oil Partners."

[58] Martin Arnold, William Wallis and Leslie Hook, "Ghana Move for Kosmos Oilfield Stake," *The Financial Times* (October 22, 2010).

[59] See United States Securities and Exchange Commission, Form S-1, Registration Statement Under the Securities Act of 1933, Kosmos Energy Ltd. (Filed March 3, 2011).

its license areas. The potential for discoveries of even more reserves indicated a potentially profitable investment. Afterward, Kosmos filed papers to make public stock offerings on the Accra Stock Exchange. In June, the same month, Tullow started selling its shares to the Ghanaian public.[60] This shift to offer company shares as a publically traded corporation distributed the corporation's liabilities and risks among its shareholders. More importantly, it gave the new corporation a means to service its debt and maintain its presence in the booming Ghanaian oil sector.

Three crucial implications emerge from the resolution of this controversy. First, Ghana protected the economic institutions that guaranteed property rights to foreign investors. This outcome has clear long-term implications for foreign direct investment and the sense that Ghana operates under the rule of law. Second, the resolution of this controversy has a direct implication for the behavior of international firms that enter the Ghanaian markets. The Ghanaian government's respect for Kosmos Energy's investments suggests that its politicians were cognizant of potential costs if they had seized the company. As a result, Ghana's reputation remains untarnished among international investors. The resolution of this controversy has been for Kosmos to trade publically on the stock exchanges in the United States and Ghana. In this fashion, the IOC is able to secure the financing to service its debt and resolve the vulnerability created by conflict with the GNPC. Third, the Kosmos Energy controversy shows the importance of understanding conditions in African petrostates; Ghana was without any question a different case than would have occurred in such countries as Equatorial Guinea, discussed next.

CLANSMEN AND CORRUPTION IN A MATURE PRODUCER: EQUATORIAL GUINEA

In Equatorial Guinea, the Obiang clan has captured key political offices. Its leaders create "identity networks consisting of an extensive web of horizontal and vertical kin-based relations"; these identity networks determine entry into elite status.[61] The clan thus forms an elementary part of an individual's identity whether through real or fictive ties. Fictive ties go beyond the immediate family to imagined relations who self-ascribe membership in a clan. In this regard, clan identity resembles ethnicity; it is a web of historical relations that are fluid and shift according to perceptions of benefit.[62] Ambitious individuals claim membership in clans or ethnic groups that provide access to

---

[60] Masahudu Ankiilu Kunateh, "Tullow Offloads 4 Million Shares on GSE," *The Chronicle* (Accra) (June 2, 2011).

[61] Kathleen Collins, "The Political Role of Clans in Central Asia," *Comparative Politics* 35, 2 (January 2003): 171; idem, "Clans, Pacts, and Politics in Central Asia," *Journal of Democracy* 13, 3 (July 2002): 142.

[62] Daniel N. Posner, "The Colonial Origins of Ethnic Cleavages: The Case of Linguistic Divisions in Zambia," *Comparative Politics* 35, 2 (January 2003): 127.

TABLE 5.2 *Corruption and Clan-Based Rule in African Petrostates*

		Corruption		
		High	Moderate	Low
Clan-based rule	High	Congo Equatorial Guinea	Gabon	Mauritania
	Moderate	Angola Chad	Sudan	
	Low	Nigeria		Ghana São Tomé and Príncipe

opportunities and influence. These weak, sometimes fictive ties confer on the elite monetary benefits and exclusivity.

In Central African petrostates, clans determine who gets access to influential positions and corrupt benefits. As Table 5.2 shows, clan-based rule is a norm among Central African petrostates and occurs in tandem with high levels of corruption. In Congo and Gabon, intermarriage has consolidated bonds between the Bongo and Sassou clans. Angola has witnessed a moderate degree of clan-based rule among the historic assimilado families of the Luanda–Benguela corridor. However, clan-based rule is most salient in Equatorial Guinea, where the Obiang clan has captured the state and used its control of state offices to an extent unrivalled among Africa's petrostates.

Elite recruitment in many African petrostates revolved around membership in a ruling clan or birth in a particular village. Although intra-clan rivalries are common in small petrostates, interclan competition, including interethnic conflicts, is far more the case in their larger counterparts. The beneficiaries of postcolonial systems thrived in circumstances where "corruption, clientelism, and 'Big Man' presidentialism – all dimensions of neopatrimonial rule – tend to go together as a package.... Indeed, these practices are so ingrained in African political life as to constitute veritable political institutions."[63] One question that we explore in this chapter is the extent to which oil revenues so embed clan politics, corrupt practices, and clientelism as to make the states resistant to reform.

In states under clan rule, presidents distribute offices and economic opportunities to clansmen and selected cronies. To enter some African markets, international companies must effectively collaborate with the ruling clique and engage brokers, who dictate to oil companies "qualified" domestic firms with which they must do business. The brokers are either close cronies or clan members; the international companies have little choice but to sign agreements with firms owned by members of the ruling clan. Often, the brokers

[63] Michael Bratton, "Formal Versus Informal Institutions in Africa," *Journal of Democracy* 18, 3 (July 2007): 98.

are the presidents' children, and the firms belong to their siblings.[64] Whereas formal rules, laws, and regulations define how the firms must behave in their contractual relations, informal institutions determine with whom and under what conditions international companies do business. It is this confluence of formal and informal institutions that decides inclusion or exclusion in the oil industry.

Clansmen and Corruption

As this book has emphasized, a country's history influences the institutional arrangements that in turn guide the behavior of individuals and groups in society. Colonial practices in Spanish Guinea involved a considerable amount of violence; these practices continued and deepened after Equatorial Guinea gained independence in 1968. Equatorial Guinea became an independent state shortly after its nationalist leaders met in Madrid to draft a constitution to codify provisions for universal suffrage and representative democracy.[65] In a thoughtful article, Campos considers the paradox of nationalist leaders from Spanish Guinea debating a democratic constitution in the capital of the authoritarian Franco regime.[66] Under the tutelage of the Spanish lawyer García Trevijano, Francisco Macías Nguema, a former mayor of Mongomo on the mainland portion of Spanish Guinea, emerged as a clear leader at the conference and later in the soon-to-be-independent state.[67] He cleverly outmaneuvered his rivals to obtain approval of the constitution and ensure his position as the leading presidential candidate.

Spain withdrew from Equatorial Guinea at independence on October 12, 1968, and Macías Nguema became its first and only elected president. Within six months, he imposed a reign of terror that lasted until his death in 1979. Macias Nguema was a particularly sadistic dictator who routinely killed his opponents, both real and imagined. He routinely ordered thousands of extrajudicial executions and reportedly had some of his victims crucified and their bodies left on display to discourage other potential rivals.[68] During his rule, more than a quarter of the population fled into exile.[69] Macias Nguema's rule was so arbitrary and brutal that one observer chose to refer to the regime's cast

---

[64] In Angola, one of the president's daughters served as a broker for foreign investors in television. In 2008, she transferred control of one of the country's television stations to her brother José Avelino Eduardo dos Santos. *Africa Confidential*, "Angola: Daughters and Generals," 49, 14 (July 4, 2008).

[65] Max Liniger-Goumaz, *Small Is Not Always Beautiful: The Story of Equatorial Guinea* (Totawa, New Jersey: Barnes and Nobles Books, 1989), 48.

[66] Alicia Campos, "The Decolonization of Equatorial Guinea: The Relevance of the International Factor," *The Journal of African History* 44 (March 2003): 111.

[67] Liniger-Goumaz, *Small Is Not Always Beautiful*, 47–50.

[68] Ken Silverstein, "U.S. Oil Politics in the 'Kuwait of Africa,'" *The Nation* (April 22, 2002): 13.

[69] Liniger-Goumaz, *Small Is Not Always Beautiful*, 51.

of characters as tropical gangsters.[70] Despite the tragic humor evident in this depiction of Equatorial Guinea's elite, Macias Nguema was a disaster for the economy and the people who depended on it for subsistence.

Macias Nguema combined economic ignorance with sociopathic rule to leave the population traumatized and poor. Before the discovery of oil, Equatorial Guinea exported cocoa, timber, palm products, and coffee to Europe. Between 1967 and 1979, its economy shrank; exports of coffee and palm products ended and lumber dropped from 360,000 cubic meters in 1968 to 6,000 cubic meters in the late 1970s.[71] Eventually, Macias Nguema's excesses became intolerable; in 1979, his nephew and army chief-of-staff, Theodore Obiang Nguema, had him arrested for treason and executed.[72] The nephew, by his own right, imposed one of Africa's most repressive regimes that like its predecessor tolerated no dissent.[73] Since assuming power, the Obiang clan has behaved with impunity, embezzled millions, and employed security forces to perpetrate human rights atrocities on its citizens.[74] The Obiang clan's rule replicated and far surpassed the brutality of Spain's colonial practices.

Equatorial Guinea is now a mature oil producer. In the late 1980s, U.S. companies began to apply for licenses to explore for oil. The first discovery was in 1990 when the U.S. firm Walter International signed a PSC to develop what the government later renamed the Alba field.[75] Marathon Oil conducted further explorations and, in March 2002, purchased all rights to the Alba field for approximately $1 billion. At the very time that Marathon was purchasing rights to the Alba field, ExxonMobil announced that it was investing $1 billion to develop the Zafiro field, estimated to hold more than 400 billion barrels at depths of 425–800 meters. Equatorial Guinea's market attracted other oil companies including Amerada Hess, Ocean Energy, and SK Corporation.[76] These discoveries and overtures from international oil companies had a transformative impact on Equatorial Guinea; it went from being an impoverished agricultural economy to a low-population petrostate.

---

[70] Robert Klitgaard, *Tropical Gangsters: One Man's Experience with Development and Decadence in Deepest Africa* (New York: Basic Books, 1990).

[71] Achille Toto Same, "Mineral-Rich Countries and Dutch Disease: Understanding the Macroeconomic Implications of Windfalls and the Development Prospects: The Case of Equatorial Guinea," World Bank Policy Research Working Paper 4595 (April 2008), 5.

[72] Adam Roberts, *The Wonga Coup: Guns, Thugs, and a Ruthless Determination to Create Mayhem in an Oil-Rich Corner of Africa* (New York: Perseus Books, 2006), 21.

[73] John R. Heilbrunn, "Equatorial Guinea and Togo: What Price Repression?" in *The Worst of the Worst: Dealing with Repressive and Rogue Nations*, ed. Robert I. Rotberg (Washington, DC: The Brookings Institution Press, 2006), 223–249.

[74] Human Rights Watch, *Well-Oiled: Oil and Human Rights in Equatorial Guinea* (New York: Human Rights Watch, July 2009).

[75] Justin Blum, "Equatorial Guinea, USA: US Oil Firms," *The Washington Post* (September 9, 2004).

[76] Information in this paragraph is from the World Bank, "Project Performance Assessment Report: Equatorial Guinea Second Petroleum Technical Assistance Project (Credit 2408-EG) (Washington, DC: the World Bank: July 2002), Annex B.

Clan Politics and Routine Violence

The capture of petrostates by clans that dominate clientelist networks has negatively influenced each country's institutional development. Collins defines a clan as "an informal organization comprising a network of individuals linked by kin and fictive kin identities."[77] Clan politics refers to practices of individuals, who, through a criterion of clan membership, capture key "gates" to the state that enable them to exclude others from political participation. Collins distinguishes further that clans are identities but clientelism and corruption are practices; clansmen are the actors who engage in clientelism and corruption.[78] This distinction is important because it differentiates practices from identity that becomes a criterion for inclusion or exclusion.

Theodore Obiang Nguema Mbasogo governed through his clan; he appointed his uncles, sons, and nephews to critical political offices. Although in 2012 he nominated his eldest son Téodorin Nguema Obiang Mangue and Ilam Milam Tang vice presidents, speculation is that Téodorin will assume the presidency when his father retires.[79] In the meantime, Obiang has implanted a regime in which his clansmen operate as brokers and use their connections to the president to seize substantial rewards.[80] Investigations in the United States and Europe suggest that by the twenty-first century, the Obiang regime resembled a criminal state; members of the clan allegedly committed a number of crimes ranging from drug smuggling and money laundering to human trafficking.[81] For just one example, during the mid-1990s, Spanish customs officials inspected a suitcase belonging to an Equatorial Guinean diplomat in which they found a substantial quantity of heroin.[82] Although the actions of a single individual hardly constitute evidence of systemic behavior, it does implicate the Obiang clan in, at a minimum, accepting criminal acts committed by officials.

After coming to office, Obiang was intolerant of opposition and perpetrated state-sponsored violence against his opponents. With time, quite possibly from Omar Bongo's tutelage, the elder Obiang understood that he needed to present his regime as less despotic. Nine years after overthrowing his uncle, Obiang began to seek closer relations with France. First, he applied to enter the French-

[77] Kathleen Collins, *Clan Politics and Regime Transition in Central Asia* (New York: Cambridge University Press, 2006), 25.

[78] Collins, *Clan Politics and Regime Transition in Central Asia*, 38.

[79] *Africa Confidential*, "Equatorial Guinea: L'Etat, c'est Nous," 54, 14 (5 July 2013).

[80] For a sensationalist depiction of this clan-based corruption, see Larry Diamond and Jack Mosbacher, "Petroleum to the People: Africa's Coming Resource Curse – and How to Avoid It," *Foreign Affairs* (September–October 2013): 86–87.

[81] Jean-François Bayart, Stephen Ellis, and Béatrice Hibou, "From Kleptocracy to the Felonious State," in *The Criminalization of the State in Africa*, eds. Jean-François Bayart, Stephen Ellis, and Béatrice Hibou (Bloomington: Indiana University Press, 1999), 25–26; Max Liniger-Goumaz, *A l'Aune de la Guinée Équatoriale: Colonisation – Neocolonisation – Démocratisation – Corruption* (Geneva: Les Éditions du Temps, 2003), 263.

[82] Santos Pascual Bikomo, "Guinea Conexión," *La Diapora* (24 de Julio de 1997).

African financial community and adopted the Central African CFA franc as the country's currency.[83] Second, he traveled to Paris, where he pledged to officials that Equatorial Guinea had elevated French to the premier level of languages spoken in the country. Surprisingly, France allocated 16 million francs in bilateral assistance for Equatorial Guinea.[84]

This close relationship soured. Throughout the 1990s, Obiang continued to arrest and incarcerate opponents at the notorious Black Beach prison.[85] This pattern of intolerance continued into the twenty-first century. For example, in 2002, police arrested and held Felipe Ondó Obiang (no relation to the president) in spite of international pleas for his release.[86] A year later, police detained Pastor Bienvenido Samba Momesori along with 110 others, and courts sentenced them to death for treason.[87] In 2005, Amnesty International issued a report detailing the horrific conditions at Black Beach, where prisoners were at risk of starvation.[88] Equatorial Guineans "live in fear of arbitrary detention, harassment, beatings, and the seizure of personal property."[89] Indeed, as late as October 2012, Obiang's regime arrested human rights activists and jailed them at Black Beach without trial or due process.[90] These actions continued during the campaign preceding the May 26, 2013, legislative elections when government officials harassed, beat, and detained opposition candidates.[91]

The Obiang Clan: Clan Politics and Entrenched Corruption

A trend in Equatorial Guinea, Gabon, Congo, and a number of other non-oil exporting states has been the rise of a clan that captures political office and plunders the economy. In a growing number of African non-petro states, dynastic rule in which a son assumes the presidency after the father's death

[83] J-M Meyer, "Afrique Centrale: Grand Ménage à la Cemac," *Jeune Afrique l'Intélligent* (1 février 2010).

[84] "Guinée Équatoriale: Le Président Obiang 'Sollicite l'Entrée dans la Francophonie'," *Le Monde* (23 Septembre 1988).

[85] Thomas Sotinel, "Vague d'Arrestations d'Opposants en Guinée-Équatoriale," *Le Monde* (19 Avril 1995).

[86] Amnesty International, "Equatorial Guinea: Possible 'Disappearance'/Fear for Safety" AFR 24/012/2003 (October 30, 2003).

[87] Amnesty International, "Equatorial Guinea: Prison Conditions/Detention without Charge/Possible Prisoner of Conscience/Fear of Torture or Ill-Treatment" AFR 24/011/2003 (November 13, 2003).

[88] Amnesty International, "Equatorial Guinea: Prisoners Starving to Death" AFR 24/006/2005 (April 14, 2005).

[89] Geoffrey Wood, "Business and Politics in a Criminal State: The Case of Equatorial Guinea," *African Affairs*, 103, 413 (2004), 561.

[90] Human Rights Watch, "Equatorial Guinea: Human Rights Lawyer 'Disappeared'" (Washington, DC: Human Rights Watch, October 24, 2012).

[91] Amnesty International, "Human Rights Concerns ahead of Equatorial Guinea elections," (May 7, 2013); Human Rights Watch, "Equatorial Guinea: Human Rights Concerns ahead of Elections: Troubling Conditions Compromise May 26 Legislative Vote" (May 7, 2013).

has taken shape. For example, in Togo, a country without oil reserves, the Gnassingbé clan has captured the state and most of the country's major productive assets.[92] In the years after Gnassingbé Eyadéma's 2005 death, Togo's economy stagnated as spontaneous violence became banal and investors shied away from the country.[93] The February 2008 death of Gabon's Omar Bongo and the succession by his son Ali represents a clear example of dynastic rule in Central Africa. In Equatorial Guinea, the president's sons, brothers, and wives own companies with which oil firms sign contracts.[94] Obiang's immediate family members are ministers and occupy other offices of state; according to the elder Obiang Nguema, anyone who is not members of the clan is a "stranger."[95] The clansmen are gatekeepers.

Because all non-clansmen were strangers, Obiang had no difficulty allowing his son Teodorino Obiang Nguema to use his position as minister of water, forests, and fisheries to seize property owned by the Bubi people on Bioko Island and grant a 200,000-hectare timber concession to the Malaysian timber company Shimmer.[96] The commission he received from this contract and other transactions enabled him to buy villas in Cape Town and Malibu.[97] The Equatorial Guinean example may be an extreme, but similar patterns of clan-based, systematic corruption occurred in other Central African regimes, as well.

Equatorial Guinea demonstrated some of the costs of extreme authoritarianism. First, it has become clear that the president and his clan siphoned off a king's fortune in resource revenues.[98] Second, the flagrant corruption of the president's son, Teodorino, prompted French prosecutors in June 2013 to validate a series of lawsuits against the younger Obiang for corruption that had been winding through the courts for years.[99] Third, the state has no agencies of horizontal accountability, a fact that makes it highly unlikely any of Obiang's children will ever be held accountable for their multiple human rights

---

[92] Fulbert Sassou Attisso, *Le Togo sous la Dynastie des Gnassingbé* (Paris: Éditions l'Harmattan, 2013), 111.

[93] Heilbrunn, "Equatorial Guinea and Togo," 223–249.

[94] United States Senate Permanent Subcommittee on Investigations, *Keeping Foreign Corruption out of the United States*, 26. See as well, Human Rights Watch, *Well Oiled*, Report 1–56432–516–4 (July 2009), 26–28.

[95] Quoted in Liniger-Goumaz, *A l'Aune de la Guinée Équatoriale*, 212.

[96] Janet Roitman and Gérard Roso, "Guinée Équatoriale: Être « Off-Shore » pour Rester « National »," *Politique Africaine* 81 (March 2001): 126.

[97] *The Financial Times*, "Taking a Cut Acceptable, Says African Minister" (October 25, 2006); Global Witness, "African Minister Buys Multi-Million Dollar California Mansion," Press Release – 08/11/2006. Retrived from http://www.globalwitness.org/media_library_detail.php/468/en/african_minister_buys_multi_million_dollar_califor.

[98] Wood, "Business and Politics in a Criminal State," 560.

[99] Nathalie Guibert, "La Guinée Équatoriale, un Partenaire aussi Stratégique qu'Encombrant," *Le Monde* (19 Juin 2013); John Reed, "Son of African Leader Linked to $35m House," *Financial Times* (November 7, 2006).

transgressions in Equatorial Guinea.[100] Meanwhile, the people live in near absolute poverty; less than half of the population has access to what the United Nations Development Programme calls an improved water source, caloric consumption is low, and human development indicators are low.[101]

Widespread corruption in Equatorial Guinea preceded the discovery of oil, but increased markedly after the state began to receive oil revenues. However, the sums of money that came available after the beginning of oil production prompted Obiang and his clan to use U.S. banks to launder money and engage in criminal activities. In two U.S. Senate Subcommittee reports on money laundering and corruption, details emerge of how the Obiang regime established a system of rule wherein they could engage in corruption with impunity. Whereas initial investigations revealed more than 60 accounts at Riggs Bank through which the Obiang clan laundered money, later reports numbered the accounts at more than 125.[102] Signatories for these accounts included the president, members of his immediate family, and selected officials.

The first Senate Subcommittee report details how, during a period of six years, the Obiang regime laundered money through accounts at Riggs Bank.[103] In the report, the authors note that "Riggs was fully aware of the corruption risks associated with the E.G. accounts." This report cites an internal Riggs Bank memo that observed, "With the establishment of a state oil company, GE Petrol, later in 2001, management of the oil sector became more opaque, and standards of governance are likely to remain poor."[104] Riggs Bank protected its profitable relationship with the Obiang clan and facilitated a series of questionable wire transfers. Officials at Riggs "failed to flag any of these transactions as suspicious at the time they occurred, and apparently asked few questions about these or any other wire transfers until the Subcommittee began investigating the E.G. accounts in March 2003, and the OCC began its E.G. examination in October 2003."[105] In early 2004, Obiang learned of the investigations; he and his henchmen closed all the accounts at Riggs Bank and transferred millions to banks around the world. Officials at Riggs Bank subsequently pleaded guilty to failure to report

[100] Human Rights Watch, *Well-Oiled*, 34.
[101] Same, "Mineral-Rich Countries and Dutch Disease," 11.
[102] United States Senate, Permanent Subcommittee on Investigations, *Money Laundering and Foreign Corruption: Enforcement and Effectiveness of the Patriot Act: Case Study Involving Riggs Bank* (Washington, DC: United States Senate Permanent Subcommittee on Investigations, July 15, 2004), 40; United States Senate, Permanent Subcommittee on Investigations, *Keeping Foreign Corruption out of the United States: Four Case Studies* (Washington, DC: United States Senate Permanent Subcommittee on Investigations, February 4, 2010), 10.
[103] United States Senate, *Money Laundering and Foreign Corruption*, 40.
[104] United States Senate, *Money Laundering and Foreign Corruption*, 47.
[105] United States Senate, *Money Laundering and Foreign Corruption*, 56.

money-laundering activities; the bank was fined a total of $41 million.[106] In May 2005, Riggs merged with PNC Bank and ceased to operate under its own name.

Evidence of systematic corruption had repercussions that went far beyond investigations in the United States and South Africa. For instance, in 2004, shortly before release of the U.S. Senate Subcommittee's report on money laundering and corruption, executives at Devon Energy decided to sell the company's 24 percent share of the Zafiro field. Devon's managers informally reported that Equatorial Guinea carried too much risk and was an investment environment best suited for other companies.[107] This lesson was not lost on Obiang; he recognized the reputational costs of the U.S. Senate report. In 2009, he hired Lanny Davis and Associates, a U.S. public relations firm, that represented his interests in Washington and internationally.[108] In effect, Obiang was seeking to reverse impressions that his state was a rogue regime that operated outside international norms. Obiang's behavior suggests that even the most predatory dictators recognize that their international image is crucial to attract foreign direct investments.

CORRUPTION AND STATE CAPTURE IN A DECLINING PRODUCER: CONGO

Declining producers are noteworthy for the fact that lengthy production has led to a consolidation of rent-seeking groups that cluster around the presidency. Throughout its postcolonial history, Congo has exhibited certain particularities. First, Congo has had historically unusual rates of urbanization. According to the World Bank, in 2010, more than 50 percent of Congo's population was living in cities.[109] This concentration of population has had implications for the vulnerability of Congo's state to urban unrest led by disgruntled labor and youth groups. Second, the World Bank reports that in 2011, Congo enjoyed an average annual per capita income of $2,270.00, which suggests a lower middle-income economy. Third, 42.3 percent of the population lives below the poverty line, a statistic that indicates extreme inequalities; a small percentage of the country enjoys an overwhelming portion of its resources.[110] Fourth, Congo's Country Performance Institutional Assessment score of 2.5 for corruption suggests that coalitions around the president manipulated politics to capture oil

---

[106] Terence O'Hara, "Riggs Bank Agrees to Guilty Plea and Fine," *The Washington Post* (January 28, 2005).

[107] Informal interview (April 10, 2008).

[108] Celia W. Dugger, "African Leader Hires Adviser and Seeks an Image Change," *The New York Times* (June 28, 2010).

[109] All data are from World Bank, *World Development Indicators 2012* (Washington, DC). Retrieved from http://data.worldbank.org/country/congo-republic.

[110] World Bank, *World Development Indicators 2010*. Retrieved from http://data.worldbank.org/topic/urban-development (accessed November 15, 2010).

rents. These statistics show that it is first necessary to consider Congo's history and second, how a failure to democratize in 1992–1998 affected subsequent outcomes. As of 2014, it is evident that the Sassou clan occupies key offices in the Congolese state and intends to stay.

Corruption and State Failure

Congo's capital, Brazzaville, was the capital of colonial French Equatorial Africa (AEF). As such, it became the administrative center from where colonial authorities pronounced policies for the AEF. Accordingly, young people moved to Brazzaville in search of employment. This population of literate youth erupted first in 1963 when strikes and street demonstrations toppled Congo's postindependence government. Congo then entered a period of coups and military governments and became a "People's Republic" in 1969. Initially, a triumvirate of military officers governed the new state that included Marien Ngouabi, Joachim Yhombi Opango, and Denis Sassou, who was perhaps the least doctrinaire member.[111] Sassou assumed power in 1979 and governed with an economic pragmatism that favored close relations with France.

Before independence, Congo exported small quantities of low-quality oil from the onshore Pointe Indienne field, which came under production in 1957.[112] Congo's people were poor; most foreign earnings came from timber exports. In the late 1960s, Elf-Erap, a subsidiary of the French national oil company Elf-Aquitaine, discovered significant reserves in Congo's offshore shelves. In 1969, Elf-Erap negotiated contracts with Congo's leaders including oil-backed loans that locked the price at $2 a barrel.[113] This practice continued long after the initial contracts; whenever Congo's president needed money, Elf's management provided oil-backed loans and protected their unrestrained access to Congo's medium to heavy sweet crude.[114] It is hardly surprising that Congo accumulated a massive public debt, much of which was from Elf's advances.[115]

It may seem curious that a putative Marxist-Leninist regime would enter commercial relations with the French national oil company. However, Young wisely cautions to avoid rapid generalizations about the country; in Congo, "Marxian dialectics are conducted on a highly sophisticated level."[116] Although

[111] Jean François de Montvalon, *Sassou Nguesso: L'Irrésistible Ascension d'un Pion de la Françafrique* (Paris: Éditions de l'Harmattan pour la Fédération des Congolais de la Diaspora, 2009), 27.

[112] Stéphane Carcillo, Daniel Leigh, and Mauricio Villafuerte, "Catch-up Growth, Habits, Oil Depletion, and Fiscal Policy: Lessons from the Republic of Congo," IMF Working Paper, WP/07/80 (April 2007), 4.

[113] Hugues Bertrand, *Le Congo: Formation Sociale et Mode de Développement Économique* (Paris: François Maspero, 1975), 214–215.

[114] John F. Clark, "The Neo-Colonial Context of the Democratic Experiment of Congo-Brazzaville," *African Affairs* 101 (April 2002): 178.

[115] Olivier Vallee, "Les Cycles de la Dette," *Politique Africaine* 31 (Octobre 1988): 15–21.

[116] Crawford Young, *Ideology and Development in Africa* (New Haven: Yale University Press, 1982), 33.

the state aligned with "capitalist" oil companies, it was simultaneously advocating Leninist democratic centralism and an economic policy consistent with central planning. This adoption of Marxist ideology crumbled in 1991 under the generational demands for democracy and a more equitable distribution of benefits.

By 1991, Sassou's children and the progeny of his many cronies matured and sought to enter employment with the state. Whereas Sassou's sons and nephews entered the Congolese state, his daughters and nieces married into ruling clans in neighboring petrostates. Sassou successfully linked his family to neighboring regimes through a practically medieval European practice of arranged marriages. His eldest daughter Edith married Omar Bongo Ondimba, Gabon's president from 1967 to 2008. Joseph Kabila, president of the Democratic Republic of Congo, married another daughter, Sandrine Nguesso. Finally, Martin Lemboumba, son of Bongo's finance minister and a baron, married Claudia Lemboumba-Nguesso. Through such alliances, Sassou established bonds with dynastic regimes in the subregion.

Failed Democracy and Stalled Development

Cronyism was rampant in Congo. Dysfunctional practices included the granting of public contracts to regime insiders as a strategy to thwart the emergence of organized dissent and increase dependence of actual or potential clients. Sassou funded these contracts through the oil-backed loans that Elf was happy to provide in exchange for discounted crude.[117] Clientelism was common in Congo; Sassou signed contracts with firms owned by political cronies as a means to distribute oil rents and maintain the regime's stability.[118] In 1990, Congo was Elf Aquitaine's third-largest supplier, pumping approximately 220,000 barrels a day, or 12 percent of the company's global production.[119] Elf's management willingly provided the oil-backed loans to Sassou, who managed the sector as if it were his private stock portfolio.[120] As a consequence, when prices declined it constituted a crisis for the Congolese state because the president used resource rents to finance his coalition.

When oil prices dropped precipitously in 1989, the regime was unable to pay salaries, and a series of strikes paralyzed Brazzaville. From February to June 1991, Sassou consented to let delegates attend a national conference; he had little choice but to placate the demonstrating groups and striking workers in Brazzaville. Once the conference was in session, the delegates declared themselves sovereign; they nominated members to a transitional government,

---

[117] Marc-Éric Gruénais, "Congo: La Fin d'une Pseudo-Démocratie," *Politique Africaine* 88 (Décembre 1997): 127.

[118] Gruénais, "Congo: La Fin d'une Pseudo-Démocratie," 125–133.

[119] Yitzhak Koula, *La Démocratie Congolaise « Brûlée » au Pétrole* (Paris: l'Harmattan, 1999), 173.

[120] Koula, *La Démocratie Congolaise « Brûlée » au Pétrole*, 174.

drafted a new constitution, and announced that Congo would hold presidential elections in 1992. The new constitution defined electoral rules on the basis of the French Fifth Republic's two-round practice, in which multiple candidates compete in the first round; if no candidate wins more than 50 percent, then the two leading candidates run in the second round. Sassou behaved passively during the conference and campaigned to stay in office.

It is possible to adduce from Sassou's actions that he never doubted he would win the presidential elections. He had allowed striking workers, students, and representatives of civil society organizations to hold the national conference. Then, after the national conference ended, he initiated a set of policies that had worked before to placate opponents and supporters alike. First, he issued an executive order to hire 12,000 new civil servants, thereby increasing the wage bill from 78 billion CFA francs to 135 billion FCFA.[121] Second, Sassou distributed a number of contracts for state-funded construction projects to his supporters.[122] This strategy diverted fiscal expenditures to networks that supported his presidential bid and away from investments that might have favored development.[123] Such strategies might have been effective in circumstances of economic expansion; in 1991, however, these policies were disastrous. The effect was that Sassou lost in the first round of voting.[124] In the second round, Pascal Lissouba, one of Sassou's oldest rivals, won.

Instability followed the elections. Almost immediately, three armed militias – the Ninja, Zulus, and Cobras – divided Brazzaville into armed camps.[125] Two bloody civil wars erupted that ended only in 1999 when Angolan troops entered from Cabinda to reinstall Sassou as president.[126] Days after the 1999 civil war in Congo ended, the government annulled the 1994 constitution and Sassou resumed his personal management of the hydrocarbon sector, effectively reversing efforts to restore Congo's competitiveness and improve oil revenue management.[127] Sassou forced his rivals and their followers into exile. Many of

---

[121] Clark, "The Neo-Colonial Context," 181.

[122] Koula, *La Démocratie Congolaise « Brûlée » au Pétrole*, 175.

[123] Gruénais, "Congo: La Fin d'une Pseudo-Démocratie," 127.

[124] Fabrice Weissman, *Élection Présidentielle de 1992 au Congo: Entreprise Politique et Mobilization Électorale* (Bordeaux: Centre d'Études d'Afrique Noire, 1993), 72. Weissman reports 59.58 percent participation in the first round of presidential voting. Pascal Lissouba came in first with 35.89 percent, Bernard Kolélas received 20.32, Denis Sassou-Nguesso 16.87, André Milongo (the transition prime minister) received 10.18, and twelve other candidates each received less than 10 percent.

[125] Rémy Bazenguissa-Ganga, "Milices Politiques et Bandes Armées à Brazzaville: Enquête sur la Violence Politique et Sociale des Jeunes Declasses," Les Études du CERI, No 13 (Avril 1996): 3.

[126] Jean-Michel Mabeko Tali, "Quelques Dessous Diplomatiques de l'Intervention Angolaise dans le Conflit Congolais de 1997," in *Les Congos dans la Tourmente*, ed. Patrice Yengo for ed. Rupture-Solidarité (Paris: Éditions Karthala, 2000), 153–164.

[127] Rina Bhattacharya and Dhaneshwar Ghura, "Oil and Growth in the Republic of Congo," IMF Working Paper WP/06/185 (August 2006): 9.

those who chose to remain behind disappeared. Amnesty International reports that at least 10,000 civilians died in Congo's civil war; in early 1999, an estimated 40,000 people fled Brazzaville to join 150,000 other refugees living in exile.[128] Revenge killings were especially common in the Pool Region, where many of Lissouba's supporters lived; Sassou's victorious troops executed anyone suspected of belonging to the militia of his rivals.[129] Sassou effectively recaptured rule through a bloody conquest and imposed a new authoritarian regime.

Corruption and State Capture

Corruption after the civil war in Congo was far reaching; Sassou manipulated the political system to ensure that his clansmen and cronies had access to revenues accruing from oil sales with breathtaking impunity. In return, they supported his regime and the Sassou family. However, by 2005, Congo's debt burden had ballooned to $8.35 billion, much of it owed to international oil companies and commercial banks.[130] The government had incurred this debt largely through oil-backed loans that mortgaged Congo's production.[131] Although his pattern of taking oil-backed loans enabled Sassou to placate his supporters with contracts paid with borrowed money, it complicated any capacity to bring transparency to Congo's oil sector. As a result, during the 2000s, the government lurched from scandal to scandal.

Sassou's management of oil revenues lacked transparency. His personal enrichment was his primary interest. Sassou had multiple bank accounts in Paris and other European capitals into which oil companies deposited funds.[132] After the civil war, Sassou resumed personal management of oil revenues, appointed cronies and clansmen to senior positions in his administration, and created the Société Nationale de Pétroles Congolais (SNPC) to participate in PSCs and manage Congo's oil reserves. He appointed Denis Gokana, a highly trained petroleum engineer and regime insider, as his special advisor, president of the SNPC, as well as chair of its board of directors. Gokana allegedly established a system to seize the oil rents that came from a number of new discoveries in deep-water fields.[133] Moreover, Gokana became a pivotal broker for oil companies wishing to explore or produce hydrocarbons in Congo.

---

[128] Amnesty International, "Republic of Congo: A Human Rights Crisis Rooted in Power Struggles," News Service: 057/99, AI Index: AFR 22/04/99.

[129] Amnesty International, "Republic of Congo: An Old Generation of Leaders in New Carnage," Amnesty International Report, AI Index: AFR 22/01/99 (25 March 1999): 18.

[130] Global Witness, *The Riddle of the Sphynx: Where Has Congo's Oil Money Gone?* (London: Global Witness Ltd., December 2005), 3.

[131] Global Witness, "The Riddle of the Sphinx," 3.

[132] Philippe Bernard, "L'Enquête sur les 'Bien Mal Acquis' par Trios Potentates d'Afrique Sera Rouvert," *Le Monde* (11 Novembre 2010).

[133] Clark, "The Neo-Colonial Context," 186.

By 2004, Congo was so deeply in debt that creditors began to seize its overseas assets, including oil tankers.[134] From all appearances, Sassou encouraged Gokana to establish a number of offshore companies to purchase oil from the SNPC, notably, Glencore Energy (UK), Sphynx (UK), Sphynx (Bermuda), and African Oil and Gas Corporation. Under Gokana's direction, these companies bought oil from the SNPC to resell later to international oil companies. These shell companies shielded revenues from banks and other oil companies to which the Congolese government owed money. With Gokana as CEO of the SNPC, Sassou distanced himself from dishonest transactions while maintaining a system that ensured his receipt of oil revenues and thereby his security in office.

Second, at the head of the SNPC's London office (SNPC-UK), Sassou appointed his eldest son, Denis Christel Sassou, who operated both as a broker and a key figure in the oil deals that allegedly defrauded Congo's creditors.[135] The SNPC-UK failed in November 2003, and thereafter Christel Sassou became the president and director general of Cotrade SA, a shell company wholly owned by the SNPC.[136] He gained a questionable notoriety in the international press in 2007 for profligate spending in trendy shopping areas in Los Angeles, Paris, and Hong Kong.[137] The impact of these stories was to erode any sympathy that Congo might have received from foreign governments and international NGOs for its crushing debt burden and multinational companies' culpability.

Congo's substantial external debt attracted "vulture funds" that bought Congo's heavily discounted private sector debt and then litigated to recover the full value. If the so-called vulture fund wins, it imposes liens and seizes properties. Perhaps the most (in)famous vulture fund was the New York firm Elliot Associates that under the name Kensington International Limited bought a substantial sum of Congo's external debt.[138] In 2005, Kensington International Limited sued in the London High Court and won a judgment against the

[134] This information comes from Global Witness, *The Riddle of the Sphynx* and evidence presented in the judgment, The Honorable Mr. Justice Cooke, "Kensington International Limited and Republic of the Congo 1. Glencore Energy, UK Limited, 2. Sphynx UK Limited, 3. Sphynx (BDA) Limited, 4. Africa Oil and Gas Corporation, and 5. Cotrade SA" (Royal Courts of Justice, Strand, London, WC2A 2LL, 28/11/2005), para 8. (Text available at *image.guardian.co.uk/sysfiles/.../KensingtonJudgmentAppro.pdf*).
[135] Global Witness, "The riddle of the Sphinx," 5.
[136] The Honorable Mr. Justice Cooke, "Kensington International," para. 41.
[137] See Lecadre Renaud, "Le Fils du President du Congo Tous Frais Payés," *Libération* (19 juillet 2007); this story based its evidence on the documents reproduced by Global Witness, "Congo: Is President's Son Paying for Designer Shopping Sprees with Country's Oil Wealth?" (26 June 2007). Retrieved from http://www.globalwitness.org/library/congo-president%E2%80%99s-son-paying-designer-shopping-sprees-country%E2%80%99s-oil-money.
[138] Lydia Polgreen, "Unlikely Ally Against Congo Republic Graft," *The New York Times* (December 10, 2007); *The Financial Times*, "Vulture Funds Aid Debt Relief Fight," (July 17 2007); The Honorable Mr. Justice Cooke, "Kensington International."

Congolese government. This lawsuit occurred after it was revealed that a supertanker owned by Glencore Energy, one of the Congolese shell companies that Gokana established, had offloaded £22.1 million in oil that it sold to BP.[139] Kensington International Limited wanted that money. Investigators found a trail of accounts that went directly back to Gokana and the Congolese government. Kensington International Limited's suit petitioned to seize the funds and other Congolese oil tankers. By the end of 2005, courts in New York, London, and Paris had passed judgments against the Congolese government and its failure to repay its debts.

The core problem was that by the end of 2004, Congo's external debt-to-GDP ratio exceeded 198 percent of GDP.[140] When successive courts ruled against the Congolese government and openly stated that the various shell companies were entities of the Congolese state, Sassou had to make serious efforts to settle with litigating creditors and reschedule Congo's external debt. In 2008, the Paris Club of creditors canceled $643 million in debt to complement the 2007 discount of 65 percent decided in London.[141] The effect of these efforts was a reduction of the external debt-GDP ratio to 56.6 percent of GDP.[142] However, the capture of Congo's most lucrative sector by an authoritarian regime that operated much like a criminal organization presented a serious dilemma confronting this declining producer's economic performance.

Congo demonstrates how historic continuities shape outcomes in African petrostates. First, its colonial history informed the arrangements that arose between Congolese political leaders and the French national oil company Elf Aquitaine. Sassou embedded informal relations in his interactions with various executives at Elf. Primarily, Sassou used his personal connections to negotiate oil-backed loans that mortgaged Congo's hydrocarbon sector to the detriment of the state. Revenue management was inefficient and favored a diversion of funds to elite politicians instead of the state's consolidated fund. These arrangements reflected inequalities in Congolese society that had persisted since colonial rule. The inequalities were evident in the continuation of an elite cadre that captured the state. In these regards, Congo lends support for this book's central contention that inequalities under colonial rule find expression in predatory political behavior that causes developmental shortfalls.

---

[139] David Leigh and David Pallister, "Investigation Urged into West African Oil Deals," *The Guardian* (December 20, 2005).

[140] IMF, "Republic of Congo: Second Review under the Three Year Arrangement under the Poverty Reduction and Growth Facility-Staff Report," IMF Country Report 10/54 (February 2010), 5.

[141] IMF, "Republic of Congo: First Review under the Three Year Arrangement under the Poverty Reduction and Growth Facility-Request for Waivers for Nonobservance of Performance Criteria and Modification of Performance Criteria-Staff Report," IMF Country Report 09/217 (July 2009), 5–6.

[142] IMF, "Congo: Second Review under the Three Year Arrangement," 5.

CONCLUSION

This chapter has noted the importance of understanding the starting conditions in African petrostates. It emphasizes first that revenue management is the developmental crucible for African petrostates. This issue is particularly important for emerging producers that often lack the bureaucracy and competent personnel to understand fundamental procedures and practices of resource revenue management. As discussed in Chapter 4, revenue management includes a complex array of royalties, income taxes, and fees that governments receive from oil companies. The principal problem for the oil-exporting state is how to mitigate corruption, assuming the leadership has an interest in doing so. The second problem is whether actors in the petrostate have sufficient public support to engage in reforms and avoid reactions such as those that occurred in Congo after Sassou lost the elections.

Second, corruption is a critical challenge that reflects the lack of state construction among Africa's oil exporters. Malfeasance was present in practically every colonial administration, whether British, French, Portuguese, or Spanish. The discussion has emphasized that dishonesty in public administration finds its origins in colonial practices and the absence of agencies to monitor and control agents of the state. Although Tignor's depictions of civil servants' dishonesty portray the behavior as common among African colonial public servants, archival and secondary historical evidence suggest that a culture of impunity was equally common among European administrators. This impunity was a consequence of the lack of supervision that left colonial officials effectively free to do whatever they wanted. Officials in the postcolonial states adopted these patterns of dysfunctional administrative behavior from colonial rule.

Third, although it might seem intuitive that corruption would occur with greater frequency in emerging producers, Ghana's experiences suggest the conditions present at the onset of production better explain levels of malfeasance in African petrostates. If, at the time of discovery, an emerging producer has agencies of accountability and norms that condemn corruption, then elected officials will likely be intolerant of graft. However, in circumstance where the bureaucracies are too small to absorb oil windfalls, lack personnel trained in revenue management, and have few oversight agencies, opportunities for corruption increase. This circumstance is evident when levels of human capital in emerging producers remain low relative to other states at similar levels of development (e.g., Equatorial Guinea and the Baltic states).

Clientelism accompanies routine violence in African petrostates. It includes relations that rest on identity, social networks, and rent seeking. As the experiences in numerous African petrostates show, clientelism is a means whereby individuals are able to capture oil wealth. Presidents retain clients to serve as brokers who, in turn, become the gatekeepers to international oil companies that hope to acquire lucrative production contracts. The arrangements that Hertog finds to be common in Saudi Arabia are present in African petrostates, as well. However, as Ghana learned, the reputational costs when brokers have opportunities to engage in ostensibly corrupt transactions may be high.

This chapter has stressed how clientelist networks recruit or serve elite clans. In African petrostates, clans represent aggregations that predate oil production and the impact of resource rents. In Africa's authoritarian mature and declining producers, clans are critical actors. For instance, in Equatorial Guinea, the Obiang clan dominated the oil sector to the exclusion of all but a tiny number of loyal supporters. The benefits of belonging to the Obiang clan are starkly apparent from the various homes that the president's son purchased in South Africa and California. Congo's Sassou retook office through violence and established a brutal, clan-based clientelist system by which he, his family, and close associates reaped extraordinary riches. This pattern of clan domination of political arrangements is no less evident in Gabon, as Chapter 6 discusses in greater detail. As we consider in the next chapter, the critical question is whether such a system has the potential to initiate elements of democracy.

6

Machine Politics, Oil, and Democracy

Chapter 5 analyzed the impact of unrestrained corruption and how it leads to inefficient revenue management in three African petrostates: Ghana, Equatorial Guinea, and the Congo Republic. It shows how these states developed procedures in managing resource windfalls that reflect their phase of production and their leaders' idiosyncrasies. The chapter pulled information from the previous chapters to illustrate the influence of a given petrostate's phase of production, role of diverse oil companies, and impact of corruption on development. This information is critical for understanding the means by which a given petrostate makes transitions toward more democratic rule. The extent of democracy in Africa's petrostate is the focus of this chapter.

This chapter proposes that political machines have emerged in many African petrostates, and these machines represent actors who are critical in the process of democratization. Political machines build on relationships among individuals and groups that predate the discovery of hydrocarbons and influence politics independently of the oil sector. The organizations that became contemporary political machines represent individuals who use them to compete for elected office and influence the distribution of fiscal expenditures. In many respects, this proposition builds on the previous discussion in Chapter 5 that examined how authoritarian leaders established political organizations to decisively shape political economic outcomes in petrostates that include Equatorial Guinea and Congo. This chapter shows how machine politics articulate the interests and complex relationships that contribute to democratization in several contemporary African petrostates, namely Nigeria (a mature producer) and Gabon (a declining producer). Whereas Nigeria has taken significant steps toward democratization, Gabon's ruling clan used the machine its patriarch established to keep power. The contrasting cases illustrate many of the impediments and achievements among Africa's petrostates.

Machine politics has been in the background of democratic transitions in Africa. For example, in their study of primaries and candidate selection in Ghana, Ichino and Nathan point out that changes in the candidate selection are more than "top-down, supply side" domination, but also a "bottom-up, demand side pressure" on the part of party members.[1] This finding is important because it denotes a growing vibrancy in the democratic pluralism active on the continent; a dynamism independent of oil production and resource revenue management. Indeed, the Ghanaian government's resolution of the Kosmos controversy discussed in Chapter 5 is further evidence that decades of political processes and representative government embed democratic institutions in African public life. Hence, changes on the continent defy simplistic arguments that oil wealth funds incumbent politicians that use the funds to ensure their longevity in office and deny democratic processes.[2]

The second part of this chapter analyzes development and democracy in Nigeria. By analyzing a mature producer with a turbulent political landscape in which competing machines present candidates for federal and state government offices, it is possible to assess the extent to which the political machines represent religious, ethnic, and social groups' interests. In 2007, competition among political actors was the causal factor that inserted a stunning level of violence in elections and called into question hopes that this multiethnic state could ever become a democracy. Chilling stories of cult groups, religious strife, and incredibly corrupt godfathers made Nigeria seem utterly lawless. However, the government's acceptance of greater levels of transparency and accountability in Nigeria's oil industry and the 2011 elections suggest a deepening of democracy. This assessment of developments in Nigerian politics suggests that the country is perhaps lurching slowly toward pluralistic, representative government.

Gabon provides a case of a stable declining producer with dwindling oil reserves where a competitive authoritarian regime has governed for decades. In Gabon, authoritarian rule rests on a clan-based political machine that effectively controls economic and social opportunities.[3] The clan's patriarch seized power in 1967 and imposed an autocracy that later included competitive elections. A gradual relaxation of political control followed elections after 1990. A formative process occurred in which fragments of democracy were present in political parties, student associations, and labor syndicates, all of which use democratic procedures in selecting their leaders.[4] Although the patriarch

[1] Nahomi Ichino and Noah L. Nathan, "Primaries on Demand? Intra-Party Politics and Nominations in Ghana," *British Journal of Political Science* 42, 4 (October 2012): 772.
[2] Michael L. Ross, *The Oil Curse: How Petroleum Wealth Shapes the Development of Nations* (Princeton: Princeton University Press, 2012), 87.
[3] Steven Levitsky and Lucan A. Way, *Competitive Authoritarianism: Hybrid Regimes after the Cold War* (New York: Cambridge University Press, 2010), 22.
[4] Richard L. Sklar, "Developmental Democracy," *Comparative Studies in Society and History* 29, 4 (October 1987): 714.

had sought to prepare the country for a post-oil economy, he also established the institutions that ensured dynastic rule. Unfortunately, after his death in 2009, his son, Ali Bongo, demonstrated some of his father's political acumen; he watched as his opponents formed ethnic political factions, consolidated his mainstream party, ran a campaign against two opponents, and won the majority of votes cast.[5] In this regard, Gabon represents a possible path for petrostates whose authoritarian leaders seek to prepare their states for post-oil economic development and protect their clans.

In Africa's petrostates, the presence of political machines has been constant since even before independence. This book argues that democratic reforms are probable. In each petrostate, to varying degrees, democracy has arrived "in fragments or parts; each fragment becomes an incentive for the addition of another."[6] These fragments of representative democracy build upon each other; their presence allows for some cautious optimism. For instance, despite high levels of corruption and other inefficiencies, politicians have eased restrictions on political organizations to create pluralism – albeit imperfect – in their respective political systems. The presence of social organizations that satisfy unmet demand disputes widely accepted notions that oil revenues enable incumbents to consolidate authoritarian rule.[7] Indeed, the increasing pluralism present even in authoritarian petrostates suggests that dictators must contend with increasingly clamorous populations. However, each of these cases demonstrates the significant challenges petrostates confront as their leaders form coalitions and use what Arriola calls pecuniary strategies to distribute benefits and hold political office.[8] Without question, demands articulated by social organizations threaten to have the familiar voracity effect; still, deeper population shifts represent factor changes that compel even entrenched dictators such as Omar Bongo Ondimba, Denis Sassou Nguesso, and others to reconsider their governing strategies.

The elements of democracy build on social relations that precede oil production and represent historic continuities. These continuities find expression in political parties, clientelist networks, and political machines that promote candidates and exclude rivals from political office.[9] For instance, Ghana's competitive politics built on traditions of ethnic blocks that dated to the colonial Legislative Assembly in which regional parties represented the government and its opposition.[10] Its arguably free elections defied stereotypes of

[5] "Gabon: A Family Legacy," *Africa Confidential* 52, 2 (January 21, 2011).
[6] Sklar, "Developmental Democracy," 714.
[7] Nathan Jensen and Leonard Wantchekon, "Resource Wealth and Political Regimes in Africa," *Comparative Political Studies* 37, 3 (September 2004): 816–841.
[8] Leonardo R. Arriola, *Multiethnic Coalitions in Africa: Business Financing of Opposition Election Campaigns* (New York: Cambridge University Press, 2013), 32.
[9] Laurent Fourchard, "A New Name for an Old Practice: Vigilantes in Southwestern Nigeria," *Africa* 78, 1 (2008): 535–558.
[10] David E. Apter, *Ghana in Transition* (Princeton: Princeton University Press, 1963), 185.

persistent authoritarian rule in African petrostates whose leaders corrupt the basic institutions of democracy. In their analysis of Nigeria's 2007 elections, Fafchamps and Vicente found that where community actors disseminated a message that condemns violence, norms emerged to mitigate brutality.[11] Finally, in Gabon, the late president's children consolidated rule through many of the same practices and organizations that had faithfully served their father. Each of these cases is indicative of particular institutions that enable their leaders to consolidate and maintain rule.

TENTATIVE DEMOCRACY IN AFRICAN PETROSTATES

Democracy, or the politician's acceptance of a possibility of losing office, has been tentative in African petrostates.[12] When production began in the countries that became oil exporters, most of the states were authoritarian regimes. Their presidents organized ostensibly competitive elections, guarding their access to wealth by which they paid members of their coalitions and the campaign expenses. Levitsky and Way have coined the term "competitive authoritarianism" to describe the "hybrid regimes" in which elections occur with regularity, albeit alongside persistent authoritarianism.[13] However, as the Freedom House indicators displayed in Table 6.1 suggest, with the exception of Ghana, the vast majority of citizens in Africa's petrostates live under ruthless dictators. Extreme authoritarian regimes govern Sudan, Equatorial Guinea, Chad, and Congo. In Angola, an oligarchy controls political economic outcomes in spite of the 2012 multiparty elections. Troubled democracies rule Nigeria and São Tomé and Príncipe. Meanwhile, in 2009 Gabon's Ali Bongo Ondimba won questionable presidential elections and consolidated his regime. Of the countries listed, only in Ghana and São Tomé and Príncipe are the people free to express their political preferences.

Although the overwhelming majority of Africa's petrostates are "Not free," this book argues that resource rents were not the causal variables in authoritarian rule and civil conflicts. These unfortunate behaviors are outcomes of grievances and relationships that preceded the discovery of oil; the availability of money through resource extraction contributed to the conflicts' intensity by facilitating the purchase of arms and the prolongation of violence. For Chad, Freedom House scores it as 7, the least-free score for political rights, and 6 for civil liberties. Although the absence of political and civil liberties is without question, the causal variables are greed and rivalries among individuals.

---

[11] Marcel Fafchamps and Pedro C. Vicente, "Political Violence and Social Networks: Experimental Evidence from a Nigerian Election," *Journal of Development Economics* 101 (March 2013): 28.

[12] Adam Przeworski, *Democracy and the Market: Political and Economic Reforms in Eastern Europe and Latin America* (New York: Cambridge University Press, 1991), 10.

[13] Levitsky and Way, *Competitive Authoritarianism*, 5.

TABLE 6.1 *Political Rights and Civil Liberties in African Petrostates*
(Freedom House Indicators 2013 – 1 = most free; 7 = least free)

Country	Political rights	Civil liberties	Status
Angola	6	5	Not free
Cameroon	6	6	Not free
Chad	7	6	Not free
Congo	6	5	Not free
Equatorial Guinea	7	7	Not free
Gabon	6	5	Not free
Ghana	1	2	Free
Mauritania	6	5	Not free
Nigeria	4	5	Partly free
São Tomé and Príncipe	2	2	Free
Sudan	7	7	Not free

Retrieved from http://www.freedomhouse.org/regions/sub-saharan-africa (2013).

Idriss Déby was Hissein Habré's military chief of staff; personal conflicts between the two men preceded Déby's defection from the government and military campaign in 1990 to chase his former patron from N'Djamena.[14] He succeeded largely as a result of assistance from the French, who had tired of Habré's excesses and saw Déby as "their man."[15] However, within a short time, internal conflicts destabilized Déby's administration as regime insiders defected to join rebel movements intent on overthrowing the regime.[16]

Conflicts in authoritarian petrostates oftentimes reflect personal animus among a small number of political actors. This animus finds its origins in long-term competition that predates hydrocarbon production. To return to Chad as our example, after Déby overthrew Habré, he appointed clansmen and others from his Bideyat Zaghawa subgroup to manage productive sectors. His governing strategy mixed co-option and repression with the effect of deepening intra-clan conflicts as evidenced by the 2007 decision of his nephews Tom and Timane Erdimi to flee N'Djaména and from the bush launch a rebellion.[17] However, the rebellion reflected more intra-clan competition, familial

[14] R. May and S. Massey, "The Chadian Party System: Rhetoric and Reality," *Democratization* 9, 3 (Fall 2002): 75. This pattern of one president's military elite defecting from the governing coalition occurred in the government that preceded Habré. In 1980, Goukoni Oueddei had a falling out with Habré, who then launched what was a successful campaign to unseat Oueddei. See P. Doornbus, "La Révolution Dérapée: la Violence dans l'est de Tchad (1978–1981)," *Politique Africaine* 7 (Octobre 1982): 11.
[15] Jean-Louis Triaud, "L'Etat Inexistant, Ingérences Extérieurs," *Le Monde Diplomatique* (Février 1992): 18.
[16] AFP, "Tchad: l'Échec Apparent de l'Offensive des Rebelles ne Marque pas la Fin du Conflit," *Le Monde* (10 Mai 2009).
[17] Jean-Philippe Rémy, "Tchad Rebellion: Le Chef des Déserteurs est un Ancien Proche du President

hostilities, and greed.[18] A perception among officials in the regime was that Déby favored certain groups and ignored the plight of others.[19] In this context, his authoritarian regime more clearly represented a continuity of past behaviors to which resource rents added a new perception of inequitable distribution of favors.

Freedom House rankings present a picture of competitive authoritarian states among Africa's oil producers. Like Chad, Equatorial Guinea and Sudan are extreme authoritarian regimes. Other "Not free" states hold periodic elections, but the autocrat decides who wins, gets the benefits, and gets nothing. In Congo, a relatively small clique resisted popular initiatives to democratize and bring more representative government. Although Freedom House ranks Congo as "Not free," the Sassou regime is hardly as repressive as the regime under Sudan's Bashir or Equatorial Guinea's Obiang Nguema.[20]

The presence of democratic institutions for extended periods prior to the discovery of oil bodes the best for continuing democracy after production begins. Among Africa's petrostates, democratic government had been the rule in Ghana for fifteen years before oil was discovered. First, although competitive elections were the norm, some practices reflected continuities from a non-democratic past. For instance, Jockers et al. first suggest that voter rolls were inflated and political competition has reverted to opponents who represent ethnic and regional parties or blocks.[21] Second, different ministries and state agencies have considerable discretion in the performance of their responsibilities. For example, during the Kufuor administration, hierarchic authority was evident in the Ministry of the Interior if less so in other ministries.[22] Whereas officials in the Serious Fraud Office had little independence from the executive branch because the president could remove them at will, appointees in other agencies had considerable discretion in their choices of investigations and activities. Such discretion was evident in the controversy over Kosmos Energy's attempt to sell its share of the Jubilee Oil Field to ExxonMobil. In this case, the GNPC had the discretion to block the sale. Although these two factors

---

Déby," *Le Monde* (14 Décembre 2005); See as well the extraordinary study by Marielle Debos, *Le Métier des Armes au Tchad: Le Gouvernement de l'Entre-Guerres* (Paris: Éditions Karthala, 2013), 91–98.

[18] Philippe Bernard et Natalie Nougayrède (avec Philippe Bolopion à l'ONU), "L'Offensive des Rebelles du Tchad Embarrasse la France," *Le Monde* (3 Février 2008).

[19] Jean-Philippe Rémy, "Le Parti du Président Tchadien Idriss Déby Lève l'Obstacle à une Présidence à Vie," *Le Monde* (29 Mai 2004); International Crisis Group, "Darfur: The Failure to Protect," Africa Report No. 89 (March 8, 2005): 12.

[20] The repression that preceded the 2013 legislative elections in Equatorial Guinea is only one example of continuing autocracy in that mature petrostate. Amnesty International, "Equatorial Guinea: Human Rights Concerns Ahead of Equatorial Guinea Elections," (May 7, 2013).

[21] Jockers et al., "The Successful Ghana Election of 2008," 96.

[22] For example, while conducting fieldwork in Ghana in 2004, it was apparent that in the Ministry of the Interior a strict hierarchic authority was present that was much different from the working relations observed in the Ministries of Justice or Finance.

hardly constitute irrefutable evidence of democracy, they do indicate a critical degree of accountability in public life.

By contrast, Nigeria's "Partly free" democracy indicates a turbulent political environment animated by patrons called godfathers who direct brutal political machines.[23] In keeping with continent-wide patterns, Nigerian politicians centralized their presidential systems to control national elections and leave smaller parties free to compete in regional and local elections.[24] However, political parties in Nigeria's thirty-six states operate as neopatrimonial political machines headed by governors who are representatives of diverse godfathers. Both the governors and their godfathers have motives to capture state governments and use their positions organizations for their personal enrichment.

Nigeria's experiences render nonsensical suggestions that patrons altruistically share their riches with their clients.[25] The political machines that emerged in post-Abacha Nigeria reflected the persistence of "grabber friendly institutions" wherein politicians profited from the absence of the rule of law, a dysfunctional civil service, and opportunities for corruption.[26] Indeed, as van de Walle forcefully states, "Clientelism cannot be redistributive"; it distributes benefits to the patron, his clan, and "immediate kin, but not to the poor within his broader lineage or ethnic group."[27] Patronage jobs in Nigeria, as elsewhere in Africa, often entailed uncompensated work; patrons required that clients pay them in kind, but offered no job security. If a client ceased to provide the patron a benefit, he or she was let go. The client was therefore subservient and vulnerable to the patrons' caprices.

Political Freedoms and Corruption

Political freedoms and corruption are negative correlates; they rarely occur simultaneously. As Table 6.2 suggests, a majority of African petrostates have both low levels of political freedom as evidenced by Freedom House 2013 rankings, and high levels of corruption as shown in Transparency International's 2012 Corruption Perception Index. Leaders of these young states are building bureaucracies from scratch; meanwhile, patrons of political machines are engineering networks to articulate their interests. Clientelist networks operate as political organizations that support patrons and their clans. In Angola,

[23] Richard L. Sklar, Ebere Onwudiwe, and Darren Kew, "Nigeria: Completing Obasanjo's Legacy." *Journal of Democracy* 17, 3 (July 2006): 100–115.

[24] Nicolas van de Walle, "Presidentialism and Clientelism in Africa's Emerging Party Systems," *The Journal of Modern African Studies* 41, 2 (June 2003): 298.

[25] Patrick Chabal and Jean-Pascal Daloz, *Africa Works: Disorder as a Political Instrument* (Bloomington: Indiana University Press, 1999), 15.

[26] Halvor Mehlum, Karl Moene, and Ragnar Torvik, "Institutions and the Resource Curse," *The Economic Journal* 116 (January 2006): 3.

[27] Nicolas van de Walle, "The Institutional Origins of Inequality in Sub-Saharan Africa," *The Annual Review of Political Science* 12 (2009): 321.

TABLE 6.2 *Corruption and Political Freedoms in African Petrostates*

		Corruption (from TI – CPI 2012 – N = 176)		
		High (135–176)	Moderate (90–135)	Low (1–89)
Political freedoms	High (Free)			Ghana (64) São Tomé and Príncipe (72)
	Moderate (Partly free)	Nigeria (139)		
	Low (Not free)	Angola (157) Cameroon (144) Chad (165) Congo (144) Equatorial Guinea (163) Sudan (173)	Gabon (102) Mauritania (123)	

Cameroon, Chad, Congo, Gabon, Mauritania, and Sudan citizens enjoy few civil liberties or political freedoms. These clientelist states are closed regimes where the president decides who enters monopolistic networks and gains access to state revenues and employment opportunities. What these rankings imply is that corruption and authoritarianism in African petrostates reflect differences in institutional frameworks.

Clientelism in African Petrostates

In many African petrostates, political leaders use clientelist networks to capture state office and insert hereditary, caciquismo-type patrimonialism in politics.[28] These behaviors occur through both formal and informal institutions. North has defined institutions as "humanely devised constraints" that may be formal, meaning laws and constitutions, or informal, including norms and self-imposed behavior; together, formal and informal institutions shape "the incentive structure of societies and specifically economies."[29] Through clientelist networks, patrons are able to conceal their goals and thereby avoid the limits that rules place on their behavior.

[28] Luis Roniger, "Caciquismo and Coronelismo: Contextual Dimensions of Patron Brokerage in Mexico and Brazil," *Latin American Research Review* 22, 2 (1987): 92; a similar attempt to embed hereditary patrimonial networks occurred in the Philippines, as well. See the depiction of patronage politics in Paul D. Hutchcroft, *Booty Capitalism: The Politics of Banking in the Philippines* (Ithaca and London: Cornell University Press, 1998), 112.

[29] Douglass C. North, "Economic Performance through Time," *The American Economic Review* 84, 3 (June 1994): 360.

The operative word in North's concept is "constraint"; institutions limit individual discretion.[30] In African petrostates, the reticence of colonial administrations to construct effective states contributed to ambiguities in formal institutions; political leaders came to office with considerable discretion in how they chose to exercise authority. Many responded more to informal institutions that operated at the social level; they failed to consider how their actions might influence the larger political arena. Helmke and Levitsky define informal institutions as *"socially shared rules, usually unwritten, that are created, communicated, and enforced outside officially sanctioned channels."*[31] They consciously fold the concept of rules into informal institutions, use the terms interchangeably, and emphasize that informal rules are exogenous to the state. An interpretation of what has occurred in African petrostates, however, suggests that politicians relax informal rules to favor clansmen and clients.[32] As is readily evident, patrons have incentives to manipulate and change informal rules to their advantage. Indeed, as Chaudhury found in Saudi Arabia, formal procedures over decision making are de facto supports for informal networks that capture crucial offices of the bureaucracy.[33] What this flexibility means is that political leaders decide the formal and informal institutional arrangements that underpin their system of government.

Because informal rules determine individual behavior within clientelist networks, competition and deal making occur among individuals who pursue material interests. For instance, influential individuals in clientelist networks alter rules to expand or restrict the criteria for inclusion. This notion of clientelism corresponds to depictions of networks in Central Asia as organizations that emerged to control access to goods in short supply.[34] People in Africa join in clientelist networks to get employment, scholarships, and status. When oil revenues decline, it is reasonable to hypothesize that leaders change the rules of inclusion to restrict access to elite status. For instance, immediately after independence in 1975, Angola's civil war started; President Agostinho Neto centralized decision making and governed through an exclusive group of advisors. These oligarchs came to resemble a *"nomenklatura"*; they controlled political processes and diverted revenues to Angola's "grand families".[35] Angola's elitist

[30] Edward L. Glaeser, Rafael La Porta, Florencio Lopes-De-Silanes, and Andrei Shleifer, "Do Institutions Cause Growth?" *Journal of Economic Growth* 9 (2004): 272.

[31] Gretchen Helmke and Steven Levitsky, "Introduction," in *Informal Institutions and Democracy: Lessons from Latin America*, eds. Gretchen Helmke and Steven Levitsky (Baltimore: The Johns Hopkins University Press, 2006), 5, emphasis in original.

[32] Elinor Ostrom, "An Agenda for the Study of Institutions," *Public Choice* 48 (1986): 5.

[33] Kiren Aziz Chaudhury, *The Price of Wealth: Economies and Institutions in the Middle East* (Ithaca and London: Cornell University Press, 1997), 172.

[34] Edward Schatz, *Modern Clan Politics: The Power of Blood in Kazakhstan and Beyond* (Seattle: University of Washington Press, 2004), 19.

[35] Manuel Ennes Ferreira, "La Reconversion Économique de la *Nomenklatura* Pétrolières," trans., Christine Messiant, *Politique Africaine* (1995): 13.

system permitted insiders to engage in corruption and indiscipline and forbid outsiders basic freedoms to join religious congregations, trade unions, or civil society organizations.[36] Its centralized presidential system embedded families and clientelist networks in the state and conferred benefits on select oligarchs who were among the MPLA's original founders.

Clientelism and Machine Politics

Clientelist networks entail a dyadic relationship between the patron, an individual of a higher socioeconomic status that provides protection and benefits to the client, who is someone from a lower status.[37] During late colonialism, clientelist networks were evident in voluntary associations active in the rapidly growing cities from which the Europeans administered their colonies.[38] Examples abound of clientelist arrangements; Cohen's memorable work on Hausa networks in Yoruba cities shows how patrons ensured their clients' loyalty by providing housing, credit, and social networks.[39] Urban immigrants, oscillating migrants, or otherwise displaced populations joined patron-client networks; they depended on the patron, who was a "big man" or woman, for benefits. In return, the client provided the patron labor, political support, and sometimes a portion of his or her earnings. Some networks endure, and in so doing they become organizations with goals of enhancing the patron's status and political influence.

Clientelist networks in Africa bear similarities to political machines common in nineteenth-century American cities. In these organizations, a patron distributed employment and favors with a goal of having influence over a population of clients, winning elections or placing compliant politicians in office, and retaining a position that provided access to wealth and power. The political machine operated through centralized authority, and members' motivations were material and not ideological.[40] In the United States, before passage of the 1888 Pendleton Act, people coveted patronage jobs in the public sector that

---

[36] Christine Messiant, *L'Angola Postcolonial*: vol. 1, *Guerre et Paix sans Démocratisation* (Paris: Éditions Karthala, 2008a), 58.

[37] For example, see René Lemarchand, "Political Clientelism and Ethnicity in Tropical Africa," *The American Political Science Review* 66, 1 (March 1972): 68–90; James C. Scott, "Patron-Client Politics and Political Change in Southeast Asia," *The American Political Science Review* 66, 1 (March 1972): 91–113.

[38] Claude Meillassoux, *Urbanization of an African Community: Voluntary Associations in Bamako, Mali* (Seattle: University of Washington Press, 1969); see as well, Kenneth Little, *West African Urbanization: A Study of Voluntary Associations in Social Change* (New York: Cambridge University Press, 1965).

[39] Abner Cohen, *Custom and Politics in Urban Africa: A Study of Hausa Migrants in Yoruba Towns* (Berkeley and Los Angeles: University of California Press, 1969).

[40] Michael Johnston, "Patrons and Clients, Jobs and Machines: A Case Study of the Uses of Patronage," *The American Political Science Review* 73, 2 (June 1979): 385.

paid higher wages than private-sector positions.[41] The classic patronage system involved a politician or boss who hired individuals from a specific population (e.g., Irish immigrants and Tammany Hall); these people worked short-term jobs on political campaigns and would turn over a portion of their salaries to the patron.[42] The client's job was secure as long as he was useful to the machine. If a client failed to make a profit, the patron either fired him or the "boss" would fire the patron.[43]

A "machine" is defined as that kind of political party which sustains its members through the distribution of material incentives (patronage) rather than non-material incentives (appeals to principle, the fun of the game, sociability, etc.). "Patronage" is customarily used to refer to all forms of material benefits which politicians may distribute to party workers and supporters.... "Patronage jobs" are all those posts, distributed at the discretion of party leaders, the pay for which is greater that the value of the public services performed. This "unearned increment" permits the machine to require that the holder perform party services as well.[44]

A party machine that predicates its actions on clientelist networks is itself a gatekeeper to individuals and firms that seek economic benefits. Ideology is secondary to the economic relationships that fund the political machine. Individuals work for the organization and support a boss or big man, who also operates in a pyramid headed by the leader of his political party. Second, patrons are brokers who possess information about access to powerful officials and opportunities. Third, patrons use a party machine to internalize information costs within the network. This information has value that the patrons control. Politicians employ clientelism as a strategy to overcome deficits in credibility about electoral promises; the political machine distributed jobs and benefits as long as it won elections.[45] Leaders of political machines used their distribution of benefits to enhance their claims to having control of contracts and opportunities. They were thereby able to attract clients, which furthered their political influence.

Whereas rent seeking and parochial interest-group activism are certainly part of the machine politics in African petrostates, clientelism also informs group behavior in support of incumbents or candidates who comply with formal rules enshrined in constitutional articles, term limits, and electoral

[41] Werner Troesken, "Patronage and Public Sector Wages in 1896," *The Journal of Economic History* 59, 2 (June 1999): 425.

[42] Ronald N. Johnson and Gary D. Liebcap, "Patronage to Merit and Control of the Federal Government Labor Force," *Explorations in Economic History* 31, 1 (1994): 92.

[43] Joseph D. Reid Jr. and Michael M. Kurth, "Public Employees in Political Firms: Part A. The Patronage Era," *Public Choice* 59, 3 (December 1988): 254.

[44] James Q. Wilson, "The Economy of Patronage," *Journal of Political Economy* 69, 4 (August 1961): 370.

[45] Philip E. Keefer, "Clientelism, Credibility, and the Policy Choices of Young Democracies," *American Journal of Political Science* 51, 4 (October 2007): 805.

processes.[46] In African petrostates, patrons use informal organizations to compete for political office, influence policy deliberations, and gain economic advantage. The most negative depictions of clientelism suggest that it coexists with a neopatrimonial state and that any capacity to move away from personal rule is bound to fail.[47] Worse, neopatrimonial states allow network leaders to provide benefits for their clients while neglecting fundamental public services for the larger population. The logic is that these states are weak and therefore prone to fail, meaning they are unable to provide their citizens with elementary public services.

Despite depictions of weak states continent wide, such accounts fail to explain the large numbers of weak African states. Moreover, the perspective that weak states are necessarily prone to fail ignores the social dynamics behind people's reasons for joining clientelist networks. For example, Cowen and Laakso criticize analyses that equate clientelism with interest group activism, rent seeking, and corruption.[48] Their criticism contrasts with Berman's perspective that clientelism is a part of an "evil triumvirate" that includes patronage, corruption, and tribalism.[49] His point is overdone; patrons organize networks to win office and retain influence. National leaders overcome challenges they encounter when attempting to project administrative power outside urban centers.[50] People have social networks to reinforce political organizations in the localities in which they live and work.

Whereas clientelist networks allocate employment opportunities to followers, their more crucial impact is as organizations that form the foundations of political machines. Johnston has perceptively noted that political machines, like men, age; the same is true of clientelist networks.[51] As patrons age, the capacity of political machines to distribute patronage jobs declines because competitors enter the arena and divert potential clients from the aging patron. In Africa, people form and enter organizations according to long-standing relations that link individuals to their larger communities. These relationships are critical bonds between displaced populations and their rural origins. However, as people leave villages and resettle in cities, their children question why they should be subservient to authority structures that influenced their parents. Clientelist

[46] Daniel N. Posner and Daniel J. Young, "The Institutionalization of Political Power in Africa," *Journal of Democracy* 18, 3 (July 2007): 127.

[47] Anne Pitcher, Mary H. Moran, and Michael Johnston, "Rethinking Patrimonialism and Neopatrimonialism in Africa," *African Studies Review* 52, 1 (April 2009): 132.

[48] Michael Cowen and Liisa Laakso, "An Overview of Election Studies," *The Journal of Modern African Studies* 35, 4 (December 1997): 73.

[49] Bruce Berman, "Ethnicity, Patronage and the African State: The Politics of Uncivil Nationalism," *African Affairs* 97, 388 (July 1998): 309.

[50] Robert Fatton, "Clientelism and Patronage in Senegal," *African Studies Review* 29, 4 (December 1986): 62. This inability of African states to project power is a theme in Herbst, *States and Power in Africa*.

[51] Johnston, "Patrons and Clients, Jobs and Machines," 396.

networks then assume increasing importance. Where clientelism was common, people reproduced both its negative and positive attributes. Although the state may exhibit authority that is patrimonial in nature, from the perspective of the actors involved, the patronage networks respond to their daily needs and form relationships that are primary.

Negative depictions of clientelism fail to account for several positive aspects of the informal networks. First, clientelist networks were traditionally a bridge for rural authorities to transfer informal rules to relatives living in cities. Although networks transmit informal rules from the countryside to the cities, they also send information in the reverse direction. Elders and patrons in villages and towns learn about practices in the cities and how political authorities use power to help or hinder their group. However, increasingly, urban populations are second- and third-generation city dwellers; their parents or grandparents migrated from rural villages. Individuals receive little or no benefit from rural relatives. As a result, rural authorities are unable to extend any authority over youth living in cities.

Networks transfer information both up and down the clientelist hierarchy with a patron at the top and clients at the bottom. Clientelist networks thereby impose authority over unemployed youth who must accept their assistance. The overall effect is to reduce social uncertainty and build social capital, a critical institution for economic development.[52] The common assumption that clientelism is a negative aspect of Africa's late-century degeneration merits a critical reevaluation. In African petrostates, the historic relations that shape decisions about who organizes and who joins clientelist networks are present in political machines.

GODFATHERS AND MACHINE POLITICS IN A MATURE PRODUCER: NIGERIA

In Africa, Nigeria is a giant; it hosts the continent's largest population and a lion's share of the oil. In addition to thirty-six states and a federal territory, the country has six geopolitical regions – the Southwest, South-South, Southeast, North Central, Northwest, and Northeast. Within each of these regions, political actors cooperate, collude, and compete for fiscal revenues and expenditures. Godfathers and their clients influence political outcomes predominantly at the state level where gubernatorial campaigns are notorious for their bloodshed. Much of what drives the competition is historic rivalries and efforts to gain a portion of the substantial sums that hydrocarbon production generates on a daily basis.

---

[52] Paul Collier and Jan Gunning, "Explaining African Economic Performance," *The Journal of Economic Literature* 37, 1 (March 1999): 65.

With reserves of approximately 37.2 billion barrels, Nigeria has more oil than all the other major African producers combined.[53] Despite serious losses to pipeline theft in the Niger Delta, called oil bunkering, in 2013 the Federal Government of Nigeria (FGN) projected production at 2.57 million barrels a day of light sweet crude. The FGN at times adopted draconian efforts to stop bunkering, but the theft acquired mythic dimensions and its perpetrators became legends.[54] Although the state received extraordinary sums from hydrocarbon production, these funds attracted rent seeking, fraud, and outright embezzlement of public funds that defied the imagination. The minister of finance in Goodluck Jonathan's administration, Ngozi Okonjo-Iweala, relates how Sani Abacha removed $2.2 billion in truckloads of cash from the Nigerian Central Bank.[55] Abacha's criminal behavior contributed to a tumultuous political milieu. Corruption amplified a culture of impunity among Nigeria's senior political officials who competed over who would control vast sums of money. Their competition could erupt in stunning violence during elections; census taking that would determine federal allocations to states, and over perceived threats or insults to religious, social, or ethnic groups.

This section presents information about the political machines that operate under godfathers who control patronage jobs and influence political campaigns in Nigeria's thirty-six states. Godfathers established political machines to secure finance through illegitimate procurement contracts, embezzlement of government resources, extortion, and complex brokerage schemes that became the subject of scandals.[56] Members in these machines came from the military cliques that dominated political offices for decades and used their positions to get access to Nigeria's substantial oil revenues. After the shift to republican democracy in 1999, former clients of the military governments surfaced and created political machines. The patrons of these machines became ever more entrenched in Nigerian politics during the 2003 campaign and robbed the 2007 elections of any veneer of legitimacy. In 2011, the machines included the multiethnic coalition in the governing PDP and other parties that competed in elections. The godfathers' continued activities attest to dynamism in Nigerian politics that presents numerous continuities as well as points of departure for this turbulent republic.

The significance of corruption and machine politics in Nigeria rests in their impacts on state legitimacy and democratization. On one hand, corruption

---

[53] Mallam Nuhu Ribadu and Olasupo Shasore San, *Report of the Petroleum Revenue Special Task Force* (Abuja: Federal Ministry of Petroleum Resources, August 2012), 33.

[54] Andrew Apter, *The Pan-African Nation: Oil and the Spectacle of Culture in Nigeria* (Chicago: University of Chicago Press, 2005), 36.

[55] Ngozi Okonjo-Iweala, *Reforming the Unreformable: Lessons from Nigeria* (Cambridge, MA: MIT Press, 2012), 85.

[56] Leena Hoffman, "Fairy Godfathers and Magical Elections: Understanding the 2003 Electoral Crisis in Anambra State, Nigeria," *The Journal of Modern African Studies* 48, 2 (June 2010): 285–310.

and machine politics call into question governing elite's political legitimacy. As Sklar observes, the Nigerian state, however, has always been the object of competition and capture.[57] In contemporary Nigeria, godfathers use their influence to seize positions that enable them to function as brokers that receive fees and commissions from international companies that want to do business in Nigeria. Governors and others who are the godfathers' clients may occupy elected office, but few assert that the elections by which they came to office were free or fair.[58] On the other hand, the emergence of different factions that compete for office and political influence reflects a violent and dynamic pluralism that pits one machine against another. As the 2007 and 2011 elections demonstrated, different machines competed at local, state, and federal levels to dominate electoral outcomes. Whereas in 2007 a tragically violent pluralism characterized the Nigerian elections, in 2011 this violence diminished significantly. The unsettling persistence of corruption sets the stage for political turmoil.

Grand Corruption in an Unsettled Democracy: The TSKJ Scandal [59]

This scandal highlights the long-term relations between international companies, military governments, and their civilian successors in a case of grand corruption. Nigeria possesses natural gas reserves estimated at 180 trillion cubic feet, making the country one of the world's top-ten producers of natural gas.[60] To exploit this resource, the Nigerian Liquid Natural Gas (NLNG) Company brought together four partners, namely, the NNPC (49 percent), Shell (25.6 percent), Total (15 percent), and ENI (10.4 percent).[61] In earlier periods, oil companies had engaged in the environmentally destructive practice of flaring, or burning off the gas. However, in the 1990s, the NLNG consortium developed the technology to supercool the gas at installations called trains. This technology involves cooling the natural gas to -162°C and shipping the liquefied gas via pipeline to be offloaded onto tankers for exportation.[62]

---

[57] Richard L. Sklar, "The Nature of Class Domination in Africa." *The Journal of Modern African Studies* 14, 4 (December 1979): 531–552.

[58] Studies of godfathers and godfatherism in Nigeria are surprisingly scarce. Olmuyiwa Olusesan Familusi, "Moral and Development Issues in Political Godfatherism in Nigeria," *Journal of Sustainable Development in Africa* 14, 7 (2012): 17.

[59] Surprisingly few analytical studies have examined the TSKJ scandal. One notable contribution is Barbara Crutchfield George and Kathleen A. Lacey, "Investigation of Halliburton Co./TSKJ's Nigerian Business Practices: A Model for Analysis of the Current Anti-Corruption Environment on Foreign Corrupt Practices Act Enforcement," *The Journal of Criminal Law and Criminology* 96, 2 (Winter 2006): 503–525.

[60] U.S. Energy Information Administration, "Nigeria" (October 16, 2012): 12.

[61] Dino Mahtani, "Gas: A Farewell to Flaring," *The Financial Times* (April 25, 2005).

[62] Vaclav Smil, *Energy at the Crossroads: Global Perspectives and Uncertainties* (Cambridge, MA: MIT Press, 2003), 47.

In 1992, the Nigerian government issued a call for bids to construct a multibillion-dollar installation of trains and an LNG pipeline from Bonny Island in Rivers State. Two large international construction consortia responded to the call-for-bid. The first was TSKJ, and it assembled Technip (France); Snamprogetti Netherlands, a subsidiary of Saipem Italy; Kellogg, Brown and Root, a U.S. firm that is part of Halliburton; and Japan Gasoline Corporation. The second consortium joined together Bechtel (United States), Chiyoda (Japan), Spibat (Emirates), and Ansaldo (Italy) under the acronym BCSA. In August 1993, TSKJ and BCSA submitted their bids to build the trains that would transform the gas into liquid form and the pipeline to transport the LNG from Bonny Island.

The original estimate for this contract was $8 billion, and it attracted widespread international attention. Senior NLNG officials received the bids that an assessment committee opened, and determined the most competitive. However, after an initial assessment, they suspended the competition without any explanation and called for a second round of bidding. Conceivably, the decision to suspend the project came from General Abacha whose attention was drawn by the sums involved in the construction of up to six LNG trains. After the second round of bidding, the NLNG awarded TSKJ the contract. According to a Nigerian parliamentary interim report, in May 1992 the tender evaluation board recommended that although BSCA submitted the lower bid, TSKJ should receive the contract for reasons of "technical superiority."

Several possible reasons account for the curious delay and reevaluation of bids; they have much to do with changes in Nigerian politics. One reason may have been the shifts that began in 1992; after a period of sectarian violence, disgruntled officers pressured General Ibrahim Babangida to resign.[63] He acceded to their demands in August 1993. His regime gave way to Chief Ernest Shonekon's interim administration. Conceivably, Shonekon had failed to build a sustainable coalition, and factions in the ever-present military demanded a greater share of the benefits from this contract. Shonekon's failure to build a supporting coalition provided Abacha the opportunity to take power and impose his brutal dictatorship.

A second possible reason might have been that Shonekon's unstable administration failed to constrain senior officials accustomed to behaving with impunity. When Dr. Pius Okigbo, chairman of the NLNG Board, abruptly resigned in 1993, he accused an executive at Shell and a senior Nigerian technical advisor of selling insider information.[64] His accusations intimated that the delay was because private firms had paid bribes to pervert the bid evaluations. A third possibility was that when Abacha seized power in November 1993, he suspended the bidding so that he might "review" the contract. Newspaper

---

[63] Rotimi Suberu, *Federalism and Ethnic Conflict in Nigeria* (Washington, DC: United States Institute of Peace Press, 2001), 41.
[64] "Nigeria: Gasmen," *Africa Confidential* 45, 13 (25 June 2004).

reports indicated that it was after Abacha took over that TSKJ allegedly began to funnel money to Nigerian officials.[65] Abacha's rise inaugurated a period when he appointed people to senior offices that would support his extraordinarily corrupt regime. Once he was confident of his security, M.D. Yusufu, chairman of the NLNG board, announced the resumption of a second round of bidding that preceded TSKJ's winning the contract.

Ten years later, investigations to uncover the trail of funds began in Nigeria, France, the United Kingdom, and the United States. From these diverse investigations, it emerged that Albert J. Stanley, an executive at Halliburton, the parent company of Kellogg, Brown, Root, feared TSKJ would lose the contract without some intervention.[66] To prevent that loss, he hired British lawyer Jeffrey Tesler and Tri-Star Company, an offshore firm licensed in Gibraltar, which eventually funneled sums in excess of $180 million to a small number of senior Nigerian officials.[67] Minutes taken at a "cultural meeting" in December 1994 list seven Nigerian officials, including petroleum minister Chief Don Etiebet and others with the phrase "cover directly" next to their names.[68] It is possible to infer that "cover directly" meant to pay these seven Nigerian officials that could have a decisive influence over who would win the contract. Given such efforts, it is hardly surprising that TSKJ won the contract.

News of the scandal first broke in France when magistrates investigating malfeasance involving Elf Aquitaine transmitted evidence of bribe paying by TSKJ to the United States Department of Justice and the United Kingdom's Serious Fraud Office.[69] Shortly thereafter, the U.S. Department of Justice indicted all four consortium partners for Foreign Corrupt Practices Act violations; each firm individually pled guilty for conspiring to pay at least $180 million in bribes to Nigerian officials to secure engineering, procurement, and construction contracts, and settled the cases for millions of dollars in fines.[70] Although the cases settled in Houston in 2010, investigations continued in Nigeria. Indeed, given the outrage expressed by Nigerian journalists, the sums

[65] Achilleus-Chud Uchegbu, "Nigeria: The Halliburton Scandal," *The Daily Champion* (Lagos), (April 10, 2009). Retrieved from http://championonlinenews.com/index.php?lang=en.

[66] Simon Romero and Craig S. Smith, "Halliburton Severs Link with 2 Over Nigeria Inquiry," *The New York Times* (June 19, 2004).

[67] Michael Peel, "Probe into KBR Role in Nigeria Bribe Case," *The Financial Times* (August 7, 2006).

[68] Thomas Catan and Michael Peel, "SEC Widens Nigeria Bribery Probe with Shell Subpoena," *The Financial Times* (October 13, 2005).

[69] Olusegun Adeniyi, "The Alleged NLNG $180 Million Bribe Scandal: The Unanswered Questions ..." *ThisDay Sunday* (September 2, 2010). Retrieved from http://www.thisdayonline.com/; see as well, Michael Peel, "Probe into KBR Role in Nigeria Bribe Case," *The Financial Times* (August 7, 2006).

[70] See the case documents on the settlements negotiated between TSKJ members at http://www.justice.gov/opa/pr/2010/June/10-crm-751.html.

that TSKJ paid officials exceeded accepted norms for bribes even in Nigeria's permissive environment.[71]

The TSKJ scandal highlights issues raised in this book. First, it was a contract that created opportunities for oil industry executives to corrupt negotiations between state agencies, in this case the NLNG, and international corporations. For Nigerian brokers, who are never too far from reminders of their countries' hardship and poverty, the contracts presented a chance to reap large "commissions." Collusion gave these officials privileged positions; oil companies treated them as equals and paid them incredible sums of money in an environment where they felt untouchable.[72] A convergence was evident in the mutual enrichment from this deal; Abacha and his cronies received facilitation fees, and TSKJ got a multibillion-dollar contract. What is critical is that this scandal did not happen in obscurity and fade away. Instead, the impunity that Nigerian officials believed they enjoyed was an illusion, and to this day they remain under investigation and the threat of indictment in Nigeria and the United Kingdom. KBR's Albert Stanley received a sentence of two and a half years for his part in the scandal. In sum, outcomes from the TSKJ scandal, like Ghana's Kosmos controversy, attest to changes in the manner in which companies conduct business in Africa.

POLITICAL MACHINES AND ELECTORAL VIOLENCE IN NIGERIA

A hegemonic party, the PDP, has dominated Nigerian national politics since the democratic transition in 1999. However, in 2013, the PDP began to fracture under the pressures of competing demands from northern politicians and their ostensible colleagues from the south. Patrons of competing political machines compete vigorously during Nigeria's elections. "Godfatherism" is a term coined to describe the patronage politics that became common in Nigeria after its 1999 democratic transition. As some have noted, "The current godfather networks of political elites have modified the more deeply divisive ethnic divisions that undermined the First and Second Republics, leading to a realignment in which godfather-led multiethnic coalitions have emerged."[73] Machines under the godfathers' patronage sponsored gubernatorial candidates and some patrons even ran for seats in the federal government's National Assembly.

The process involved agreements that in exchange for financial support and campaign workers, the candidates/clients promised their patrons money, contracts, and key appointments. As stated, many godfathers were former military

---

[71] Constance Ikokwu, "NLNG Bribery Scandal: British Police Arrest Lawyer," *ThisDay Online* (Lagos) (March 7, 2009). On the cultural norms for corruption, see the excellent study by Daniel Jordan Smith, *A Culture of Corruption: Everyday Deception and Popular Discontent in Nigeria* (Princeton: Princeton University Press, 2007).

[72] Gobind Nankani, "Development Problems of Mineral Exporting Countries," World Bank Staff Working Paper No. 354 (Washington, DC: The World Bank, 1979), 8.

[73] Sklar et al., "Nigeria," 105.

officers or civilian clients of the military regimes that governed Nigeria from 1966 to 1999. These big men had accumulated incredible wealth that they used to fund their political machines and dominate Nigeria's political landscape. In practically, in every state, at least one godfather promotes the political career of a godson who campaigns for governor. Indeed, even in President Goodluck Jonathan's home of Bayelsa State, few disputed the influence of Diepreye Alamieyeseigha despite his arrest and incarceration for embezzlement of millions.[74] Alamieyeseigha's prominence has faded and the flamboyant King A.J. Turner reportedly exerts considerable sway over the president.[75]

In numerous Nigerian states, godfathers ' political machines and the parties they support operate without an ideological orientation; their goals are to build an organization that can win elections and extract wealth from the state. Violence was a strategic choice of individuals active in Nigerian politics. Whether elections, census taking, or decisions over the apportionment of public resources, these processes resulted in brutal outbreaks. People's fears of not receiving their fair share had roots in long-standing ethnoregional hatreds, sectarian conflicts, long periods of military rule, and a civil war.[76] A resort to violence became the preferred strategy of elite politicians to intimidate opponents, win political office, and acquire wealth.[77] It was irrelevant to these individuals that their actions denied a vast majority of Nigeria's people any benefits from a half-century of oil production. Worse, the high levels of corruption rendered the Nigerian state illegitimate. In the Niger Delta, this lack of legitimacy contributed to an extremely volatile and dangerous situation in which groups contested the controversial derivation principle by which the federal government apportions oil revenues.[78] Violence was a routine strategy; it was inseparable from electoral competition, sectarian hatred, and the explosive vigilantism of armed militias that erupted during the 2007 elections, lending a salience to its role in Nigerian politics.

Nigeria is unique among Africa's petrostates for its multiple ethnic divisions, social cleavages, religious conflicts, and the complexity of its political system. The complexity of Nigerian politics stems from the inequities enshrined under colonial administrations. Political competition developed though staggered democratization; first British authorities extended universal suffrage to the Lagos Town Council elections of 1950, then to the Eastern Region during the 1954 parliamentary elections; men could vote in the Western Region's

---

[74] In the Bayelsa State capital, Yenagoa, the main boulevard in the city is the Isaac Adaka Boro Expressway, also called the Alamieyeseigha Road.

[75] Ekanpou Enewardideke, "King Robert Ebizimor's Epic Portrait of A.J. Turner." *The Vanguard* (June 17, 2012).

[76] Toyin Falola, *Colonialism and Violence in Nigeria* (Bloomington and Indianapolis: Indiana University Press, 2009), 171.

[77] Peter M. Lewis, *Growing Apart: Oil, Politics, and Economic Change in Indonesia and Nigeria* (Ann Arbor: The University of Michigan Press, 2007), 78.

[78] Suberu, *Federalism and Ethnic Conflict in Nigeria*, 63–68.

regional elections in 1956, and adult male suffrage was granted in the north during the federal elections of 1959.[79] This democracy in stages influenced the emergence of factions, particularly around influential national leaders that led the regional parties, namely Obafemi Awolowo, Nnamdi Azikiwe, and Ahmadu Bello. By the same token, democracy in stages necessarily created an elite leadership that shared few commonalities with the mass of common Nigerians. During this period of staggered democratization, it is critical to recall that although oil production had begun, it had a minor impact on Nigerian fiscal revenues or elite competition. The driving force behind political competition had its origins in the ethnoregional factionalism that divided Nigeria's governing elite.

Factionalism in contemporary Nigerian society continues to be a competition among big men who use political machines and violence to get some share of the nearly $100 billion the FGN receives from oil production. Competition for the presidency in 2015 has increased with the coalition in the All Progressives' Congress that assembles members of the major opposition parties.[80] In this strategic mix, there is continuity for Nigerian society; the competition among leaders from the key regions is indicative of long-present coalitions. For instance, electoral rivalries were common sources of violence between Awolowo and his principle rival, Samuel Ladoke Akintola; both employed "thugs" to intimidate their rival's followers.[81] During electoral campaigns in the late twentieth century, godfathers behaved much as their predecessors did at the end of British colonialism; they hired violent individuals to beat their rivals. In this critical aspect, the godfathers' political machines represent more continuity than discontinuity. They operate in a fashion similar to strategies that Awolowo, Azikiwe, and Bello adopted as they competed against one another. Joseph's analysis of multiethnic clientelist networks that were crucial actors in Second Republic "prebendal" politics is useful for considering the composition of the political machines that godfathers built to compete in democratic elections in contemporary Nigeria.[82] An ability to compensate clients who support patrons remains at the base of many political economic interactions.

---

[79] Richard L. Sklar, *Nigerian Political Parties: Power in an Emergent African Nation* (Princeton: Princeton University Press, 1963), 30–31.

[80] The APC is a coalition of the Action Congress of Nigeria, the All Nigeria Peoples Party, the All Progressives Grand Alliance, and the Congress for Progressive Change. See *Africa Confidential*, "Nigeria: Inside the presidential fight," 54, 14 (5 July 2013).

[81] Laurent Fourchard, "A New Name for an Old Practice: Vigilantes in Southwestern Nigeria," *Africa* 78, 1 (2008): 28.

[82] Richard A. Joseph, *Democracy and Prebendal Politics in Nigeria: The Rise and Fall of the Second Republic* (New York: Cambridge University Press, 1987), 61; Hoffman, "Fairy Godfathers and Magical Elections," 291. For a contrary argument – that godfathers are agents who promote narrow ethnic interests – see Kamal Bello, "God-Fatherism in the Politics of Nigeria: Continuity and Change," *Canadian Social Science* 7, 2 (2011): 258.

Cult Groups and Violent Gangs

Criminal gangs in twenty-first-century Nigeria have adopted a characterization as "cult groups," indicating the leadership of an individual who decides the gang members' actions. The original cult groups were "confraternities" and self-help associations that university students organized during the 1950s. However, during the 1990s criminal gangs adopted the mantle of cult groups to legitimate their activities in the popular mind.[83] These violent gangs find their origins in the socioeconomic decline that deepened under Abacha's dictatorship; they are criminal organizations active in drug trafficking, petroleum smuggling, and the infamous "419" scams.[84] Members of these gangs are often clients of patrons who co-opt them and direct their activities "not merely as vandals but also as vanguards."[85] Others join cult groups in response to under- or unemployment; in the gangs, they make a living by kidnapping, extortion, theft, and oil bunkering.[86]

It is oil bunkering that provides the greatest profits for cult group members. As Watts remarks, "The organization of the oil theft trade, which by 2004 was a multibillion dollar industry involving high ranking military, government officials and merchants, drew upon the local militia to organize and protect the tapping of pipelines and the movement of barges through the creeks and ultimately offshore to large tankers."[87] Once offloaded on supertankers, the crude has entered the international spot market, where it is untraceable and the criminals may sell it for substantial profit. Although direct evidence is lacking, it is probable that the substantial amounts of money earned through oil bunkering have attracted international criminal organizations that participate in the sale of crude oil siphoned from pipelines in the Niger Delta.[88]

With so much money at stake, it is hardly surprising that violent competition between rival gangs was common during the first decade of the twenty-first century. Approximately 100 gangs are active in the Niger Delta. Among these gangs, at least ten competed for leadership; Chief Ateke Tom's Niger Delta Vigilante and Alhaji Mujahid Dokubo-Asari's Niger Delta People's Volunteer Force were perhaps the most prominent.[89] Both these organizations received

---

[83] Jonathan Matusitz and Michael Repass, "Gangs in Nigeria: An Updated Examination," *Crime, Law, and Social Change* 52, 5 (November 2009): 501.

[84] Peter M. Lewis, "From Prebendalism to Predation: The Political Economy of Decline in Nigeria," *The Journal of Modern African Studies* 34, 1 (March 1996): 90.

[85] David Pratten, "'The Thief Eats His Shame': Practice and Power in Nigerian Vigilantism," *Africa* 78, 1 (2008): 70.

[86] Yomi Oruwari, "Youth in Urban Violence in Nigeria: A Case Study of Urban Gangs from Port Harcourt," Niger Delta Economies of Violence Working Paper No. 14 (University of California, Berkeley: Institute of International Studies, 2006), 3.

[87] Michael J. Watts, "Imperial Oil: The Anatomy of a Nigerian Oil Insurgency," Niger Delta Economies of Violence Working Paper No. 18 (University of California, Berkeley: Institute of International Studies, 2008), 15.

[88] Ribadu and San, *Report of the Petroleum Revenue Special Task Force.*

[89] Matusitz and Repass, "Gangs in Nigeria," 500.

funds from senior politicians in the Port Harcourt-Okira-Kalabari region that they used to buy arms, pay off Nigerian military, and engage in kidnapping, banditry, and other criminal activities.[90] Ateke Tom reportedly netted substantial revenues from oil that he pilfered by tapping a pipeline from a refinery and running a tributary pipeline directly to his hideout in Rivers State.[91] His clever strategy indicated inventiveness as well as a shocking sense of impunity among gang leaders. After the 2009 amnesty, Ateke Tom continued to exert political pressure from his position as a leader of a militant group and prominent Ijaw activist.

Once the amnesty for Niger Delta militants went into effect in 2009, some of the leaders, notably Dokubo-Asari, who entered mainstream politics as president of the Ijaw Council in Bayelsa State and a leader of the PDP's South-South regional faction. In May 2013, Dokubo-Asari took national attention when he threatened that he was ready to fight "bullet for bullet" to defend Goodluck Jonathan's presidency.[92] Dokubo-Asari's threats are indicative of the subcurrents of ethnic competition in Nigeria. Indeed, the cult groups active in the South-South region are only one set of actors among a plethora of violent groups that increase instability and uncertainty in the subregion.[93]

The prospect of expulsion from one of the cult groups means nothing less than loss of status, unemployment, and destitution. As a consequence, the stakes are high. In Nigeria's turbulent democracy, elections have included incidents of fierce combat between different gangs who support godfathers. Gangs include young men from the Niger Delta as well as the other cult groups that are active in Southwestern Nigeria, such as the Oodua People's Congress (OPC). Frederick Fasehun established the Yoruba-based OPC in 1994 after Abacha arrested and jailed Chief Moshood Abiola on trumped-up charges, the real reason being that Abiola had probably won the 1993 presidential elections.[94] In 1999, a splinter faction led by Gani Adams radicalized the OPC; Adams accused Igbo merchants of having taken over the Alaba market in Lagos and called for their expulsion from Southwestern Nigeria, with violence if necessary.[95]

Cult groups included a number of people who established monopolistic criminal organizations with the sole purpose of making money through illegal

---

[90] Michael J. Watts, "Petro-Insurgency or Criminal Syndicate? Conflict, Violence and Political Disorder in the Niger Delta," Niger Delta Economies of Violence Working Paper No. 16 (University of California, Berkeley: Institute of International Studies, 2006), 22.

[91] BBC, "Nigeria oil rebel pipeline found," BBC (March 11, 2008).

[92] Emma Amaize and Akpokona Omafuaire, "2015: Dokubo Vows to Fight Opposition, Bullet for Bullet," *The Vanguard* (May 22, 2013).

[93] Emma Arubi, "Tension in Delta as Ijaw Youths Kill 4 Itsekiri," *The Vanguard* (July 03, 2013).

[94] Yvan Guichaoua, "The Making of an Ethnic Militia: The Oodua People's Congress in Nigeria," CRISE Working Paper No. 26 (Oxford: Centre for Research in Inequality, Human Security and Ethnicity, November 2006), 9.

[95] Wale Adebanwi, "The Carpenter's Revolt: Youth, Violence and the Reinvention of Culture in Nigeria," *The Journal of Modern African Studies* 43, 3 (September 2005): 359.

activities.[96] Cult groups tended to be unstable; in the early twenty-first century, the Hizbah, the Egbesu Boys, and the Bekassi Boys from Aba in Abia State were among their members. Although the Bekassi Boys gang started as a civic organization, it soon became a criminal organization.[97] Their members participated in racketeering organizations that provided protection, and under a threat of kidnapping and violence extorted payment from oil companies in the Niger Delta. Although competing cult groups try to monopolize criminal activities in a given subregion, they also engage in both plunder and protection, or what Mehlum et al. have called the "protection screw."[98] The protection screw implies that the gangsters participate in outright theft of oil and demanding payments from oil companies as a protection racket. These gangs differ markedly from criminal organizations such as the Sicilian mafia, which enforced property rights to ensure their monopoly over protection.[99] The cult groups were indifferent to stabilizing property rights; they engaged in criminal activities that stretched from Nigeria throughout West Africa, Europe, and even North America. Their actions so increased uncertainty in the oil sector that they compelled many international companies to cease production, declare a force majeure in the execution of their contracts, and otherwise exit the Nigerian market. Indeed, an inability to stem these criminal activities prompted Shell and ChevronTexaco to sell some of their onshore assets in the Niger Delta in 2013.[100]

In the background of the Niger Delta conflict is competition among oil companies from various countries around the world. These companies seek oil mining leases (OMLs) and percentage shares of production contracts. Their competition for Nigeria's oil blocs creates incentives for deals with domestic groups that might influence deliberations over the awarding of coveted licenses and contracts. Although no evidence exists of Asian NOCs interfering in Nigerian domestic politics, the CNOOC's reported efforts to purchase 6 billion barrels of Nigerian crude for $30–$50 billion (between $50 and $83 a barrel) indicates just how high the stakes in this competition have become.[101] Second, this offer was indicative of an intense battle to dominate the quality reserves in Nigeria. In sum, conflicts in the Niger Delta, although tragic for its

[96] Thomas C. Schelling, "Economics and Criminal Enterprise," *The Public Interest* 7 (Spring 1967): 63.

[97] Kate Meagher, "Highjacking Civil Society: The Inside Story of the Bekassi Boys Vigilante Group of South Eastern Nigeria," *The Journal of Modern African Studies* 45, 1 (2007): 93.

[98] Halvor Mehlum, Karl Ove Moene, and Ragnar Torvik, "Plunder and Protection Inc.," *Journal of Peace Research* 39, 4 (July 2002): 448.

[99] Diego Gambetta, *The Sicilian Mafia: The Business of Private Protection* (Cambridge, MA: Harvard University Press, 1993).

[100] For one example, see Benoît Faucon, "Nigerian Oil Thefts Prompt Shell to Act," *Wall Street Journal* (April 12, 2013); Chineme Okafor, "Chevron to Sell 40% Stake in Two Oil Blocks," *ThisDay* (June 12, 2013).

[101] Tom Burgis, "China Seeks Big Stake in Nigerian Oil," *The Financial Times* (September 28, 2009).

inhabitants, permit the potential entry of new players among the international oil companies.

Godfathers, Political Machines, and Presidential Elections

By the time of Sani Abacha's death in June 1998, the Nigerian state had practically collapsed. The Abacha regime had been extraordinarily predatory; it diverted large sums of money to personal accounts the president and his cronies controlled, disregarding social-sector expenditures.[102] Clientelist networks were pervasive; big men used their positions to manipulate politics so they could engage in flagrantly corrupt behavior. Security officers, local officials, and "barons" engaged in high-profit schemes that involved the sale of crude oil bunkered the Niger Delta.[103] Meanwhile, violent gangs roamed the countryside terrorizing common citizens. In the Niger Delta and Southwestern Nigeria, cult groups openly contested the state's monopoly on the means of violence. Many groups operated under the protection of patrons for whom they served as enforcers, and they imposed terror in towns and cities. In the North, fundamentalist groups, notably the Boko Haram, attacked "non-believers" and aggravated a sense of instability.[104] Conceivably, the Nigerian state risked collapse, but the causes of conflict were more in long-term competition among diverse groups; oil played a secondary role.

In the months that followed former General Olusegun Obasanjo's 1999 election, politicians attempted to reverse the failures that had occurred under Abacha. The challenges were daunting because Obasanjo confronted individuals with a direct stake in preserving the status quo. Foremost among those who were contesting the state's hegemony were the godfathers, the former military officers, and civilians who had plundered the state during the Abacha regime. As the crisis in Anambra State after the 2007 elections showed, the stakes of keeping unfettered access to resources and influence in national politics encouraged individuals such as Chief Chris Uba to engage in outlandish behavior.[105] His principal challenge was to ensure that his elected clients honored his agreement to compensate the machine adequately. When Dr. Chris Ngige reneged on his pledges, godfather Uba retaliated with litigation, smear campaigns, and violence.[106]

---

[102] Lewis notes that between 1988 and 1993, the Abacha regime diverted $12.2 billion to off-budget accounts, a sum that equaled 20 percent of total earnings. Lewis, "From Prebendalism to Predation," 92.

[103] Ribadu and San, *Report of the Petroleum Revenue Special Task Force*, 123.

[104] Adam Nossiter, "Killings in Nigeria Are Linked to Islamic Sect," *The New York Times* (October 18, 2010).

[105] Hoffman, "Fairy Godfathers and Magical Elections," 306.

[106] Mamman Lawan, "Abuse of Powers of Impeachment in Nigeria," *The Journal of Modern African Studies* 48, 2 (June 2010): 325.

Events in Anambra State after the 2003 gubernatorial election aptly illustrate the influence of Nigeria's godfathers.[107] Chris Uba had funded Ngige's campaign in which his gangs had served as foot soldiers during the electoral season. In return for Uba's help, Ngige agreed, reportedly in writing, to provide his godfather with contracts and money. As a condition for his backing, Uba had required Ngige to sign a resignation letter that Uba would produce should Ngige fail to honor their agreement. Immediately after the elections, Uba demanded over £16 million and, probably to his astonishment, the newly elected governor refused. The godfather produced the resignation letter and tried to remove Ngige from office. A crisis ensued that only ended after the intervention of traditional religious authorities. Ngige remained in office, but Uba retained significant leverage over the governor. This incident highlighted the godfathers' extraordinary power and how political machines influenced outcomes in state governments around Nigeria. Such clashes played out even further in the 2007 presidential elections that many observers deemed neither free nor fair.

In 2006, the supposedly reformist President Obasanjo attempted to reverse constitutional term limits that denied him a third term. On May 16, 2006, the Nigerian senate ended his attempt to change the Federal Constitution, and Obasanjo's bid for a third term ended.[108] Upon hearing the announcement that Obasanjo could not run, candidates scrambled for campaign finance and assembled political organizations. Among their benefactors were the godfathers that sponsored candidates and mobilized militia to get control of the electoral processes in their states.[109] Within a short period, godfathers sent their cult groups into battle, pushing Nigeria once again toward anarchy. Nigeria's 2007 elections were extraordinarily violent by any measure; campaign strategies included kidnapping, beatings, and threats.[110]

The elections were primarily a contest between Obasanjo's chosen successor, Alhaji Umaru Yar'Adua for the PDP and General Mohammed Buhari's All Nigerian Peoples Party. In April 2007, the Nigerians cast votes in 36 states and 774 local governments. It was no surprise that Obasanjo's PDP swept the elections; Yar'Adua received 24,638,063 votes or over 70 percent of the electorate; he defeated 24 other candidates led by his two closest rivals, General Buhari and Alhaji Abubakar Atiku, who received a combined count of 9,243,143 or less than 27 percent. Yar'Adua's PDP had won twenty-nine of the thirty-six governorships and an overwhelming majority in the

---

[107] The description of this incident comes from Smith, *A Culture of Corruption*, 125–130, and Hoffman, "Fairy Godfathers and Magical Elections," 285–310.

[108] Dino Mahtani, "Nigerian Senate Rules Out Third Term for Leader," *The Financial Times* (May 17, 2006).

[109] International Crisis Group, "Nigeria's Elections: Avoiding a Political Crisis," Africa Report No 123 (March 28, 2007): 9.

[110] National Democratic Institute, *Final NDI Report on Nigeria's 2007 Elections* (Washington, DC: The National Democratic Institute, 2008), 26.

congressional elections.[111] However, multiple reports on the elections support a conclusion that they had been fraught with "massive irregularities and electoral malpractices," and were inexcusably violent, blatantly corrupt, and in effect, "a charade."[112]

When international observers condemned the 2007 presidential elections as neither free nor fair, President Elect Yar'Adua conceded that opponents were free to challenge elections in the courts;[113] nothing happened. The elections thus "cast a harsh and very public light on patterns of violence, corruption, and outright criminality that have come to characterize Nigeria's political system – and on the extent to which officials and institutions at all levels of government accept, encourage, and participate in those abuses."[114] To a tragic extent, the patronage system that emerged among the political machines in Nigeria has hoisted into positions of prominence godfathers who sponsored political candidates in return for contracts, opportunities, and influence. An effect has been the splintering of Nigeria's political arena into fiefdoms dominated by godfathers who demonstrate little interest in economic development or democracy.

Despite this pessimistic assessment, international observers praised the April 2011 elections as free and fair. According to Akhaine, "A distinct level of political will and patriotism, buttressed by meaningful contributions from citizens, the civil service, and the military all came together to make Nigeria's 2011 elections a success story."[115] Whereas the 2007 elections had fostered violent competition among various factions, in 2011, diverse groups campaigned with relative calm for office. The peaceful electoral process had positive implications for Nigeria's democratic future that implied a probability that the country would enjoy pluralist elections. In these elections, political machines emerged and assembled groups and individuals who campaigned for elected office. This competition indicates a probability that cross-cutting cleavages long present in Nigerian society have shifted the "giant" toward democratic elections.

A CLAN-BASED POLITICAL MACHINE: GABON

French oil companies found oil in colonial Gabon in the Ozouri field in 1956. According to 2011 estimates, Gabon possesses reserves that contain approximately 3.7 billion barrels.[116] Oil became the primary source of government

[111] J. Shola Omotola, "'Garrison' Democracy in Nigeria: The 2007 General Elections and the Prospects of Democratic Consolidation," *Commonwealth and Comparative Politics* 47, 2 (April 2009): 195.

[112] National Democratic Institute, *Final NDI Report on Nigeria's 2007 Elections*, 65.

[113] Matthew Green, "Court Challenge Tests Yar'Adua Ambitions," *Financial Times* (December 6, 2007).

[114] Human Rights Watch, *Criminal Politics*, 16.

[115] Sylvester Odion Akhaine, "Nigeria's 2011 Elections: The 'Crippled Giant' Learns to Walk," *African Affairs* 110, 441 (October 2011): 649.

[116] Cheikh Gueye, "Gabon's Experience Managing Oil Wealth," in *Oil Wealth in Central Africa: Policies for Inclusive Growth*, eds. Bernardin Akitoby and Sharmini Coorey (Washington, DC: The International Monetary Fund, 2012), 197.

revenue and represented a substantial portion of Gabon's overall GDP.[117] Gabon began its postindependence under a concessionary fiscal regime that paid the government via royalties; this regime shifted to PSCs in 1982 and resource revenues paid to the Direction Générale des Hydrocarbures were in the form of royalties, cost oil, and profit oil, as discussed in Chapter 3.[118] Management of this absolutely critical sector, however, rested in the central government, specifically under the president and his appointees. Hence, economic development in Gabon attests to the primacy of politics.

Political machines emerged in Africa around neopatrimonial leaders who captured the petrostate to seek wealth and influence in their countries. In Gabon, Albert Bernard Bongo (he would later take the name Omar Bongo Ondimba) established a political machine that endured for more than three decades. He became an extraordinarily wealthy man and succeeded in embedding his clan into the elite positions in Gabon. Bongo was born in December 1935 in Lewai, a modest village in Southeastern Gabon. He was a member of the Téké people, one of the three major ethnic groups in Gabon. A talented student, Bongo finished his secondary education, joined the colonial civil service, and moved to Brazzaville, the capital of French Equatorial Africa. In Brazzaville, Bongo began a lifelong association with Freemasonry that he continued and deepened after his return to Libreville.

His ability to establish important relationships came to the attention of Léon M'ba. In 1963, the then-President M'ba named the talented twenty-eight-year-old Bongo his chief of staff.[119] Two years later, M'ba designated Bongo his successor. The aging M'ba made this decision in spite of Jacques Foccart's discomfort with what he perceived to be Bongo's autocratic tendencies; Foccart expressed his discomfort to M'ba in various meetings between 1965 and 1967.[120] Having put Bongo in charge of national defense, M'ba evidently saw his chief of staff as capable of leading the country, especially after an attempted coup in 1964 that failed only because of French intervention.[121] Jean-Hilaire Aubame, M'ba's long-time rival since before independence, tried to take power from what he considered a Fang presidency with a Batéké chief of staff.[122] Bongo used the coup attempt to establish an authoritarian state in

---

[117] World Bank, "Republic of Gabon: Public Expenditure Management and Financial Accountability Review (PEMFAR)," Poverty Reduction and Economic Management Unit (PREM3), Africa Region (Washington, DC: The World Bank, September 20, 2006), 10.

[118] Gueye, "Gabon's Experience Managing Oil Wealth," 199.

[119] Omar Bongo, *Blanc Comme Nègre: Entretiens avec Airy Routier* (Paris: Éditions Grasset & Fasquelles, 2001), 32–34.

[120] Jacques Foccart, *Tous les Soirs avec de Gaulle: Journal de l'Elysée – I: 1965 – 1967* (Paris: Librairie Arthème Fayard, 1997), 58.

[121] Bongo, *Blanc Comme Nègre: Entretiens avec Airy Routier*, 65.

[122] Claude Wauthier, *Quatre Presidents et l'Afrique: De Gaulle, Pompidou, Giscard d'Estaing, Mitterrand* (Paris: Éditions du Seuil, 1995), 125.

Gabon.[123] Hence, when M'ba died in 1967, Bongo succeeded him as president and immediately began to build a political machine to dominate Gabonese politics and society.

The 1964 attempted coup apparently convinced Bongo that security was crucial, and he actively discouraged political competition.[124] Most importantly, he set up a political machine that distributed opportunities to a select number of relatives or members of his inner cadre. Ostensibly, it was through the Parti Démocratique gabonaise (PDG) that the president established in 1968 as his primary political organization. It comprised trade unions, student associations, and business groups under a banner of party-affiliated organizations. Anyone who wished to succeed in Gabon had to transit in some manner through the PDG. However, the foundation on which the regime functioned was an autocracy that Bongo dominated, and after several decades used to employ his more than fifty children, their spouses, and members of his clan. In effect, the PDG provided an organization that citizens joined; meanwhile, the Bongo system embraced an exclusive coalition that received fortunes; the common Gabonese remained agrarian and poor.[125]

The "Bongo System"[126]

By the time Bongo died in 2009, members of his machine had long enjoyed an impunity that allowed them to accumulate millions of Euros. Bongo's organization rested on five crucial elements of rule. First, he distributed senior offices according to ethnicity; his prime minister was Fang, the National Assembly's president was Myènè, and Bongo was a member of the Téké group.[127] Second, Bongo ruled through a coalition of loyal followers. For example, Georges Rawiri and Léon Mébiane were ministers of state, Michel Teale was his military chief of staff, and the intellectual Jean Ping drafted treatises to justify the PDG's rule and the distribution of economic benefits to supporters and potential opponents.[128] His machine depended on a neopatrimonial system on the

[123] Jean-François Obiang, *France-Gabon: Pratiques Clientélaires d'État dans les Relations Franco-Africaines* (Paris: Éditions Karthala 2007), 129; see as well, Douglas A. Yates, *The Rentier State in Africa: Oil Rent Dependency and Neocolonialism in the Republic of Gabon* (Trenton, NJ: Africa World Press, 1996), 114.

[124] Obiang, *France-Gabon*, 131; Bongo, *Blanc Comme Nègre: Entretiens avec Airy Routier*, 76.

[125] David E. Gardinier, "Gabon: Limited Reform and Regime Survival," in *Political Reform in Francophone Africa*, eds. John F. Clark and David E. Gardinier (Boulder: Westview Press, 1997), 148.

[126] The term "Bongo System" is from Pierre Péan, *Affaires africaines* (Paris: Librarie Arthème Fayard, 1983), 93.

[127] Obiang, *France-Gabon*, 139.

[128] Jacques Foccart, *Foccart Parle: Entretiens avec Philippe Gaillard* (Paris: Librairie Arthème Fayard, 1995), 281; Gardinier, "Gabon: Limited Reform and Regime Survival," 146.

basis of personal rule that a network of loyal barons supported.[129] Third, in his domestic politics, Bongo used the PDG as the sole political party. In so doing, he followed the example of Côte d'Ivoire's Félix Houphouët-Boigny, whose single party controlled Ivoirian politics after independence. Like Houphouët, Bongo used the PDG for elite recruitment and as an instrument to restrict access to the political arena.

International agreements with French firms constituted the fourth element of the Bongo system. His regime maintained and deepened bilateral economic agreements that M'ba had signed before independence. Bongo extended guarantees to the French national oil company Elf Aquitaine that it could count on continued access to Gabon's oil.[130] In his foreign policy, Bongo reinforced personal relations with French President Charles de Gaulle, Jacques Foccart, and Pierre Guillaumat, head of Elf Aquitaine; he even made contributions to French political parties.[131] This pattern of support and campaign contributions for the governing French president and whoever managed Elf Aquitaine continued throughout Bongo's lengthy administration. Indeed, after "the collapse in Brazzaville, the historic fiefdom of French influence in Equatorial Africa, the explosion in Côte d'Ivoire repositioned Gabon as the pillar of the French influence in Central Africa."[132] Accordingly, President Ali Bongo Ondimba has carefully protected his close relations with French mining and oil companies.

The Bongo system depended on oil revenues that funded the political machine and financed a system of rewards for regime insiders. Outsiders, such as agricultural producers who contributed few tax revenues, were a burden and a drain on oil wealth; accordingly, they received practically nothing, and most lived in extreme poverty.[133] Because Bongo's Gabon was a rentier economy, his machine could ignore impoverished people in the countryside without political or economic repercussions. It is likely that in Gabon's post-oil environment, various networks inside and outside the state may carry greater relevance for opportunities and wealth.

Family and clan relations constituted the fifth element of the Bongo system. Over time, Bongo's many children replaced some barons in the key appointments of the Gabonese state. Foremost was his eldest daughter and chief of

---

[129] Michael Bratton and Nicolas van de Walle, "Neopatrimonial Regimes and Regime Transitions in Africa," *World Politics* 46, 4 (July 1994): 458. On the Bongo barons, see Jean-Pierre Tuquoi, "La bande à Bongo," *Le Monde* (27 Novembre 2005); see also the biographies in "Gabon: Les 50 Hommes et Femmes qui Comptent," *JA l'Intelligent* No 2191 (11 Janvier 2003): 51–83.

[130] Péan, *Affaires Africaines*, 96–98.

[131] On French-Gabonese relations, a popular literature has appeared under the theme of françafrique. Perhaps the first example is Péan's contribution in *Affaires africaines*; see as well, François-Xavier Verschave, *La Françafrique: Le Plus Long Scandale de la République* (Paris: Éditions Stock, 1998).

[132] Florence Bernault and Joseph Tonda, "Le Gabon: Une dystopia tropicale," *Politique Africaine* 115 (Octobre 2009): 15.

[133] Yates, *The Rentier State in Africa*, 155; The World Bank, "Republic of Gabon: Poverty in a Rent-Based Economy," Report 16333-GA, vol. 2 (Washington: The World Bank, 1997), 18.

staff, Pascaline, who, before entering government service, had attended the University of Southern California and the prestigious French graduate school the École nationale d'administration. As chief of staff, she was the ultimate gatekeeper who controlled access to the president.[134] Second, Bongo's wife Edith Lucie Sassou Bongo Ondimba, daughter of Denis Sassou-Nguesso, took care to ensure the security of her children. She was a discrete influence over the president's decisions. Third, Omar Bongo's son Ali rotated through numerous ministerial positions; when his father died in 2009, he became the president. Other key children include Jeff Bongo, Christian Bongo, Anicet Bongo, Martin Bongo, and children from liaisons outside either of his marriages. His more than fifty children are active at various decision-making levels in policy circles and businesses. For instance, like his father, Ali Bongo is influential in Gabon's Masonic order that ensured close relations with French investors.[135] He and his many siblings represent critical continuities in Gabonese politics.

Masonic Networks in Gabon

Freemasonry has long been a critical element of elite recruitment in Gabon. Since colonialism, the leaders of many francophone African states were freemasons.[136] French freemasons who belonged to the Grand Loge de France opened l'Orient de Saint Louis du Sénégal, Africa's first lodge, in February 1824.[137] Other lodges soon followed; in 1904, lodges opened in Libreville and Brazzaville.[138] Advocates of colonialism, Jules Ferry, Léon Gambetta, and Maurice Viollette, publisher of the *Annales Coloniales* and chairman of the Union of Socialist Free Masons, sought "evolved Africans" as recruits for Masonic lodges.[139] However, during the 1930s divisions in France between leftist and conservative political parties led dissident freemasons of the Grand Orient de France to establish the conservative Grand Loge National de France (GLNF).[140] After World War II, Gaullist politicians joined the GLNF as an alternative to the socialist Grand Orient de France (GODF). This lodge rapidly spread to Africa and recruited a number of young elites.

---

[134] Tuquoi, "La Bande à Bongo."

[135] Christophe Boltanski, "Ali Bongo Grand Maître du Gabon: La franc-maçonnerie est l'un des piliers du régime gabonaise." *Nouvel Observateur* (29 Octobre 2009).

[136] Axel Augé, "Jeunes, Jeunesse et Intégration des Élites Politique au Gabon: La Place des Trajectoires Sociales Individuelles," *Afrique Contemporaine* 213 (Hiver 2005a): 197–215.

[137] Daniel Béresniak and Joseph Badiila with Jean Moreau, *Les Francs-Maçons et l'Afrique* (Paris: Éditions Detrad, 2008), 34.

[138] Joseph Badila, La Franc-Maçonnerie en Afrique Noire: Un Si Long Chemin Vers la Liberté, l'Égalité, la Fraternité (Paris: Éditions Detrad, 2004), 24–26.

[139] Georges Odo, *La Franc-Maçonnerie en Afrique* (Paris: Éditions Maçonniques de France, 2000), 26–29.

[140] Pierre Chevallier, *Histoire de la Franc-Maçonnerie française*, vol. 3, *La Maçonnerie: l'Église de la République (1877–1944)* (Paris: Fayard, 1974), 165.

Elite French politicians and business executives meet at Masonic lodges to informally discuss production contracts and economic arrangements.[141] In the lodges, they might meet prominent African freemasons including Cameroon's Paul Biya, Congolese Sassou-Nguesso, Chadian Déby, Burkinabè Blaise Compaoré, Central African Republic's François Bozizé, Nigerien Mamadou Tandja, and Senegalese President Abdoulaye Wade.[142] As France encountered increasing competition from North American and Asian oil companies, these informal bonds became increasingly important. It is hardly surprising that French freemasons included such individuals as Andre Tarallo, Charles Pasqua, and Fernand Wibaux on the right and Roland Dumas, Pierre Joxe, and Loïk le Floch Prigent on the left.[143] Given the dynamic nature of competition among various oil companies in Africa, the role of Masonic recruitment is part of a larger pattern of building identities for francophone African leaders.

Omar Bongo wove Masonic lodges into Gabonese politics; he embedded members of the semi-secret organization in the state and as key players in his system of rule.[144] To join Bongo's political machine, ambitious individuals had to belong to the Masonic network; Masonic connections were essential in building personal relations with diplomats and executives employed by Elf.[145] Bongo himself benefitted from personal relations with various French presidents, their staffs, and close friendships with fellow Masons.[146] Even minor officials had to join the Grand Loge du Gabon.[147] After Omar Bongo's death, Ali Bongo succeeded him as Grand Master of Gabon's Masonic order.[148] Indeed, an understanding of the persistence of freemasonry as a sociopolitical force in Gabon is critical to any explanation of democracy and development in the Central African petrostate.

Pressures to Democratize in Gabon

In 1990, pressures to democratize increased in francophone Africa. The Berlin Wall had fallen and Benin held its famous 1990 national conference that moved the country toward an ostensibly democratic transition. Rawiri, with characteristic prescience, advised Bongo to hold a national conference and announce his intention to allow multiparty elections.[149] A national conference preceded

---

[141] Sophie Coignard, *Un État dans l'État: Le Contre Pouvoir Maçonnique* (Paris: Albin Michel, 2009), 277.

[142] Boltanski, "Ali Bongo Grand Maître du Gabon."

[143] A substantial literature exists in the French media about the freemasons' secretive nature and the elite politicians who enter the orders.

[144] Axel Eric Augé, *Le Recrutement des Élites Politiques en Afrique Subsaharienne: Une Sociologie de Pouvoir au Gabon* (Paris: Éditions de l'Harmattan, 2005b), 217–219.

[145] Obiang, *France-Gabon*, 128.

[146] Péan, *Affaires Africaines*, 93.

[147] Augé, *Le Recrutement des Élites Politiques en Afrique Subsaharienne*, 214.

[148] Boltanski, "Ali Bongo Grand Maître du Gabon."

[149] Gérard Conac, "Les Processus de Démocratisation en Afrique," in *L'Afrique en Transition vers le Pluralisme Politique*, ed. Gérard Conac (Paris: Economica, 1993), 37.

announcements of elections that would follow the rules in France's Fifth Republic. In November 1993, Bongo won 51.07 percent of the votes in the first round.[150] Although it is impossible to know whether the elections were fair, the decision to open political space for competing parties introduced norms of competitive authoritarianism into Gabonese politics.

The 1993 elections opened the gates to competition, and over the next decade Bongo's political machine came under attack from disgruntled barons who used their clientelist networks to establish political parties to contest his rule. His barons' children had grown into adults who demanded benefits for themselves and their families. These people represented the emergence of a nascent middle class, the members of which wanted greater voice and political representation. For example, former baron Zacharie Myboto's daughter, Chantal, had intimate relations with the president, her sister Suzanne had married Landry Bongo, and another sister, Yolande, married one of Bongo's nephews.[151] Myboto organized an opposition party to run for president in the 2005 elections. Although he lost the elections by a significant margin, his campaign represented a first attempt by a former baron to pry political office away from the exclusive Bongo political machine.

Bongo's reaction to increasing competition illustrated shifts in Gabon's political landscape. For instance, during the 2005 campaign, the president tried to silence his opponents when he asked the Paris government to share the names of Gabonese political candidates who, while in France, spoke out against his administration or its relationship with French interests.[152] He warned his opponents that they would face prosecution for defamation upon their return to Libreville. Second, he used the powers of incumbency to visit hitherto ignored regions; helicopters would land in remote locations and Bongo, his Moroccan bodyguards, soldiers from the presidential guard, and clansmen would disembark, hand out gifts to local populations, and then depart.[153] Third, Bongo had come to understand that international observers would not believe election results that showed 99 percent of the votes in favor of any one candidate. However, he was unwilling to subject his position to a second round of voting should he receive less than 51 percent of the vote. Accordingly, the reported 2005 election results gave Bongo 79 percent of the vote, Pierre Mamboundou 13.5 percent, and Myboto only 6.5 percent; a number of other candidates shared the rest.[154] His machine prevailed and set forth the conditions for Ali Bongo's succession.

---

[150] AFP, "Le Président Gabonais Omar Bongo Ondimba, Doyen des Chefs d'Etat Africains" (29 Novembre 2005).

[151] Tuquoi, "La Bande à Bongo."

[152] Philippe Bernard, "M. Bongo Veut Faire Taire l'Opposition à Paris," *Le Monde* (22 Septembre 2005).

[153] Jean-Pierre Tuquoi, "Au Pouvoir au Gabon Depuis 1967, Omar Bongo s'Offre dans les Urnes un Nouveau Septennat," *Le Monde* (27 Novembre 2005).

[154] AFP, "Réélection sans Surprise du President Omar Bongo Ondimba au Gabon," *Le Monde* (30 Novembre 2005).

Whereas practices that ensure transparency and accountability underlie legitimate governments, in Gabon these concepts are quite foreign. It is in obscurity that oil revenues enter the treasury, decisions are made as to who may withdraw funds from government accounts, and who participates in contractual negotiations. Bongo, his clan, and cronies amassed a fortune during his rule. For example, when Transparency International filed lawsuits in France that accused Bongo of sheltering corruptly acquired gains in French banks, he ignored the litigation as just another maneuver – harassment by his opponents.[155] An appeals court in Paris dismissed these charges with the comment that the courts in France had no jurisdiction over foreign heads of government.[156] Transparency International's efforts must have seemed an illegitimate attempt to impose foreign notions of accountability on the Gabonese state. Indeed, the subsequent decision to reopen the case threatens to make public the extent of the clan's fortune and its attempts to hide ill-gotten gains.[157]

When Omar Bongo Ondimba died on June 8, 2009, he left behind a neopatrimonial political machine. After all, Gabon was his fiefdom; he managed its oil wealth as if it were entirely his own; its citizens were his subjects upon whom he would, on rare occasions, bestow his presence. To quote the obituary from the British weekly *The Economist*:

On the Atlantic coast of Gabon, white sand beaches slope out into the ocean. That sand, in which few tourists leave their footprints, was Omar Bongo's. Elephants and buffalo stroll down to the water, and leatherback turtles make their nests: his elephants, his buffalo, his turtles. Oil rigs and gas flares punctuate the horizon: his oil, 3.2 billion barrels in proven reserves. Eastwards, the silver carriages of the world's most expensive railway rattle five times a week through his hardwood forests between Libreville, the capital, and Franceville, in his homeland, carrying loads of his manganese or piled high with his *okoumé* and *ozigo* logs, bound mostly for China. Mr. Bongo made no distinction between Gabon and his private property.[158]

Democracy and a Post-Oil Gabon

The prospects for democracy in post-oil Gabon are fragile, and depend on the government's willingness to open the political economy to a variety of actors. Although Gabon has enjoyed the highest per capita income in Africa,

---

[155] This story that detailed the seizure of 4.2 million euros in various bank accounts in Paris first broke in Bordeaux's daily newspaper, "Les Comptes d'Omar Bongo Saisit à Paris," *SudOuest* (26 février 2009). Other papers, notably *Le Figaro* and *Le Monde*, quickly picked up the story.

[156] AFP, "Biens Mal Acquis: La Justice Refuse l'Ouverture d'une Enquête," *Libération* (29 Octobre 2009).

[157] Philippe Bernard, "L'Enquête sur les 'Bien Mal Acquis' par Trios Potentates d'Afrique Sera Rouvert," *Le Monde* (11 Novembre 2010).

[158] Rex Features, "Omar Bongo Ondimba, President of Gabon, Died on June 8, Aged 73," *The Economist* (June 18, 2009).

the wealthiest quintile of its population receives half of the national income.[159] Although this income distribution may resemble even developed economies, the difference in the level of poverty equals levels found in the poorest African countries. The Bongo clan's near absolute domination of politics resulted in this misdistribution of wealth; funds paid for the extraction of hydrocarbons enriched the governing coalition and its elite politicians. In 2012, estimates were that Gabon's declining oil reserves might be productive for another forty years. However, the governing clique has come under pressure for more inclusive rule, more equity in expenditure distribution, better budget management, and an improved business climate.[160]

Ali Bongo confronts two contradictory choices. First, he needs to improve his non-oil economic performance. An improvement in non-oil growth means the state may expect a dependence on taxes for its fiscal revenues. This dependence on tax revenues means that citizens need to support the state. Hence, Bongo's political system will need to be more inclusive. Second, he needs to ensure that his opponents do not expel him and his clan from the administration. The Bongo clan's strategy has encouraged regime insiders to create ostensibly rival political parties. For example, Victoire Lasséni Duboze, a regime insider who had served as a minister, was a candidate for the presidency. She had resigned from the ruling PDG ostensibly to run against Ali Bongo. Duboze competed against a number of candidates including Paul Mba Abessole (Le Rassemblement pour le Gabon – the majority party), Pierre Mamboundou (L'Union du Peuple Gabonaise), and Zacharie Myboto (L'Union Gabonaise pour la Démocratie et le Développement). This strategy prevents the emergence of a viable candidate who could unify the opposition. Having numerous candidates campaign for the presidency ensured that Ali Bongo would receive more than fifty percent in the first round of the 2009 elections. The opposition remained fragmented, and Ali Bongo handily won the elections.

Once in office, Ali Bongo effectively employed the strategies of rule his father had perfected. A critical difference, however, and one that is indicative of creeping democracy, is the increasing number of political parties, some of which represent productive non-oil economic sectors. For example, the loggers had established a party called the Rassemblement National des Bûcherons (RNB; the National Woodcutters' Rally). This party grouped actors in Gabon's tropical wood sector. Although Gabonese timber production declined in the early twenty-first century, reportedly because of blatant inefficiencies and corruption, the political power of the RNB and its offshoots remains a potent force that the Bongo government acknowledges.[161] How political competition changes when the oil is gone is contingent on the extent to which incremental

---

[159] IMF, "Ghana: 2010 Article IV Consultation – Staff Report" (Washington: International Monetary Fund, May 2011), 4.
[160] Gueye, "Gabon's Experience Managing Oil Wealth," 211–212.
[161] AFP, "Le Secteur du Bois, Stratégique pour l'Économie Gabonaise, en Plein Crise."

democratization in a context of competitive authoritarianism occurs. However, demands for more inclusive rule from within the governing clan and others outside may be expected to increase as Gabon's population grows and people want more opportunities for themselves and their children.

CONCLUSION

This chapter has addressed the relationship between political machines and democratic institutions in African petrostates. It has evaluated this relationship in the context of whether a state is a mature (Nigeria) or declining producer (Gabon). The issue of machine politics matters because political organizations take their impetus from historic relationships and use machines to create neo-patrimonial regimes. Each of these cases has particularities that make them somewhat distinct, but similar in their political and economic development.

Ghana provides a contrasting case. Ghanaian economic performance had been impressive even before Tullow Oil discovered the reserves in the Jubilee field. As an emerging producer, the West African petrostate might have expected destructive rent-seeking coalitions, general economic instability consistent with the Dutch disease, and authoritarianism. However, Ghana is an outlier in Africa and among African petrostates; it is a democratic state. First, Ghana has a number of democratic institutions that include a professional and independent Electoral Commission, an independent judiciary, and a popular self-awareness among its citizens that it is a democratic polity.[162] For these reasons, it is plausible to conjecture that Ghana's trajectory may more closely resemble that of Norway than Chad. Second, its two-party system dates to the end of the colonial period. The National Democratic Congress (NDC) and the New Patriotic Party (NPP) resemble blocks of voters that have been present in Ghana since before independence.[163] Voter alignments have been more complicated than an assertion of simple continuities would imply, however; regions that had been considered NPP voted for the NDC and in other regions the inverse occurred.[164] These events point to an embedded democracy that bodes positively for the emerging producer's capacity to manage the oil revenues with a minimum of economic and political dislocations.

By contrast, Nigeria's experiences with abundant natural resources date to the late 1950s when the country was still a crown colony. Nigeria is a mature producer with various agencies and offices effectively managing the hydrocarbon sector. Although oil production actually began in 1957, prospecting for oil and other minerals had been constant during the later years

---

[162] Levitsky and Way, *Competitive Authoritarianism*, 303.

[163] Staffan Lindberg and Minion K.C. Morrison, "Exploring Voter Alignments in Africa: Core and Swing Voters in Ghana," *The Journal of Modern African Studies* 43, 4 (December 2005): 584.

[164] Kevin S. Fridy, "The Elephant, Umbrella, and Quarreling Cocks, Disaggregating Partisanship in Ghana's Fourth Republic," *African Affairs* 106, 423 (April 2007): 282.

of British colonialism. After the sustained oil boom of the 1970s, talented and ambitious individuals either entered the armed forces or left government service "in favor of intermediary and rentier activity" in the Nigerian economy.[165] Unfortunately, the military's capture of the Nigerian state embedded authoritarian impulses that found their extreme expression in Abacha's autocracy. Abacha's death opened an arena into which political machines entered and created the violent competition that characterized Nigerian politics in the 2007 elections.

Although it is tempting to suggest that the godfathers and their political machines are a recent phenomenon facilitated by the rough politics of the Obasanjo years, machine politics has operated in Nigeria since the late colonial period. The machines organized by the pre-independence leader had a significant impact on electoral competition. Contemporary machines provided employment and security for clients, and the godfathers grew infamously rich. Nigeria's political machines challenge the state's hegemony over the means of violence, but they are pluralist factions that constitute the basis of parties in a complex federal system. Indeed, the 2011 elections represented a clear divergence from the violence and corruption that had tainted the 2007 vote. As Lewis trenchantly notes:

Nigeria's 2011 elections offered its citizens the most competitive and transparent contest in decades. Innovations in election administration and the political commitment of national leaders helped to produce dramatic improvements in the selection of Nigerian officeholders. The polls also produced significant losses for the ruling party and potentially fostered a more pluralistic political landscape.[166]

Gabon has shown how political change occurs after decades of stable, authoritarian leadership. The Bongo system successfully implanted political institutions that enriched the clan and its supporting oligarchs. However, population growth, largely as a result of economic prosperity, caused a sizeable portion of the population to demand more political representation. In effect, Gabon's president established a political machine that he used to ensure the status first of his children, and second of his cronies. The machine operates smoothly as indicated by Ali Bongo's electoral victory in 2009. What remains to be understood is the concessions that Ali Bongo will make to retain power for himself and his clan after the oil is depleted.

These cases illustrate the considerable challenges of implementing democracy that confront petrostates, regardless of whether they are emerging, mature, or declining producers. However, changes in Nigeria and Gabon are indicative of larger shifts across Africa and especially in its petrostates. How leaders of

---

[165] Tom Forrest, *The Advance of African Capital: The Growth of Nigerian Private Enterprise* (Charlottesville: University Press of Virginia, 1994), 243.

[166] Peter M. Lewis, "Nigeria Votes: More Openness, More Conflict," *Journal of Democracy* 22, 4 (October 2011): 74.

African petrostates adjust institutional arrangements in politics and economics is critical to the countries' prospects for democracy. These arrangements shape the development and consolidation of democracy as states move through the cycles of being an emerging, then a mature, and finally a declining producer.

Conclusion: Oil, Democracy, and Development in Africa

This book has teased out a story of tentative and fragile democracy and economic development in African petrostates. Democracy and development are probable outcomes in oil exporting states as they move through their phases of production. However, attaining these outcomes is contingent on the political and economic conditions present at the onset of hydrocarbon production. The productive cycle of an oil reserve is long enough to result in subtle transformations. Subtle economic changes include the emergence of a nascent middle class and pockets of capital accumulation. Political changes include demands for more representative government and basic liberties and that the leadership agree to compromises. Oil revenues thus have a transformative effective on the leaders' willingness to fund social-sector services that reduce poverty. Education and health care become more widely available, so literacy rates rise and people live longer. Finally, economic performance in different petrostates has varied. In some countries, spending the oil wealth benefitted only a few; in others, oil contributed to more inclusive economic opportunities for the general population.[1] Although the record appears to be uneven, when we look at performance since the time of discovery, even among the weaker African oil economies development has occurred. In short, democracy and development follow in subtle and obvious fashions the expansion and maturation of resource-based economies.

A THEMATIC APPROACH

Instead of a case-by-case analysis, this book takes a thematic approach that explores key variables to explain democracy and development in African

---

[1] Bernardin Akitoby and Sharmini Coorey, "The CEMAC's Macroeconomic Challenges," in *Oil Wealth in Central Africa: Policies for Inclusive Growth*, eds. Bernardin Akitoby and Sharmini Coorey (Washington, DC: The International Monetary Fund, 2012), 3.

petrostates. First, it looked at the different histories of these countries and considered how those historical variables have influenced contemporary outcomes. Second, the analysis has outlined the competition that has driven the oil companies to collude with African leaders in their efforts to win contracts. Third, the phase of production is crucial in any attempt to explain the conditions in a state as it progresses from the discovery of hydrocarbons to the point where oil corporations pump the last commercially recoverable barrel from the well. The central message is that oil production is a dynamic process that presents numerous junctures at which policymakers may lead the country in distinct directions.

Having set forth the context in Africa's oil exporters, Chapters 5 and 6 assessed how politicians react to payments of windfalls and the subtle pressures on these states to open their political systems to more representative government. In both chapters, the theme of corruption informs the analysis. Chapter 5 used the phase of production to frame its analysis of how corruption influences development and revenue management. The first case, an emerging producer, is Ghana and the Kosmos Energy controversy that occurred in 2009–2010. Although it might have appeared in 2009 that Ghana was poised to fall into a pattern of political interference and public malfeasance, the controversy's resolution suggests that the state would avoid the corruption pitfall. Resolution of this controversy is therefore indicative of how the starting point for receipt of oil revenues – Ghana was already a functioning democracy – has a distinct impact on political economic outcomes. Equatorial Guinea is the second example presented here of a country that encounters dilemmas of corruption. The crucial difference is that clan-based rule in Equatorial Guinea has embedded corruption in official transactions, thereby contributing to a progressive impoverishment of the population. Finally, the declining producer is Congo, where a regime on the basis of clientelism dominated the country's political economy. Whereas the president's clan was influential, security in office was a result of coalition support.

Representative democracy has a strong impact on a petrostate's ability to manage hydrocarbon revenues efficiently. In Chapter 6, the emergence of political machines and nascent democracy informs the analytic perspective. To provide background, evidence was presented that clan-based rule and clientelism were elements of a growing pluralism in African petrostates. Clientelist networks, common throughout Africa since well before independence, are the organizational foundations on which individuals build political parties. Both formal and informal institutions shape the manner in which clientelism operates. The chapter examined how corruption influenced the machine politics that emerged in Nigeria's turbulent elections in the early twenty-first century. Rewards for engaging in corruption, and getting away with it, are immense. At base, the capacity of patrons to gain control of political machines informs their capital accumulation on an astounding scale. Given the payoffs for securing elected office, violence is a tactic political rivals use with shocking impunity.

Baseline conditions at the time companies discover hydrocarbons and begin extraction are far more relevant for understanding the trajectories of African petrostates than snapshots of their current situations. Oil provides revenues that political leaders may use for a variety of expenditures including social-sector services such as education and health care. A rising middle class has emerged in response to opportunities in providing needed services or to work as employees in the hydrocarbon sector. These people articulate these demands for education and health care. As Sassou learned in Congo, policymakers ignore the hopes of a rising middle class at their own risk.

Politically, the availability of money from oil production encourages people to organize and seek access to that wealth. As citizens organize, a consequence is evident in the growing number of voluntary associations and political pluralism that has emerged in a number of African petrostates. Employment opportunities, better social-sector services, and multiparty political competition are unambiguous benefits that have come with oil production. This book, writ large, agrees with Haber and Monaldo's assertion that "to the degree that we detect any statistically significant relationships, they point to a resource blessing: increases in natural-resource income are associated with increases in democracy."[2] And these increases in democracy mirror improvements in economic development.

The production and sale of oil increases a country's economic activity and wealth that lead to a number of changes. First, service industries emerge in the domestic market to satisfy demand for banking, housing, security, and a variety of other goods and products the oil industry requires. In many circumstances, members of the president's clan own the businesses that fulfill oil companies' needs. In various countries, demand shifts as the producer matures and new firms owned by non-clansmen take advantage of opportunities. Second, expansion of the oil sector has ripple effects throughout society as evident in an improvement in health care, education, and living conditions. These improvements have long-term impacts on population growth. As populations grow, people demand a relaxation of restrictions on commercial activities and political organizations. In short, as petrostates receive more revenues they develop, both politically and economically.

It is crucial to understand the conditions in these countries when production began. In many African petrostates, the discovery of oil occurred in countries that had experienced civil war, ethnic conflict, authoritarian rule, and a stunted public sector. The poorest of these states lacked a bureaucracy to manage the revenues. Effective interest mediation, representative government, and managerial capacity required that the leaders of these states build the organizations and define the rules to overcome these shortfalls. As Larsen notes, even

[2] Stephen Haber and Victor Menaldo, "Do Natural Resources Fuel Authoritarianism? A Reappraisal of the Resource Curse," *The American Political Science Review* 105, 1 (February 2011): 3.

in Norway, a democratic state with an effective bureaucracy, management of oil revenues posed clear challenges.[3] In deeply impoverished African states, bureaucracies are illusory; their central banks exist only in name and ministries lack agencies to manage revenues. Perhaps most crucial is the absence of rules and norms that enable the petrostate to manage the oil sector.

The discovery of oil creates a sudden demand for regulations, banking, and rules to manage this new industry. For sure, economic development in African petrostates has been difficult and seemingly slow; many of these countries were extremely poor when they emerged from colonial domination. Then, the starting point when most of these African petrostates began to export oil and receive revenues is really the relevant benchmark for understanding their trajectories. This concluding chapter discusses comparatively the themes of the book: first, one must consider the historical roots of political and economic behavior in African petrostates. Second, the conclusion compares the violence that is common in African petrostates. Finally, the experiences with corruption continue among African oil exporters. Having considered these themes in a comparative light, this conclusion ends with a brief discussion of policy implications for petrostates.

PROPOSITION I: HISTORY EMBEDS POLITICAL AND ECONOMIC BEHAVIOR IN PETROSTATES

This book has argued that historic events embedded clientelism in African petrostates. Whether under Portuguese, British, French, or Spanish colonial administrations, subjects created clientelist networks to respond to the dislocations and uncertainties caused by urbanization, shifting authority patterns, and violence under colonial rule. Rather than arguing that clientelism was a dysfunctional political practice and a direct contradiction of "modernity,"[4] this book portrays clientelism as a foundation of pluralist politics. In history, clientelist networks were organizations that people voluntarily joined to bring order to the uncertainties brought by the profound changes imposed under colonial rule. In contemporary African petrostates, clientelist networks weave a fabric of social organizations that constitute basic elements of democracy.[5]

Colonialism had an extraordinary impact on those African societies over which the administrations imposed their rule. These profound effects empowered individuals and groups who used their positions to foster dependence

---

[3] E. Røed Larsen, "Are Rich Countries Immune to the Resource Curse: Evidence from Norway's Management of Its Oil Riches," *Resources Policy* 30 (2005): 75–68.

[4] Jean-François Médard, "Le Rapport de Clientèle: de Phénomène Sociale à l'Analyse Politique," *Revue Française de Science Politique* 26, 1 (1976): 104.

[5] Richard L. Sklar, "Developmental Democracy," *Comparative Studies in Society and History* 29, 4 (October 1987): 714.

and domination.[6] In Algeria, for instance, Lowi finds that French colonialism changed the rules that governed land-tenure practices.[7] Controls over land necessarily uprooted some populations and excluded others from their agricultural livelihoods. As a consequence, people had little choice but to migrate from their rural homes to growing urban centers. New social relations prompted Algerians to establish organizations whose patrons developed clientelist networks that provided alternatives to French authority.[8] By the time French engineers discovered significant oil reserves, the clientelist networks in Algeria had already taken shape. As in African petrostates, the introduction of oil revenues was an intermediate variable; preexisting social relations formed the bonds for subsequent organizations.

The centrality of clan and client as a historical production was no less important in the Middle East. For example, Crystal describes how British administrators in Kuwait created rivalries within the ruling family to set one faction against another as a means of dominating these societies.[9] Herb discusses how the Al Saud clan's strategy was to marginalize rivals in Saudi Arabia; the royal clan thereby constructed a bureaucratic state that permitted some networks to flourish and denied others access to positions of influence.[10] This system of rule in Saudi Arabia created the conditions that Hertog refers to as "segmented clientelism" – "parallel and often strictly separate" networks shared in an oil-funded distributional system.[11] Although these strategies worked in Saudi Arabia, clans in some African petrostates built clientelist systems that defined membership through fictive and real relations that harkened to colonial rule and precolonial societies. Common to all these networks is the element of exclusivity wherein some groups reaped rewards through inclusion and others got nothing.

In most African colonies, European authorities removed the kings and chiefs from office and replaced them with compliant individuals. The result of these practices was the creation of new influential networks in these societies. An unanticipated effect was the emergence of parallel authority structures; one included individuals whose power was in traditional organizations and the other people who worked in colonial bureaucratic administrations.[12]

---

[6] James C. Scott, "Patron-Client Politics and Political Change in Southeast Asia." *The American Political Science Review* 66, 1 (March 1972): 94.

[7] Miriam R. Lowi, *Oil Wealth and the Poverty of Politics: Algeria Compared* (New York: Cambridge University Press, 2009), 51.

[8] Hugh Roberts, "Demilitarizing Algeria," Carnegie Papers 86 (May 2007): 7.

[9] Jill Crystal, *Oil and Politics in the Gulf: Rulers and Merchants in Kuwait and Qatar* (New York: Cambridge University Press, 1990), 43.

[10] Michael Herb, *All in the Family: Absolutism, Revolution, and Democracy in Middle Eastern Monarchies* (Albany: New York University Press, 1999), 57.

[11] Steffen Hertog, *Princes, Brokers, and Bureaucrats: Oil and the State in Saudi Arabia* (Ithaca and London: Cornell University Press, 2010a), 12.

[12] Richard L. Sklar, "The African Frontier for Political Science," in *Africa and the Disciplines: The Contribution of Research on Africa to the Social Sciences and Humanities*, eds. Robert H. Bates,

After independence, the parallel authorities interacted uncomfortably in what Erdman and Engel have termed an "invasion of informal personal relations into the formal structures of legal rational relations"; this invasion also reflected the assertion of informal authority through clientelist networks in African petrostates.[13] Hence, in Africa, the prevalence of formal and informal institutions in states speaks to a diarchy that was evident in various colonies. Domination over individuals thus shifted from traditional authorities to big men or godfathers, where traditional authorities' attempts to allocate employment and land alienated the youth and contributed to social unrest and violence.[14] These alienated youth were prime candidates for recruitment into violent gangs that did the patrons' bidding.

The emergence of political machines has been a process that occurred in numerous African petrostates with several important differences. In Gabon, Omar Bongo used machine politics to consolidate his single-party regime effectively and defeat his rivals after he permitted multiparty competition. Through the PDG, he distributed benefits to loyal supporters and clansmen. Bongo's political machine was largely inclusive and served as an organizational precondition of socioeconomic mobility.

Machine politics in Nigeria drew impetus from the extraordinary rewards electoral success promised. Nigerian godfathers used clientelist networks to build their machines to further their political goals.[15] In turn, the machines became elements of political party organization at the local levels. A multiplicity of political machines animated a growing pluralism in Nigerian society. This interpretation of political machines rejects the notion that a split has occurred between informal actors in society and administrative personnel in the state. Often, the very people managing informal networks are themselves key actors in the political economy. This convergence of informal and formal institutions is evident in petrostates where clientelist networks form constitutive elements of political parties.

Historical processes are the bases of clientelism in African petrostates where distortions embedded in African societies by colonial authorities contributed to conflicts among big men. Those individuals that colonial French administrators designated as notables used informal clientelist networks to enhance their

V.Y. Mudimbe, and Jean O'Barr. (Chicago: University of Chicago Press, 1993), 83–111.

[13] Gero Erdmann and Ulf Engel, "Neopatrimonialism Reconsidered: Critical Review and Elaboration of an Elusive Concept," *Commonwealth & Comparative Politics* 45, 1 (February 2007): 104.

[14] Human Rights Watch, *Criminal Politics: Violence, and "Godfathers" and Corruption in Nigeria,* 19, no. 16(A). New York: Human Rights Watch (October 2007); William Reno, "Old Brigades, Money Bags, New Breeds, and the Ironies of Reform in Nigeria." *Canadian Journal of African Studies* 27, 1 (April 1993): 71.

[15] Leena Hoffman, "Fairy Godfathers and Magical Elections: Understanding the 2003 Electoral Crisis in Anambra State, Nigeria," *The Journal of Modern African Studies* 48, 2 (June 2010): 285–310.

political status and social influence. After independence, people joined these patronage networks on the basis of social relations; someone they knew from their neighborhood, village, or town introduced them to the patron. Clientelist networks built on established organizations that represent members of age cohorts, merchants in business groups, student and youth associations, religious congregations, and professional societies. These organizational impulses are hardly unique to African petrostates; clientelist networks are a common means by which individuals in complex societies are able to find order. A reaction to the entrenched instability was authoritarianism, which itself led to further disorder.[16]

PROPOSITION II: STATES WITH HISTORIES OF ROUTINE VIOLENCE BEFORE THE ONSET OF OIL PRODUCTION CONTINUE TO EXPERIENCE SOCIAL UNREST AFTERWARD

This book has emphasized that colonialism and its legacy of violence are the root causes of routine brutality in African petrostates. The extended wars in Angola, Sudan, and Chad, and the low-intensity conflicts in Nigeria and Equatorial Guinea originated in practices that occurred under colonial regimes and continued after independence. For the majority of the people living in these societies, violent social conflicts erupted with considerable regularity. When these states began to receive revenues from hydrocarbon extraction, their politicians chose to distribute the benefits unevenly. It was this unequal distribution of scarce resources that leaders of different factions cited as cause for conflict.

Brutality was a likely outcome of interactions between common citizens and the colonial state. During the colonial period, Africa's contemporary petrostates received paltry investments in schools and training for their citizens that might have enabled them to define the political and economic institutions necessary for state construction. For example, Portugal's second colonization of Angola stalled and reversed institutional development that had occurred during the nineteenth century. All Angolans were thereafter subject to arbitrary seizure and forced conscription on colonial work details; the most unfortunate went to São Tomé and Príncipe. When Portugal withdrew from Africa, leaders of Angola's splintered nationalist movements chose to go to war. For these individuals, a chilling level of brutality had been part of their lives since fleeing the arbitrary exactions of the Portuguese colonial state and its secret police. Constant violence since the late nineteenth century had contributed to a society in which people lived in strife that continued even after the civil war ended in 2002.

Violence is both a legacy of colonialism and a common strategy of rule in postcolonial Africa. The cases discussed in this book support the proposition

---

[16] Bates, *When Things Fell Apart*, 34.

that contemporary states reproduce the legacies of violence regardless of whether or not a country becomes a petrostate. Violence is a behavior that reflects actions in the past. For example, the history of Southeastern Nigeria includes the horrific experiences of the civil war in Biafra. This history of violence might account for the capricious aggression in the Niger Delta, where the armed militias have sown terror. In part, this violence responds to the oil companies' careless disregard of citizens' basic human rights.[17] In other respects, it is a consequence of mismanaged oil revenues, widely practiced corruption, unemployment, and a sense of despair among the subregion's youth. The effect has been an emergence of cult groups that assemble young men who have engaged in an undeclared war against both the oil companies that operate in the Niger Delta and the Nigerian federal government.[18] Regardless of causal explanations, the situation in the Niger Delta indicates a volatility that surpassed other oil producers that are not at war.

The events in Nigeria bear clear parallels to outcomes in Indonesia, another oil-exporting giant.[19] In both Nigeria and Indonesia, inequalities were a source of conflict, mismanagement, and pervasive corruption. These inequalities entrenched institutions that contributed to autocratic rule and endemic poverty. The extent of poverty in both these states accompanies extreme inequalities in the distribution of benefits. From Smith's work on the Suharto regime in Indonesia, it is possible to draw parallels to Sassou Nguesso's Congo.[20] Both petrostates distributed government contracts as effective prebends for which regime insiders competed. In Nigeria, as in Congo, the distribution of government contracts was a common form of paying off cronies and maintaining the military regime in office.[21] The exclusive allocation of wealth poses a challenge for Africa's oil exporters because elite politicians have children who want influential positions in the petrostate.

In African petrostates, multiple clientelist networks tend to be closely linked to the governing clan. The clan retains control over rent-based rewards, leaving desolate the non-oil sector producers for whom opportunities are limited and exclusive. In the worst cases (e.g., Equatorial Guinea), the political class is extraordinarily exclusive; only members of the president's clan and the children of his cronies are able to gain access to resource wealth. As a result, members of the inner circle that surrounds the president and his clan engage in

---

[17] Michael J. Watts, "Petro-Insurgency or Criminal Syndicate? Conflict, Violence and Political Disorder in the Niger Delta," Niger Delta Economies of Violence Working Paper No. 16 (University of California, Berkeley: Institute of International Studies, 2006).

[18] Michael Peel, *A Swamp Full of Dollars: Pipelines and Paramilitaries at Nigeria's Oil Frontier* (Chicago: Lawrence Hill Books, 2010), 73.

[19] Peter M. Lewis, *Growing Apart: Oil, Politics, and Economic Change in Indonesia and Nigeria* (Ann Arbor: The University of Michigan Press, 2007).

[20] Benjamin Smith, *Hard Times in the Lands of Plenty: Oil Politics in Iran and Indonesia* (Ithaca: Cornell University Press, 2007), 184.

[21] Lewis, *Growing Apart*, 105.

grand corruption. Favored individuals jealously guard access to opportunities. It is therefore understandable that insiders resort to violence. To fall from favor is to enter forced retirement or even arrest and incarceration for treason or corruption. However, hydrocarbon extraction is hardly causal; the origins of competition and conflict are evident in colonial rule that failed to define rules and norms that would have facilitated equitable income distribution and conflict mediation. Instead, inequalities led to the emergence of informal networks that persisted after colonialism and simmering conflicts.

PROPOSITION III: CORRUPTION LEVELS CHANGE IN PETROSTATES AS THEY DEVELOP

This book shows that African petrostates may be differentiated according to practices of inclusion or exclusion. Inclusion meant access to illicit gains. Such practices had a direct impact on the petrostate's non-oil sector and political economic development. In African petrostates, the governing clan dominated multiple clientelist networks and limited opportunities. Clans and clientelist networks collaborated with oil companies to restrict economic opportunities and political influence. The political class was necessarily exclusive. As a result, grand corruption implicated members of the inner circle that surrounded the president. Favored individuals jealously guarded their access to opportunities because to fall from favor is to enter forced retirement or even arrest and incarceration for corruption.

Although it is tempting to assert that over time oil production leads to lower levels of corruption, this assertion appears to be incorrect. Corruption continues to be a persistent problem in African petrostates. It is evident that oil autocrats are simultaneously pulled in multiple directions. One option is to capture revenues for personal gain. When there are no constraints on the leaders, they have incentives to be predatory and corrupt. However, as politicians deepen their relationships with international investors and become more attuned to the world economy, a need emerges to present an image of stability and a minimum of probity in their economic management. Then new norms of accountability and due diligence enter the leaders' calculations and "constrain the actions of power-holders and oblige them to respect the rights and wishes of their constituents."[22] Such changes take considerable lengths of times, but as governments accumulate wealth, democracy tentatively takes root.

For countries that discovered oil after independence, the extent of decolonization influenced relations between national oil companies and the governments. For example, Congo's leaders adopted Marxism-Leninism after 1963. It had little impact on the leadership's close relationships with the French national oil company Elf Aquitaine. Production continued throughout the period and even during the 1997 civil war. Several weeks after the war's end,

[22] Sklar, "Developmental Democracy," 713.

Elf-Congo announced the discovery of two deep-sea fields that would increase Congo's production for a short period. These examples speak to the oil companies' continued influence and their priority status among foreign investors in African petrostates. Their influence was, in turn, affected by the phase of production and the size of the African petrostate; an oil company enjoys far greater status when the government has only just begun to receive oil rents than when it has been receiving the rents for a lengthy period.

Among oil producers, close commercial and economic relations with oil companies demonstrated the difficulties of decolonization. All too often, personal relations were evident in contractual agreements signed between oil companies and African petrostates. In an important sense, the reproduction of contractual agreements suggests a deferred process of decolonization. In part, this reflects the more tumultuous relationship between colonial ministries and elite African politicians. For example, even during colonialism, political elites from Nigeria's regions formed clientelist networks to act collectively. A pattern of big men that dominated competitive factions located in particular states became embedded in late twentieth-century Nigerian politics.

CONCLUSION

Oil production leads to an expansion of a country's economy and resource revenues increase societal wealth. These increases are evident in the organization of service industries, notably in banking, housing, security, and distribution networks of consumer goods. Non-oil producers move into niches such as middlemen to distribute consumer goods, security officers who might have been former or current police officers, and staff hired to work in banks and ministries. However, this process takes time because at the onset of production, in most cases, the state was without sufficient civil servants, banks lacked competent personnel, and police were part of a repressive apparatus. In countries such as Equatorial Guinea, members of the president's clan become the service providers that respond to oil companies' needs for housing, security, and entertainment. However, by 2010, countries such as Nigeria have booming information and distribution networks that benefit from the oil sector but remain independent. In other countries, unmet demand encourages firms that respond to new opportunities.

The oil sector's expansion has ripple effects throughout the society, as is evident in improvements in health care, education, and urban living conditions. Moreover, as studies of Ghanaian public-sector investments have shown, these strategies are a significant means to offset Dutch disease effects in the tradeables sector.[23] Such strategies have failed to be uniform in all African petrostates. Gabon, for instance, did not enact similar policies to reduce Dutch

---

[23] Jihad Dagher, Jan Gottschalk, and Rafael Portillo, "Oil Windfalls in Ghana: A DSGE Approach," IMF Working Paper WP/10/116 (May 2010): 31.

disease effects and its oil sector developed to the detriment of what had been functional mining and agricultural sectors.[24] Although Gabon has suffered a process of deindustrialization, its low levels of corruption and high levels of per capita GDP suggest that the Bongo administration improved human capital stocks. These improvements have long-term positive effects and people call for a relaxation of restrictions on commercial activities and political organizations. In short, experiences in Gabon suggest that as petrostates receive more revenues they develop, both politically and economically.

This book has emphasized that the starting point for Africa's petrostates is the benchmark to begin an evaluation of issues of development and democracy. To make this argument, the book presents evidence on the historical context among the countries that became petrostates. Second, it focuses on how the strategies of corporations seeking to extract oil in Africa has an impact on the developmental trajectories of these countries. The impact, however, is conditioned by the phase of production – whether a country is an emerging, mature, or declining producer. Finally, two chapters presented evidence from five specific cases in Africa. These incidents and examples buttress the argument that African petrostates are both developing and coming under representative and pluralist democratic rule.

---

[24] Ali Zafar, "What Happens When a Country Does Not Adjust to the Terms of Trade Shocks? – The Case of Oil-Rich Gabon," World Bank Policy Research Working Paper 3403 (September 2004): 10.

Bibliography

Acemoglu, Daron, Simon Johnson, and James A. Robinson. 2003. "An African Success Story: Botswana." In *In Search of Prosperity: Analytic Narratives of Economic Growth*, 80–119. Edited by Dani Rodrik. Princeton: Princeton University Press.

    2001. "The Colonial Origins of Comparative Development: An Empirical Investigation." *The American Economic Review* 91, 5 (December): 1369–1401.

    2002. "Reversal of Fortune: Geography and Institutions in the Making of the Modern World Income Distribution." *The Quarterly Journal of Economics* 117, 4 (November): 1231–1294.

Acemoglu, Daron and James A. Robinson. 2006. *Economic Origins of Dictatorship and Democracy*. New York: Cambridge University Press.

    2012. *Why Nations Fail: The Origins of Power, Prosperity, and Poverty*. New York: Crown Publishing.

Adebanwi, Wale. 2005. "The Carpenter's Revolt: Youth, Violence and the Reinvention of Culture in Nigeria," *The Journal of Modern African Studies* 43, 3 (September): 339–365.

Adebanwi, Wale and Ebenezer Obadare. 2011. "When Corruption Fights Back: Democracy and Elite Interest in Nigeria's Anti-Corruption War." *The Journal of Modern African Studies* 49, 1 (June): 185–213.

Adekanye, J. Bayo. 1997. "The Military." In *Transition Without End: Nigerian Politics and Civil Society Under Babangida*, 55–80. Edited by Larry Diamond, Anthony Kirk-Greene, and Oyeleye Oyediran. Boulder: Lynne Rienner Publishers Inc.

Adeniyi, Olusegun. 2010. "The Alleged NLNG $180 Million Bribe Scandal: The Unanswered Questions." *ThisDay Sunday* (September 2, 2010). Retrieved from http://www.thisdayonline.com/.

AFP. 2009. "Biens mal Acquis: La Justice Refuse l'Ouverture d'une Enquête." *Libération* (29 Octobre).

    2005. "Le Président Gabonais Omar Bongo Ondimba, Doyen des Chefs d'Etat Africains." 29 Novembre.

    2004. "Pressé par le FMI, le Gabon Restructure sa Filière Bois (Papier d'Angle)." *Le Monde* (21 Décembre).

2005. "Réélection sans Surprise du President Omar Bongo Ondimba au Gabon." *Le Monde* (30 Novembre).

2004. "Le Secteur du Bois, Stratégique pour l'Économie Gabonaise, en Plein Crise." *Le Monde* (21 Décembre).

2009. "Tchad: L'Échec Apparent de l'Offensive des Rebelles ne Marque pas la Fin du Conflit." *Le Monde* (10 Mai).

Africa Confidential. 2012. "Angola: Marques Takes Them On." *Africa Confidential* 53, 2 (20 January).

2013. "Equatorial Guinea: L'Etat, c'est Nous." *Africa Confidential* 54, 14 (5 July).

2011. "Gabon: A Family Legacy." *Africa Confidential* 52, 2 (January 21).

Aghion, Philippe, Peter Howitt, and David Mayer-Foulkes. 2005. "The Effective of Financial Development on Convergence: Theory and Evidence." *The Quarterly Journal of Economics* 120, 1 (February): 173–222.

Agyare, Dr. Jemima. 2010. "Transparency, Accountability and Participation: A Formula to Enhance the Governance of Ghana's Petroleum Sector." *The Guardian* (Accra) (August 2). Retrieved from http://ghanaian-chronicle.com August 2, 2010.

Akhaine, Sylvester Odion. 2011. "Nigeria's 2011 Elections: The 'Crippled Giant' Learns to Walk," *African Affairs* 110, 441 (October): 649–655.

Alba, Eleodoro Mayorga. 2009. "Extractive Industries Value Chain." Extractive Industries for Development Series #3. Africa Region Working Paper Series #125 (Washington, DC: The World Bank, March).

Alden, Chris. 2007. *China in Africa*. New York: Zed Books.

Alexeev, Michael and Robert Conrad. 2009. "The Elusive Curse of Oil." *The Review of Economics and Statistics* 91, 3 (August): 586–598.

Almeida, Henrique. 2009. "Angolan President's Family Taint Corruption Fight." *Reuters* (December 3).

Alvarez, Mike, José Antonio Cheibub, Fernando Limongi, and Adam Przeworski. 1996. "Classifying Political Regimes." *Studies in Comparative International Development* 31, 2 (Summer): 3–36.

Akitoby, Bernardin and Sharmini Coorey. 2012. "The CEMAC's Macroeconomic Challenges." In *Oil Wealth in Central Africa: Policies for Inclusive Growth*, 3–16. Edited by Bernardin Akitoby and Sharmini Coorey. Washington, DC: The International Monetary Fund.

Amaize, Emma and Akpokona Omafuaire. 2013. "2015: Dokubo Vows to Fight Opposition, Bullet for Bullet." *The Vanguard* (May 22).

Amnesty International. 2007. *Above the Law: Police Accountability in Angola*. AFR 12/005/2007. New York: Amnesty International (September).

2013. "Equatorial Guinea: Human Rights Concerns ahead of Equatorial Guinea Elections." (May 7).

2003. Equatorial Guinea. "Possible 'Disappearance'/Fear for Safety." AFR 24/012/2003 (October 30).

2003. "Equatorial Guinea: Prison Conditions/Detention without Charge/Possible Prisoner of Conscience/Fear of Torture or Ill-Treatment." AFR 24/011/2003 (November 13).

2005. "Equatorial Guinea: Prisoners Starving to Death." AFR 24/006/2005 (April 14).

2009. *Nigeria: Petroleum, Pollution, and Poverty in the Niger Delta*. AFR 44/017/2009. New York: Amnesty International (June).

1999. "Republic of Congo: A Human Rights Crisis Rooted in Power Struggles." News Service: 057/99, AI Index: AFR 22/04/99.

1999. Republic of Congo: An Old Generation of Leaders in New Carnage. AFR 22/01/99. New York: Amnesty International (25 March).

2003. *Republic of Congo: A Past that Haunts the Future.* AFR 22/001/2003. New York: Amnesty International (April).

Amodu, Taiwo and Desmond Mgboh. 2013. "NGF Chair: Jonathan, Amaechi in Final Showdown." *The Sun* (May 24).

Andrade, Mário de. 1999. "Sur la Première Generation de MPLA: 1948–1960, Entretiens avec Christine Messiant," *Lusotopie*: 185–221.

Andrew, C.M. and A.S. Kanya-Forstner. 1974. "The French Colonial Party and French Colonial War Aims 1914–1918," *The Historical Journal* 17, 1 (March): 79–106.

Ansprenger, Franz. 1989. *The Dissolution of the Colonial Empires.* New York: Routlege.

Apter, Andrew. 2005. *The Pan-African Nation: Oil and the Spectacle of Culture in Nigeria.* Chicago: University of Chicago Press.

Apter, David E. 1963. *Ghana in Transition.* Princeton: Princeton University Press.

Arnold, Martin, William Wallis and Leslie Hook. 2010. "Ghana Move for Kosmos Oilfield Stake." *The Financial Times* (October 22).

Arriola, Leonardo R. 2013. *Multiethnic Coalitions in Africa: Business Financing of Opposition Election Campaigns.* New York: Cambridge University Press.

Arubi, Emma. 2013. "Tension in Delta as Ijaw Youths Kill 4 Itsekiri." *The Vanguard* (July 03).

Atenga, Thomas. 2003. "Gabon: Apprendre à Vivre sans Pétrole." *Politique Africaine* 92 (December): 117–128.

Attisso, Fulbert Sassou. 2013. *Le Togo sous la Dynastie des Gnassingbé.* Paris: Éditions l'Harmattan.

Augé, Axel Eric. 2005a. "Jeunes, Jeunesse et Intégration des Élites Politique au Gabon: La Place des Trajectoires Sociales Individuelles," *Afrique Contemporaine* 213 (Hiver): 197–215.

2005b. *Le Recrutement des Élites Politiques en Afrique Subsaharienne: Une Sociologie du Pouvoir au Gabon.* Paris: Éditions l'Harmattan.

Auty, Richard M. 2001a. "Conclusions: Resource Abundance, Growth Collapses, and Policy." In *Resource Abundance and Economic Development*, 315–327. Edited by R. M. Auty. New York: Oxford University Press.

1997. "Does Kazakhstan Oil Wealth Help or Hinder the Transition?" Development Discussion Paper No. 615. Harvard University: Harvard Institute for International Development (December).

2001b. "Introduction and Overview." In *Resource Abundance and Economic Development*, 3–16. Edited by R. M. Auty. New York: Oxford University Press.

1997. "Natural Resource Endowment, the State and Development Strategy," *Journal of International Development* 9, (4): 651–663.

1995. *Patterns of Development: Resources, Policy and Economic Growth.* New York: Edward Arnold.

2001c. "The Political State and the Management of Mineral Rents in Capital Surplus Economies: Botswana and Saudi Arabia." *Resources Policy* 27, 2 (June): 77–86.

Ed. 2001d. *Resource Abundance and Economic Development.* New York: Oxford University Press.

Auty, Richard M. and Alan Gelb. 1986. "Oil Windfalls in a Small Parliamentary Democracy: Their Impact on Trinidad and Tobago." *World Development* 14, 9 (September): 1161–1175.

2001. "Political Economy of Resource Abundant States." In *Resource Abundance and Economic Development*, 126–144. Edited by R. M. Auty. New York: Oxford University Press.

Auty, Richard M. and Nicola Pontara. 2008. "A Dual-Track Strategy for Managing Mauritania's Projected Oil Rent." *Development Policy Review* 26, 1 (January): 59–77.

Azarya, Victor and Naomi Chazan. 1987. "Disengagement from the State in Africa: Reflections on the Experience of Guinea and Ghana." *Comparative Studies in Society and History* 29, 1 (January): 106–131.

Babadagli, Tayfun. 2007. "Development of Mature Oil Fields – A Review," *Journal of Petroleum Science and Engineering* 57: 221–246.

Badila, Joseph. 2004. *La Franc-Maçonnerie en Afrique Noire: Un Si Long Chemin Vers la Liberté, l'Égalité, la Fraternité.* Paris: Éditions Detrad.

Baiôa, Manuel, Paulo Jorge Fernandes, and Filipe Ribeiro de Meneses. 2003. "The Political History of Twentieth-Century Portugal." *E-Journal of Portuguese History* 1, 2 (Winter): 4. http://www.brown.edu/Departments/Portuguese_Brazilian_Studies/ejph/html/issue2/html. Accessed 14 July 2007.

Baland, Jean-Marie and Patrick Francois. 2000. "Rent-Seeking and Resource Booms," *Journal of Development Economics* 61: 527–542.

Baniafouna, Calixte. 1995. *Congo Démocratie: Les Déboires de l'Apprentissage.* Paris: Éditions l'Harmattan.

Barboza, David, Andrew Ross Sorkin, and Steve Lohr. 2005. "China's Oil Set Back: The Overview; Chinese Company Drops Bid to Buy U.S. Oil Concern." *The New York Times* (August 3).

Barnard, Chester. 1938/1968. *The Functions of the Executive.* Cambridge: Harvard University Press.

Barnett, Steven and Rolando Ossowski. 2002. "Operational Aspects of Fiscal Policy in Oil Producing Countries." IMF Working Paper WP/02/177.

Barzel, Yoram. 2000. "Property Rights and the Evolution of the State," *Economics of Governance* 1, 1 (March): 25–51.

Bates, Robert H. 1981. *Markets and States in Tropical Africa.* Berkeley and Los Angeles: University of California Press.

2008. *When Things Fell Apart: State Failure in Late Century Africa.* New York: Cambridge University Press.

Baunsgaard, Thomas. 2003. "Fiscal Policy in Nigeria: Any Role for Rules?" IMF Working Paper WP/03/155. Washington: The International Monetary Fund (July).

2001. "A Primer on Mineral Taxation," IMF Working Paper WP/01/139. Washington, DC: The International Monetary Fund (September).

Baunsgaard, Thomas, Mauricio Villafuerte, Marcos Poplawski-Ribeiro, and Christine Richmond. 2012. "Fiscal Frameworks for Resource Rich Developing Countries." IMF Staff Discussion Note SDN/12/04 (May 16).

Bayart, Jean-François. 1989. *L'État en Afrique: La Politique du Ventre.* Paris: Fayard.

Bayart, Jean-François, Stephen Ellis, and Béatrice Hibou. 1999. "From Kleptocracy to the Felonious State." In *The Criminalization of the State in Africa*, 1–31. Edited by Jean-François Bayart, Stephen Ellis, and Béatrice Hibou. Bloomington: Indiana University Press.

Bazenguissa-Ganga, Rémy. 1996. "Milices Politiques et Bandes Armées à Brazzaville: Enquête sur la Violence Politique et Sociale des Jeunes Declasses." Les Études du CERI, No 13 (April).

BBC. 2009. "France Halts African Leaders Case."(29 October).

——— 2008. "Nigeria Oil Rebel Pipeline Found." (March 11).

Beblawi, Hazem. 1987. "The Rentier State in the Arab World." In *Nation State and Integration in the Arab World*, Volume II: *The Rentier State*, 85–98. Edited by Hazem Beblawi and Giacomo Luciani Beckenham. Kent, UK: Croom Helm Ltd.

Becker, Gary S. 1968. "Crime and Punishment: An Economic Approach." *The Journal of Political Economy* 76, 2 (March–April): 169–217.

Bekker, Peter H.F. 2003. "International Decisions: Land and Maritime Boundary between Cameroon and Nigeria (*Cameroon v. Nigeria*; Equatorial Guinea Intervening). *The American Journal of International Law* 97, (2): 387–398.

Bello, Kamal. 2011. "God-Fatherism in the Politics of Nigeria: Continuity and Change." *Canadian Social Science* 7, (2): 256–260.

Bender, Gerald J. 1978. *Angola under the Portuguese: The Myth and the Reality*. Berkeley and Los Angeles: University of California Press.

Benjamin, Nancy, Shantayanan Devarajan, and Robert Weiner. 1989. "The Dutch Disease in a Developing Country: Oil Reserves in Cameroon." *The Journal of Development Economics* 30, 1 (January): 71–92.

Béresniak Daniel and Joseph Badiila with Jean Moreau. 2008. *Les Francs-Maçons et l'Afrique*. Paris: Éditions Detrad.

Berle, Adolf A. and Gardiner C. Means. 2009. *The Modern Corporation and Private Property*. Tenth printing. New Brunswick, NJ: Transaction Publishers.

Berman, Bruce. 1998. "Ethnicity, Patronage and the African State: The Politics of Uncivil Nationalism," *African Affairs* 97, 388 (July): 305–341.

Bernard, Philippe. 2010. "L'Enquête sur les 'Bien Mal Acquis' par Trios Potentates d'Afrique Sera Rouvert." *Le Monde* (11 Novembre).

——— 2005. "M. Bongo Veut Faire Taire l'Opposition à Paris." *Le Monde* (22 Septembre).

Bernard, Philippe and Henri Dubief. 1985. *The Decline of the French Republic 1914–1938*. Translated by Anthony Foster. New York: Cambridge University Press.

Bernard, Philippe and Natalie Nougayrède (with Philippe Bolopion à l'ONU). 2008. "L'Offensive des Rebelles du Tchad Embarrasse la France." *Le Monde* (3 Février).

Bernault, Florence. 1996. *Démocraties Ambiguës en Afrique Centrale: Congo-Brazzaville, Gabon: 1940–1965*. Paris: Éditions Karthala.

Bernault, Florence and Joseph Tonda. 2009. "Le Gabon: Une Dystopia Tropicale." *Politique Africaine* 115 (Octobre): 15.

Berry, Sara S. 1975. *Cocoa, Custom, and Socioeconomic Change in Rural Western Nigeria*. New York: Oxford University Press.

Bertrand, Hugues. 1975. *Le Congo: Formation Sociale et Mode de Développement Économique*. Paris: François Maspero.

Bhattacharya, Rina and Dhaneshwar Ghura. 2006. "Oil and Growth in the Republic of Congo." IMF Working Paper WP/06/185 (August).

Biegelman, Martin T. and Daniel R. Biegelman. *Foreign Corrupt Practices Act Compliance Guidebook*. Hoboken, NJ: John Wiley and Sons Inc., 2010.

Bienen, Henry. 1988. "Nigeria: From Windfall Gains to Welfare Losses?" In *Oil Windfalls: Blessing or Curse?*, 227–261. Edited by Alan Gelb and Associates. New York: Oxford University Press for the World Bank.

Bikomo, Santos Pascual. 1997. "Guinea Conexión." *La Diapora* (24 de Julio).

Birmingham, David. 2002. "Angola." In *A History of Postcolonial Lusophone Africa*, 137–184. Edited by Patrick Chabal, David Birmingham, Malyn Newitt, Gerhard Siebert, and Elisa Silva Andrade. Bloomington: Indiana University Press.

2006. *Empire in Africa: Angola and Its Neighbors*. Athens, OH: Ohio University Press.

Blattman, Christopher and Edward Miguel. 2010. "Civil War," *The Journal of Economic Literature* 48, 1 (March): 3–57.

Blum, Justin. 2004. "Equatorial Guinea, USA: US Oil Firms." *Washington Post* (September 9).

Boltanski, Christophe. 2009. "Ali Bongo Grand Maître du Gabon: La Franc-Maçonnerie est l'un des Piliers du Régime Gabonaise." *Nouvel Observateur* (29 Octobre).

Bongo, Omar. 2001. *Blanc Comme Negre: Entretiens avec Airy Routier*. Paris: Éditions Grasset & Fasquelle.

Boone, Catherine. 2003. *Political Topographies of the African State: Territorial Authority and Institutional Choice*. New York: Cambridge University Press.

Bourguignon, François and Mark Sundberg. 2006. "Absorptive Capacity and Achieving the MDGs." UNU-WIDER Research paper No. 2006/47. Helsinki, Finland: United Nations University-World Institute for Development Economics Research.

Bratton, Michael. 2004. "The 'Alternation Effect' in Africa." *Journal of Democracy* 15, 4 (October): 147–158.

2007. "Formal Versus Informal Institutions in Africa." *Journal of Democracy* 18, 3 (July): 96–110.

Bratton, Michael and Nicolas van de Walle. 1997. *Democratic Experiments in Africa: Regime Transitions in Comparative Perspective*. New York: Cambridge University Press.

1994. "Neopatrimonial Regimes and Regime Transitions in Africa." *World Politics* 46, 4 (July): 453–489.

Bräutigam, Deborah. 2008. "Contingent Capacity: Export Taxation and State-Building in Mauritius." In *Taxation and State Building in Developing Countries: Capacity and Consent*, 135–159. Edited by Deborah Bräutigam, Odd-Helge Fjeldstad, and Mick Moore. New York: Cambridge University Press.

Bräutigam, Deborah, Odd-Helge Fjeldstad, and Mick Moore, Eds. 2008. *Taxation and State Building in Developing Countries: Capacity and Consent*. New York: Cambridge University Press.

Bray, John. 2003. "Attracting Reputable Companies to Risky Environments: Petroleum and Mining Companies." In *Natural Resources and Violent Conflict: Options and Actions*, 287–352. Edited by Ian Bannon and Paul Collier. Washington, DC: The World Bank.

Brownlee, Jason. 2007. "Hereditary Succession in Modern Autocracies." *World Politics* 59, 4 (July): 595–628.

Budina, Nina, Gaobo Pang, and Sweder van Wijnbergen. 2007. "Nigeria's Growth Record: Dutch Disease or Debt Overhang?" World Bank Policy Research Working Paper 4256 (June).

Buijtenhuijs, Robert. 1989. "Chad: The Narrow Escape of an African State." In *Contemporary West African States*, 49–58. Edited by Donal Cruise O'Brien, John Dunn, and Richard Rathbone. New York: Cambridge University Press.

———. 1993. *La Conference Nationale Souveraine du Tchad: Une Essai d'Histoire Immediate.* Paris: Éditions Karthala.

———. 1998. *Transition et Elections au Tchad: Restauration Autoritiare et Recomposition Politique.* Paris: Éditions Karthala.

Burgis, Tom. 2009. "China Seeks Big Stake in Nigerian Oil." *The Financial Times* (September 28).

———. 2012. "U.S. to Probe Cobalt Oil Links in Angola." *The Financial Times* (February 21).

Burgis, Tom and William Wallis. 2009. "China in Push for Resources in Guinea." *The Financial Times* (October 11).

Butt, Simon. 2009. "'Unlawfulness' and Corruption under Indonesian Law." *The Bulletin of Indonesian Economics* 45 (2): 179–198.

Caiden, Gerald E. 1993. "From the Specific to the General: Reflections on the Sudan." *Corruption and Reform* 7 (3): 205–213.

Campos, Alicia. 2003. "The Decolonization of Equatorial Guinea: The Relevance of the International Factor." *The Journal of African History* 44 (March): 95–116.

Carcillo, Stéphane, Daniel Leigh, and Mauricio Villafuerte. 2007. "Catch-Up Growth, Habits, Oil Depletion, and Fiscal Policy: Lessons from the Republic of Congo," IMF Working Paper, WP/07/80 (April).

Carneiro, Francisco. 2007. *Angola: Oil, Broad-Based Growth, and Equity.* Washington, DC: The World Bank.

Catan, Thomas and Michael Peel. 2005. "SEC Widens Nigeria Bribery Probe with Shell Subpoena." *The Financial Times* (October 13).

Chabal, Patrick. 2002. "Lusophone Africa in Historical and Comparative Perspective." In *A History of Postcolonial Lusophone Africa*, 3–134. Edited by Patrick Chabal, David Birmingham, Malyn Newitt, Gerhard Siebert, and Elisa Silva Andrade. Bloomington: Indiana University Press.

Chabal, Patrick, David Birmingham, Malyn Newitt, Gerhard Siebert, and Elisa Silva Andrade. 2002. *A History of Postcolonial Lusophone Africa.* Bloomington: Indiana University Press.

Chabal, Patrick and Jean-Pascal Daloz. 1999. *Africa Works: Disorder as a Political Instrument.* Bloomington: Indiana University Press.

Chahabi, H.E. and Juan J. Linz. 1998. "A Theory of Sultanism 1 and 2: A Type of Nondemocratic Rule." In *Sultanistic Regimes*, 3–48. Edited by H.E. Chahabi and Juan J. Linz. Baltimore: The Johns Hopkins University Press.

Chalk, Nigel. 1998. "Fiscal Sustainability with Non-Renewable Resources," IMF Working Paper, WP/98/26. Washington, DC: International Monetary Fund.

Chandler, Alfred D. Chandler. 1992. "Organization Capabilities and the Economic History of the Industrial Enterprise." *Journal of Economic Perspectives* 6, 3 (Summer): 79–100.

———. 1990. *Scale and Scope: The Dynamics of Industrial Capitalism.* Cambridge: Harvard University Press.

———. 1962. *Strategy and Structure Chapters in the History of the American Industrial Enterprise.* Cambridge, MA: MIT Press.

1977. *The Visible Hand: The Managerial Revolution in American Business.* Cambridge: Harvard University Press.

Chaudhury, Kiren Aziz. 1997. *The Price of Wealth: Economies and Institutions in the Middle East.* Ithaca and London: Cornell University Press.

Chenery, Hollis B. and Nicholas G. Carter. 1973. "Foreign Assistance and Development Performance, 1960–1970." *The American Economic Review* 63, 2 (May): 459–468.

Chernow, Ron. 2004. *Titan: The Life of John D. Rockefeller.* New York: Vintage Books.

Chevallier, Pierre. 1974. *Histoire de la Franc-Maçonnerie française.* volume 3, *La Maçonnerie: l'Église de la République* (1877–1944). Paris: Fayard.

Choi, Jin-Wook. 2007. "Governance Structure and Administrative Corruption in Japan: An Organizational Network Approach." *Public Administration Review* (September–October): 930–942.

Chronicle (Accra). 2010. "Row Over Sale of Shares to Exxon: Kosmos Breaks Silence: 'We Broke no Laws'" (July 27). Retrieved from http://ghanaian-chronicle.com August 2, 2010).

Clarence-Smith, W.G. 1979. *Slaves, Peasants, and Capitalists in Southern Angola 1840–1926.* New York: Cambridge University Press.

1994. "African and European Cocoa Producers on Fernando Poo, 1880s to 1910s." *The Journal of African History* 35, (2): 179–199.

1980. "Review Essay: Class Structure and Class Struggles in Angola in the 1970s." *Journal of Southern African Studies* 7, 1 (October): 109–128.

Clark, John F. 2002. "The Neo-Colonial Context of the Democratic Experiment of Congo-Brazzaville." *African Affairs* 101 (April): 171–192.

Clark, Martin. 2008. "Ghana's Deep-Water Potential." *Petroleum Economist* (May).

Cockett, Richard. 2010. *Sudan: Darfur and the Failure of an African State.* New Haven: Yale University Press.

Cohen, Abner. 1969. *Custom and Politics in Urban Africa: A Study of Hausa Migrants in Yoruba Towns.* Berkeley and Los Angeles: University of California Press.

Coignard, Sophie. 2009. *Un État dans l'État: Le Contre Pouvoir Maçonnique.* Paris: Albin Michel.

Coleman, James S. 1958. *Nigeria: Background to Nationalism.* Berkeley and Los Angeles: University of California Press.

Colgan, Jeff D. "Oil and Revolutionary Governments: Fuel for International Conflict." *International Organization* 64, 4 (Fall 2010): 661–694.

Collier, David and Steven Levitsky. 1997. "Democracy with Adjectives: Conceptual Innovation in Comparative Research." *World Politics* 49, 3 (April): 430–451.

Collier, Paul. 2007. *The Bottom Billion: Why the Poorest Countries are Failing and What Can Be Done about It.* New York: Oxford University Press.

1999. "Learning from Failure: The International Finance Institutions as Agencies of Restraint in Africa." In *The Self-Restraining State: Power and Accountability in New Democracies,* 313–330. Edited by Andreas Schedler, Larry Diamond, and Marc Plattner. Boulder: Lynne Rienner Publishers, Inc.

2010. *The Plundered Planet: Why We Must – and How We Can – Manage Nature for Global Prosperity.* New York: Oxford University Press.

Collier, Paul, V.L. Elliott, Havard Hegre, Anke Hoeffler, Marta Reynal-Querol, and Nicholas Sambanis. 2003. *Breaking the Conflict Trap: Civil War and Development Policy*. New York: A Copublication of the World Bank and Oxford University Press.

Collier, Paul and Jan Willem Gunning. 1999. "Explaining African Economic Performance." *Journal of Economic Literature* 37,1 (March): 64–111.

2008. "Sacrificing the Future: Intertemporal Strategies and Their Implications for Growth." In *The Political Economy of Economic Growth in Africa: 1960–2000*, volume 1, 202–224. Edited by Benno J. Ndulu, Stephen A. O'Connell, Robert H. Bates, Paul Collier, and Chukwuma C. Soludo. New York: Cambridge University Press.

Collier, Paul and Anke Hoeffler. 2005. "Democracy and Resource Rents." Mimeo, Department of Economics, Oxford University (26 April).

2000. "Greed and Grievance in Civil Wars," World Bank Working Paper (Washington, DC: The World Bank).

Collier, Paul and Stephen A. O'Connell. 2008. "Opportunities and Choices." In *The Political Economy of Economic Growth in Africa: 1960–2000*, 1: 76–136. Edited by Benno J. Ndulu, Stephen A. O'Connell, Robert H. Bates, Paul Collier, and Chukwuma C. Soludo. New York: Cambridge University Press.

2005. "Resource Rents, Governance, and Conflict." *The Journal of Conflict Resolution* 49, 4 (August): 625–633.

Collins, Kathleen. 2006. *Clan Politics and Regime Transition in Central Asia*. New York: Cambridge University Press.

2002. "Clans, Pacts, and Politics in Central Asia." *Journal of Democracy* 13, 3 (July): 137–152.

2004. "The Logic of Clan Politics: Evidence from the Central Asia Trajectories." *World Politics* 56, 2 (January): 224–261.

2003. "The Political Role of Clans in Central Asia." *Comparative Politics* 35, 2 (January): 171–190.

Conac, Gérard. 1993. "Les Processus de Démocratisation en Afrique." In *L'Afrique en Transition vers le Pluralisme Politique*, 11–41. Edited by Gérard Conac. Paris: Economica.

Conklin, Alice. 1997. *A Mission to Civilize: The Republican Idea of Empire in France and West Africa* (Stanford: Stanford University Press).

Cooke, The Honorable Mr. Justice. 2005. "Kensington International Limited and Republic of the Congo 1. Glencore Energy, UK Limited, 2. Sphynx UK Limited, 3. Sphynx (BDA) Limited, 4. Africa Oil and Gas Corporation, and 5. Cotrade SA" (Royal Courts of Justice, Strand, London, WC2A 2LL, 28/11/2005), para 8.

Cooper, Frederick. 2005. *Colonialism in Question: Theory, Knowledge, History*. Berkeley and Los Angeles: University of California Press.

Coquery-Vidrovitch, Catherine. 1979. "Colonisation ou Impérialisme: La Politique Africaine de la France Entre les Deux Guerres," *Le Mouvement Social* 107 (April–June): 51–76.

1975. "L'Impact des Intérêts Coloniaux: S.C.O.A. et C.F.A.O dans l'Ouest Africain, 1910–1965." *Journal of African History* 16, 4 (October): 595–621.

1993. "La Ville Coloniale « Lieu de Colonisation » et Métissage Culturel." *Afrique Contemporaine* (4): 11–22.

Corden, W. Max and Peter Neary. 1982. "Booming Sector and De-Industrialisation in a Small Open Economy." *The Economic Journal* 92, 3688 (December): 825–848.

Corra, Mamadi and David Willer. 2002. "The Gatekeeper," *Sociological Theory* 20, 2 (July): 180–207.

Cossé, Stéphane. 2006. "Strengthening Transparency in the Oil Sector in Cameroon: Why Does It Matter?" IMF Policy Discussion Paper PDP/06/2 (March).

Cowen, Michael and Liisa Laakso. 1997. "An Overview of Election Studies." *The Journal of Modern African Studies* 35, 4 (December): 717–744.

Cragg, Wesley and William Woof. 2002. "The U.S. Foreign Corrupt Practices Act: A Study of Its Effectiveness." *Business and Society Review* 107 (1): 98–144.

Crystal, Jill. 1990. *Oil and Politics in the Gulf: Rulers and Merchants in Kuwait and Qatar*. New York: Cambridge University Press.

Dadieh, Cyril Kofie. 2009. "The Presidential and Parliamentary Elections in Ghana, December 2008." *Electoral Studies* (28): 642–673.

Dagher, Jihad, Jan Gottschalk, and Rafael Portillo. 2010. "Oil Windfalls in Ghana: A DSGE Approach," IMF Working Paper WP/10/116 (May).

Daily Campion. 2005. "Editorial." *Daily Champion* (Lagos) (5 September).

Dalmazzo, Alberto and Guido de Blasio. 2001. "Resources and Incentives to Reform: A Model and Some Evidence on Sub-Saharan African Countries," IMF Working Paper, WP/01/86.

Daniel, Philip. 1995. "Evaluating State Participation in Mineral Projects: Equity, Infrastructure and Taxation." In *Taxation of Mineral Enterprises*. Edited by James M. Otto. Boston: Graham & Trotman/Martinus Nijhoff.

   2002. "Petroleum Revenue Management: An Overview." Paper prepared for Workshop on Petroleum Revenue Management (Washington, DC: The World Bank, October 23–24).

Daniel, Philip, Brenton Goldsworthy, Wojciech Maliszewski, Diego Mesa Puyo, and Alistair Watson. 2010. "Evaluating Fiscal Regimes for Resource Projects: An Example from Oil Development." In *The Taxation of Petroleum and Minerals: Principals, Problems and Practices*, 187–240. Edited by Philip Daniel, Michael Keen, and Charles McPherson. New York: Taylor, Francis and Routledge.

Davis, Graham A. 1995. "Learning to Love the Dutch Disease: Evidence from the Mineral Economies." *World Development* 23, 10 (October): 1765–1779.

Davis, Jeffrey, Rolando Ossowski, James Daniel, and Steven Barnett. 2001. "Stabilization and Savings Funds for Nonrenewable Resources: Experience and Fiscal Policy Implications," IMF Occasional Paper 205.

Davis, Jeffrey, Rolando Ossowski, and Annalisa Fedelino. 2003. "Fiscal Challenges in Oil-Producing Countries: An Overview." In *Fiscal Policy and Implementation in Oil-Producing Countries*, 1–10. Washington, DC: The International Monetary Fund.

Debos, Marielle. 2013. *Le Métier des Armes au Tchad: Le Gouvernement de l'Entre-Guerres*. Paris: Éditions Karthala.

Denny, L.M. and Donald I. Ray. 1989. "São Tomé and Príncipe." In *Mozambique São Tomé and Príncipe: Economics, Politics, and Society*, 119–204. Edited by Bogdan Szajkowski. New York: Pinter Publishers Ltd.

Desposato, Scott W. 2006. "How Informal Electoral Institutions Shape the Brazilian Legislative Arena." In *Informal Institutions and Democracy: Lessons from Latin*

America, 56–68. Edited by Gretchen Helmke and Steven Levitsky. Baltimore: The Johns Hopkins University Press.

Diamond, Larry and Jack Mosbacher. 2013. "Petroleum to the People: Africa's Coming Resource Curse – and How to Avoid It." *Foreign Affairs* (September–October): 86–98.

Djik, Han van. 2007. "Briefing: Political Deadlock in Chad." *African Affairs* 106, 425 (October): 697–703.

Dogbevi, Emmanuel K. 2010. "Kosmos Energy under investigation for corruption in Ghana." *Ghana Business News* (January 8).

Doornbus, P. 1982. "La Révolution Dérapée: la Violence dans l'est de Tchad (1978–1981)." *Politique Africaine* 7 (Octobre): 5–13.

Dugger, Celia W. 2010. "African Leader Hires Adviser and Seeks an Image Change." *The New York Times* (June 28).

Dunning, Thad. 2008. *Crude Democracy: Natural Resource Wealth and Political Regimes*. New York: Cambridge University Press.

Durrer, E.J. and G.E. Slater. 1977. "Optimization of Petroleum and Natural Gas Production – A Survey." *Management Science* 24, 1 (September): 35–43.

Dyer, Geoff and Kate Mackenzie. 2009. "Chinese Groups Court West for Partnerships." *The Financial Times* (April 19).

Easterly, William. 2001. "The Middle Class Consensus and Economic Development." *The Journal of Economic Growth* (6): 317–335.

Easterly, William and Ross Levine. 1997. "Africa's Growth Tragedy: Policies and Ethnic Divisions." *The Quarterly Journal of Economics* 112, 4 (November): 1203–1250.

Edzodzomo-Ela, Martin. 2000. *Mon Projet pour le Gabon: Comment Redresser un Pays Ruiné par Trois Décennies de Mauvaise Gestion*. Paris: Éditions Karthala.

Eifert, Benn, Alan Gelb, and Nils Borje Tallroth. 2003. "Natural Resource Endowments, the State and Development Strategy." In *Fiscal Policy and Implementation in Oil-Producing Countries*, 82–122. Edited by Jeffrey Davis, Rolando Ossowski, and Annalisa Fedelino. Washington, DC: The International Monetary Fund.

Enewardideke, Ekanpou. 2012. "King Robert Ebizimor's Epic Portrait of A.J. Turner." *The Vanguard* (June 17) (http://www.vanguardngr.com/)

Engel, Eduardo and Rodrigo Valdés. 2000. "Optimal Fiscal Strategy for Oil Exporting Countries," IMF Working Paper, WP/00/118. Washington, DC: The International Monetary Fund (June).

Engelbert, Pierre. 2009. *Africa: Unity, Sovereignty, and Sorrow*. Boulder: Lynne Rienner Publishers Inc.

Engelbert, Pierre and James Ron. 2004. "Primary Commodities and War: Congo-Brazzaville's Ambivalent Resource Curse." *Comparative Politics* 37, 1 (October): 61–81.

Engerman, Stanley L. and Kenneth Sokoloff. 1997. "Factor Endowments, Institutions, and Differential Paths of Growth among New World Economies: A View from Economic Historians of the United States." In *How Latin America Fell Behind: Essays on the Economic Histories of Brazil and Mexico, 1800–1914*, 260–304. Edited by Stephen Haber. Stanford: Stanford University Press.

2002. "Factor Endowments, Inequality, and Paths of Development among New World Economies." *Economia* 3 (Fall): 41–109.

England, Andrew and William Wallis. 2012. "Angola Sets Up Fund to Preserve Oil Riches." *The Financial Times* (October 17).

Erdmann, Gero and Ulf Engel. 2007. "Neopatrimonialism Reconsidered: Critical Review and Elaboration of an Elusive Concept." *Commonwealth and Comparative Politics* 45, 1 (February): 95–119.

European Union, Election Observation Mission. 2011. "Nigeria: Final Report: General Elections" (April).

Fabrikant, Robert. 1975. "Production Sharing Contracts in the Indonesia Petroleum Industry." *Harvard International Law Journal* 2 (Spring): 303–351.

Fafchamps, Marcel and Pedro C. Vicente. 2013. "Political Violence and Social Networks: Experimental Evidence from a Nigerian Election." *Journal of Development Economics* 101 (March): 27–48.

Falola, Toyin. 2009. *Colonialism and Violence in Nigeria*. Bloomington and Indianapolis: Indiana University Press.

    2001. *Violence in Nigeria: The Crisis of Religious Politics and Secular Ideologies*. Rochester: University of Rochester Press.

Familusi, Olmuyiwa Olusesan. 2012. "Moral and Development Issues in Political Godfatherism in Nigeria," *Journal of Sustainable Development in Africa* 14, 7 (2012): 11–25.

Fasano, Ugo. 2000. "Review of the Experience with Oil Stabilization and Savings Funds in Selected Countries," IMF Working Paper, WP/oo/112. Washington, DC: The International Monetary Fund (January).

Fatton, Robert. 1986. "Clientelism and Patronage in Senegal." *African Studies Review* 29, 4 (December): 61–78.

Faucon, Benoît. 2013. "Nigerian Oil Thefts Prompt Shell to Act." *Wall Street Journal* (April 12).

Fearon, James D. "Counterfactuals and Hypothesis Testing in Political Science." *World Politics* 43 (January 1991): 169–195.

Ferreira, Manuel Ennes. 1995. "La Reconversion Économique de la *Nomenklatura* Pétrolières." Translated by Christine Messiant. *Politique Africaine* (March): 11–26.

The Financial Times. 2006. "Taking a Cut Acceptable, Says African Minister" (October 25).

Fishman, Robert. 1990. "Rethinking State and Regime: Southern Europe's Transitions to Democracy." *World Politics* 42, 4 (April): 422–440.

Fjeldstad, Odd-Helge. 2002. "Fighting Fiscal Corruption: The Case of the Tanzanian Revenue Authority." WP 2002:3. Bergen, Norway: The Chr. Michelsen Institute.

Foccart, Jacques. 1997. *Tous les Soirs avec de Gaulle: Journal de l'Elysée – I: 1965 – 1967*. Paris: Librairie Arthème Fayard.

Follorou, Jacques. 2012. "Loïk Le Floch-Prigent et la Fable du Trésor Ivoirien." *Le Monde* (28 Septembre).

Forbes, Alex. 2008. "Scramble for Assets Goes Global." *Petroleum Economist* 75, 2 (February).

Forrest, Tom. 1994. *The Advance of African Capital: The Growth of Nigerian Private Enterprise*. Charlottesville: University Press of Virginia.

Fourchard, Laurent. 2008. "A New Name for an Old Practice: Vigilantes in Southwestern Nigeria." *Africa* 78 (1): 16–40.

Frestad, Denis. 2010. "Corporate Hedging under a Resource Rent Tax Regime." *Energy Economics* 32 (March): 458–468.

Freund, William. 1986. "Theft and Social Protest among the Tin Miners of Northern Nigeria." In *Banditry, Rebellion, and Social Protest in Africa*, 49–63. Edited by Donald Crummey. Portsmouth, NH: Heinemann Educational Books Inc.

Fridy, Kevin S. 2007. "The Elephant, Umbrella, and Quarreling Cocks, Disaggregating Partisanship in Ghana's Fourth Republic." *African Affairs* 106, 423 (April): 281–305.

Frieden, Jeffry A. 1994. "International Investment and Colonial Control: A New Interpretation." *International Organization* 48, 4 (Autumn): 559–593.

Fritz, Verena, Kai Kaiser, and Brian Levy. 2009. *Problem Driven Governance and Political Economy Analysis: Good Practice Framework*. Washington: The World Bank.

Frynas, Jedrzej George. 2004. "The Oil Boom in Equatorial Guinea." *African Affairs* 103 413 (October): 227–546.

2000. *Oil in Nigeria: Conflict and Litigation between Oil Companies and Village Communities*. Piscataway, NJ: Transaction Publishers.

Frynas, Jedrzej George, Geoffrey Wood, and Ricardo M.S. Soares de Oliveira. 2003. "Business and Politics in Sao Tomé and Príncipe: From Cocoa Monoculture to Petro-State." *African Affairs* 102, 406 (January): 25–50.

2003. "Business and Politics in Sao Tomé and Príncipe: From Cocoa Monoculture to Petro-State." *Lusotopie*: 33–58 (updated and revised version).

Gaillard, Philippe. 1995. *Foccart Parle: Entretiens avec Philippe Gaillard*. Paris: Fayard.

Gambetta, Diego. 1993. *The Sicilian Mafia: The Business of Private Protection*. Cambridge, MA: Harvard University Press.

Gardinier, David E. 1997. "Gabon: Limited Reform and Regime Survival." In *Political Reform in Francophone Africa*, 145–161. Edited by John F. Clark and David E. Gardinier. Boulder: Westview Press.

Gary, Ian. 2009. *Ghana's Big Test: Oil Challenge to Democratic Development*. Boston: Oxfam America (February).

Gary, Ian and Nikki Reisch. 2005. *Chad's Oil: Miracle or Mirage: Following the Money in Africa's Newest Petrostate*. Baltimore: Catholic Relief Services.

Geddes, Barbara. 1994. *Politician's Dilemma: Building State Capacity in Latin America*. Berkeley and Los Angeles: University of California Press.

Gelb, Alan, and Associates. 1988. *Oil Windfalls: Blessing or Curse?* New York: Oxford University Press for the World Bank.

Gelb, A., J.B. Knight, and R.H. Sabot. 1991. "Public Sector Employment, Rent Seeking and Economic Growth." *Economie Journal* 101 (September): 1186–1199.

George, Barbara Crutchfield and Kathleen A. Lacey. 2006. "Investigation of Halliburton Co./TSKJ's Nigerian Business Practices: A Model for Analysis of the Current Anti-Corruption Environment on Foreign Corrupt Practices Act Enforcement." *The Journal of Criminal Law and Criminology* 96, 2 (Winter): 503–525.

Geslin, Jean-Dominique. 2002. "Les Certitudes de Teodoro Obiang Nguema: Propos Recueillis à Malabo." *Jeune Afrique l'Intélligent* 2186 (2 au 8 Décembre): 32–33.

Ghana, Republic of. 2004. "Among the Republic of Ghana, Ghana National Petroleum Corporation, Kosmos Energy Ghana HC, and the EO Group in Respect of West

Cape Three Points Block Offshore Ghana." (July 22, 2004). Accra: Government Print Office.

1983. Ghana National Petroleum Corporation Act. Accra: Government Print Office.

2010. Management of Ghana National Petroleum Corporation (GNPC), "Status Report on the Jubilee Field Oil and Gas Development (Tano Deepwater and West Cape Three Points)." Retrieved from www.gnpcghana.com/ (accessed July 30, 2010).

1983. Provisional National Defense Council Law 64. Accra: Government Print Office.

Ghura, Dhaneshwar. 1997. "Private Investment and Endogenous Growth: Evidence from Cameroon," IMF Working Paper WP/97/165 (December).

Glaeser, Edward L., Rafael La Porta, Florencio Lopes-De-Silanes, and Andrei Shleifer. 2004. "Do Institutions Cause Growth?" *Journal of Economic Growth* (9): 271–303.

Glaser, Antoine. 2011. "Un Système du Gouvernement Parallèle." *Le Nouvel Observateur* (27 Janvier à 2 Février): 26.

Global Witness. 2006. "African Minister Buys Multi-Million Dollar California Mansion," Press Release – 08/11/2006. Retrived from http://www.globalwitness.org/media_library_detail.php/468/en/african_minister_buys_multi_million_dollar_califor.

2007. "Congo: Is President's Son Paying for Designer Shopping Sprees with Country's Oil Wealth?" (26 June). Retrieved from http://www.globalwitness.org/library/congo-president%E2%80%99s-son-paying-designer-shopping-sprees-country%E2%80%99s-oil-money.

2005. *The Riddle of the Sphynx: Where Has Congo's Oil Money Gone?* London: Global Witness Ltd. (December).

1999. *A Crude Awakening: The Role of the Oil and Banking Industries in Angola's Civil War and the Plunder of State Assets.* London: Global Witness Ltd. (December).

Goldsmith, Arthur A. 1999. "Africa's Overgrown State Reconsidered: Bureaucracy and Economic Growth." *World Politics* 51, 4 (July): 520–546.

Granitz, Elizabeth and Benjamin Klein. 1996. "Monopolization by 'Raising Rivals' Costs': The Standard Oil Case." *The Journal of Law and Economics* 39, 1 (April): 1–47.

Green, Matthew. 2007. "Court Challenge Tests Yar'Adua Ambitions." *Financial Times* (December 6).

Greif, Avner. 2006. *Institutions and the Path to the Modern Economy: Lessons from Medieval Trade.* New York: Cambridge University Press.

Gruénais, Marc-Éric. 1997. "Congo: La Fin d'une Pseudo-Démocratie." *Politique Africaine* 88 (Décembre): 125–133.

Gueye, Cheikh. 2012. "Gabon's Experience Managing Oil Wealth." In *Oil Wealth in Central Africa: Policies for Inclusive Growth*, 197–212. Edited by Bernardin Akitoby and Sharmini Coorey. Washington, DC: The International Monetary Fund.

Guibert, Nathalie. 2013. "La Guinée Équatoriale, un Partenaire aussi Stratégique qu'Encombrant." *Le Monde* (19 Juin).

Guichaoua, Yvan. 2006. "The Making of an Ethnic Militia: The Oodua People's Congress in Nigeria," CRISE Working Paper No. 26. Oxford: Centre for Research in Inequality, Human Security and Ethnicity (November).

Guirauden, Denis. 2004. "Legal, Fiscal and Contractual Framework." In *Oil and Gas Exploration and Production: Reserves, Costs, and Contracts*, 179–218. Edited by Jean-Pierre Favennec. Translated by Jonathan Pearse. Paris: Editions Technip.

Gylfason, Thorvaldur. 2001. "Natural Resources, Education, and Economic Development." *European Economic Review* (45): 847–859.

Gyimah-Boadi, Emmanuel. "Ghana's Uncertain Political Opening." *Journal of Democracy* 5, 2 (April 1994): 75–86.

Gyimah-Boadi, E. and H. Kwasi Prempeh. "Oil, Politics, and Ghana's Democracy." *Journal of Democracy* 23, 3 (July 2012): 94–108.

Haber, Stephen and Victor Monaldo. 2011. "Do Natural Resources Fuel Authoritarianism? A Reappraisal of the Resource Curse." *The American Political Science Review* 105, 1 (February): 1–26.

Hager, David and Matt Gibson. 2001. *The Norwegian Government Petroleum Fund: Annual Performance Measurement Report for 2000*. London: Bacon and Woodrow Investment Services Limited (18 May).

HalliburtonWatch. 2010. "Interim Report: The Halliburton/TSKJ/NLNG Investigations." Retrieved from www.halliburtonwatch.org/news/nigeria_parliament_report.pdf (accessed 29 October 2010).

Harrigan, Kathryn Rudie. 1988. "Joint Ventures and Competitive Strategy." *Strategic Management Journal* 9, 2 (March–April): 141–158.

Harris, Ron. 2000. *Industrializing English Law: Entrepreneurship and Business Organization, 1720–1844*. New York: Cambridge University Press.

Hart Group. 2006. *Nigeria Extractive Industries Transparency Initiative: Final Report*. London: Hart Group.

Heilbrunn, John R. 2006. "Equatorial Guinea and Togo: What Price Repression?" In *The Worst of the Worst: Dealing with Repressive and Rogue Nations*, 223–249. Edited by Robert I. Rotberg. Washington, DC: The Brookings Institution Press.

2004. "Ghana: Anti-Corruption Diagnostic." Unpublished report commissioned by GTZ Accra (October).

2005. "Oil and Water? Elite Politicians and Corruption in France." *Comparative Politics* 37, 3 (April): 277–292.

Hellermann, Pauline von. 2010. "The chief, the youth, and the plantation: communal politics in southern Nigeria," *The Journal of Modern African Studies* 48, 2 (June): 259–283.

Helmke, Gretchen and Steven Levitsky. 2006. "Introduction." In *Informal Institutions and Democracy: Lessons from Latin America*, 1–30. Edited by Gretchen Helmke and Steven Levitsky. Baltimore: The Johns Hopkins University Press.

Herb, Michael. 1999. *All in the Family: Absolutism, Revolution, and Democracy in Middle Eastern Monarchies*. Albany: New York University Press.

2005. "No Representation without Taxation? Rents, Development, and Democracy." *Comparative Politics* 37, 3 (April): 297–316.

Herbst, Jeffrey. 1994. "Ghana in Comparative Perspective." In *Economic Change and Political Liberalization in sub-Saharan Africa*, 182–198. Edited by Jennifer Widner. Baltimore: The Johns Hopkins University Press.

2004. "Let Them Fail: State Failure in Theory and Practice – Implications for Policy." In *When States Fail: Causes and Consequences*, 302–318. Edited by Robert I. Rotberg. Princeton: Princeton University Press.

2000. *States and Power in Africa: Comparative Lessons in Authority and Control*. Princeton: Princeton University Press.

Hertog, Steffen. 2010a. *Princes, Brokers, and Bureaucrats: Oil and the State in Saudi Arabia*. Ithaca and London: Cornell University Press.

2010b. "The Sociology of the Gulf Rentier Systems: Societies of Intermediaries." *Comparative Studies in Society and History* 52, 2 (April): 282–318.

Hirschman, Albert O. 1959. *The Strategy of Economic Development*. New Haven: Yale University Press.

Hodges, Tony. 2004. *Angola: Anatomy of an Oil State*. Second edition. Bloomington and Indianapolis: Indiana University Press.

Hoffman, Leena. 2010. "Fairy Godfathers and Magical Elections: Understanding the 2003 Electoral Crisis in Anambra State, Nigeria." *The Journal of Modern African Studies* 48, 2 (June): 285–310.

Hook, Leslie, Anousha Sakoui, and Stephanie Kirchgaessner. 2012. "Cnooc Heeds Lessons of Failed Unocal Bid." *The Financial Times* (July 24).

Hopkins, A.G. 1966. "Economic Aspects of Political Movements in Nigeria and in the Gold Coast 1918–1939." *The Journal of African History* 7, 1 (January): 133–152.
1973. *Economic History of West Africa*. New York: Columbia University Press.

Hoyos, Carola. 2006. "National Oil Companies: Majors Have a Tough Job." *The Financial Times*. 29 May.
2007. "The New Seven Sisters: Oil and Gas Giants Dwarf Western Rivals." *The Financial Times* (11 March).

Hugon, P. 1996. "Sortir de la Recession et Preparer l'Après-Pétrole: Le Préalbre Politique: Le Cameroun dans L'Entre-Deux." *Politique Africaine* 62, (Juin): 35–44.

Human Rights Watch. 2007. *Criminal Politics: Violence, and "Godfathers" and Corruption in Nigeria*, 19, no. 16(A). New York: Human Rights Watch (October).
2013. "Equatorial Guinea: Human Rights Concerns ahead of Elections: Troubling Conditions Compromise May 26 Legislative Vote" (May 7).
2004. *Some Transparency, No Accountability: The Use of Oil Revenues in Angola and Its Impact on Human Rights*. New York: Human Rights Watch 16, 1A (January).
2003. *Sudan, Oil, and Human Rights*. New York: Human Rights Watch.
2009. *Well-Oiled: Oil and Human Rights in Equatorial Guinea*. New York: Human Rights Watch (July).

Hutchcroft, Paul D. 1998. *Booty Capitalism: The Politics of Banking in the Philippines*. Ithaca and London: Cornell University Press.

Ichino, Nahomi and Noah L. Nathan. 2012. "Primaries on Demand? Intra-Party Politics and Nominations in Ghana." *British Journal of Political Science* 42, 4 (October): 769–791.

Igbikiowubo Hector and Luka Binniyat. 2006. "South Korea Beats India to Nigeria's Blocks 321 and 323." *The Vanguard* (Lagos) (March 14). Retrieved from http://allafrica.com (accessed 14 March 2006).

Ikokwu, Constance. 2009. "NLNG Bribery Scandal: British Police Arrest Lawyer," *ThisDay Online* (Lagos) (March 7) (http://www.thisdayonline.com/).

International Crisis Group. 2005. "Darfur: The Failure to Protect." Africa Report No. 89 (March 8).

International Monetary Fund. 2003. "Angola: Staff Report for the 2003 Article IV Consultation" (July 14).
2003. "Equatorial Guinea: Selected Issues and Statistical Annex" (October 29).
2013. "Gabon: 2012 Article IV Consultation." IMF Country Report 13/55 (March).
2005. "Gabon: Staff Report for the 2005 Article IV Consultation for the Government of Gabon, Third Review under the Stand-By Arrangement, and Review of Financing Assurances" (March 16).

1999. "Gabon: Statistical Appendix." Country Report No. 99/12 (February).

2004. "Ghana Enhanced Initiative for Highly Indebted Poor Countries – Completion Point Document." IMF Country Report No. 04/209 (July).

2011. "Ghana: Staff Report for the 2010 Article IV Consultation" (May 2011).

2012. "Nigeria: 2011 Article IV Consultation – Staff Report." IMF Country Report 12/194 (July).

2009. "Nigeria: 2009 Article IV Consultation – Staff Report." IMF Country Report 09/315 (November).

2011. "Republic of Congo: Fifth and Sixth Reviews under the Three-Year Arrangement under the Extended Credit Facility and Financing Assurances Review – Staff Report." IMF Country Report 11/255 (August).

2009. "Republic of Congo: First Review under the Three Year Arrangement under the Poverty Reduction and Growth Facility-Request for Waivers for Nonobservance of Performance Criteria and Modification of Performance Criteria-Staff Report." IMF Country Report 09/217 (July).

2011. "Republic of Congo: Joint IMF/World Bank Debt Sustainability Analysis" (July 15).

2010. "Republic of Congo: Second Review under the Three Year Arrangement under the Poverty Reduction and Growth Facility-Staff Report." IMF Country Report 10/54 (February).

Jaffe, Amy Myers and Ronald Soligo. 2007. "The International Oil Companies." Houston: The James A. Baker III Institute for Public Policy of Rice University.

Jensen, Nathan and Leonard Wantchekon. 2004. "Resource Wealth and Political Regimes in Africa." *Comparative Political Studies* 37, 3 (September): 816–841.

Jensen, W.G. 1968. "The Importance of Energy in the First and Second World Wars." *The Historical Journal* 11, 3 (September): 538–554.

Jiang, Julie and Jonathan Sinton. 2011. *Overseas Investments by Chinese National Oil Companies: Assessing the Drivers and Impacts.* Paris: OECD/International Energy Agency.

Jockers, Heinz, Dirk Kohnert, and Paul Nugent. 2010. "The Successful Ghana Election of 2008: A Convenient Myth." *The Journal of Modern African Studies* 48, 1 (March): 95–115.

John-Nambo, Joseph. 1994. "Parodie d'Élection Présidentielle au Gabon." *Politique Africaine* 53: 133–138.

Johnson, Douglas H. 2003. *The Root Causes of Sudan's Civil Wars.* Bloomington and Indianapolis: Indiana University Press.

2008. "Why Abyei Matters: The Breaking Point of Sudan's Comprehensive Peace Agreement." *African Affairs* 107, 426 (January): 1–19.

Johnson Ronald N. and Gary D. Liebcap. 1994. "Patronage to Merit and Control of the Federal Government Labor Force." *Explorations in Economic History* 31, 1 (January): 91–119.

Johnston, Daniel. 1994. *International Petroleum Fiscal Systems and Production Sharing Contracts.* Tulsa, OK: PennWell Publishing Company.

Johnston, David. 2007. "How to Evaluate the Fiscal Terms of Oil Contracts." In *Escaping the Resource Curse,* 53–88. Edited by Macartan Humphreys, Jeffrey D. Sachs, and Joseph E. Stiglitz. New York: Columbia University Press.

Johnston, Michael. 1979. "Patrons and Clients, Jobs and Machines: A Case Study of the Uses of Patronage." *The American Political Science Review* 73, 2 (June): 385–398.

2005. *Syndromes of Corruption: Wealth, Power, and Democracy*. New York: Cambridge University Press.

Jones, G. Gareth. 1977. "The British Government and the Oil Companies 1912–1924: The Search for an Oil Policy." *The Historical Journal* 20, 3 (September): 647–672.

Jones Luong, Pauline and Erika Weinthal. 2010. *Oil is Not a Curse: Ownership Structure and Institutions in Soviet Successor States*. New York: Cambridge University Press.

2001. "Prelude to the Resource Curse: Explaining Oil and Gas Development Strategies in the Soviet Successor States and Beyond." *Comparative Political Studies* 34, 4 (May): 367–399.

Joseph, Richard. 1987. *Democracy and Prebendal Politics in Nigeria: The Rise and Fall of the Second Republic*. New York: Cambridge University Press.

Kalyvas, Stathis N. 2006. *The Logic of Violence in Civil War*. New York: Cambridge University Press.

Karl, Terry Lynn. 1997. *The Paradox of Plenty: Oil Booms and Petro-States*. Berkeley and Los Angeles: University of California Press.

Katz, Menachem, Ulrich Bartsch, Harinder Malothra, and Milan Cuc. 2004. *Lifting the Oil Curse: Improving Petroleum Revenue Management in Sub-Saharan Africa*. Washington, DC: The International Monetary Fund.

Kea, Ray A. 1986. "'I Am Here to Plunder on the General Road': Bandits and Banditry in the Pre-Nineteenth Century Gold Coast." In *Banditry, Rebellion, and Social Protest in Africa*, 109–132. Edited by Donald Crummey. Portsmouth, NH: Heinemann Educational Books.

Keefer, Philip E. 2007. "Clientelism, Credibility, and the Policy Choices of Young Democracies," *American Journal of Political Science* 51, 4 (October): 804–821.

Keefer, Philip and Stuti Khemani. 2012. "Do Informed Citizens Receive More ... or Pay More? The Impact of Radio on the Government Distribution of Public Health Benefits." Policy Research Working Paper 5952. Washington, DC: The World Bank (January).

Khan, Sarah Ahmad. 1994. *Nigeria: The Political Economy of Oil*. Oxford: Oxford University Press.

Khanna, Jyoti and Michael Johnston. 2007. "India's Middlemen: Connecting by Corrupting." *Crime, Law, and Social Change* 48, 3–5 (December 2007): 151–168.

Kimble, David. 1963. *A Political History of Ghana: The Rise of Gold Coast Nationalism 1850–1928*. New York: Oxford University Press.

King, Gary, Robert Keohane, and Sidney Verba. 1994. *Designing Social Inquiry: Scientific Inference in Qualitative Research*. Princeton: Princeton University Press.

Klitgaard, Robert. 1990. *Tropical Gangsters: One Man's Experience with Development and Decadence in Deepest Africa*. New York: Basic Books.

Knack, Stephen and Philip E. Keefer. 1995. "Institutions and Economic Performance: Cross Country Test with Alternative Institutional Measures." *Economics and Politics* 7 (November): 207–227.

Konings, Piet. 2005. "The Anglophone Cameroon Nigeria Boundary: Opportunities and Conflicts." *African Affairs* 104, 415 (April): 275–301.

Kopytoff, Jean Herskovitts. 1965. *A Preface to Modern Nigeria: The "Sierra Leonians" in Yoruba, 1830–1890*. Madison: The University of Wisconsin Press.

Koranteng, Adu. 2009. "Ghana to Discover More Oil and Gas." *The Statesman* (Accra) (April 9). Retrieved from http://www.thestatesmanonline.com/ (accessed April 11, 2009).

Koula, Yitzhak. 1999. *La Démocratie Congolaise « Brûlée » au Pétrole*. Paris: l' Éditions l'Harmattan.

Krueger, Anne O. 1974. "The Political Economy of the Rent-Seeking Society." *The American Economic Review* 64, 3 (June): 291–303.

Kunateh, Masahudu Ankiilu. 2011. "Tullow Offloads 4 Million Shares on GSE." *The Chronicle* (Accra) (June 2).

Lam, Ricky and Leonard Wantchekon. 1999. "Dictatorships as Political Dutch Disease." Economic Growth Center Discussion Paper 795. New Haven: Yale University (January).

Landes, David S. 2006. *Dynasties: Fortunes and Misfortunes of the World's Great Family Businesses*. New York: Viking Penguin.

Lanne, Bernard. 1998. *Histoire Politique du Tchad de 1945 à 1958: Administration, Partis, Élections*. Paris: Éditions Karthala.

1984. "Le Sud, l'Etat et la Révolution." *Politique Africaine* 16 (Décembre): 30–44.

Larsen, E. Røed. 2005. "Are Rich Countries Immune to the Resource Curse: Evidence from Norway's Management of Its Oil Riches." Resources Policy 30: 75–68.

Laske, Karl. 2000. *Ils se Croyaient Intouchables*. Paris: Éditions Albin Michel.

2000. "L'Ex-Monsieur l'Afrique d'Elf Entendu." *Libération* (5 Avril).

Lawan, Mamman. 2010. "Abuse of Powers of Impeachment in Nigeria." *The Journal of Modern African Studies* 48, 2 (June 2010): 311–338.

Lederman, Daniel and William F. Maloney, eds. 2007. *Natural Resources: Neither Curse nor Destiny* Stanford: Stanford University Press and the World Bank.

Lefranc, Georges. 1965. *Histoire du Front Populaire (1934–1938)*. Paris: Payot.

Leigh, David and David Pallister. 2005. "Investigation Urged into West African Oil Deals." *The Guardian* (December 20).

Leith, J. Clark. 2005. *Why Botswana Prospered*. Montreal: McGill-Queen's University Press.

Lemarchand, René. 2003. "The Democratic Republic of the Congo: From Failure to Potential Reconstruction." In *State Failure and State Weakness in a Time of Terror*, 29–70. Edited by Robert I. Rotberg. Washington, DC: Brookings Institution Press.

1972. "Political Clientelism and Ethnicity in Tropical Africa." *The American Political Science Review* 66, 1 (March): 68–90.

Levitsky, Steven and Lucan A. Way. 2010. *Competitive Authoritarianism: Hybrid Regimes after the Cold War*. New York: Cambridge University Press.

2002. "The Rise of Competitive Authoritarianism." *Journal of Democracy* 13, 3 (April): 51–65.

Levy, Brian and Pablo T. Spillar. 1996. "A Framework for Resolving the Regulatory Problem." In *Regulations, Institutions, and Commitment: Comparative Studies of Telecommunications*, 1–35. Edited by Brian Levy and Pablo T. Spillar. New York: Cambridge University Press.

Lewis, Peter M. 1996. "From Prebendalism to Predation: The Political Economy of Decline in Nigeria." *The Journal of Modern African Studies* 34, 1 (March): 79–103.

2007. *Growing Apart: Oil, Politics, and Economic Change in Indonesia and Nigeria*. Ann Arbor: The University of Michigan Press.

2011. "Nigeria Votes: More Openness, More Conflict." *Journal of Democracy* 22, 4 (October): 60–74.

Lindberg, Staffan. 2006. *Democracy and Elections in Africa.* Baltimore: The Johns Hopkins University Press.

Lindberg, Staffan and Minion K.C. Morrison. 2005. "Exploring Voter Alignments in Africa: Core and Swing Voters in Ghana." *The Journal of Modern African Studies* 43, 4 (December): 565–586.

Liniger-Goumaz, Max. 2003. *A l'Aune de la Guinée Équatoriale: Colonisation – Neocolonisation – Démocratisation – Corruption.* Geneva: Les Éditions du Temps.

1989. *Small Is Not Always Beautiful: The Story of Equatorial Guinea.* Translated by John Wood. Totowa, NJ: Barnes and Noble Books.

Little, Kenneth. 1965. *West African Urbanization: A Study of Voluntary Associations in Social Change.* New York: Cambridge University Press.

Lowi, Miriam R. 2009. *Oil Wealth and the Poverty of Politics: Algeria Compared.* New York: Cambridge University Press.

Luong, Pauline Jones and Erika Weinthal. 2010. *Oil is Not a Curse: Ownership Structure and Institutions in Soviet Successor States.* New York: Cambridge University Press.

Maass, Peter. 2005. "A Touch of Crude." *Mother Jones* (January/February).

Mabeko-Tali, Jean-Michel. 2005. *Barbares et Citoyens: L'Identité Nationale à l'Épreuve des Transitions Africaines – Congo-Brazzaville.* Angola and Paris: l' Éditions l'Harmattan.

2000. "Quelques Dessous Diplomatiques de l'Intervention Angolaise dans le Conflit Congolais de 1997." In *Les Congos dans la Tourmente*, 153–164. Edited by Patrice Yengo for Rupture-Solidarité. Paris: Éditions Karthala.

Mahoney, James and Dietrich Rueschemeyer. 2008. "Comparative Historical Analysis: Achievements and Agendas." In *Comparative Historical Analysis in the Social Sciences*, 3–38. Edited by James Mahoney and Dietrich Rueschemeyer. New York: Cambridge University Press.

Mahtani, Dino. 2006. "Doubts over Nigeria's Oil Block Awards." *Financial Times* (February 14).

2005. "Gas: A Farewell to Flaring." *The Financial Times* (April 25).

2006. "Nigerian Senate Rules Out Third Term for Leader." *The Financial Times* (May 17).

2006. "Nigeria Vows to Investigate $90 Million Oil Deal." *Financial Times* (October 31).

2006. "Oil Development: New Players Struggle for Funds." *The Financial Times* (May 15).

Mamdani, Mahmood. 2001. "Beyond Settler and Native as Political Identities: Overcoming the Political Legacy of Colonialism." *Comparative Studies in Society and History* 43, 4 (October): 651–664.

1996. *Citizen and Subject: Contemporary Africa and the Legacy of Late Colonialism.* Princeton: Princeton University Press.

Marcel, Valérie with John V. Mitchell. 2006. *Oil Titans: National Oil Companies in the Middle East.* Washington: Brookings Institution Press.

Marcum, John A. 1978. *The Angolan Revolution*, volume II. *Exile Politics and Guerilla Warfare (1962 – 1976).* Cambridge, MA: MIT Press.

Marseille, Jacques. 1984. *Empire Colonial et Capitalisme Français: Histoire d'un Divorce* Paris: Éditions Albin Michel.

Matusitz, Jonathan and Michael Repass. 2009. "Gangs in Nigeria: An Updated Examination." *Crime, Law, and Social Change* 52, 5 (November): 495–511.

May, Roy and Simon Massey. 2002. "The Chadian Party System: Rhetoric and Reality." *Democratization* 9, 3 (Fall): 72–91.

M'Bokolo, Elikia. 1982. "French Colonial Policy in Equatorial West Africa in the 1940s and 1950s." In *The Transfer of Power in Africa: Decolonization, 1940–1960*, 173–210. Edited by Prosser Gifford and Wm. Roger Louis. New Haven: Yale University Press.

McGee, John. 1958. "Predatory Price Cutting: The Standard Oil (N.J.) Case." *The Journal of Law and Economics* 1, (October): 137–169.

McPherson, Charles. 2003. "National Oil Companies." In *Fiscal Policy Formulation and Implementation in Oil-Producing Countries*, 184–203. Edited by J.M. Davies, R. Ossowski, and A. Fedelino. Washington, DC: The International Monetary Fund. (2003).

Meagher, Kate. 2007. "Highjacking Civil Society: The Inside Story of the Bekassi Boys Vigilante Group of South Eastern Nigeria." *The Journal of Modern African Studies* 45 (1): 89–115.

Médard, Jean-François. 1976. "Le Rapport de Clientèle: de Phénomène Sociale à l'Analyse Politique." *Revue Française de Science Politique* 26, (1): 103–131.

1982. "The Underdeveloped State in Tropical Africa: Political Clientelism or Neo-Patrimonialism?" In *Private Patronage and Political Power: Political Clientelism in the Modern State*, 162–192. Edited by C. Clapham. London: Francis Pinter Ltd.

Mehlum, Halvor, Karl Moene, and Ragnar Torvik. 2006. "Institutions and the Resource Curse." *The Economic Journal* 116, (January): 1–20.

2002. "Plunder and Protection Inc.," *Journal of Peace Research* 39, 4 (July): 447–459.

Meillassoux, Claude. 1969. *Urbanization of an African Community: Voluntary Associations in Bamako, Mali*. Seattle: University of Washington Press.

Melby, Eric D.K. 1981. *Oil and the International System: The Case of France, 1918–1969*. New York: Arno Press.

Messiant, Christine. 2006. *1961. L'Angola Colonial, Histoire et Société: Les Prémisses du Mouvement Nationaliste*. Bâle, Switzerland: P. Schlettwein Publishing.

2008a. *L'Angola Postcoloniale 1. Guerre et Paix sans Democratization*. Paris: Éditions Karthala.

2008b. *L'Angola Postcoloniale 2. Sociologie Politique d'une Oléocratie*. Paris: Éditions Karthala.

2000. "Éditorial: l'Angola? Circulez, il n'y Rien à Voir!" *Lusotopie*: 9–26.

1999. "La Fondation Eduardo dos Santos (FESA): A Propos de « l'Investissement » de la Société Civile par le Pouvoir Angolais." *Politique Africaine* 73 (March): 82–102.

1998. "Protestantisme en Situation Coloniale: Quelles Marges." *Lusotopie* 245–256.

Meyer, J-M. 2010. "Afrique Centrale: Grand Ménage à la Cemac," *Jeune Afrique l'Intélligent* (1 février).

Mayeur, Jean-Marie and Madeleine Rebérioux 1987. *The Third Republic from its Origins to the Great War 1871–1914*. Translated by J.R. Foster. New York: Cambridge University Press.

Montvalon, Jean François de. 2009. *Sassou Nguesso: L'Irrésistible Ascension d'un Pion de la Françafrique*. Paris: Éditions l'Harmattan for Fédération des Congolais de la Diaspora.

Moore, Mick. 2008. "Between Coercion and Contract: Competing Narratives on Taxation and Governance." In *Taxation and State Building in Developing Countries: Capacity and Consent*, 34–63. Edited by Deborah Bräutigam, Odd-Helge Fjeldstad, and Mick Moore. New York: Cambridge University Press.

Morrison, Minion K.C. 2004. "Political Parties in Ghana through Four Republics" A Path to Democratic Consolidation." *Comparative Politics* 36, 4 (July): 421–442.

Myerson, Roger B. 2009. "The Autocrat's Credibility Problem and Foundations of the Constitutional State." *The American Political Science Review* 102, 1 (February): 125–139.

Nakhle, Carole. 2010. "Petroleum Fiscal Regimes: Evolution and Challenges." In *The Taxation of Petroleum and Minerals: Principles, Problems, and Practice*, 89–221. Edited by Philip Daniel, Michael Keen, and Charles McPherson. New York: Routledge.

Nankani, Gobind. 1979. "Development Problems of Mineral Exporting Countries." World Bank Staff Working Paper No. 354. Washington, DC: The World Bank.

National Democratic Institute. 2008. *Final NDI Report on Nigeria's 2007 Elections*. Washington, DC: The National Democratic Institute.

Nevinson, Henry W. 1905. "The New Slave Trade: Introductory – Down the West Coast." *Harpers Monthly Magazine* 111, 663.

1905. "The New Slave Trade: Introductory II – West African Plantation Life To-Day." *Harpers Monthly Magazine* 111, 664.

1905. "The Slave-Trade of To-Day: Part III. *Harpers Monthly Magazine* 111, 665.

1905. "The Slave-Trade of To-Day: Part IV – 'The Hungry Country'." *Harpers Monthly Magazine* 111, 665.

1905. "The Slave-Trade of To-Day: Part V – Down to the Coast." *Harpers Monthly Magazine* 111, 666.

1905. "The Slave-Trade of To-Day: Part VI – The Slaves at Sea." *Harpers Monthly Magazine* 112, 668.

1906. "Through the African Wilderness." *Harpers Monthly Magazine* 112, 669.

Newbury, Colin W. Ed. 1971. *British Policy towards West Africa: Selected Documents 1875–1914 with Statistical Appendices 1800–1914*. London: Oxford at the Clarendon Press.

1978. "Trade and Technology in West Africa: The Case of the Niger Company, 1900–1920." *The Journal of African History* 19, 4: 551–575.

Newitt, Malyn. 1995. *A History of Mozambique*. Bloomington: Indiana University Press.

2003. "São Tomé and Príncipe: Decolonization and its Legacy, 1974–90." In *The Last Empire: Thirty Years of Portuguese Decolonization*, 37–52. Edited by Stewart Lloyd-Jones and Antonio Costa Pinto. Portland, OR: Intellent Books.

Nicholls, Tom. 2005. "NOCs 1 IOCs 0." *Petroleum Economist* 72, 4 (April 1): 4–9.

Nigeria, Federal Government. 2011. "Nigeria Sovereign Investment Authority (Establishment) Act, 2011." Abuja: Federal Government of Nigeria.

Nolutshungu, Sam C. 1996. *Limits of Anarchy: Intervention and State Formation in Chad*. Charlottesville: University of Virginia Press.

North, Douglass C. 1994. "Economic Performance through Time." *The American Economic Review* 84, 3 (June): 359–368.

1990. *Institutions, Institutional Change and Economic Performance*. New York: Cambridge University Press.

1982. *Structure and Change in Economic History.* New York: W.W. Norton.

North, Douglass C. and Barry R. Weingast. 1989. "Constitutions and Commitment: The Evolution of Institutions Governing Public Choice in Seventeenth-Century England." *The Journal of Economic History* 64, (4): 803–832.

Nossiter, Adam. 2010. "Killings in Nigeria Are Linked to Islamic Sect." *The New York Times* (October 18).

Nowell, Gregory P. 1994. *Mercantile States and the World Oil Cartel, 1900–1939.* Ithaca: Cornell University Press.

Nwanma, Vincent. 2007. "Nigeria: 'Last-Minute' Offer of 45 Oil Blocks Draws Criticism." Retrieved from http://www.rigzone.com/news/article.asp?a_id=43514 accessed 5–04–2007.

Obiang, Jean-François. 2007. *France-Gabon: Pratiques Clientélaires d'État dans les Relations Franco-Africaines.* Paris: Éditions Karthala.

Odo, Georges. 2000. *La Franc-Maçonnerie en Afrique.* Paris: Éditions Maçonniques de France.

O'Donnell, Guillermo. 1994. "Delegative Democracy." *Journal of Democracy* 5, 1 (January): 55–69.

Odunyi, Mike. 2005. "Nigeria is Building a New Crop of Indigenous Operators." *Alexander's Gas and Oil Connection* 10, 14 (July 2005).

2005. "Oil Blocks Sale to Fetch N337 bn." *This Day* (Lagos) (September 5).

Oelbaum, Jay. 2004. "Ethnicity Adjusted? Economic Reform, Elections, and Tribalism in Ghana's Fourth Republic." *Commonwealth and Comparative Politics* 42, 2 (July): 242–273.

Ogunsanya, Mogalaji and Harold Thomas. 2004. "Unblocking the Blockages: Challenges for Nigerian Education." *Journal of Developing Societies* 20, 1–2 (June): 79–88.

O'Hara, Terence. 2005. "Riggs Bank Agrees to Guilty Plea and Fine." *The Washington Post* (January 28).

Okafor, Chineme. 2013. "Chevron to Sell 40% Stake in Two Oil Blocks." *ThisDay* (June 12).

Okonjo-Iweala, Ngozi. 2012. *Reforming the Unreformable: Lessons from Nigeria.* Cambridge, MA: MIT Press.

Olivier de Sardan, J.-P. 1996. "L'Économie Morale de la Corruption en Afrique." *Politique Africaine* 63 (Octobre): 97–118.

Olson, Mancur, Jr. 1993. "Dictatorship, Democracy, and Development." *The American Political Science Review* 87, 3 (September): 567–576.

Olson, Mancur, Jr. 1982. *The Rise and Decline of Nations: Economic Growth, Stagflation, and Social Rigidities.* New Haven: Yale University Press.

Omotola, J. Shola. 2009. "'Garrison' Democracy in Nigeria: The 2007 General Elections and the Prospects of Democratic Consolidation." *Commonwealth and Comparative Politics* 47, 2 (April): 194–220.

Organization for Economic Cooperation and Development. 2011. *Convention on Combating Bribery of Foreign Public Officials in International Business Transactions and Related Documents.* Paris: OECD.

Oruwari, Yomi. 2006. "Youth in Urban Violence in Nigeria: A Case Study of Urban Gangs from Port Harcourt." Niger Delta Economies of Violence Working Paper No. 14. University of California, Berkeley: Institute of International Studies.

Osborne, D.K. 1976. "Cartel Problems." *The American Economic Review* 66, 5 (December): 835–844.

Ostrom, Elinor. 1986. "An Agenda for the Study of Institutions." *Public Choice* (48): 3–25.

Otto, James, Craig Andrews, Fred Cawood, Michael Dogett, Pietro Guj, Frank Stermole, John Stermole, and John Tilton. 2006. *Mining Royalties: A Global Study of Their Impact on Investors, Government, and Civil Society*. Washington, DC: The World Bank.

Otto, James, Maira Luisa Batarseh, and John Cordes. 2000. *Global Mining Taxation Comparative Study*. Golden, CO: Institute for Global Resources Policy and Management, The Colorado School of Mines (March).

Péan, Pierre. 1983. *Affaires Africaines*. Paris: Librarie Artème Fayrd.

Pearson, Scott R. 1970. *Petroleum and the Nigerian Economy*. Stanford: Stanford University Press.

Peel, Michael. 2010. *A Swamp Full of Dollars: Pipelines and Paramilitaries at Nigeria's Oil Frontier*. Chicago: Lawrence Hill Books.

2006. "Probe into KBR Role in Nigeria Bribe Case." *The Financial Times* (August 7).

Pegg, Scott. 2009. "Chronicle of a Death Foretold: The Collapse of the Chad-Cameroon Pipeline Project." *African Affairs* 108, 431 (April): 311–320.

Pepinsky, Thomas B. 2009. *Economic Crises and the Breakdown of Authoritarian Regimes: Indonesia and Malaysia in Comparative Perspective*. New York: Cambridge University Press.

Persell, Stuart Michael. 1983. *The French Colonial Lobby 1889–1938*. Stanford: Hoover Institution Press.

Perham, Margery. 1968. *Lugard: The Maker of Modern Nigeria: The Years of Authority 1898–1945*. Hamden, CT: Archon Books.

Perham, Margery and Mary Bull. Editors. 1963. *Frederick Lugard, The Diaries of Lord Lugard*, vol. 4, *Nigeria, 1894–5 and 1898*. Evanston, IL: Northwestern University Press.

Persson, Torsten, Gérard Roland, and Guido Tabellini. 1997. "Separation of Powers and Political Accountability." *The Quarterly Journal of Economics* 112, 4 (November): 1163–1202.

Persson, Torsten and Guido Tabellini. 2004. "Constitutional Rules and Fiscal Policy Outcomes." *The American Economic Review* 94, 1 (March): 25–45.

2003. *The Economic Effect of Constitutions*. Cambridge, MA: MIT Press.

Petroleum Economist. 2008. "Ghana: Jubilee Field Larger than Expected." *Petroleum Economist* (June).

2005. "News Brief: Nigeria." *Petroleum Economist* (May).

Petry, Martin and Naygotimti Bambé. 2005. *Le Pétrole du Tchad: Rêve ou Cauchemar pour les Populations*. Paris: Éditions Karthala.

Pfeffer, Jeffrey and Philip Nowak. 1976. "Joint Ventures and Interorganizational Interdependence." *Administrative Science Quarterly* 21, 3 (September): 398–418.

Pierson, Paul. 2003. "Big, Slow-Moving, and … Invisible: Macrosocial Processes in the Study of Comparative Politics." In *Comparative Historical Analysis in the Social Sciences*, 177–207. Edited by James Mahoney and Dietrich Rueschemeyer. New York: Cambridge University Press.

Petry, Martin and Naygotimti Bambé. 2000a. "Increasing Returns, Path Dependence, and the Study of Politics." *The American Political Science Review* 92, 2 (June): 251–267.

2000b. "The Limits of Design: Explaining Institutional Origins and Change." *Governance* 13, 4 (October): 475–499.

Pinto, António Costa. 2006. "'Chaos' and 'Order': Preto, Salazar and Charismatic Appeal in Inter-War Portugal." *Totalitarian Movements and Political Religions* 7, 2 (June): 203–214.

Pitcher, M. Anne. 2002. *Transforming Mozambique: The Politics of Privatization, 1975–2000.* New York: Cambridge University Press.

Pitcher, Anne, Mary H. Moran, and Michael Johnston. 2009. "Rethinking Patrimonialism and Neopatrimonialism in Africa." *African Studies Review* 52, 1 (April): 125–156.

Polgreen, Lydia. 2012. "Change Unlikely from Angolan Election, but Discontent Simmers." *The New York Times* (August 31).

2007. "Unlikely Ally Against Congo Republic Graft." *The New York Times* (December 10).

Politi, James. 2005. "CNOOC Funding for Unocal Scrutinised." *The Financial Times* (29 June).

Porter, Michael E. 1985. *Competitive Advantage: Creating and Sustaining Superior Performance.* New York: The Free Press.

1990. *The Competitive Advantage of Nations.* New York: The Free Press.

1991. "Toward a Dynamic Theory of Strategy." *Strategic Management Journal* 12 (Winter): 95–117.

Posner, Daniel N. 2003. "The Colonial Origins of Ethnic Cleavages: The Case of Linguistic Divisions in Zambia." *Comparative Politics* 35, 2 (January): 127–146.

2004. "The Political Salience of Cultural Difference: Why Chewas and Tumbukas are Allies in Zambia and Adversaries in Malawi." *The American Political Science Review* 98, 4 (November): 529–545.

Posner, Daniel N. and Daniel J. Young, 2007. "The Institutionalization of Political Power in Africa." *Journal of Democracy* 18, 3 (July): 126–140.

Pratt, Joseph A. 1980. "The Petroleum Industry in Transition: Antitrust and the Decline of Monopoly Control in Oil." *The Journal of Economic History* 40, 4 (December): 815–837.

Pratten, David. 2008. "'The Thief Eats His Shame': Practice and Power in Nigerian Vigilantism." *Africa* 78, 1 (February): 64–83.

Przeworski, Adam. 1991. *Democracy and the Market: Political and Economic Reforms in Eastern Europe and Latin America.* New York: Cambridge University Press.

Przeworski, Adam, Michael E. Alvarez, José Antonio Cheibub, and Fernando Limogi. 2000. *Democracy and Development: Political Institutions and Well-Being in the World, 1950–1990.* New York: Cambridge University Press.

Przeworski, Adam and Fernando Limongi. 1993. "Political Regimes and Economic Growth." *Journal of Economic Perspectives* 7, 3 (Summer): 51–69.

Quinlan, Martin. 2005. "Equatorial Guinea: developing high margin LNG." *Petroleum Economist* (May).

2005. "Nigeria: Looking for Explorers." *Petroleum Economist* (May).

Radon, Jenik. 2005. "The ABCs of Petroleum Contracts: License-Concession Agreements, Joint Ventures, and Production-Sharing Agreements." In *Covering Oil: A Reporter's Guide to Energy and Development*, 61–85. Edited by Svetlana Tsalik and Anya Schiffrin. New York: Open Society Institute.

Reed, John. 2006. "Son of African Leader Linked to $35m House." *Financial Times* (November 7).

Reed, Kristin. 2009. *Crude Existence: Environment and the Politics of Oil in Northern Angola.* Berkeley and Los Angeles: University of California Press.

Reid Jr., Joseph D., and Michael M. Kurth. 1988. "Public Employees in Political Firms: Part A. The Patronage Era." *Public Choice* 59, 3 (December): 253–262.

Rémy, Jean-Philippe. 2004. "Le Parti du Président Tchadien Idriss Déby Lève l'Obstacle à une Présidence à Vie." *Le Monde* (29 Mai).

2005. "Tchad Rebellion: Le Chef des Déserteurs est un Ancien Proche du President Déby." *Le Monde* (14 Décembre).

Renaud, Lecadre. 2007. "Le Fils du President du Congo Tous Frais Payés." *Libération* (19 Juillet).

Reno, William. 1993. "Old Brigades, Money Bags, New Breeds, and the Ironies of Reform in Nigeria." *Canadian Journal of African Studies* 27, 1 (April): 66–87.

2005. "The Politics of Violent Opposition in Collapsing States." *Government and Opposition* 40, 2 (Spring): 127–151.

2011. *Warfare in Independent Africa.* New York: Cambridge University Press.

1998. *Warlord Politics and African States.* Boulder: Lynne Rienner Publishers, Inc.

République Française. 1943. Département de Pool, Rapport Politique Année 1942. N°425. ANSOM. AEF 4(2) D75 (Brazzaville, le 27 mars).

1936. Ministère des Colonies. "Dépêches Ministérielles de l'Okoumé." No 5983. ANSOM. AEF 1B 473 (7 Décembre).

1948. Territoire du Gabon. Rapport Politique, Année 1947, Chefferie – Faits Importants, Assemblées de Chefs. ANSOM. AEF 4 (1) D55.

République Gabonaise. 2012. *Plan Stratégique Gabon Emergent: Vision 2015 et Orientations Stratégiques 2011–2016.* Libreville: République Gabonaise, Juillet.

Rex Features. 2009. "Omar Bongo Ondimba, President of Gabon, Died on June 8, Aged 73." *The Economist* (June 18).

Ribadu, Mallam Nuhu and Olasupo Shasore San. 2012. *Report of the Petroleum Revenue Special Task Force.* Abuja: Federal Ministry of Petroleum Resources (August).

Rice, Xan. 2009. "Nigeria Begins Amnesty for Niger Delta Militants." *The Guardian* (August 6).

2012. "Nigeria Plans Big Boost to Sovereign Fund." *The Financial Times* (October 3).

Rigzone. 2010. "Kosmos Cancels ExxonMobil's $4B Deal for Ghana Assets." Retrieved from http://www.rigzone.com/news/article.asp?a id=97477 (accessed August 18, 2010).

2009. "KBR Pleads Guilty in Bonny Island Bribes Case." Retrieved from http://www.rigzone.com/news/article.asp?a_id=72822 (accessed February 12, 2009).

Roberts, Adam. 2006. *The Wonga Coup: Guns, Thugs, and a Ruthless Determination to Create Mayhem in an Oil-Rich Corner of Africa.* New York: Perseus Books.

Roberts, Hugh. 2007. "Demilitarizing Algeria." Carnegie Papers 86 (May).

Roberts, Richard and Kristin Mann. 1991. "Law in Colonial Africa." In *Law in Colonial Africa,* 3–58. Edited by Richard Roberts and Kristin Mann. Portsmouth, New Hampshire: Heinneman Educational Books, Inc.

Robinson, James A. 2002. "*State and Power in Africa* by Jeffrey I. Herbst: A Review Essay." *Journal of Economic Literature* 40 (June): 510–519.

Robinson, James A., Ragnar Torvik, and Thierry Verdier. 2006. "Political Foundations of the Resource Curse." *Journal of Development Economics* 79 (April): 447–468.

Roche, François. 2003. *TotalFinaElf: Une Major Française.* Paris: Editions le Cherche Midi.

Rodrik, Dani. 2007. *One Economics Many Recipes: Globalization, Institutions, and Economic Growth.* Princeton: Princeton University Press.

Roitman, Janet and Gérard Roso. 2001. "Guinée-Équatoriale: Être « Off-Shore » pour Rester « National »." *Politique Africaine* 81 (Mars): 121–142.

Romer, Christina D. 1990. "The Great Crash and the Onset of the Great Depression." *The Quarterly Journal of Economics* 105, 3 (August): 597–624.

Romero, Simon and Craig S. Smith. 2004. "Halliburton Severs Link with 2 Over Nigeria Inquiry." *The New York Times* (June 19).

Roniger, Luis. 1987. "Caciquismo and Coronelismo: Contextual Dimensions of Patron Brokerage in Mexico and Brazil." *Latin American Research Review* 22 (2): 71–99.

Rose-Ackerman, Susan. 1999. *Corruption and Government: Causes, Consequences, and Reform.* New York: Cambridge University Press.

  2004. "Establishing the Rule of Law." In *When States Fail: Causes and Consequences,* 182–221. Edited by Robert I. Rotberg. Princeton: Princeton University Press.

Ross, David A. 1965. "The Career of Domingo Martinez in the Bight of Benin 1833–1864." *Journal of African History* 6, 1 (March): 79–90.

Ross, Michael L. 2001a. "Does Oil Hinder Democracy?" *World Politics* 53, 3 (April): 325–361.

  2012. *The Oil Curse: How Petroleum Wealth Shapes the Development of Nations.* Princeton: Princeton University Press.

  1999. "The Political Economy of the Resource Curse." *World Politics* 51, 2 (January): 297–322.

  2001b. *Timber Booms and Institutional Breakdown in Southeast Asia.* New York: Cambridge University Press.

Rudie-Harrigan, Kathryn. 1988. "Joint Ventures and Competitive Strategy." *Strategic Management Journal* 9, 2 (March–April): 141–158.

Russell, Alec. 2007. "Angola Offers Timeframe for Sonangol Shake-Up." *The Financial Times* (October 11).

Rutman, Gilbert, Bernadette de Bonpros-Bainville, Dominique Ausseur, Pierre Castillon, Frédéric Cegarra, Jean-Marie Gerbeaux, Jean Gérin, Roman Gozalo, Didier Hiard, Philippe Jacques, Jacques Jaisson, Jean Lecendreaux, Jean-Pierre Roche, Jacques Sampré, and Jean Vergne. 1998. *Elf Aquitaine des origines à 1989.* Paris: Fayard.

Sachs, Jeffrey D. and Andrew M. Warner. 2001. "The Curse of Natural Resources." *European Economic Review* (45): 827–838.

  1997. "Natural Resource Abundance and Economic Growth." Center for International Development and Harvard Institute for International Development (November).

  1999. "Natural Resource Abundance and Economic Growth." National Bureau of Economic Research Working Paper No. 5398.

Sala-i-Martin, Xavier and Arvind Subramanian. 2003. "Addressing the Natural Resource Curse: An Illustration from Nigeria," IMF Working Paper WP/03/139 (July).

Same, Achille Toto. 2008. "Mineral-Rich Countries and Dutch Disease: Understanding the Macroeconomic Implications of Windfalls and the Development Prospects: The Case of Equatorial Guinea." World Bank Policy Research Working Paper 4595 (April).

Sandbrook, Richard. 2000. *Closing the Circle: Democratization and Development in Africa.* New York: Zed Books Ltd.

1985. *The Politics of Africa's Economic Stagnation.* New York: Cambridge University Press.

Sarraut, Albert. 1921. *La Politique d'Association.* Paris: Payot.

Satre, Lowell J. 2005. *Chocolate on Trial: Slavery, Politics, and the Ethics of Business.* Athens, OH: Ohio University Press.

Schatz, Edward. 2004. *Modern Clan Politics: The Power of Blood in Kazakhstan and Beyond.* Seattle: University of Washington Press.

Schelling, Thomas C. 1967. "Economics and Criminal Enterprise." *The Public Interest* 7 (Spring): 61–78.

Scott, James C. 1972. "Patron-Client Politics and Political Change in Southeast Asia." *The American Political Science Review* 66, 1 (March): 91–113.

Seibert, Gerhard. 2003a. "The Bloodless Coup of July 16 in São Tomé e Príncipe." *Lusotopie:* 245–260.

2006. *Comrades, Clients and Cousins: Colonialism, Socialism and Democratization in São Tomé and Príncipe.* Boston: Koninklijke Brill NV.

1997. "Le Massacre de Février 1953 à São Tomé e Príncipe: Raison d'Être du Nationalisme Santoméen." *Lusotopie:* 173–192.

1995. "A Políca num Micro-Estado: São Tomé e Príncipe ou os Conflitos Pessoais e Políticos na Génese dos Partidos Políticos." *Lusotopie:* 239–250.

1996. "São Tomé e Príncipe: Military Coup as a Lesson." *Lusotopie:* 71–80.

2003b. "São Tomé and Príncipe: Recent History and Economy." *Africa South of the Sahara* (London).

Sen, Amartya. 1999. *Development as Freedom.* New York: Alfred Knopf.

2009. *The Idea of Justice.* Cambridge: The Belknap Press of Harvard University Press.

Servant, Jean-Christophe. 2003. "Offensive sur l'or Noir Africaine." *Le Monde Diplomatique* (Janvier): 19.

Shankleman, Jill. 2006. *Oil, Profits, and Peace: Does Business Have a Role in Peacemaking?* Washington, DC: United States Institute of Peace Press.

Shleifer, Andrei and Robert W. Vishny. 1993. "Corruption." *The Quarterly Journal of Economics* 108, 3 (August): 599–617.

1992. "Pervasive Shortages under Socialism." *RAND Journal of Economics* 23, 2 (Summer): 237–246.

Sklar, Richard L. 1993. "The African Frontier for Political Science." In *Africa and the Disciplines: The Contribution of Research on Africa to the Social Sciences and Humanities,* 83–111. Edited by Robert H. Bates, V.Y. Mudimbe, and Jean O'Barr. Chicago: University of Chicago Press.

1987. "Developmental Democracy." *Comparative Studies in Society and History* 29, 4 (October): 686–714.

1979. "The Nature of Class Domination in Africa." *The Journal of Modern African Studies* 14, 4 (December): 531–552.

1963. *Nigerian Political Parties: Power in an Emergent African Nation.* Princeton: Princeton University Press.

Sklar, Richard L., Ebere Onwudiwe, and Darren Kew. 2006. "Nigeria: Completing Obasanjo's Legacy." *Journal of Democracy* 17, 3 (July): 100–115.

Smil, Vaclav. 2003. *Energy at the Crossroads: Global Perspectives and Uncertainties.* Cambridge, MA: MIT Press.

Smith, Benjamin. 2007. *Hard Times in the Lands of Plenty: Oil Politics in Iran and Indonesia*. Ithaca: Cornell University Press.

Smith, Daniel Jordan. 2007. *A Culture of Corruption: Everyday Deception and Popular Discontent in Nigeria*. Princeton: Princeton University Press.

Smith, Ernest E. and John S. Dzienkowski. 1989. "A Fifty-Year Perspective on World Petroleum Arrangements." *Texas International Law Journal* 24, (1): 1–50.

Smith, Robert. 1979. *The Lagos Consulate 1851–1861*. Berkeley and Los Angeles: University of California Press.

Smith, Stephen and Antoine Glaser. 1992. *Ces Messieurs Afrique: Le Paris-Village du continent noir*. Paris: Calman Lévy.

1997. *Ces Messieurs Afrique: Des Réseaux aux Lobbies*. Paris: Calmann-Lévy.

Soares de Oliveira, Ricardo. 2007. "Business Success, Angola-Style: Postcolonial Politics and the Rise of Sonangol." *The Journal of Modern African Studies* 45 (4): 595–619.

2011. "Illiberal Peacekeeping in Angola." *The Journal of Modern African Studies* 49, 2 (March): 287–314.

2007. *Oil and Politics in the Gulf of Guinea*. New York: Columbia University Press.

Söderling, Ludvig. 2006. "After the Oil: Challenges Ahead in Gabon." *Journal of African Economies* 15, 1 (March): 117–148.

2002. "Escaping the Curse of Oil? The Case of Gabon," IMF Working Paper, WP/02/93.

Sokoloff, Kenneth and Stanley L. Engerman. 2000. "History Lessons: Institutions, Factors Endowments, and Paths of Development in the New World." *Journal of Economic Perspectives* 14, 3 (Summer): 217–232.

Soni-Benga, Paul. 2001. *La Guerre Inachevée du Congo-Brazzaville (15 Octobre 1997– 18 Décembre 1998)*. Paris: Éditions l'Harmattan.

Sotinel, Thomas. 1995. "Vague d'Arrestations d'Opposants en Guinée-Équatoriale." *Le Monde* (19 Avril)

Soudan, François. 2006. "Le Mystérieux M. Obiang." *Jeune Afrique* (9 Octobre).

2001. "Sassou a-t-il Change?" *Jeune Afrique l'Intélligent* 2136 (18 au 24 Décembre): 38–41.

Stern, Babette. 2000. "Le Tchad a Acheté des Armes avec l'Argent du Pétrole." *Le Monde* (22 Novembre).

Stone, Gilbert. 1920. "The Mining Laws of the West African Colonies and Protectorates." *Journal of Comparative and International Law* 2 (3): 259–266.

Suberu, Rotimi. 2001. *Federalism and Ethnic Conflict in Nigeria*. Washington, DC: United States Institute of Peace Press.

Svensson, Jakob. 2008. "Absorption Capacity and Disbursement Constraints." In *Reinventing Foreign Aid*, 311–332. Edited by William Easterly. Cambridge, MA: MIT Press.

Swanson, Philip, Mai Oldgard, and Leiv Lunde. 2003. "Who Gets the Money? Reporting Resources Revenues." In *Natural Resources and Violent Conflict: Options and Actions*, 43–96. Edited by Ian Bannon and Paul Collier. Washington, DC: The World Bank.

Tali, Jean-Michel Mabeko. 2000. "Quelques Dessous Diplomatiques de l'Intervention Angolaise dans le Conflit Congolais de 1997." In *Les Congos dans la Tourmente*, 153–164. Edited by Patice Yengo for Rupture-Solidarité. Paris: Éditions Karthala.

Tarbell, Ida M. 2009. *The History of the Standard Oil Company*, volumes I and II. New York: Cosimo Classics.

Taylor, Ian. 2006. "China's Oil Diplomacy in Africa." *International Affairs* 82, 5 (September): 937–959.

Thelen, Kathleen. 2004. *How Institutions Evolve: The Political Economy of Skills in Germany, Britain, the United States, and Japan*. New York: Cambridge University Press.

Thiery, Guillaume. 2011. "Partis Politiques et Élections de 2011 au Nigeria: l'Action Congress of Nigeria en Champagne." *Afrique Contemporaine* (239): 89–103.

Thomas, Martin. 2005. "Albert Sarraut, French Colonial Development, and the Communist Threat, 1919–1930." *The Journal of Modern History* 77 (December): 917–955.

Tignor, Robert. 1993. "Political Corruption in Nigeria Before Independence," *The Journal of Modern African Studies* 31, 2 (June): 175–202.

Tilly, Charles. 1992. *Coercion, Capital, and European States: AD 990–1992*. Cambridge, MA: Blackwell Publishers.

Timmons, Jeffrey F. 2005. "The Fiscal Contract: States, Taxes, and Public Services." *World Politics* 57, 4 (July): 530–567.

Tirole, Jean. 1992. "Persistence of Corruption." Institute for Policy Reform Working Paper 152 (October).

Tornell, Aaron and Philip R. Lane. 1999. "The Voracity Effect." *The American Economic Review* 89, 1 (March): 22–46.

Triaud, Jean-Louis. 1992. "Au Tchad, la Démocratie Introuvable." *Le Monde Diplomatique* (Février): 18.

Troesken, Werner. 1999. "Patronage and Public Sector Wages in 1896." *The Journal of Economic History* 59, 2: 424–446.

Tulipe, Simon. 2004. "Le Bassin Tchadien à l'Épreuve de l'or Noir: Réflexions sur la «Nouvelle Donne Pêtrole Politique» en Afrique Centrale." *Politique Africaine* 94 (Juin): 59–81.

Tuquoi, Jean-Pierre. 2005. "Au Pouvoir au Gabon Depuis 1967, Omar Bongo s'Offre dans les Urnes un Nouveau Septennat." *Le Monde* (27 Novembre).

   2005. "La bande à Bongo." *Le Monde* (27 Novembre).

Uchegbu, Achilleus-Chud. 2009. "Nigeria: The Halliburton Scandal." *The Daily Champion* (Lagos) (April 10, 2009). Retrieved from http://championonlinenews.com/index.php?lang=en.

United Nations Environmental Programme. 2011. *Environmental Assessment of Ogoniland*. New York: UNEP.

United States Geological Survey. 2009. "2008 Minerals Yearbook: Cameroon and Cape Verde." Washington, DC: U.S. Department of the Interior (November).

U.S. Energy Information Administration. 2012. "Nigeria." (October 16).

Vail, Leroy and Landeg White. 1980. *Capitalism and Colonialism in Mozambique*. Minneapolis: University of Minnesota Press.

Vallee, Olivier. 1988. "Les Cycles de la Dette." *Politique Africaine* 31 (Octobre): 15–21.

Vanasco, Rocco R. 1999. "The Foreign Corrupt Practices Act: An International Perspective." *Managerial Auditing Journal* 14, (4–5): 161–165.

Van de Walle, Nicolas. 2001. *African Economies and the Politics of Permanent Crisis, 1979–1999*. New York: Cambridge University Press.

2004. "The Economic Correlates of State Failure: Taxes, Foreign Aid, and Policies." In *When States Fail: Causes and Consequences*, 94–115. Edited by Robert I. Rotberg. Princeton: Princeton University Press.

2009. "The Institutional Origins of Inequality in Sub-Saharan Africa." *The Annual Review of Political Science* (12): 307–327.

2003. "Presidentialism and Clientelism in Africa's Emerging Party Systems." *The Journal of Modern African Studies* 41, 2 (June): 297–321.

Verschave, François-Xavier. 1998. *La Françafrique: Le Plus Long Scandale de la République*. Paris: Éditions Stock.

2000. *Noire Silence: Qui Arrêtera la Françafrique?* Paris: Éditions les Arènes.

Vicente, Pedro C. 2010. "Does Oil Corrupt? Evidence from a Natural Experiment in West Africa." *Journal of Development Economics* 92, 1 (May): 28–38.

Vines, Alex, Lillian Wong, Markus Weimer, and Indira Campos. 2009. *The Thirst for Africa's Oil: Asian National Oil Companies in Nigeria and Angola*. London: A Chatham House Report (August).

Wallerstein, Immanuel. 2003. "Citizens All? Citizens Some! The Making of the Citizen." *Comparative Studies in Society and History* 45, 4 (October): 650–679.

Wallis, John Joseph. 2006. "The Concept of Systematic Corruption in American History." In *Corruption and Reform: Lessons from American Economic History*, 23–62. Edited by Edward L. Glaeser and Claudia Goldin. Chicago: University of Chicago Press.

Wallis, William. 2009. "Ghana Pledges Open Accounting as It Prepares for Oil Revenues." *The Financial Times* (December 4).

2009. "Ghana Seeks Way Out of Oil Dispute." *The Financial Times* (July 19).

2010. "Oilfield Dispute Fires Up Ghana-US Match." *The Financial Times* (June 27).

"Review of Ghana's Oil Contract Holds Up Funding." *The Financial Times* (August 5).

2010. "Oil Riches to Test Trail-Blazer Ghana." *The Financial Times* (May 31).

Wallis, William and Martin Arnold. 2010. "'Sweat Equity' Probe Tests Ghana's Oil Jackpot." *The Financial Times* (January 7).

Wallis, William, Martin Arnold, and Brooke Masters. 2010. "Corruption Probe into Oil Partners." *The Financial Times* (January 8).

Watts, Michael J. 2008. "Blood Oil: The Anatomy of a Petro-Insurgency in the Niger Delta, Nigeria." Niger Delta Economies of Violence Working Paper No. 22. University of California, Berkeley: Institute of International Studies.

2008. "Imperial Oil: The Anatomy of a Nigerian Oil Insurgency." Niger Delta Economies of Violence Working Paper No. 18. University of California, Berkeley: Institute of International Studies.

1994. "Oil as Money: The Devil's Excrement and the Spectacle of Black Gold." In *Money, Power and Space*. 406–445. Edited by Stuart Corbridge, Ron Martin, and Nigel Thrift. Cambridge, MA: Blackwell Publishers.

2006. "Petro-Insurgency or Criminal Syndicate? Conflict, Violence and Political Disorder in the Niger Delta." Niger Delta Economies of Violence Working Paper No. 16. University of California, Berkeley: Institute of International Studies.

Wauthier, Claude. 1995. *Quatre Presidents et l'Afrique: De Gaulle, Pompidou, Giscard d'Estaing, Mitterrand*. Paris: Éditions de Seuil.

Weber, Max. 1978/1968. *Economy and Society: An Outline of Interpretive Sociology*. Edited by Guenther Roth and Claus Wittich. Berkeley and Los Angeles: University of California Press.

Wei, Shang-Jin. 2000. "How Taxing is Corruption on International Investors?" *The Review of Economics and Statistics* 82, 1 (February): 1–11.

Weinthal, Erika and Pauline Jones Luong. 2001. "Energy Wealth and Tax Reform in Russia and Kazakhstan." *Resources Policy* 27, 4 (December): 215–223.

Weidenbaum, Murray and Samuel Hughes. 1996. *The Bamboo Network: How Expatriate Chinese Entrepreneurs are Creating a New Economic Superpower in Asia*. New York: The Free Press.

Weissman, Fabrice. 1993. *Élection Présidentielle de 1992 au Congo: Entreprise Politique et Mobilization Électorale*. Bordeaux: Centre d'Etudes d'Afrique Noire.

Whitaker, C.S. 1970. *The Politics of Tradition, Continuity and Change in Northern Nigeria 1946–1966*. Princeton: Princeton University Press.

Wiegand, Johannes. 2004. "Fiscal Surveillance in a Petro Zone: The Case of CEMAC." IMF Working Paper, WP/04/8 (January).

Wienthal, Erika and Pauline Jones Luong. 2001. "Energy Wealth and Tax Reform in Russia and Kazakhstan." *Resources Policy* 27, 4 (December): 215–233.

Wijnbergen, Sweder van. 1984. "The 'Dutch Disease': A Disease after All?" *The Economic Journal* 94 (March): 41–55.

Wilkins, Mira. 2005. "Multinational Enterprise to 1930: Discontinuities and Continuities." In *Leviathans: Multinational Corporations and the New Global History*, 45–79. Edited by Alfred D. Chandler, Jr. and Bruce Mazlish. New York: Cambridge University Press.

Wilkinson, Steven I. 2004. *Votes and Violence: Electoral Competition and Ethnic Riots in India*. New York: Cambridge University Press.

Wilks, Ivor. 1975. *Asante in the Nineteenth Century: The Structure and Evolution of a Political Order*. New York: Cambridge University Press.

Wilson, James Q. 1961. "The Economy of Patronage." *Journal of Political Economy* 69, 4 (August): 369–380.

Wintrobe, Ronald. 1998. *The Political Economy of Dictatorship*. New York: Cambridge University Press.

Wood, Geoffrey. 2004. "Business and Politics in a Criminal State: The Case of Equatorial Guinea." *African Affairs* 103 (413): 547–567.

Woolcock, Michael, Lant Pritchett, and Jonathan Isham. 2001. "The Social Foundations of Poor Economic Growth in Resource Rich Countries." In *Resource Abundance and Economic Development*, 76–92. Edited by R.M. Auty. New York: Oxford University Press.

World Bank. 2005. *Angola: Public Expenditure Management and Financial Accountability*. Report No. 29036-AO. Washington, DC: The World Bank (February 16).

   1997, *Helping Countries Combat Corruption: The Role of the World Bank* Washington, DC: the World Bank, September.

   1997. Republic of Gabon: Poverty in a Rent-Based Economy." Report 16333-GA. Two Volumes. Washington, DC: The World Bank.

   2006. Republic of Gabon: Public Expenditure Management and Financial Accountability Review (PEMFAR). Poverty Reduction and Economic Management Sector Unit (PREM3). Africa Region. Washington, DC: The World Bank (September 20).

   2012. World Development Indicators. Washington, DC: The World Bank. Retrieved from http://data.worldbank.org/data-catalog/world-development-indicators various dates.

Yates, Douglas A. 1996. *The Rentier State in Africa: Oil Rent Dependency and Neocolonialism in the Republic of Gabon.* Trenton, NJ: Africa World Press, Inc.

Yengo, Patrice. 2006. *La Guerre Civile du Congo-Brazzaville, 1993–2002: « Chacun Aura sa Part ».* Paris: Éditions Karthala.

Yergin, Daniel. 1991. *The Prize: The Epic Quest for Oil, Money, and Power.* New York: The Free Press.

2011. *The Quest: Energy, Security, and the Remaking of the Modern World.* New York: The Penguin Press.

Youde, Jeremy. 2005. "Economics and Government Popularity in Ghana." *Electoral Studies* 24, 1 (March): 1–16.

Young, Crawford. 1994. *The African Colonial State in Comparative Perspective.* New Haven: Yale University Press.

1982. *Ideology and Development in Africa.* New Haven: Yale University Press.

1976. *The Politics of Cultural Pluralism.* Madison: The University of Wisconsin Press.

Zafar, Ali. 2004. "What Happens When a Country Does Not Adjust to Terms of Trade Shocks? The Case of Oil-Rich Gabon." World Bank Policy Research Working Paper 3403 (September).

Government Documents

United States Senate Minority Staff of the Permanent Subcommittee on Investigations. 2004. *Money Laundering and Foreign Corruption: Enforcement and Effectiveness of the Patriot Act: Case Study Involving Riggs Bank.* Washington, DC: United States Senate Permanent Subcommittee on Investigations (July 15).

United States Senate Permanent Subcommittee on Investigations. 2010. *Keeping Foreign Corruption out of the United States: Four Case Studies.* Washington, DC: United States Senate Permanent Subcommittee on Investigations (February 4).

Archives

Archives Nationale du Togo – ANT (Lomé)
Archives Nationale de France – ANF (Paris)
Archive Nationale de France Section Outre-Mer – ANSOM (Aix-en-Provence)

Index

Diamond, Larry, 13n.47
Direct taxes, 106
Dodd-Frank Act of 2010, 31, 77
Dokubo-Asari, Alhaji Mujahid, 202
Domestic national oil companies (DNOCs), 89, 95
dos Santos, Jose Eduardo, 129, 151
dos Santos, Jose Filomeno, 147
Dunning, Thad, 16n.60
Dutch disease, 2, 14, 16, 68, 113, 121, 139, 144, 159, 160, 216, 228

Easterly, William, 7, 7n.27, 150n.13
Easterly, William and Ross Levine, 120n.32
Éboué, Félix, 44, 45n.30
Economic growth in China, 135
Edusie, Kwame Bawuah, 161
Eifert, Benn, Alan Gelb, and Nils Borje Tallroth, 160n.38
Elf Aquitaine, 2, 19, 31, 78n.8, 91, 140
Elf Aquitaine and Congo, 179, 227
Elf Aquitaine and Gabon, 210
Emerging producer, 17, 20, 90, 109, 111, 114, 120, 121, 123, 124, 126, 129, 133, 143, 144, 147, 156, 157, 158, 160, 180, 216, 220
Engerman, Stanley L. and Kenneth L. Sokoloff, 6, 40
EO Group, 160, 161, 162, 164
Equatorial Guinea, 118, 119, 124, 133, 150, 157, 165, 166, 167, 168, 170, 171, 172, 181
Equatorial Guinea – Black Beach prison, 170
Equatorial Guinea – clan politics, 165
Equatorial Guinea – colonialism in Spanish Guinea, 116
Equatorial Guinea – contracts, 91
Erdimi, Tom and Timane Erdimi, 155, 186
Extractive Industries Transparency Initiative, 23, 99
Exxon, 162n.45
Exxon – ExxonMobil, 3
ExxonMobil, 33, 90, 92, 117n.25, 161, 162, 168, 187

Fabrikant, Robert, 101n.116
Falola, Toyin, 27n.90
Ferry, Jules, 42, 51, 211
Forced labor, 49
Foreign Corrupt Practices Act, 79, 79n.10, 79n.11, 80, 124, 163, 196n.59, 198
Fourchard, Laurent, 184n.9, 201n.81

France, 214
France and Gabonese electoral competition, 213
Francisco Macias Nguema, 118
Freedom House, 158, 185, 186t. 6.1, 187, 188
Freemasonry among French elites, 211, 212
Freemasonry in francophone Africa, 211, 212
Freemasonry in Gabon, 208, 211
French Colonial Lobby, 42, 42n.23
French Colonial Ministry, 44
French colonialism, 50
French colonialism – forced labor laws, 40, 50, 53
French colonialism – Politique d'association, 116

Gabon, 140, 142, 183, 207, 208, 214, 215, 217
Gabon – democracy, 215
Gabon – democracy prospects, 214
Gabon – elections 2005, 213n.154
Gabon – elite recruitment, 211
Gabon – obituary, Omar Bongo Ondimba, 214
Gabon – political machines, 224
Ghana, 1, 66n.133, 126, 156, 157, 158, 159n.35, 160n.40, 163n.53, 183, 187
Ghana – democracy, 216
Ghana – development and democracy, 158
Ghana – electoral fraud and block voting, 158
Ghana – Jubilee Field, 159, 159n.36, 160, 161, 161n.41, 187, 216
Ghana – Kosmos Controversy, 159, 160, 161, 164, 183
Ghana – Oil Sector Legislation, 4n.19
Ghana National Petroleum Corporation (GNPC), 159n.36, 160
Ghanaian democracy, 126
Glaser, Antoine, 28n.95, 141n.104
Glaser, Antoine and Stephen Smith, 31n.103
Gokana, Denis, 177
Gold Coast Colony, 48, 66
Grand corruption, 196, 227
Grand corruption in Equatorial Guinea, 227
Gyimah-Boadi, Emmanuel, 25n.82

Haber, Stephen and Victor Monaldo, 13
Habré, Hissein, 3
Halliburton – TSKJ investigation, 31n.106
Heavily Indebted Poor Country, 140
Heilbrunn, John R., 31n.104, 91n.67, 128n.60, 128n.61, 168n.73
Helmke, Gretchen and Steven Levitsky, 190
Herb, Michael, 16n.60